To the previous generation of Cryers,

Donald, Pauline, and Mary,

and to the next, Julia and Erica, and to Dixie Goss

Being Alive
and Having to Die

BEING ALIVE
AND HAVING TO DIE

The Spiritual Odyssey of
Forrest Church

DAN CRYER

St. Martin's Press
New York

www.stmartins.com

Library of Congress Cataloging-in-Publication Data

Cryer, Dan.
    Being alive and having to die : the spiritual odyssey of Forrest
Church / Dan Cryer. — 1st ed.
       p. cm.
    Includes bibliographical references and index.
    ISBN 978-0-312-59943-0
    1. Church, F. Forrester. 2. Unitarian Universalist Association—
Clergy—Biography. I. Title.
    BX9869.C53C79 2011
    289.1092—dc23
    [B]   2011025859

First Edition: November 2011

10 9 8 7 6 5 4 3 2 1

Contents

ACKNOWLEDGMENTS

Special thanks to my family: Dixie Goss, my wife, intellectual partner, resident techie, and witty co-conspirator; my cheerleading daughters, Julia and Erica Cryer; David and Britt Cryer; Jon and Judy Cryer; Kathy and David Keller; Kay Callentine, Mary Jo Garrison, and Loretta and Tom Spinar.

More special kudos to my indefatigable and accurate transcriber, Jan Mach; my agent, Betsy Lerner, who believed in this project before any other publishing professional and gave me a green light to do it my way; and my editor, George Witte, for his confidence in me and his patience. Thanks also to the St. Martin's publicity staff, in particular Joan Higgins and Sarit Schneider; to copy editor John McGhee; and to my former *Newsday* colleague Mary Voboril, for her meticulous reading of the manuscript. While writing this book, I met Peter Havholm, emeritus professor of English at my alma mater, the College of Wooster. Peter read every line with an editor's skeptical eye and a friend's compassionate heart.

Forrest Church not only gave generously of his time but granted access to many of his personal papers and permission to quote from them.

Both he and Carolyn Buck Luce gave permission to reproduce family photos. I could not have written this book without their assistance.

Former *UU World* editor Tom Stites, former UUA president John Buehrens, Professor Paul Rasor, and Guy Quinlan and Mary-Ella Holst proved indispensable guides through all matters Unitarian Universalist. Patrick and Debbie Shea welcomed me into their home in Salt Lake City, as did Patrick and Martha Maher in Arlington, Virginia, and Jim and Lee Blue in Darnestown, Maryland.

I received repeated encouragement from Sue and David Taylor, Anhared and John Stowe, Bonnie Havholm, Alexandra Mezey, Elizabeth O'Brien, Nancy Braund Boruch, Carolyn Jackson, Vic Henschel and Judy Samuelson, Susan Richman, Robin Bossert, Frank and Rose Patton, Eric Lamm and Marye Elmlinger, Ronald Speight, Erica Marcus, Sheryl McCarthy and Len Hollie, Mary Voboril and Jim Robbins, Marilyn Goldstein, James Kindall, Peg Wreen, Blamo Jaurey, and Peter and Carolyn Horn.

Thanks to Frank Church's biographers Rod Gramer and LeRoy Ashby, and to my fellow writers Joseph Berger, Susan Jacoby, Julie Salomon, Todd Gitlin, Barbara Fisher, and Laura Pedersen for help of various kinds.

At the Unitarian Church of All Souls, New York City, a special salute to Rev. Galen Guengerich and Annie Gorycki, and to Lorraine Allen for guiding me through the labyrinth of the All Souls Archives. At the Unitarian Universalist Association in Boston, Christopher Walton, Kathleen Montgomery, John Hurley, Janette Lallier, and Beth Miller all offered a helping hand.

Librarians and archivists provide indispensable aid to writers. I want to acknowledge the help of Alan Virta, Mary Carter, and Jim Duran at the Boise State University Library, and Garry Wenske, executive director of the Frank Church Institute, Boise State University, for setting up my Idaho interviews; Gloria Korsman, Clifford Wunderlich, and Michelle Gautier at Andover-Harvard Theological Library; Rodney L. Petersen at Boston Theological Institute; Molly Molloy and Patricia

E. White of Stanford University Libraries; Jane Goldstein, Carolyn Waters, and Brandi Tambasco at the New York Society Library; Seth Kasten, Burke Library, Union Theological Seminary; and Amy Hague and Kelly Anderson, Sophia Smith Collection, Smith College.

For my research on Bethesda, Maryland, thanks to local historian William Offutt; Debra Heibein Rankin, director, Montgomery County Historical Society; and at Walt Whitman High School, Assistant Principal Jennifer Webster and librarian Barbara Steele. Gary S. Lutzker permitted a visit to Frank and Bethine Church's former home there.

I wish to thank several professors of history, theology, and sociology of religion for providing a road map to religion in late-twentieth-century America: Paul Rasor, Virginia Wesleyan College; Gary Dorrien and Donald Shriver, Union Theological Seminary; Jon Butler, Yale University; Nancy Ammerman, Boston University; Courtney Bender, Columbia University; Gerald Marwell, New York University; Harvey Cox, Harvard University; Rhys Williams, University of Cincinnati (now at Loyola University, Chicago); and James Davison Hunter, University of Virginia.

Finally, a tip of the hat to my late-night companions: W. S. Merwin, Jane Hirshfield, Adam Zagajewski, and Charles Wright.

The religious quest is not about discovering "the truth" or "the meaning of life," but about living as intensely as possible here and now. The idea is not to latch onto some superhuman personality or to "get to heaven" but to discover how to be fully human.

—KAREN ARMSTRONG

BEING ALIVE
AND HAVING TO DIE

Introduction

The goal of life is to live in such a way that
our lives will prove worth dying for.

—FORREST CHURCH

W hen Rev. Forrest Church preached at the Unitarian Church of All Souls, his soaring, light-filled sanctuary on New York's Upper East Side, nearly every pew was filled.

This was a congregation that once included Herman Melville and William Cullen Bryant and members of the city's nineteenth-century social elite, and now attracted investment bankers and corporate lawyers, actors and professors, teachers and social workers from the entire region. Well-scrubbed and often well-heeled, they were a cross-section of metropolitan high achievers. Music drew them as much as well-crafted sermons. The superb thirty-voice choir, laced with professional singers, had once boasted a young soprano named Renée Fleming.

On this day, February 3, 2008, Reverend Church stood in the pulpit with an unmistakable air of command. Six foot two, bearded and bespectacled, wearing the scarlet robe of a Harvard Ph.D., he was every inch the scholarly and ecclesiastical authority. Yet his engaging smile also conveyed a pastor's kindness. That the smile occasionally broadened into a mischievous grin, as he told a joke at his own expense, suggested that he was as human as his listeners. Their frailties were his.

Church had been inspiring his congregation for nearly thirty years. In that time he had dealt in public with the crises most people face only in private. After falling in love with one of his married parishioners, he managed to survive a humiliating, career-threatening scandal and divorce. Ten years later, he confessed that he had finally stopped drinking after a life-long battle with alcoholism.

As Church ascended the pulpit on that bright, cold Sunday morning, only a few insiders had any inkling of what was to come. As he spoke, he took on the air of a family physician. In measured, calm tones, he delivered dire news. He was both doctor and patient. His most potent nemesis had come back with a vengeance. The esophageal cancer treated and sent into remission two years before had spread to his liver and lungs and was now terminal. The remainder of his life would be measured not in years, but in months. In the pews, some wept. Others hugged their companions as if the news were their own.

The sermon, "Love and Death," proclaimed a familiar theme, evocative of their pastor's much-quoted definition of religion—"our human response to the dual reality of being alive and having to die." This, his listeners knew, was not morbid stuff at all, but an urgent summons to live life abundantly.

Ever an optimist—he liked to say that he was born "sunny-side up"—Church began with a story about the absentminded minister who failed to inform his staff about his forthcoming sermon title. Consequently, it was billed as "The Great Mystery . . . What Dr. Barr will be preaching about is a mystery, but we're certain that it will be great."

Death was the great mystery, he continued, the inevitable bookend to that other mystery, the good fortune of birth. "I didn't become a minister until I performed my first funeral," he recalled. "When death or dying comes calling at the door, like a bracing wind it clears our being of pettiness. It connects us to others. More alert to life's fragility, we reawaken to life's preciousness."

The preeminent Unitarian Universalist clergyman from 1985 through 2009—profiled by *Esquire, People,* and *New York* magazine—Church was not only a consummate preacher but an eloquent author, theologian, public intellectual, and opponent of the religious right. In an age of conservative ascendancy, he stood steadfast as a brilliant beacon of liberal religion. At ease before television cameras—whether being interviewed by Bill Moyers or standing side by side with Dan Rather as America mourned after the September 11 terrorist attacks—he held forth on the intricacies of church-state relations and the misguided notion that the United States was a Christian nation. Public speaking was in his DNA. His father, Frank Church of Idaho, had been a Jeremiah in the U.S. Senate, sounding alarms about an out-of-control CIA and the futility of the Vietnam War.

While the senator's oratory could sometimes seem a little bombastic, the younger Church spoke in a more intimate, conversational tone. He connected to people in the pews the way FDR had related to listeners to the radio. He had a knack for making parishioners feel that he was speaking directly to them.

On this day he cited one of them, Damon Brandt, whose book of photographs, *Hospice,* chronicles his father's final days. "Damon's unsentimental yet deeply moving record touches the heart," Church said. "Why does it move those who never knew Damon's father? Because his death is our death too. We are never closer than when we ponder the great mystery that beats at the heart of our shared being . . .

"If we insulate ourselves from death we lose something precious, a sense of life that does know death, that elevates human to humane, that reconciles human being with human loss.

"The word *human* has a telling etymology: *Human, humane, humility, humus.* Dust to dust, the mortar of mortality that binds us fast to one another . . .

"How do we respond when we get a terminal sentence? Far too often with, 'What did I do to deserve this?'

"'Nothing.' The answer is 'Nothing.' Against unimaginable odds, we have been given something that we didn't deserve at all, the gift of life, with death as our birthright . . .

"When those we love die, a part of us dies with them. When those we love are sick, we too feel the pain. Yet all of this is worth it. Especially the pain. Grief and death are sacraments, or can be. A sacrament symbolizes communion, the act of bringing us together."

And then Church returned to the photographs: "A man is dying. He has been given but a few sweet days to live. His wife and children gather at his bedside. They reminisce. They hold hands. They laugh. They cry. They wait. Their hearts tremble with love.

"Damon's pictures tell life's deepest story. And each carries the same meaning. The most eloquent answer to death's 'no' is love's 'yes' . . . The only question worth asking is 'Where do we go from here?' And part of the answer is 'together.'"

Church was performing the duties of pastor. Instead of lamenting his own death, he was consoling his listeners. Today many of them were in tears.

Before he died, Church told the congregation, he hoped to achieve three goals. He would finish a short book, *Love and Death*, summing up his pastoral theology. He would escort his daughter, Nina, down the aisle on her August wedding day. And on September 23, he would celebrate his sixtieth birthday, coinciding with his thirty years of service at All Souls. "It would be remarkably unimaginative," he jested, "for me to die at fifty-nine, as my father and grandfather each did before me."

The minister ended his sermon, as he always did, with words of comfort: "Amen. I love you. And may God bless us all." The congregation responded, as it rarely did, with a standing ovation.

Forrest Church cannot be understood outside the context of his high-profile political family. His father was a prominent Democratic senator who knew how to win elections in a conservative state. His mother, Bethine, daughter of onetime Idaho governor Chase Clark, had the gregarious, work-the-room instincts of a natural politician. One legacy for their son was a commitment to liberalism, even against overwhelming odds. But the result of the couple's endless rounds of politicking was to hand over young Forrest to caretakers who often left him to his own devices. Out of benign neglect, he became what he called a "free-range kid"—independent, uncomfortable in groups he did not lead, unwilling to play by the usual rules.

As the son of a famous father, Forrest Church rebelled for a time and struggled to find his own way. He might have had a clear path to success following in his father's footsteps, but he eventually found in religion a subject that matched his talents with his passion.

In retrospect, Church's role as one of the nation's foremost advocates of liberal religion is clear. He did not take up the torch from William Sloan Coffin, who in the 1960s and '70s defined liberal Protestantism with his pro-civil-rights and anti–Vietnam War activism. Though Church once aspired to be "the Coffin of my generation," he was not a prophet, marching in the streets and engaging in civil disobedience. The 1980s and '90s demanded a different sort of leadership. So he was a thinker, a framer of politico-religious debates. Like William Ellery Channing, his nineteenth-century Unitarian forebear, he assumed the multiple roles of pastor, theologian, and public intellectual.

At a time when Jerry Falwell and Pat Robertson preached a rigid fundamentalism, Church discerned the divine light streaming into a universal cathedral, not merely from one window, but from many. God "was not God's name," but "our name for that which is greater than all and yet present in each." When they thundered about heaven and hell, he proclaimed, "Whether or not there is life after death, surely there is love after death." For Church, Jesus was not divinity but the greatest of all moral teachers. The essence of the Nazarene's teachings was not salvation but our duty to serve humanity. The Bible wasn't the inspired word of God but a treasure trove of stories, fables, proverbs, and, above all, wisdom. His was a theology of love rather than wrath. Broad in sweep yet nondoctrinal, his appeal stretched a hand to Americans weary of orthodoxy and open to new varieties of spirituality.

Church was equally eloquent in reminding his countrymen that the determination to keep church and state at arm's length was anything but an assault on religion. It was not only a vital heritage from the Founding

Fathers, but essential to keeping the peace in today's America. As the per-
centage of mainstream Protestants declined and that of evangelicals rose,
pressures to cross previously clear-cut boundaries increased. So, at every
opportunity, Church spoke out against such breaches as prayer in public
schools and state funding of religious institutions. Churches flourished best,
he argued, when they were free of state oversight. And only a thoroughly
secular government could deal equitably with America's unprecedented
religious pluralism.

Similarly, in his magisterial *So Help Me God: The Founding Fathers and the
First Great Battle Over Church and State,* Church attacked the myth that the
United States was a Christian nation. The Falwells, Robertsons, and their
ilk failed to grasp that deist leaders like Washington and Jefferson were
more akin to Forrest Church than to any fundamentalist. One of Church's
earliest religious inspirations, in fact, was the so-called Jefferson Bible, that
president's edited Gospel version of *The Life and Morals of Jesus of Nazareth,*
which omitted miracles and resurrection.

Over the course of his career, Church wrote fourteen books, co-
authored one, and edited ten more. In them, religion and politics continually jostle each other. These great subjects form the bookends of his life
and thought. What is astonishing about this corpus is the range of the author's mind and interests. Never content to write one sort of book, he leap-
frogged from memoir to personal essay to political analysis to theology to
history. Few religious figures of his time moved so easily in such disparate
worlds.

This book is not an authorized biography, in the sense that neither Forrest
Church nor his family censored it or had final control over its content.
But it could not have been done without the cooperation of Reverend
Church, who consented to seventeen lengthy interviews, and his family.
As a member of All Souls since 1994, I had come to know him through
his sermons, his books, and his public presence in the media—but not in
an intimate way. But throughout a nearly two-year process, he proved
unusually thorough, insightful, and candid, thus ushering me into his

inner sanctum. He also granted me access to a collection of memorabilia, ranging from letters to school report cards to unpublished poetry, and introduced me to a host of people who had known him in various stages of his life. Given this entrée, I was able to conduct 180 additional interviews. Among the key players in this story, only his first wife, Amy Furth, and Michael Luce, the former husband of Church's second wife, Carolyn Buck Luce, declined to participate.

My conversations with Church began after the announcement of his terminal illness, in his All Souls office, in effect a shrine to liberalism. Here was his father's desk from the U.S. Senate. On one wall were a framed print of Norman Rockwell's painting *Freedom of Worship* (based on Franklin Roosevelt's Four Freedoms speech) and photos of Church posed with Ted Kennedy, Arthur Schlesinger, Cornel West, Nelson Mandela, Bill and Hillary Clinton, and other liberal icons. Here also were family photos, bookshelves lined with works of history and religion, and a whimsical sign with the motto "Run Forrest Run" from the movie *Forrest Gump*.

Thereafter, our conversations took place at Church's nearby apartment. Here he would stretch out on a couch, sometimes with one of his cats—Rudy, the Angora, or Jedidiah, a Maine coon—sprawled on his chest, and engage in what he considered a "fine, valedictory thing to do," to examine who he was and what had made him that way. When I asked tough questions, he did not hold back, try to hide his flaws, or make excuses for his mistakes. A dying man, he had made peace with himself. He hoped to "ace the death test."

One

Free-Range Kid

Since rules weren't imposed at home,
I've always been resistant to rules.
—FORREST CHURCH

Forrest Church nearly missed his appointment with life. His parents, Frank and Bethine Church, had decided to put off having children until Frank completed his education. But thanks to 1940s-era "under-the-counter birth control that did not work," the next Church generation arrived ahead of schedule. Had birth control done its appointed job for six months longer, he would not have arrived at all.[1]

Ever since Frank Church's youth in Boise, Idaho, he had set his sights on a career in politics. In his wife, Bethine Clark Church, he found the perfect partner. Daughter of Chase Clark, a onetime governor of the state, she commanded the connections, the campaigning skills, and the audacity to make her husband's abstract dreams a reality. He was a big thinker, an orator, a policy wonk. She was the good mixer, the spirited organizer, the gregarious hostess. So acute were her political instincts that one day she would be known as Idaho's "third senator."

When Bethine learned that she was pregnant, in January 1948, Frank was midway through his first year at Harvard Law School. The couple lived in a cramped fourth-floor walkup in Boston and commuted together to Cambridge, where she worked in the library at Radcliffe College.

Despite Frank's excellent grades—he made law review by the end of the second term—things weren't going well. The winter of 1947–48, one of the most severe in the region's memory, spread a cloak of misery. Frank was so immersed in his studies that Bethine felt ignored, and Frank shot back that she didn't understand the pressures to succeed. Their discontent sometimes boiled over into quarrels. Meanwhile, the aches in Frank's back wouldn't go away. Their physician, dismissing the symptoms as the result of stress, prescribed aspirin. Eventually, because neither Frank nor Bethine was thrilled with living on the East Coast and because Frank's political future clearly lay in the West, he decided to transfer to the law school at Stanford, his alma mater.

Back in Boise for the summer, the couple moved in with Bethine's parents. To cheer them up, "Pop" Clark bought them a new yellow Packard convertible to replace another that had been stolen in Boston. Frank Forrester Church IV, whom everyone would call "Twig" and as an adult would be known as Forrest, was born on September 23, 1948. He was a healthy baby who soon beamed his smile on everyone in sight. A few weeks later the couple drove off to their new life in California, rented a small house with a garden and patio, and Frank resumed his studies.

But, as Forrest Church would later say, trapdoors have a way of opening in front of us when we least expect them. In February of the following year, Frank's increasing pain sent him to the hospital for an operation on a "strangulated testicle." Six hours later he faced an unexpected and terrifying diagnosis. He was informed that he had testicular cancer and that it had spread extensively. His life expectancy was no more than three to six months. Fortunately, after a later diagnosis of a less lethal form of cancer, doctors gave him the option of experimental X-ray therapy after he had healed from the initial operation. During the next five weeks, Frank and Bethine fought to keep depression at bay, their bright hopes beyond reach. Neither could imagine a future without the other. They resolved that if the treatment failed, they would leave Twig in the care of grandparents, fly to Europe, and commit suicide together by driving off a cliff. Once into the grueling treatment—daily megadoses of radium—Frank slogged through days of nausea and appetite loss. His weight dwindled to ninety pounds. After seven weeks, he was pronounced cured, but at an enormous cost. The doctors estimated that ten to fifteen years had been shaved off his life span. And he was no longer able to sire children.

Forrest Church had been conceived just in time. If his parents had been able to follow their original plan of waiting until after law school, he would never have been born.

According to Bethine, Frank emerged from this ordeal vowing to "play for high stakes, for the things he believed in, no matter what the cost." And she would always be at his side, urging him on, an exuberant partner on the campaign trail.

But what was the impact on their son? When Frank was first hospitalized, Bethine called on an aunt, Mabel Patterson, a hotel manager in San Francisco, to tend to six-month-old Twig. Then, during the weeks of radiation that followed, friends in Palo Alto helped with the baby so that Bethine could give full attention to her ailing husband. The pattern was set early.

For his first nine years, Forrest Church would have the luxury of being an adored only child. Unquestionably, his parents loved him, but neither was especially devoted to parenting. Their eyes were riveted on the political prize. So they frequently handed off Twig to their parents and others, who gave him enormous latitude to do what he wanted. As a result, their son evolved into an independent-minded, free-range child. He feigned illness in order to skip school, preferred the games he invented to prepackaged ones, ruled like a lord over his little clique of playmates. He dropped out of the regimented Cub Scouts and never took part in organized sports. Since most of Twig's cousins lived far away, when Sunday dinners or Christmas celebrations saw him in the company of grandparents, he held a fixed spot at the center of their world, the little kid whose cute ways could be endlessly chuckled over and applauded.

"I was spoiled by freedom, so it became my watchword," Forrest Church observed near the end of his life. "I did tend to get my way . . . That gave me a sense of exceptionalism that carried through to a kind of renegade quality, a kind of bad-boy quality that never turned into being so bad that you get into trouble, but into being a maverick. Since rules weren't imposed at home, I have always been resistant to rules . . . Now, what does that lead to? It leads to someone who is irrepressible and irresponsible, someone who is creative and not very disciplined unless the discipline is associated with the act of creation. At which point I become absolutely focused."[2]

Character, they say, is destiny. But one should never underestimate the power of destiny's sly first cousin, sheer luck. In one of those random oddities of history, both Frank Church and Bethine Clark could trace their ancestry to the *Mayflower*. Centuries before their families made their way to Idaho, they helped found an English colony in Massachusetts. John Howland, a young indentured servant, was the lucky one. He nearly botched his transatlantic voyage of 1620. Foolishly venturing out on deck during a fierce storm, he was swept into the sea. Fortunately—for Forrest Church's destiny—he managed to grab a trailing halyard and was hauled back onto the ship. When his master died a year later, Howland was granted his freedom and, probably, a share of the estate. He married Elizabeth Tilley, who had endured the *Mayflower* passage along with her parents, John and Elizabeth, as well as the pestilence that struck them down that first harrowing winter. The enterprising Howland went on to become a merchant and one of Plymouth's foremost citizens. Blessed with ten children and a prodigious eighty-eight grandchildren, the Howlands established Bethine Clark's American line.

Frank Church's American forebears sprang from the union of Richard Church, who arrived from England in the 1630s, and Elizabeth Warren. Like Howland and Tilley, Elizabeth's father, Richard Warren, had been one of the signers of the Mayflower Compact. Richard and Elizabeth Church's son, Benjamin, would win fame during King Philip's War of 1675–76 as "America's first Indian fighter." More than most of his peers, he respected his tribal neighbors and learned from them, including their unorthodox military tactics, and vowed to treat them like human beings.

Nonetheless, when confronted with the body of King Philip himself—known as Metacom among his people—he ordered it drawn and quartered, in revenge for the chief's alleged misdeeds. Philip's head was later placed on a palisade of Plymouth's fort, a warning to Native Americans of the price of rebellion against English domination.[3]

However storied or morally ambiguous the colonial beginnings of the Churches and Clarks, the Clarks could claim a far more substantial recent heritage. Bethine was from one of Idaho's leading Democratic families. Chase, her father, rose from the posts of state representative, state senator, and mayor of Idaho Falls to a one-term governorship during 1941–42. President Roosevelt later appointed him to the federal district court in Boise. Barzilla Clark, Bethine's uncle, had been mayor of Idaho Falls and governor during the thirties. In the same period, Bethine's cousin D. Worth Clark served two terms in Congress and one in the U.S. Senate.

After studying law at the University of Michigan in the opening decade of the twentieth century, Chase Clark set up a practice in Mackay, a rough-and-tumble town in eastern Idaho where barroom quarrels often erupted into fistfights. Here he met and married Jean Burnett, a quiet eighteen-year-old whose father owned a meat market. Clark's everyday clients were ranchers and farmers embroiled in disputes over land and water rights. More lucrative fees came from his corporate clients, the Empire and White Knob copper companies. By the late 1920s Clark was well off, his legal earnings supplemented by substantial investments in land and stocks. The Crash of '29, however, took most of his wealth, though he did manage to hang on to Robinson Bar, a dude ranch in the Sawtooth Mountains that would prove seminal in Forrest Church's early life. In any event, the Clark family moved to Idaho Falls and started over.

Jean, a teetotaling Presbyterian, eventually became head of the state's Woman's Christian Temperance Union. No self-righteous, axe-wielding Carrie Nation, she was, according to her daughter, "never harsh or unforgiving of those who drank." She had, in fact, an open heart toward the down-and-out. As an elderly woman, she even spoke warmly about the bordello madam whose compassion for girls in need of medical help or an extra dollar was legendary in Mackay. The gentle, forgiving Jean would be as frequent a caretaker for the young Forrest Church as his own mother.

In 1909, Jean had given birth to a boy. But the infant lived less than a day, and she nearly died, too. Consequently, as Bethine's birth approached fourteen years later, the Clarks drove to Salt Lake City in search of more sophisticated medical care. Jean Bethine Clark emerged safely into the world on February 19, 1923. She would be a beloved only child. "Because [Pop] had always wanted a son," Bethine wrote, "I became his boy and companion as well as his 'princess.' Pop talked with me about everything, which was unusual for a father and a daughter in those days . . . [He] thought no dinner table discussion was much good without a great roaring conversation of taboo subjects—religion, politics, or one of his law cases—everything except sex."[4]

As for her eventual husband, Frank Church III was born in Boise on July 25, 1924. Nicknamed Frosty, he was a frail child, continually fending off attacks of bronchitis. His father, Frank, owned a sporting-goods store and then a small apartment building, while his mother, Laura, minded the two boys, Frank and Richard, who was nine years older. Laura was outgoing, her husband emotionally remote and unsmiling. Solid, cautious middle-class citizens, without high aspirations, they nonetheless produced sons whose ambitions took them far from Idaho. One would become a U.S. senator, the other a U.S. Naval Academy graduate and career military officer.

Since his father was a devout Catholic, young Frank began his formal education at a parochial school. But after enduring too much bullying from stronger boys, he was allowed to transfer to a public school. Gifted with a bright mind and an inquisitive nature, he began to thrive. While his peers stuck their noses into comic books, he pored over the newspaper. In 1938, he responded to a request from the *Boise Capital News* for essays on the proposition "Should the United States keep out of foreign troubles?" Following in the footsteps of his Republican hero, Idaho's Senator William Borah, he wrote a polished brief for isolationism. The newspaper's readers may have been astonished to learn that the author of this essay was a mere fourteen-year-old, but the Churches were not. Discussions of this sort were an everyday staple in their household. At this young age, Church vowed to duplicate Borah's achievement as chairman of the Foreign Relations Committee in the U.S. Senate. Thoughtful, outgoing, and chatty, Frank developed into an outstanding debater at Boise High School, leading his team to the state championship. In 1941, as a junior, he triumphed over 108,000 contestants to win the American Legion National High School Oratorical Contest, in Charleston, South Carolina. His reward was a four-thousand-dollar college scholarship. Back home at Boise High, his feat paid off again. The skinny nonathlete was elected student body president over the star quarterback.

By now Frank differed markedly from his father. Frank Sr. was a lifelong Republican who voted Democrat only once, for FDR in 1932, and regretted it ever after. "I learned all about the Democrats so I could argue with Dad," the senator once noted. "I ended up by converting myself." He also cast aside his father's Catholicism. According to his older brother, young Frank "questioned everything." In this light, the church of Rome seemed too dogmatic, run by "self-righteous people" who were "wrong about a lot of things." His father's shopkeeper world was altogether too small to accommodate Frank's emerging worldview and ambitions. Looking back, he thought of his father, according to Forrest, as "a very dear and sweet man, a kind man," but too cautious, too conservative, too averse to risk.[5]

Frank Church and Bethine Clark were hardly an inevitable match. He grew up Catholic and Republican. She was a Presbyterian and a Democrat. In this era, differences like these could be insurmountable barriers. But by 1940, when they met at a high school government convention, his Catholicism was behind him and her commitment to Presbyterianism was tepid at best. Both were avid supporters of the New Deal. Her family moved to the capital in January of the next year, as Chase Clark took over the governorship. Bethine, a senior, was a newcomer to Boise High, where Frank was a year younger and a junior. But given his growing stardom and their mutual interest in politics, the age difference hardly mattered.

She was drawn into his orbit, and he into the heady world of the Clarks. Soon both the Clark and Church households were gathering places for Frank and his buddies. Bright, ebullient Bethine, the only female, was treated like "one of the boys." Almost every Sunday evening the gang would join the Clarks to eat leftovers, bask in the glow of the governor, and discuss state government or the war in Europe.

Although Frank and Bethine dated, their relationship was as much intellectual companionship as romance, and both went out with others. Following graduation, Bethine attended Boise Junior College. For several years thereafter, distance kept them apart. When she went east to the University of Michigan, Frank headed west to Stanford. He spent only two quarters there—long enough to establish himself as the university's ablest debater—before resolving to enlist in the U.S. Army in 1942. For most of his tour of duty, Lieutenant Church served as an intelligence officer in Southeast Asia and China. Meanwhile, Bethine majored in sociology, honed her sculpting skills, and acted in plays. Letters flew back and forth, more chatty than flirty. Bethine found a steady beau in Ann Arbor, then one who attended West Point. While still vowing his devotion, Frank nonetheless suggested she not "wait for him," whereupon a heartbroken Bethine became engaged to the cadet. Frank heard the news while home on leave and acted with military dispatch. He countered with his own proposal, and his sweetheart accepted immediately. "I think we both realized like a bolt of lightning that we had always loved each other," Bethine wrote. After graduating from Stanford with honors in political science, Frank Church married Bethine Clark on June 21, 1947, in an outdoor wedding at Robinson Bar Ranch. The next stop: Harvard Law School.[6]

After Stanford and Harvard, the Churches had to readjust to life in the provinces: Boise in the 1950s was a decidedly unsophisticated place. The city attracted politicos, lobbyists, and bureaucrats as the state capital, but aside from that base, it was little more than a largish town. In the 1950 census, its population was just over 34,000. It had no dial telephone service until July 1952—to make a call before that date, you had to call an operator—and not a single television station until November of that year. It could boast of no universities and few cultural amenities. Moreover, town fathers and business leaders resisted industrialization. Instead of factories, Boise had several corporate headquarters: Morrison-Knudsen, the construction giant that built the Hoover Dam and other vast projects, and Boise Cascade, eventually a multinational empire, but then a timber company.

What Boise possessed in spades was the Mountain West good life—an unpretentious, easygoing spirit, clean streets and broad shade trees, a low crime rate, and quick access to the outdoors. Trout streams, deer hunting grounds, and mountain hiking trails were just minutes away. A 1947 profile in *The Saturday Evening Post* raved about the town's personification of "pioneer America, with a go-to-hell glint in one eye and a howdy pardner gleam in the other . . . People don't care a hang how much dough you've got or who your old man was." Vices were few. In Boise, and throughout the state, saloons were illegal; drinking outside the home was confined to licensed bottle clubs. Gambling was also prohibited. Thus it chose, according to the *Post* writer, not to compete with Reno for "the lucrative divorce trade." What's more, the city had no red-light district, and police blotters "seldom record darker deeds than loitering or overtime parking. For two years no killing has marred the peace." In short, Boise was a clean-cut, smaller Salt Lake City. Mormons, in fact, made up one sixth of the population. There were also four thousand Basques (initially drawn to Idaho's sheep ranches) who were well integrated into the majority community, and small numbers of Chinese, Japanese, and African-Americans, who were not.[7]

On November 2, 1955, a few months after Forrest Church's seventh birthday, Boise's calm was shattered by the unexpected presence of another minority. *The Idaho Statesman* story bearing the headline THREE BOISE MEN ADMIT SEX CHARGES only hinted at the nature of the scandal. Over the next two years, a handful of men, including a well-known local banker, were convicted of violating laws against sodomy and sentenced to prison. It's hardly surprising that homosexuality, here as elsewhere in 1950s America, was taboo. Nor, in the age of McCarthy, was the hysteria and denunciation that followed. Sex between men was uniformly reviled as a symptom of moral depravity or mental derangement. After the story appeared, Boiseans flooded the newspaper and police department with rumors of same-sex orgies and molested boys. What's more striking is the underlying straitjacket of conformity exposed by these events. "Boise was a very lonely place for nonconformists," psychiatrist Dr. John Butler, then head of the mental health division of the state's department of health, observed a decade later. "Liberals, for example, had no one to talk to. I don't just mean political liberals, but any kind. Just to find people who were interested in the arts, in music, people who read novels of quality and essays, was almost an impossible task." Butler eventually quit the post in frustration. In Idaho, the very concept of mental illness and its treatment was under continual attack. The word *expert*, a Butler ally contended, was "one of the worst insults you can use in Boise."[8]

Amid all the tumult, one voice of reason was a young lawyer with his eye on the U.S. Senate. At a community meeting held in December 1955, Frank Church spoke out, along with Dr. Butler, the head of the state prison, and other officials. By the standards of his time and place, Church's views were enlightened and measured. While urging an end to rumor-mongering, he had no doubt that homosexuality was "a problem," but one whose extent was exaggerated. Though Church's involvement in the issue was admittedly minor, it's worth noting that he was not afraid to air his opinion.[9]

After living with Bethine's parents for a few years, the Churches were able to buy a tiny house of their own on Logan Street, a cul-de-sac ideal for raising children. Just behind them were Carl and Spice Burke, with three kids, and next to the Burkes were Jim and Lois Bruce, with three more. Jim Bruce, also an attorney, would one day rise to the presidency of the Idaho Power Company.[10]

For the boy Forrest, Logan Street was the locus of simple small-town pleasures, unclouded by controversy: "I can remember popping tar bubbles in the driveway on hot summer afternoons . . . endless hours in a little wading pool with Chris Burke and Jimmy Bruce . . . trips to the drugstore to buy little plastic packets of miniature cowboys and Indians." Invariably, Forrest was the leader of the pack. He was two years older than Chris, and Jimmy proved a willing follower. "I tended to call the shots, not unhappily for them, but nonetheless I got my way an unseemly amount of the time," he said.

Like his father, though, Forrest was not physically strong and had no talent for sports. So Jimmy, a shorter but much tougher lad, took charge when anyone threatened his best friend. If Jimmy happened to be elsewhere, however, Forrest was in jeopardy. Bethine remembers one neighborhood scamp who loved nothing better than pummeling other kids: "I saw him pounding on Forrest, and so I said to Forrest, 'Forrest, if you'd just hit him once, it would stop this because you're bigger than he is. Why don't you do that?' He said, 'Why, Mother? I'm not mad at him.' "[11]

If Forrest's temperament was gregarious and cheerful, his curious and thoughtful mind gave him an inward focus. Once he learned to read, he devoured boys' classics like the Hardy Boys and Tom Swift series. But he enjoyed nothing better than making up his own board games and playing them for hours on end. There were war games, baseball games, games with fantastical creatures, and political games complete with elaborate campaign strategies. "I would set up the rules," he said, "make the pieces, and I would play them with myself. I guess you could call that a fantasy life in its own way. I didn't need much external entertainment. With my friends, I would have them play my games with me. I was imperious [but] . . . I think they had a good time there."[12]

Roosevelt School—named for Teddy, not Franklin—was just a few blocks from home. During the primary grades, Forrest's achievement and social skills were uniformly praised. For years after that, though, schoolwork simply did not receive his full attention. Forrest drifted, dreamed, dallied, never working hard, never putting his intelligence to much of a test. "I have little memory of learning anything at school and little memory of being bored there," he said. "I would never push myself to the

point of pain . . . Whenever I came to a fork in the path, I took the gen-
tler or shaded lane." Oddly enough, his parents never demanded more of
their son. Once when his mother did complain to a teacher about a string
of Cs and Ds, her concern wasn't so much Forrest's performance as the
reasons for his punishment. "So I had a sense of only being accountable
to myself," he said, "and . . . I did not discipline myself to perform or to
excel."

Aside from parental inattention, two other factors account for Forrest's
habit of getting by instead of doing well. One was illness, or feigned illness. On many days, he simply wasn't in school. Forrest's elementary
school report cards reveal a startling story: In first grade, he was absent 25
percent of the time, in second grade 33 percent.

"All I had to do was say I had a sniffle and [Mother] would let me stay
home," Forrest reported. Given this wink and nod, he could skip an entire week. "I would have a sniffle and I would sit around in a draft all day
Monday and get a legitimate cold by Tuesday, and that would last all the
way through Wednesday. And that would convince my mother that I
wouldn't have to go back to school on Thursday or Friday because I might
get sick again."

Bethine acknowledged her role as enabler: "Frank always said to me,
'Bethine, you are really a sucker. I don't think he's that sick.' "[13]

Politics subverted Forrest's scholastic record as well. In 1952, when
Forrest turned four, Frank Church launched his political career by winning election as head of the Idaho Young Democrats. He was on a fast
track that would propel him to the U.S. Senate. Two years later, when
Forrest began his formal schooling, his father was actively drumming up
support for that post, crisscrossing the state with Bethine. To help finance
the campaign, the Churches sold their little house and moved back in with
Bethine's parents. In 1956, Church survived a difficult primary, narrowly
defeating perennial populist challenger Glen Taylor, and then charged
past incumbent Herman Welker, an ultraconservative Republican, to win
the Senate seat. He won despite the Democrats' minority status in Idaho

and the enormous popularity of the reelected President Eisenhower. Church was just thirty-two, one of the youngest senators in American history.[14]

Once Frank Church went to the Senate, his son's education suffered from geographical whiplash. In that era, the congressional session that began in January was finished by August or September. The result was that, from third grade through ninth grade, Forrest would attend Boise schools during the fall semester and Washington-area schools in the spring. Since the latter's standards were far higher than the former's, the A and B student in Boise, exerting the same effort in the nation's capital, dropped to C-level mediocrity. Given the higher bar, he was not inclined to jump.[15]

Forrest not only bounced back and forth between Boise and D.C. Throughout boyhood and youth, he had another residence. His "summer home" was his grandparents' Robinson Bar Ranch, in central Idaho. A seventy-acre dude ranch for tourists drawn to mountain scenery and horseback riding, it was also a paradise for kids. Forrest's frequent companion there was his pal Jimmy Bruce. Their days were carefree and unstructured. They rode horses. They fished in Warm Springs Creek, a tributary of the Salmon River. They swam in two pools, one a natural hot spring. They fed the chickens and got in the way of the housekeepers. They joked with wranglers, the teenage boys in charge of the horses. Forrest and Jimmy occupied a room in the main lodge, an unadorned log structure with guest rooms, a lounge, and a dining hall, until they grew older and graduated to outlying bunkhouses.

"I was an accidental Idahoan," Forrest recalled. "I did have a horse, but I wasn't a good rider. I did have a BB gun, but I couldn't hit the broad side of the barn. I did fish a bit and go out in the outdoors, but I wasn't a natural outdoorsman."

Forrest's parents did not summer at Robinson Bar and rarely visited. In their son's early years, they were busy campaigning. Later they were busy governing. Forrest's minder on the ranch was Beulah Reeves, his maternal grandmother's half-sister. Because she was preoccupied with managing the ranch, she was not likely to put Forrest on a very short leash. "I was kind of a pet child at the ranch," he said. "[Jimmy and I] just ranged free."[16]

A free-range kid is not necessarily free of anxiety. It's telling that Forrest's most intense childhood memories fairly scream with the fear of losing his peripatetic parents. One was a recurring nightmare in which he and his father are driving up a steep mountain road. Frank Church smiles and waves as he spots familiar faces, acknowledging them along the way. He's feeling so cheery that he breaks into song. As father and son climb higher and higher, however, the son begins to be filled with dread. Suddenly, a huge logging truck swerves into their lane, and the car is swept off the road and over a cliff. "My fear was not for myself," the adult Forrest claimed. "It was for my father, reckless, buoyant, unconcerned, beautiful, singing as we plummeted toward our doom."[17] This boy clearly anticipated the pain of possibly *losing* that buoyant, beautiful father.

Another memory involved his equally precious mother. Children of the Cold War era will never forget the duck-under-your-desk drills supposedly designed to shield them from atomic-bomb fallout. (Nothing, of course, could have saved them, but this bit of fakery was intended to soothe a child's fears.) Informed that he would have an eleven-minute warning before any such attack, fourth grader Forrest decided, if he were about to die, he'd rather do so in the arms of his mother. Instead of ducking, one day he ran the short distance home to Bethine.[18]

Insecurity is also the central theme of the story Bethine liked to tell about Forrest and Brownie, a dilapidated toy monkey long past its prime. As Frank Church's first senatorial primary election drew to a close, in August 1956, the young politician decided that he needed a break from the stress. So he and the family, including the Clarks, drove to Lake Tahoe, where they stayed in a motel. On the way home, Forrest suddenly realized that he'd left his beloved Brownie behind and begged that they retrieve it. Frank and Bethine didn't want to bother, but kindly Pop Clark insisted that they drive back to the motel. Sure enough, the manager had found the monkey and not discarded it. "It looked too terrible not to be important," he joked.[19]

Psychologists tell us that blankets and similar items function for young children as reassuring totems of parental love. Most kids have enough confidence to give them up by the time they enter school. When this incident occurred, though, Forrest was just five weeks shy of his eighth birthday and about to enter third grade. Not surprisingly, he was not the only anxious member of the family. In the general election that fall, Bethine would be continually at her husband's side. But her son, left in the care of Mom and Pop in Boise, remained in her thoughts: "I kept thinking, 'I have a child at home—what am I doing?' (a thought I would have frequently throughout our lives together)."[20]

The most searing of Forrest's childhood memories was a stark, recurring passion play of abandonment and death. It went like this. Act One: a bitter argument with his mother over some trifle. Act Two: a tearful, self-pitying retreat to his bedroom. Act Three: a fantasy of escape that ends badly. After wandering outdoors into a wintry landscape, Forrest succumbs to the cold, dying alone and unloved in a snowdrift. "My parents hadn't missed me. They didn't even notice I had run away." Finale: his mother hears his sobs, opens his bedroom door, takes him into her arms, and reassures him that, indeed, she loves her boy.[21]

Mother and son were locked in a long-running drama that would be transformed during adolescence into a father-son struggle. Bethine overflowed with exuberance, generosity, and compassion. But she was also strong-willed and emotionally domineering. "She's the only person I know," Forrest once said, "who can fill three rooms at once." Her husband once toasted her as "a hurricane" and "a volcano" before adding that she was also "a jewel." Bethine's steadfast devotion to her husband's career, legendary in Idaho and Washington, necessarily meant that she frequently delivered her son to the care of her mother, "a pushover . . . a real softie," according to Forrest, or to equally easygoing housekeepers. Whenever Bethine's attention was elsewhere, as it often was, Forrest could do as he pleased. Because he became accustomed to that long leash, he felt stifled and frustrated when it was shortened. Having been granted great freedom, he could not abide its temporary suspension. Hence long periods of benign neglect punctuated now and then by teary dustups and reconciliation.[22]

"I think I felt the danger of being subsumed in [my mother], being a part of her, so I became apart from her," Forrest said. "And not as rebellion, but simply so I could cultivate my own persona. And I got away with that because she didn't notice me when I wasn't in the room . . . It was something my mother abetted because she wanted to be free, too. In a strange way, our mutual desire to be free kept us out of one another's hair."[23]

When the freshman senator and his family arrived in the nation's capital, early in 1957, they initially rented a small house in the District of Columbia. Forrest completed the second half of third grade at Horace Mann, a highly regarded public school also attended by Vice President Richard Nixon's daughters, Tricia and Julie. But Frank and Bethine soon set their sights on a bigger, newer house. They found one in Bethesda, Maryland, within easy commuting distance of the Senate.

The Bethesda of the late fifties spoke the language of upper-middle-class ease. It was a place designed to escape the rigors of the workday, to enjoy a backyard barbecue, to golf at nearby country clubs. Its sophistication made Boise seem even more insular than it was in fact. You could send your kids to first-class public schools. You were surrounded by an educated elite of politicians, government managers, physicians, and scientists. Some newcomers arrived because they sought brand-new homes, which were largely unavailable in older, neighboring Chevy Chase. Some were passengers on the great ship *White Flight* seeking refuge from the District of Columbia. In Bethesda, you rarely saw blacks or Asians, unless they happened to be diplomats. Jews were buying homes here, even if some golf clubs still excluded them. Pockets of modest homes housed cops and carpenters, but they served, by contrast, to underscore the community's essentially upscale character.[24]

To be sure, Bethesda was not immune to population pressures as post-war America surged into the suburbs. The metropolitan Washington area grew faster during the fifties than any other in the nation except for Houston and Los Angeles. Still, Bethesda's downtown, unlike today's high-rise, commercial magnet, retained a sleepy, small-town ambience. It consisted primarily of two movie theaters, a burger joint, a bowling alley, a pancake house, and a couple of unpretentious restaurants. The only institutions setting this placid bedroom community apart from any other were the U.S. Naval Hospital and the National Institutes of Health on sprawling campuses just outside downtown. It was not until the late 1960s that the area evolved into a major research-and-development center, anchored by GE, RCA, Applied Research, and Booz Allen.[25]

The Bethesda home the Churches found was on a cul-de-sac in the brand-new subdivision of Kenwood Park (not to be confused with nearby Kenwood, Bethesda's most exclusive address). The brick-and-frame split-level at 6704 Pemberton Street sat on a third of an acre that backed into the Kenwood Golf and Country Club. It had not only the eat-in kitchen Bethine wanted but a two-car garage, four bedrooms, commodious living and dining rooms, a study and den, and a finished basement and tree-filled backyard where Forrest could play.

This was not the kind of imposing residence you might expect of a U.S. senator's family, but it suited the Churches. Frank Church was not rich. He came to the Senate as a young lawyer who had spent far more time politicking than practicing, and he never made a lot of money until he left the Senate in 1981. Not grand, the Pemberton Street house echoed the Churches' informal, convivial style. Bethine and Frank's motley guest lists threw together foreign diplomats, news reporters, Idaho friends, and the occasional celebrity. Democratic senators from the West—Gale McGee (Wyoming) or George McGovern (South Dakota)—would show up. Theodore Bickel, the actor and folksinger, would strum his guitar and lead the group in song. Marlon Brando would head downstairs to play pool with the senator, decisively demonstrating that he was a better actor than pool shark.[26]

Less than a year after the Churches moved from Boise, and three days before Forrest's ninth birthday, they greeted an unexpected addition to the family. Frank and Bethine had wanted to adopt a child for several years, but they were startled to learn, on September 20, 1957, that a newborn boy was suddenly available. They took him home that day. Chase, named after Bethine's father and soon dubbed "Spud," would complete the family. Though delighted to welcome the baby, Bethine felt she needed more help with child care. So in Boise, her parents lent a hand; in Bethesda, she relied on live-in housekeepers. Most would come and go, but Jean Cyr served as Bethine's right hand for nearly a decade. A native of Maine with French-Canadian roots, Cyr was initially a diamond in need of polishing. Bethine had to teach her to speak standard English, to answer the phone, to drive, and to cook. Once up to speed, though, she performed her duties quite well. No more than ten years older than Forrest, she was less a surrogate mother figure than an amiable big sister who made sure he was cared for but largely kept out of his way. Chase was her primary responsibility. Bethine, confident that her older son was on the right track, focused most of her maternal attention on Spud. As a result, Forrest's already independent role in the family constellation solidified and took on a life of its own.[27]

As Forrest Ping-Ponged between Boise and Bethesda—Roosevelt School, followed by East Junior High; Radnor School, then Western Junior High—his grades continued to flip between outstanding and mediocre. As he advanced into adolescence, however, the sociability that was evident early on began to flourish. One manifestation of his popularity surfaced in January 1963, just before Forrest was scheduled to leave East Junior High for the second semester in Bethesda: One hundred classmates signed a petition pleading, unsuccessfully, with his parents to let him stay in Idaho for the remainder of the academic year.

One suspects that Forrest's ability to discern the prevailing winds and stay blithely on course proved a necessary survival skill. It was also, of course, the family business. A moderately liberal Democrat in conservative Idaho constantly navigated treacherous waters. In any event, the basement on Pemberton Street in Bethesda evolved into a daily after-school hangout for Forrest's growing circle of friends. Just as their parents had, Bethine and Frank proved to be amiable hosts for a steady stream of teenagers.

By ninth grade, Forrest and Peter Fenn had become best friends. The attachment would be permanent. Fenn's father, Dan, a former lecturer at Harvard Business School, served as an aide to President Kennedy, and later would run the John F. Kennedy Presidential Library in Boston. After Dan Fenn and his wife divorced, Peter and his three younger siblings were left in their father's care. So Peter was drawn not only to Forrest's bright flame but also to Bethine's gregarious maternal embrace. She would come to regard him as her third son, and he would overlook her occasional flares of temper. Soon Peter was showing up at the Church dinner table nearly as often as at his own. When the Churches headed for vacation in the Blue Ridge Mountains or Cape Hatteras, Peter was part of the family.[28]

The gang that trooped into the basement to shoot pool, scarf down chocolate chip cookies, and crank up the stereo—Forrest, Peter, Phil Dahan, Bob Watkins, and Seiichi Tsurumi, among others—were neither misfits nor the coolest kids in school. They were hip to the Beatles and the rock scene, but they weren't as cool as jocks. They were certainly smart, but hardly grinds. They weren't part of the most popular crowd, but they embodied a playful, nerdy, almost anarchic outsider wit that would have given them a much greater sheen just a few years down the road.

The group's insouciant ringleader choreographed their most note-worthy amusement, the Endless Monopoly Game. Forrest vowed that he and his buddies could get themselves into the *Guinness Book of World Records*. All they had to do was surpass the hours for the longest Monopoly game ever recorded. Board games were one of Forrest's passions, and he had the posse necessary to make the feat happen. So over a long holiday weekend, the boys played and played, moving the action from Forrest's basement to the family convertible to someone else's house. No one remembers how many hours were finally clocked, but they did break the record. A photo that appeared in *The Washington Post* depicted a gaggle of teens gathered around the car and the Monopoly board. Once they'd had enough, they drove to the high school parking lot and burned the board, the pieces, and the Monopoly dollars. Their fame was short-lived. Soon another band of goofy enthusiasts eclipsed their record, and they never made it into *Guinness* after all.[29]

Forrest and company were basically teenage innocents. They went bowling. They hung out in the cafeteria before school to play hearts or poker. In winter, they jumped the fence behind Forrest's house and went sledding on the country club fairways. When they reached driving age, they cruised around town looking for girls or sometimes went for beers in the District, where the drinking age was eighteen instead of twenty-one. Forrest wasn't much of a drinker yet, though Jimmy Bruce remembers the godawful hangovers they suffered at Robinson Bar Ranch after an experiment with a mixture of high-potency liquors. Another time, the pair received tongue-lashings from their parents for mooning drivers in downtown Boise.[30]

Girls provoked Forrest's shy side. It wasn't that he didn't date. He did. But his effervescent bonhomie and smile disguised a lack of confidence in the presence of the opposite sex. As Forrest headed out to his first high school dance, Marlon Brando happened to be visiting. "You aren't nervous, are you?" the Hollywood idol asked the obviously nervous ninth grader. His odd bit of advice: Gather people around you, start talking, and make big, grand gestures. Soon you'll attract a crowd and feel more sure of yourself. "The secret to all success is gesticulation," he declared. One suspects that the admonition proved more fruitful in the pulpit than at the prom.[31]

In Forrest's experience, dating was most easily mastered by means of a two-pronged strategy: picking a steady girlfriend and keeping his pal Peter by his side. Most often, he would double-date with Peter, escorting Lisa Stratton, daughter of Congressman Samuel Stratton of upstate New York, to a movie or a dance. Forrest partnered with Lisa for two historic events: the Beatles' debut American concert, at the Washington Coliseum on February 11, 1964, and, the following January, the inaugural balls for

President Lyndon Johnson. Later, Forrest would date Kathy Kiilsgaard, a
student at nearby Walter Johnson High School.[32]

In response to Montgomery County's soaring population, Bethesda
teens, who had previously attended Walter Johnson or Bethesda–Chevy
Chase (BCC) High Schools, greeted a new school of their own in the fall
of 1962. With one glorious exception, Walt Whitman High looked like
every other functional brick school building built in the sixties. Its gym
was a Buckminster Fuller–designed geodesic dome, looking from the
outside, one observer remarked, like a giant igloo.

BCC, until then the premier public high school in the county that
boasted the highest per-capita income in the nation, soon faced stiff
competition from Whitman. The upstart possessed ample resources of its
own. Eighty percent of its students' fathers, according to a 1965 report,
had attended or graduated from college; a third had gone on to graduate
school. More than three fourths were professionals or managers. Given
these advantages, the results weren't surprising. For the class of 1963, the
mean for those in the National Merit scholarship competition was the
ninetieth percentile; one fifth scored in the ninety-ninth percentile.
Today, Whitman High consistently ranks among the nation's best public high schools, but its aspirations for elite status were evident from its
founding.[33]

If Walt Whitman High School called for excellence, Forrest wasn't
listening. Now full-time in Bethesda, his classroom performance charted
his on-again, off-again approach to conventional learning. Although the
future writer achieved straight As in world history and U.S. history, he
maintained only a B average in English, and the rest of his record was
sprinkled with Bs and Cs.[34]

However uneven a student, Forrest seemed destined for politics. At
the dinner table, public issues prevailed over every other topic. Forrest's
relationship with his father consisted mainly of witty banter over Capitol
Hill wins and losses. The boy was learning the craft; the father was passing the torch, obliquely and without pushing. Whenever Frank Church
ran for reelection, as in 1962, Forrest would take part in the obligatory

family photo ops. And in an age predating cell phones and text messages, he and Peter spent one summer as pages on the floor of the U.S. Senate, delivering messages from one senator to another.

At Whitman, Forrest sang in the chorus of *H.M.S. Pinafore*, enjoyed Bridge Club, and presided over Chess Club. But his primary focus was politics. Forensic League and Hi-Y Club (and a public-speaking course) helped hone his oratorical skills. Although he lost a race for the junior class presidency, he was elected to other offices of the student government for three successive years. In his senior year, he led Jeff Fryman's successful campaign for student body president. Fryman, a maverick intellectual cynical about student government, was determined to shake things up. For one thing, he appointed another maverick, Forrest Church, as chairman of the Ways and Means Committee. Essentially the financial arm of student government, the group raised money by running the concession stands at football and basketball games.

Compared with the other student government officers, mostly exquisitely good-looking girls, Forrest said, "Jeffrey and I were like weeds in a very carefully cultivated garden . . . I smoked my pipe during those meetings, or I would knit."

His grandmother Clark had taught him to knit. His parents, hoping he would steer clear of cigarettes, had allowed him a pipe. The image—eccentric, raffish, rule-bending, and gender-tweaking—is telling.[35]

In September 1965, for a senior English assignment, Forrest dashed off an essay entitled "My Future." Its content shows that politics was the very sea he swam in. Its style demonstrates a casual, slovenly approach to schoolwork:

"An environment that has enveloped me, as a result of my father and his occupation," the essay begins, "is the general factor that has contributed most highly to my future plans and present ideals." His experience as a Senate page, he went on, was "the final persuasion I needed for a self-compulsion towards a similar goal my father had already reached . . . my life revolves around politics."[36]

No matter how awkward the prose, the meaning was clear. Forrest

would follow in his father's footsteps. However, Frank Church unknow-
ingly conveyed another legacy that would not be clarified for years. Every
senator in those days was given a copy of the so-called Jefferson Bible,
The Life and Morals of Jesus of Nazareth, a version of the New Testament
Gospels edited by Thomas Jefferson to cleanse it of miracles and other
notions that offended his Enlightenment-era deism. In Jefferson's render-
ing, Jesus was a good and wise moral teacher. There was no room for
Jesus as the Christ, the son of God who was resurrected from the dead.

This clear-eyed vision meshed neatly with what was, in Forrest
Church's view, essentially a secular humanist household. Having given
up on Catholicism, Frank Church embraced an unspoken credo best
summed up in Jefferson's words: "It is in our deeds and not in our words
that our religion must be read." Bethine Church's Presbyterianism was
lukewarm at best, heated up only at holiday time. She sometimes attended
church in Boise, rarely in Bethesda. It was Bethine's more devout mother
who taught Forrest his bedtime prayers. In his boyhood, Forrest picked
up stray bits of Bible lore at Sunday school from time to time. His occasional forays to a Presbyterian youth group in Bethesda are best defined
as expeditions to scope out girls.

Intellectual curiosity, not Christian devotion, drew Forrest to the Jefferson Bible. At the time, he was ten or eleven years old, lingering over
the family library while skipping school. It was the first time he had read
any of the Bible, and he was ignorant of Jefferson's Unitarian leanings.
Using a yellow marker, he highlighted in the family's Revised Standard
Version those passages that Jefferson had included in his reduction, carefully noting what was left in and what was left out. The omissions were
striking, but their import still eluded him.

"It was like a game, a puzzle," Forrest recalled. "And it was fascinating
to me. But its half-life was very short in terms of gripping my consciousness. Whether a seed was planted then that was on a slow gestation . . . I
don't know."[37]

If religion's role in Forrest Church's upbringing was minimal, a powerful moral vision nonetheless loomed large. Frank and Bethine shared a

deeply felt belief in justice, fairness, and equality in human relations. Their benevolence was not the abstract variety that loved "humanity" while ignoring the human beings in front of them. One of Frank's staff members regarded him as the kindest of human beings, a man who "never failed to say thank you . . . never raised his voice at a staff member . . . never berated one person in front of another." Bethine cheerfully considered her Pemberton Street house as a home-away-from-home for many of Forrest's high school and college friends. With enough casseroles stuffed in the freezer, she could feed them all. When the family of Seiichi Tsurumi, whose father was a Japanese diplomat, was about to move back to Tokyo, the Churches invited him to live with them so that he could remain at Whitman for his final semester of high school.[38]

In the political realm, this spirit of open-minded goodwill was expressed in an initially moderate Democratic progressivism that grew more pointedly liberal over the years. As a shrewd politician, Senator Church knew just how far to the left he could lean. To avoid offending conservative Idahoans, he shunned gun control. Yet he consistently backed wilderness protection laws opposed by mining and timber companies and ranchers. On civil rights and Vietnam, the senator staked out positions out of step with many of his white, my-country-right-or-wrong constituents.

As Forrest came of age, in the early sixties, the African-American struggle for equal status in America took on a new urgency. Blacks and their allies battled to integrate schools and dismantle walls of discrimination in employment and housing. They went to court, organized, marched, and sat in. A fourteen-year-old Forrest played a bit part in that history, turning up at the Washington Mall on August 23, 1963, for the great march that culminated in Martin Luther King's "I Have a Dream" speech.

Few blacks lived in Idaho, yet Frank Church was their committed advocate in Washington. His efforts were crucial to passage of the Civil Rights Bills of 1957, 1964, and 1965. In the eyes of some activists, though, he did not go far enough. But he was not constantly peering over his shoulder at voters in Idaho. According to Church's biographers, his natural bent was "for the middle ground, for building coalitions, and for what seemed politically tenable. Compromise, to him, was the very stuff of legislation."[39]

For a while, this balancing act would mark the senator's approach to the Vietnam War as well. He had entered the Senate as a traditional Cold Warrior, but his views began to shift as he surveyed a world in flux. The United States, he believed, should not prop up just any Third World dictator in the name of anticommunism. If the nation followed that course, it would inherit the dubious mantle of colonialism. Increasingly, he saw the Vietnam conflict in those terms, as an unwinnable quagmire. In public, he remained cautious, supporting the Tonkin Gulf Resolution, an act that legitimized President Johnson's aggressive war policies. It was a vote Church soon regretted. By late 1964, his deepening doubts came to light in the radical magazine *Ramparts*. The resulting flak came at him from all sides—the president, fellow senators, Idaho voters, his father-in-law, even Bethine. "I fought him tooth and toenail for three months," she wrote, "because I felt strongly that President Johnson knew better." Early the next year she came around to his point of view. Meanwhile, he declined to vote to cut off funds for the troops, as the Democratic senators Morse (Oregon) and Gruening (Alaska) had—that would be political suicide— but he was willing to write opinion pieces challenging administration policy in such national forums as *The New York Times* and *The Washington Post*. By Forrest's final semester of high school, in 1966, Church and fellow senators on the Foreign Relations Committee were holding hearings that amounted to a national teach-in on Vietnam.[40]

Forrest wasn't yet focused on Vietnam. He was thinking about where to apply to college. He approached the matter the same way he approached every academic endeavor at this time, casually and carelessly. Without consulting his parents and without visiting a single campus, he picked out Stanford and three public universities: Wisconsin, North Carolina, and Colorado. To his father's longtime friend Carl Burke he wrote a letter, in longhand on lined notebook paper, requesting a recommendation to

Stanford, his "first choice school." Burke's letter to the university, while offering mere generalities about the applicant, noted that the boy's father was a Stanford alumnus. Although Forrest's SAT scores were strong—749 in math and 624 in verbal by his senior year—he graduated only 114th in a Whitman High class of about 600. Seventeen members of his class, but not Forrest, were National Merit Scholar finalists. By his own admission, Forrest Church made the cut at Stanford "by virtue of being my father's son."[41]

Two

Ticking Time Bomb

There are moments in history when the sense of extremity takes on a life of its own . . .
Was not the old order, however one understood it, passing?

—TODD GITLIN, ON THE YEAR 1967

On the day before his eighteenth birthday, Forrest Church and thirteen hundred other freshmen filed into Stanford's Memorial Auditorium for their official welcome to college. Their hosts were the student body president, the chaplain, and the university president.

David Harris had unexpectedly vaulted to student leadership the previous spring by calling for the elimination of fraternities, legalization of marijuana, and an end to university cooperation with conduct of the Vietnam War. The bearded Harris—dressed in the now de rigueur student uniform of work shirt, jeans, and granny glasses—exhorted his fellow students to redefine education, not as something passively done to them, but as a life-changing process initiated on their own. Then the dean of the chapel took to the podium. The Reverend Davie Napier's "The Gospel According to the Beatles," with its evocation of "all the lonely people," earned him a standing ovation. It remained for President Wallace Sterling, a former history professor, to stand up for the status quo. No matter how eager for reform, students were obliged to obey the law and to respect the guiding hand of reason. "Candor and impulse," he said, "are not viable substitutes for analysis and judgment."[1]

In the fall of 1966, Stanford University was on the cusp of change. In the next four years its students would indeed shed the role of passive educational consumers and take to the streets, demonstrating for educational reform and against the Vietnam War. Sex, drugs, and rock 'n' roll would shake up student life. Through it all, impulse would wrestle with reasoned judgment. By Forrest Church's final college term, in the spring of 1970, antiwar protests would virtually shut the campus down.

The Stanford of Frank Church's era, the 1940s, had been a solid regional university. By the time his son arrived, however, it was rocketing into national prominence, if not quite at the pinnacle it occupies today. Wallace Sterling, president from 1949 to 1968, and his provost from 1955 to 1965, the hard-driving electrical engineering professor Fred Terman, had transformed their sleepy campus into a leading research university. Terman saw the future, and it was no longer an ivory tower but an alliance of government, business, and academia. He refashioned Stanford along Cold War lines, with a premium placed on "applied knowledge" and defense-related technology. Two of the university's iconic scientific institutions were built under his aegis: the two-mile-long Stanford Linear Accelerator, and "the Dish," a 150-foot-diameter radio antenna in the surrounding foothills, a joint venture between the Stanford Research Institute and the U.S. Air Force. The meticulous Terman kept a notebook to record every professor's productivity. Little wonder that humanities professors despised him, while departments of engineering, physics, biochemistry, and quantitative-oriented political science soared to world renown. By the mid-sixties five Nobel Prize laureates adorned the faculty.[2]

Forrest Church's Stanford was bucolic enough to retain the nickname "The Farm." Its 8,800 acres were graced by buildings in the Spanish Mission style, with red-tile roofs, sandstone walls, and arch-covered walkways. Fountains, it seemed, were everywhere. It was a sun-filled paradise for outdoor lunches, lolling on the grass, or a Frisbee toss between classes. No longer content to offer a fashionable education to California children of privilege, Stanford now admitted only one of every five applicants to its eucalyptus groves. It lagged only slightly behind Harvard and Yale in enticing Merit Scholars. Across San Francisco Bay, in Berkeley, the University of California already flashed a more bohemian style, part countercultural, part politically radical. A few years earlier the Free Speech movement—with its denunciations of the university as a factory for producing student robots—had changed Berkeley's profile dramatically. At Stanford, fraternities continued to dominate the scene. So far, David Harris was the exception to Stanford's apple-cheeked wholesomeness. As one professor remarked, "They're just nice upper-class kids. You're more like an obstetrician than a teacher here."[3]

Still, niceness could take these kids far afield. In the early sixties, Stanford was the leading supplier of graduates for the Peace Corps. Each spring nearly 10 percent of the senior class signed up and headed abroad. On the domestic front, the evolving crusade for civil rights beckoned. Allard Lowenstein, who later sparked the "Dump Johnson" movement, briefly appeared on the Stanford stage, in title an assistant dean of men and political science instructor, but in truth a Johnny Appleseed for liberal activism. Every issue this charismatic provocateur touched, David Harris observed, became "a pressing question of emergency proportions." At Lowenstein's prompting, more Stanford students traveled to Mississippi in 1963–64 to volunteer in historic, and dangerous, campaigns to register black voters than those of any other school. One of those sojourners was Harris. He was so radicalized by the experience that he soon dismissed Lowenstein's liberalism as timid and ineffective.[4]

On the night of October 20, 1966, the clash between old and new Stanford took its first dramatic turn. A swarm of Delta Tau Delta fraternity brothers surrounded Harris on campus, threw him to the ground, and shaved off the long hair they found so offensive. Harris surprised his captors by not resisting, and then began preaching to them about educational reform. Taken aback, they spared his beard and skulked away. *The Stanford Daily*'s accounts in the next few days heralded changing times. Harris was deemed the hero, the frat boys Neanderthals. That fall, on every front, it seemed, the old order was collapsing. The local chapter of Sigma Chi broke with the national organization to pledge a black student. Fiery orator Stokely Carmichael was scheduled to highlight "Black Power Day." Concerts by the emerging bands Jefferson Airplane and the Grateful Dead introduced the seductions of psychedelic rock. Wilbur Hall, the freshmen men's dorm, hosted a "happening" featuring another new San Francisco–based group, Big Brother and the Holding Company, with a whiskey-voiced singer named Janis Joplin. Trancos House, the section of Wilbur that housed Forrest Church and ninety other frosh, invited party guests to "return to the womb"—sandboxes, Tinkertoys, and finger paints included.[5]

In Trancos, Forrest shared a room with Hans Dankers, who had been valedictorian at a Bay Area high school. Already an antiwar activist, Hans was aware of Senator Church's opposition to the war well before arriving on campus. Once there, he discovered that the senator's son "Twig" he had read about was to be his roommate. Their shared relish for easygoing wit and humor made the two a good match. Hans rigged up a curtain of "love beads" for the perfect entrance to their bohemian pad. Scavenging on campus, they found a discarded plaster sculpture of a headless man to adorn the middle of the room. On the overhead light they attached the phrase "Sex Is Not Love." After Christmas break, Forrest hauled a saddle back from Idaho to add a zany Western touch.[6]

Forrest was not the only scion of celebrity in residence. Secretary of State Dean Rusk's daughter, Peggy, would scandalize some by marrying an African-American man. Win Brown, son of Winthrop Brown, ambassador to South Korea, would rent a house with Forrest and others during their junior and senior years. Sarah Spaght, daughter of Shell Oil chairman Monroe Spaght, would become Win's girlfriend and later wife. Next door to Forrest and Hans lived a future celebrity, Stanford's freshman quarterback, Jim Plunkett, who would eventually lead the Oakland Raiders to the Super Bowl.

In this turbocharged environment, there was no way Forrest could be quite the ringleader he had been in Bethesda. He was surrounded by too many valedictorians, star athletes, and student body presidents. All the same, Hans and Forrest's room soon emerged as a popular hangout. Lively debate over Vietnam took turns, and sometimes overlapped, with the pounding rhythms of the latest rock album. Forrest would corral passersby to come in and hear music proclaimed the greatest ever. At the start of his Stanford years, it was the Beatles; by the end, it would be Gustav Mahler. Stanford friends uniformly remember Forrest as smart, curious, thoughtful, voluble, witty, fun-loving, gregarious, and, above all, enthusiastic. This last trait was his most definitive.[7]

"I always have been a serial enthusiast," Church said. "Whatever I pledged my troth to, I did completely. I plumbed it as deeply as I possibly could, and immersed myself in it. And the odd thing would be that, three weeks later, it could have changed entirely . . . That is what has given me the necessary breadth to be a professional amateur, which is what I am . . . That explains, more than anything else, my passionate eclecticism."[8]

Spurred on by this lava flow of enthusiasm, Forrest sometimes tended to pontificate. Dialogue gave way to monologue. Pipe in hand, surrounded by an audience lapping up his opinions, he could seem full of himself. "Some people didn't know what to make of him or how to handle him," one classmate recalls. "There's just so much energy, and he's so articulate. One could sit in a room with Forrest and just talk forever." Another found his penchant for political discussion intimidating. Yet Kim Dunster, who dated him that fall, remembers a different Forrest, a young man willing to listen, deeply respectful of other's people's opinions.[9]

Paradoxically, Forrest had a shy side, usually hidden. Like some gregarious types, he could feel out of place when not the center of attention. Certain unstructured social situations, perfect for small talk, made him perfectly uncomfortable. Girls intimidated him, too, though those he dated rarely sensed his insecurity. He dodged that weakness by keeping a steady girl close at hand.[10]

Politics, by contrast, seemed like home. Bred to the life, Forrest gravitated naturally to running for office. In the first two weeks of freshman year, he entered the race to represent Trancos in the Legislature of the

Associated Students of Stanford University (LASSU). His opponent, Patrick Shea, relied on humor, putting over dorm urinals campaign signs saying, "Your future is in your hands. Go to bat for Pat." Forrest's more polished oratory, however, carried the day. Shea, sensing a kindred spirit in the victor, quickly became a friend. Following an eventual LASSU presidency, a Rhodes Scholarship, and Harvard Law School, he would join Senator Church's staff.[11]

A few months after this initial victory, Trancos members elected Forrest their house president. Not wanting both jobs, he resigned from LASSU and was replaced by another of his chums, Chris Norgaard. Forrest's father was delighted to hear of his son's presidency, calling it a "feather in your cap," but less pleased that Forrest, who had found ROTC to be "a morale killer," had chosen to drop out of the student military program: "As always, you make a very plausible case," the father wrote. "But I think you should have discussed this with me before making your decision. I can only hope it turns out for the best." The tone of this busy man's letters to Forrest, dictated and typewritten by a secretary, was respectful but sometimes distant. Comfortable with giving advice, he had a harder time conveying the extraordinary kindness for which he was famous. He knew that his son needed the occasional nudge. During a visit to San Francisco with Forrest to meet his father, Kim Dunster was surprised that the senator made a point of speaking with her alone, determined to get a sense of what his son was "planning to do with his life." She was offended that the senator didn't understand "how focused and compassionate" Forrest was. For both father and son, as they separately navigated the treacherous shoals of the late sixties, the sense of not quite knowing what to make of each other would only grow.[12]

Oddly enough, David Harris's war with the American military system eased Forrest Church's temporary entry into Stanford's student political system. What Forrest would "do with his life," for much of his freshman year, was to have a go at the family business. In February 1967, Harris stepped down from his LASSU presidency to protest the draft full-time. In short order, he dropped out of school and began leading the

Resistance. With Harris's second in command assuming leadership of LASSU, the job of vice president fell vacant. Overflowing with self-confidence, Forrest jumped into the race. According to *The Stanford Daily,* he was the first freshman in university history to run for a general student body office.[13]

Given the liberal tenor of the times, nearly every candidate claimed the banner of reform—from revamping liberal education to co-ed dorms to student representation in university governance. Forrest stood squarely in the middle of the pack, solemnly urging Stanford to be "a part of society, and not an island of its own." A *Daily* columnist scoffed that in Forrest's vague platform "the word freshman pops up in the most unusual places." His appeal "must perforce be limited to a shortsighted segment of that class." Nonetheless, the chutzpah-stoked freshman came in third among seven candidates, narrowly missing being included in a runoff for the position. When the normal electoral cycle resumed a few months later, Forrest plunged into the fray again. This time, he ran as the vice presidential candidate with graduate business student Pete Hansen. Theirs was an even more moderate platform, advocating a "change of old educational habits" through a "respectful and responsible confrontation with faculty and administration." Church's youthful "enthusiasm" was deemed the perfect complement to Hansen's experience. The pair proposed, among other things, that freshman grades be stricken from students' permanent records, along with the usual boilerplate about co-ed dorms and experimental modes of learning. Their platform emphasized that though both were "essentially opposed" to the war in Vietnam, LASSU officers should not use their positions as "a podium to express their personal views." In a press release to the *Daily,* Hansen and Church further underscored their distance from radicals like Harris: "We do not agree with the concept of student power . . . We substitute instead the concept of student influence." In the May election, Hansen and Church's careful moderation carried them only so far. Out of five slates they came in second.[14]

Throughout 1967, Senator Church worried about his son. Forrest's grades were disappointing. Cs in freshman English and math and science

courses were somewhat offset by Bs in other courses and As in a freshman seminar called "America in Transition." Perhaps Forrest was spending too much time running for office instead of hitting the books. In any
event, Frank urged his son not to let an election loss "get you down. Your
life has so many dimensions, opportunities and challenges, and campus
politics is one outlet among many." (In truth, Forrest viewed the LASSU
races as more of an adventure, a testing of his political muscle, than anything serious, but he was reluctant to let his father know that.) In September, the senator suggested that Forrest's greatest strength could be an
Achilles' heel: "Now, don't let any of your enthusiasms run away with
you. Strive for some semblance of balance and this should prove to be a
good year for you." By the next month, however, the contemporary drug
scene had him unnerved. Beer was one thing, but pot and acid presented
a "menace to life and health, quite beyond anything before. I know you
will keep your head," he wrote Forrest, "but I can't help worrying. After
all, life's not so bad even if it gets humdrum on occasion. Anyhow, the
notion that there is an escape hatch is a fantasy and a fraud."[15]

Senator Church had good reason to worry. America was in the throes
of epochal change. His World War II generation found the Age of Aquar-
ius inexplicable, but it could be equally baffling for the young. All the old
rules seemed tossed away. The time-honored route to the good life—work
and study hard, get a good job, get married and have children—was suddenly passé. In its place, Timothy Leary offered the impish injunction
to "turn on, tune in, and drop out." Social critics, from street-corner
pamphleteers and rock lyricists to university theorists and bestselling authors, launched an unrelenting assault on established values. Education
was an exercise in brainwashing, marriage a straitjacket, pursuing a career
an eternity of following mindless orders. Reason, the very bulwark of
Western civilization, was itself suspect. After all, reason—in the form of
JFK and Lyndon Johnson's brainy advisers—had led directly to the madness of Vietnam. The antidote was liberation, and nothing embodied
liberation more than the sirens of sex, drugs, and rock 'n' roll. Drugs
posed the most potent threat to tradition. If LSD and other hard drugs

proved unpredictable, bringing on either ecstasy or horror, marijuana reliably transported you to immediate bliss. By the late sixties, pot had migrated from the ghetto, barrio, and jazz joint to become ubiquitous on college campuses.

Forrest Church ignored his father's warning about marijuana. It's not clear when, but at some point he joined the many Stanford classmates who smoked pot. It became a regular experience for him, and hardly a guilty pleasure. Given the time and place, it was simply what one did, as common as beer drinking had been for his father's generation. His encounter with LSD would come a bit later.[16]

As much as rock 'n' roll, the Vietnam War was Forrest's collegiate background music. Antiwar fervor escalated every year he spent at Stanford. The subject of endless dorm-room bull sessions, the war prompted Forrest to invite several classmates to take a weekend trip to Boise. They were eager to meet a senator bold enough to lead the charge against Lyndon Johnson's folly. They returned to campus impressed by Church's unpretentious, down-to-earth manner and his courage in taking a stand so unpopular with his constituents.[17]

However unmistakable Forrest's antiwar views, he remained gun-shy about engaging in collective protest. The first significant opportunity arose when Hubert Humphrey arrived at Stanford on February 20, 1967, for a question-and-answer session with a panel of students at Memorial Auditorium. When he began defending the war, in his customary loquacious, combative manner, a host of students and professors wearing white peace armbands rose up and walked out. Afterward, protestors surrounded Humphrey's limo, chanting "Shame! Shame!" One of Forrest's activist friends, Bob Yeager, will never forget the moment: staring into the face, just a few feet away behind the glass, of a terrified vice president of the United States.[18]

Forrest was not present for this event. Nor did he take part in the sit-in during May 1968 against the expulsion of students who had demonstrated against CIA recruiting on campus. Nor in the massive Vietnam Moratorium marches of 1969. Nor in the nine-day occupation that year of Stanford's Applied Electronics Lab, which conducted secret military research. This was a curious position for someone outraged about the war's corrosive impact on American life, someone who by now defined America as "an imperialist empire, wanton in its disregard" of small nations like Vietnam. He supported friends like Pat Shea and Bob Yeager, who put their bodies on the line, but he simply could not join them. Except for the historic March on Washington in 1963, Forrest participated in no marches or demonstrations of any kind, and he was never arrested for civil disobedience.

If Forrest didn't like to play by the rules, what better way to do that than by publicly thumbing his nose at authority? Why didn't he do so? Because, he said, he feared even more the loss of identity, the loss of control, that being part of the mass required. In a throng, he was no longer in charge. What's more, he loathed confrontation. He was still the kid who refused to fight back. Sitting in would have rendered him vulnerable on both counts. "Almost everything I did politically," he said, "I did almost as a loner. I am crowd-averse." This wasn't a trait he was proud of, and he knew it smacked of arrogance. It was simply who he was.[19]

Forrest's friends believed he was also looking over his shoulder at his parents. According to Pat Shea, "Forrest's instinct was to be an observer." Forrest may have earned the nickname "Moral Man" because of his penchant for analytical reflection on ethical-political issues, but when talk shifted to action, Shea said, his deference to family brought him up against "the boundary line of acceptability." Chris Norgaard put the matter directly: "There was a tension within Forrest about how far he could go so as not to embarrass or jeopardize his father's career." For now, he kept himself in check.[20]

Forrest wasn't just Moral Man, of course. He was also a high-spirited, fun-loving college freshman. By the end of the year, Forrest and six friends, including Norgaard, banded together to pledge Theta Xi fraternity. The freshmen resolved to be accepted en masse, or they would look elsewhere for a fraternal home. Since Theta Xi was one of the weaker fraternities, far outside the social fast lane, it agreed to the group's unusual demand. Later that year Forrest learned that he and his father not only shared the same fraternity but lived in the same room at the frat house.

Within this Gang of Seven, Dalton Denton was Forrest's closest college friend. "He introduced me to scotch and Beethoven," Forrest wrote, "two habits he had picked up at Exeter . . . He was the closest thing to a sophisticate that I had ever encountered." According to Norgaard, Denton was tall and slim, preppy handsome behind horn-rim glasses, and "urbane but not pretentious." His manner was self-assured, his smile dazzling. "If there wasn't a party happening," classmate Carla Berg said, "he'd make one." In all things social, Denton's sophistication outshone Forrest. His gentlemanly manners made him a magnet to co-eds. Soon he and Carla became an item, often double-dating with Forrest and Kim Dunster. Forrest's description of Denton—"blithe of spirit, serious about things but not at all somber"—applied just as well to himself. Both young men charged full-throttle into pursuits both serious and blithe. They took turns probing the depths, then jesting and playing with each other. They were brothers.[21]

In the fall of 1967, at the start of sophomore year, Forrest and his pledge class moved into the Theta Xi house. His feelings about fraternities were already ambivalent. In fact, his plan had called for his buddies to "take over" the organization, whatever that meant, but Hell Week quickly put that naïveté to rest. One night after a particularly raucous party, the pledges were wakened at three a.m. and ordered outside in their underwear. Stuffing a piece of liver inside his shorts was but the first act Forrest refused to perform. Everything that followed amounted to low-key hazing by fraternity standards, but Forrest found it all uniformly humiliating. He declined to play by these rules. Two weeks later, he deserted his buddies to hermit himself in an apartment in the foothills beyond campus. "Dalton was hurt and angry when I left," Forrest wrote. "He accused me of petulance and unwarranted pride. I accused him of succumbing to a foolish, childish set of rules and rites." Then the brothers stopped speaking to each other.[22]

The rest of that year Forrest felt estranged from friends. But just before spring break, in March 1968, he and Denton reconciled. One day they drove back and forth between Stanford and the sea, wrestling with the great questions of life and death. In a burst of romantic fervor, "part of a desperate attempt to feel life deeply," Forrest declared that he didn't expect to live beyond the age of twenty-five. Denton, more at peace with himself, urged Forrest simply to accept who he was. In a kind of blessing, he quoted Saint Augustine: "Love, and do what you will." But it was Denton who died soon thereafter. While on a ski trip to Aspen, Colorado, with other students—but not the sports-averse Forrest—he fell ill and retreated from the slopes. When his friends returned at the end of the day, they found him dead. Denton had died of pneumonia.

Denton's death was the defining moment of Forrest's young life. Never before had he brushed so closely against life's random unfairness. This was not just the stuff of Romantic poets and rock lyrics. He had lost a love. He nearly dropped out of school. For weeks, he was filled with grief and rage. He would pound his hand into a wall until he could no longer bear the pain. "I had no context for dealing with this rage," Forrest said. "I couldn't believe the inanity of every conversation or every action I saw." From this enormous early loss, he eventually extracted a sense of life's fragility and preciousness. Denton's death would be the bridge "to a more dedicated search which led through history and philosophy into religion, and only a long time later to God." In the meantime, God was far away, and grief and rage fueled already smoldering discontents. Abroad, the horrors of Vietnam only worsened. Closer to home, student government seemed worthy only of parody.[23]

Enter Vicky Drake. A Stanford co-ed who moonlighted as a topless dancer in a local bar, Drake ran for student body president in the May '68 election. She signed up Forrest, who had made a name for himself as a comer in student politics, as her campaign manager. Forrest's duties were minimal, as were the candidate's clothes. The pouty-lipped blonde would flounce into a men's dorm lounge wearing a trench coat, accompanied by her husband, a diminutive Charlie Chaplin lookalike. A tape player–

bearing Forrest would crank up the music. And Drake would shed her coat and dance, wearing only a G-string. Part sheer adolescent rebellion, part anarchic wail in the wake of his friend's death, this was Forrest's "Yippie moment." He was laughing to hide his pain.[24]

When campaign posters of a nude Ms. Drake appeared all over campus, most of the Stanford community took it in stride. A campus wit defined the Drake campaign as a series of "visual utterances." *The Stanford Daily* published a bit of student doggerel in her honor. One columnist was not amused, grousing that Drake wasn't so much topless as brainless. The paper's editorial board suggested that student government mattered so little that no one need bother voting. But in the heaviest turnout in years, Vicky Drake ran second in a runoff with Denis Hayes, later famous as the founder of Earth Day. Then her fifteen minutes of fame stretched into a half hour. The September 1968 issue of *Playboy* featured a lot of photos of the naked beauty along with a little bit of text. "Although she lost the election," the piece concluded, "in our book Vicky's every inch a winner." As for Forrest, he was called into Provost Richard Lyman's office for a tongue-lashing about making a farce of student government, but emerged otherwise unscathed. Ridicule was exactly what he'd intended. His alienation from traditional American institutions and values was at its peak.[25]

Senator Church had warned about LSD's "menace to life and health." But in the spring of 1968, overwhelmed by angst and goaded by curiosity, Forrest decided to try it. Acid was readily available, and so were fellow travelers to assure his safety. Pat Shea, who did not partake, would serve as "designated driver"; Bob Yeager, who had used the drug before, would trip along with the neophyte Forrest. The result was a classic "good trip," complete with fits of giggling and the metamorphosis of the ordinary into the extraordinary. The trio wandered around campus, delighting in such exotica as garbage-can lids and sugar packets. Once in the car, with Pat driving, they discovered another marvel: traffic lights could actually turn themselves into biplanes. Up in the foothills, Forrest and Bob danced around like forest sprites. A beatific Forrest approached Pat, saying, "You have to experience this! This is love expanding my mind!"[26]

Little wonder that Forrest was dubbed "the ticking time bomb" that summer, when he joined his parents in Boise. Senator Church's staff never knew when his erratic bohemianism might harm his father, who was running for reelection in a tough campaign against ultraconservative Congressman George Hansen. Not that the experienced Church was running scared. His campaign slogan distanced the senator from the Johnson administration, portraying him as "Idaho's voice of independence." Thus, even Church's unpopular stance on Vietnam was turned on its head, transforming him into an iron-willed Marlboro Man standing up to the president of the United States. At the same time, he assailed federal gun-control laws and paid close attention to Idaho-friendly issues like agriculture and water rights.

This was also the man who in February, in a slashing Senate speech titled "Torment in the Land," rebuked the government for its "dangerous delusion of American omnipotence" in foreign affairs. The Vietnam War, he asserted, "brutalizes our culture," while the impact of racial discrimination threatened to explode into civil unrest. Usually, Church avoided confrontational politics, which, according to his biographers, he believed "ultimately destroyed the middle ground, reasonability, and the art of democratic persuasion." Yet this moderation rarely undermined the courage of his convictions. In the wake of Hansen's attacks on Church's pro-civil-rights record, the senator joined with neighbors in Bethesda to push for racial integration of the Kenwood Country Club.[27]

While in Boise, the Churches lived in the Clarks' big house on Idaho Street. During previous elections Forrest had been an integral part of the family portrait, expected to wear a smile and show up for parades and rodeos. This time he opted out. Forrest's hair was shaggy; his beard stretched to Rasputin-like proportions. He rigged out the hot, dank basement as his summer pad, painting the pipes in psychedelic black and red, silver and gold. While the stereo blasted out Cream and the Beatles, he smoked pot and pored over *The Communist Manifesto* and volumes of Russian history. (At Stanford, he had just completed courses on twentieth-century Russia and Communist China.) On the surface at least, he may have qualified as the most seditious person in Idaho. Congressman Hansen's staff was on to something; they spread rumors about Forrest's "San Francisco Hippy Club." Never mind that no self-respecting hippie would join anything deemed a club.[28]

Stan Zuckerman, a college student who worked on Frank Church's 1968 campaign and later became a psychoanalyst in Boise, remembered Forrest being so ambivalent about his father that he was paralyzed. He was torn between admiring his father and regarding him, in the idiom of the era, as a "sellout" who hadn't done enough to get the United States out of Vietnam. After spending several summers (in Boise and Bethesda) with Forrest and his family, Zuckerman came to define Forrest as a kind of orphan. His parents were so preoccupied with politics that their older son got lost in the shuffle. This was the downside of being the ever-independent, free-range kid. Even as he yearned to be free of his parents, he silently screamed for their attention, Zuckerman thought.[29]

The time bomb nearly exploded when Stan, Forrest, and his Bethesda girlfriend Kathy Kiilsgaard and a few other free spirits drove into the mountains of central Idaho to party. They swam in Red Fish Lake and sang Beatles tunes off key. And they drank and drank. Cases of beer were followed by watermelons laced with vodka. According to Zuckerman, Forrest grew very drunk, began shouting at Kathy, and then jumped into his Mustang and drove off "like a madman." Zuckerman, fearing Forrest would hurt himself or others, got into a car in pursuit. Forrest roared past U.S. Forest Service troopers, then raced in and out of a gas station (in the process breaking off the hose, which he'd left connected to the car). Driving back to the party site, he rammed through barricades set up by the troopers. Zuckerman had to plead with them not to arrest the senator's son. He agreed to take the keys away from Forrest, and they agreed to look the other way. "The senator's been real good to us," they explained. Senator Church's pro-conservation politics, it turns out, paid off in ways he never realized.[30]

During this period Forrest and his father were almost completely es-tranged. They could barely talk to each other. "My passions were so high and my experience and knowledge so thin," Forrest wrote much later. "I had stopped wearing a watch. I had stopped reading the newspaper. Every-thing that he had devoted his life to struck me as superficial and yet, when we talked, his advantage over me was great. He was thinking and I was feeling . . . When I could not explain what I felt, when he tripped up my arguments with logic, I was wounded and angry . . . Once I even burst into tears. I hated myself for this, for my inability to express adequately in words the truth I so deeply felt; and I hated my father for exposing this weakness by his quiet, if impatient, questioning. Ultimately, the only re-sponse left to me was simply to retreat into a vale of self-righteousness."[31]

Who could calm the troubled waters? Bethine intervened, to little avail. She had an explosive temper, but Peter Fenn, who was working on the campaign while sharing the basement pad with Forrest, gave her high marks for keeping her cool in this period. Jerry Brady, a young staff member who had gone to law school at Berkeley, tried to bridge the gap between bewildered father and alienated son. But Fenn was better posi-tioned to play the go-between. The senator usually kept his emotions well under control, but during a campaign stop in Idaho Falls, Fenn ob-served a clearly angry Frank Church. What kind of son, he demanded of Peter, wouldn't stand by his father in this election? Doesn't Forrest care if I win or lose? Doesn't he love me? Fenn explained that Forrest's disaffec-tion wasn't personal. Martin Luther King and Robert Kennedy had just been assassinated. The whole political system was "just a crock."[32]

It wasn't personal, of course, except that Forrest was desperately try-ing to forge an identity of his own. "You're the son of a famous person," Fenn explained years later. "You're trying to find out what the hell you want to do with your life. You're trying to find out if you're good at any-thing, or whether you're just Frank Forrester Church the Fourth."

By late summer, a truce was brokered, if not yet a full reconciliation. Bethine's mother, a gentle woman whom Forrest adored, persuaded her grandson to trim his hair and shave off that nasty beard. Forrest further agreed to go to Robinson Bar Ranch to film a TV campaign ad with the senator and a group of college students. In the piece, which lasted about fifteen minutes, Forrest appeared clean-shaven and soft-spoken, a model of filial loyalty. What viewers didn't see was a behind-the-scenes under-current of raw emotion.

One day the senator invited Peter and Forrest to take an afternoon walk at the ranch. Along the way they discussed issues, their differences surfaced, and they argued a bit. It was a rerun of Idaho Falls, with Peter acting as middleman, but this time the scenario ended on a positive note. Tears welled up in both father and son. They embraced. The crisis was over, the time bomb defused. Despite Richard Nixon's huge victory in the state that November, Frank Church was sent back to the Senate with 61 percent of the vote.[33]

Forrest's final two years at Stanford were marked by paradox. The more heated the campus grew with debate and confrontation, the more he retreated. Conflict-averse, he lived off-campus, ignored student poli-tics, and bore down on his studies. And he began a relationship with the woman who would become his wife.

For most of sophomore year, Forrest had lived alone. Without the lively presence of Dalton Denton, socializing seemed pointless. He was part hermit, part impish prankster. At the start of junior year, however, Win Brown recruited Forrest to join a few other men, including Chris Norgaard, in renting a house in Los Altos, ten miles south of Palo Alto. All of Stanford, it seemed, was moving off-campus. Many students set up communes, with shared meals and shared sex based on countercultural principles. This, however, was no commune, just a group of guys who enjoyed hanging out with one another. Certainly, the pet goat named Mildred (alongside two cats and a dog) lent a waggish air to the enter-prise; pot smoking was commonplace; and a communal dinner brought everyone to the same table once a week or so.[34]

"It was not self-important or overly self-absorbed," Win Brown's girl-friend, Sarah Spaght, said. "People saw each other when they could and enjoyed evenings and smoked the odd joint together and listened to music.

Sometimes we'd drink wine because we had concluded that wine was cheaper than milk . . . It was a nice remove from the politics of the campus."[35]

Indeed, activist students such as Gary Maes regarded their friend Forrest as AWOL. While they were on campus manning the barricades, Forrest's absence "seemed like a breach of faith. We've got a revolution going on here, and what's he doing, off contemplating his navel?"[36]

Among other things, Forrest was contemplating the symphonies of Gustav Mahler. As a birthday present (in September of 1968 or 1969), Frank and Bethine gave him a complete set, performed by the New York Philharmonic under Leonard Bernstein. It became a cherished possession, and he and Win Brown set out to absorb every measure of these Late Romantic masterworks. They would listen for hours, and then discuss the possible meanings. According to Brown, Forrest's curiosity was endless, his ability to teach himself masterful. Mahler was only one segment of this musical self-education: "He started with Bach and worked his way all the way through to modern composers . . . reading about them, listening to their music." Because he loved the music so passionately, he decided to take piano lessons. But after two brief and humiliating attempts, then and a year or so later, he realized that his talents lay elsewhere.[37]

At the university, Forrest's courses were now heavy on history and literature. Finally, achievement matched ability; most of his grades were As. He rounded out his history major with several seminars. English courses ranged from Shakespeare to American literature to contemporary drama. Enthralled by several courses on Russian literature in translation, he took another in the Russian language. Four quarters of Spanish completed his foreign-language requirement. His favorite course was an introduction to poetry, taught by William M. Chace, later president of Wesleyan University and Emory University. "That's when I started writing," Forrest said. "He helped give me a voice." For the time being, his was the voice of doggerel.[38]

Forrest held on to some of this juvenilia, perhaps as a reminder of how young and foolish he once was. These poems are filled with fantasy ("Rapping on my toadstool / Stood a dreary Nhome [sic] from Slithe") or sexual yearning ("Youthful body begs carresses [sic] / Yet her shadow holds me shy") or early death ("betty bouncer's recipe will lead you finally to your grave / . . . I will blink and burp and bid farewell to all this crap"). Most striking, though, is a clear disgust with the American political scene. "America #2" cites the murders of Robert Kennedy and JFK and laments that "laws were forgotten before they were written." In several poems, the American flag symbolizes a misbegotten war and unthinking patriotism. Decades later, taking back the flag from the right wing would become central to his political-religious mission.[39]

In the first weeks of Forrest's junior year, Amy Furth came into his life as a counterweight to all this angst. She was tall, good-looking, doe-eyed, ash-blond, and just a freshman. Amy hailed from an affluent family in Lafayette, east of Berkeley. Her father, Gordon, had been valedictorian of his class at Berkeley and editor of the student newspaper. He married its managing editor, Nina Wynne, earned an MBA at Harvard, and went to work for the accounting firm Arthur Andersen. In 1956, he joined the executive ranks of Marcona Corporation, a giant San Francisco–based mining and shipping company with assets from New Guinea to Peru. From 1960 to 1964, when Amy turned fourteen, the family lived in Lima, Peru.[40]

Forrest and Amy quickly became devoted and inseparable. He nicknamed her the Doob. Amy may have officially resided in a dorm, but by the following year she was living most of the time with Forrest. Her Los Altos housemates came to recognize Amy's endearing qualities—kindness, authenticity, intelligence, and quiet grace. She possessed a steadying calm and self-control that balanced Forrest's boisterous effervescence. In some ways, she seemed older, more intense and serious than he. She respected boundaries. The men would joke that they'd better not do something because Amy thought they shouldn't. "She had a sense that, if left to our own devices, we would be irresponsible," Win Brown said. "And she was right."[41]

Opportunities for going astray abounded. For the class of 1970, their final spring quarter was especially turbulent, marked by the most campus violence in Stanford's history. In one episode after another, debate gave way to force. At the end of March, a faculty vote to grant partial credit for ROTC courses prompted student rioters to break windows at ROTC headquarters, the president's office, and other campus buildings. A few days after sheriff's deputies arrested two dozen people at a sit-in at the Old Union in late April, arsonists burned down a section of the Center for Advanced Study in the Behavioral Sciences. In May, the U.S. invasion of Cambodia touched off pitched battles between window-smashing Stanfordites and club-wielding policemen. The killing of four students on May 4 by panicked National Guardsmen, at Kent State in Ohio, further inflamed student outrage. Demanding an end to business as usual, collegiate leaders across the nation called for a moratorium on classes. According to *The Stanford Daily*, at the height of the strike only 20 percent of classes were meeting in the university's School of Humanities and Sciences.[42]

Forrest's account of this period in his first book, *Father and Son*, exaggerates the extent of his youthful rebellion. He was not, in fact, "manning the barricades" to shut down the university, nor was he living in a "commune." These were not his chosen roles. But the book honestly records his deep estrangement from an "insane war" and the "fraud" of conventional politics. Only later could Forrest speak with pride of his father's efforts to work within the system to end the war. That spring Senator Church reached across the aisle to collaborate with Senator John Sherman Cooper, Republican of Kentucky, to cut off funds for U.S. troops in Cambodia after June 30. Their Cooper-Church Amendment passed in the Senate, only to die in a House-Senate conference committee.[43]

Taking advantage of a shut-down university came naturally to Forrest Church. He couldn't abide lectures, so his attendance in such courses was catch-as-catch-can anyway. "I was creating a unique identity for myself," he said, "and that was going to be done independently of institutions and authorities." He preferred seminars, where he could showcase his flair for discussion and debate. In the wake of Cambodia, most of his classes weren't meeting at all. Three of his four professors dispensed with grades that term and simply recorded a "pass." All the same, he managed to graduate "with distinction."[44]

But what to do next year? And how could Forrest avoid the draft? His housemates vividly recall Forrest's howl of protest in December 1969 when he learned that he had drawn a low number in the draft lottery and so would likely serve in the despised military unless he found a way out. He prepared four alternative plans. The first made no sense at all. He was accepted to Stanford's law school. But he had absolutely no interest in the law, and law school enrollment would not have kept him out of the draft anyway. Second, he followed in the footsteps of earlier Stanford idealists by signing up for the Peace Corps. This seemed like a safe bet, but he also opted for the one sure thing, divinity school, whose students remained exempt from the draft, lottery or no lottery. He was accepted by the Pacific School of Religion, in Berkeley, which had come to his attention because a PSR professor, Wayne R. Rood, was serving as acting dean of the Stanford chapel. Finally, Forrest explored the possibility of becoming a conscientious objector. This would keep him out of the military and busy changing military hospital bedpans. However praiseworthy among antiwar crusaders, CO status might also detonate the Forrest Church "time bomb." His father would pay the price in his 1974 reelection campaign.[45]

None of these options was wholly satisfying. Further complicating Forrest's confusion was the belief that the times were truly revolutionary and the future highly unpredictable. "We were not living to plan a future," he said. "We were living year to year." At the time, only two things were crystal-clear. Forrest was determined to avoid the draft, and to marry Amy Furth.[46]

Gordon Furth, by now executive vice president of Marcona, wasn't initially keen on the idea. After all, his daughter was a mere nineteen and her college education only half complete. And though Forrest was the son of a U.S. senator, he seemed to lack direction. Ultimately, Furth gave in, and the couple was married in the Furths' huge backyard on May 30,

1970. By and large, the affair followed convention. Forrest wore formal wear and appeared clean-shaven except for a mustache. Amy did without a veil and adorned her hair with flowers. Rev. Wayne Rood officiated before three hundred guests, including several U.S. senators. Frank Church himself nearly missed the ceremony because of hectic negotiations over the amendment to limit U.S. forces in Cambodia. "We were afraid a filibuster would keep him at the Senate," Amy's mother told *The New York Times*.[47]

Only the vows written by Forrest and Amy flouted tradition. Despite "a world of turmoil torn by violence," they promised to nurture their love and to be good parents. Amy vowed to "try always to meet all people without violence." More incendiary was Forrest's pledge "never to bear arms, nor to serve in the military." When Bethine learned that morning that Amy and Forrest planned to hand out leaflets bearing these pacifist vows to wedding guests, she was apoplectic. If word got out, she feared a media frenzy. Already the Cooper-Church Amendment was being damned as "defeatist, disloyal, and worse." She made her own vow, to skip the ceremony. Then Senator Church, always adroit at compromise, arranged a middle ground acceptable to all parties: the vows would remain, but they would not be circulated to guests. In the aftermath, political damage was limited. Only the newspaper in Twin Falls, Idaho, and the armed forces publication *Stars and Stripes* paid any notice.[48]

At the time of the wedding, Forrest and Amy had been accepted by the Peace Corps and were scheduled to begin training in July. Senator Church's former aide, Jerry Brady, arranged a plum assignment for them. Now assistant director of the Corps, Brady had recently scoured the Caribbean for possible placements and found one in the Grenadines, on the island of Bequia, a chic vacation spot for well-to-do tourists. As a Church loyalist, Brady later acknowledged, he was doing his best "to help [Forrest] not go to war—by any means necessary." But Peace Corps service, whether set on an idyllic isle or not, might only defer young men from the military. It would not exempt them. After completing their service, they could still be drafted. In fact, some insistent draft boards were ordering volunteers back from abroad in the middle of their Peace Corps tours of duty. What's more, this option would have interrupted Amy's education.[49]

So Forrest looked elsewhere for relief. In late July, following a honeymoon in St. Croix, he filed for conscientious objector status with his Boise draft board. This was risky business, indeed, not only because of the obvious political ramifications, but because gaining CO status was as unusual as sighting Vietcong soldiers along the Ho Chi Minh Trail. It rarely happened. This was because successful applicants had to be opposed to involvement in all wars, not just the Vietnam War, and their opposition had to be based on "religious training and belief." Forrest had trouble on both counts.

The essay Forrest submitted to his draft board twisted fact. It emphasized his Christian upbringing, though neither parent cared much for religion, and his attendance at church was infrequent. At college, he wrote, he had encountered thinkers who challenged his faith. But, in the end, "Christianity has withstood the test of my wanderings, and I have returned to the teaching of Christ as the closest expression of my thought . . . with a stronger belief in God." This was simply not true. At the time he did not accept any God concept. The vague "conscience as spiritual consciousness" that Forrest cited was more an indication of his spiritual restlessness than of theological resolution. Even less did he hail, as implied, the man Jesus as Christ, the son of God. One genuine note surfaced in his mention of Dalton Denton. His friend's death, Forrest wrote, pushed him to "search inwardly for that part of my own being that might be immortal."[50]

Forrest's CO packet also included a copy of his wedding vows and several supporting letters. Senator Church wrote that, while he did not agree with his son's pacifism, he regarded it as sincere, in keeping with his lack of interest in guns and abhorrence of violence. In a similar vein, Amy Furth Church described her new husband as "a truly gentle soul." In an effort to help Forrest pass the religious litmus test, Wayne Rood's well-meaning letter probably made matters worse. Forrest, he noted, did not "use words like 'God' or 'divine' often, but his reverence for Life is clearly spiritual in grounding and religious in quality."[51]

From the start, the CO gambit was unlikely to pass muster. Forrest was simply not a full-fledged pacifist. If pressed, he would have to admit that his opposition was to the Vietnam War, not to all wars. Forrest soon rescinded his application. Perhaps he could not stomach his own disingenuousness. Unquestionably, his action would have threatened his father's career. His essay and Rood's letter, however, did point to a bent that was spiritual, if not exactly religious.

The origins of Forrest's spirituality were something of a mystery, even to himself. They certainly did not lie in a family that put religion at the center of their lives. Frank and Bethine respected it, but mostly at a distance. Forrest's boyhood smattering of religious instruction did not make a deep impression. His encounter with the Jefferson Bible was significant only in retrospect. Certainly, the death of Dalton Denton was the pivotal event of his early life, etching into his consciousness life's precarious knife edge. In the larger world, the Vietnam War and the counterculture provoked continual debate about right and wrong, the nature of the good life, and the responsibilities of citizens. "I had come to hate politics," Forrest wrote. "I was desperately looking for something to believe in."[52]

Yet his thinking about religion remained inchoate, largely because it did not emerge from a clearly defined Christian perspective. He was not focusing on or reacting against, say, his mother's Presbyterianism. There was simply not enough there to inspire reflection. At Stanford, his readings in philosophy and religion were haphazard and unfocused. He took no courses in those fields. But he had been drawn to Wayne Rood's religious and philosophical speculation at Memorial Church. Like all his serial enthusiasms, this one grew out of a restless probing. Unlike them, it lasted all his life.

All this rumination did not take place in a vacuum. Being a very social animal, Forrest passed on what he had learned, whether his audience wanted to hear it or not. "All my time at Stanford," he recalled, "I am told that people called me Reverend Church. I was preachy. I did a lot of pastoral counseling, and I use the word 'pastoral' in quotes, because it was not God-grounded . . . I was really preaching to myself. But at some point my love of philosophy and my love of history joined, and I found myself most fascinated by the history of religion, of belief and believers . . . And that's what just set me on fire."[53]

Having run out of alternatives, Forrest Church headed to the Pacific School of Religion. "There's no question," he later acknowledged, "that I went to divinity school to avoid the draft."[54] Many of his contemporaries, outraged by U.S. involvement in the Vietnam War, did the same. But in Forrest's case, the escape from military service would lead to a life of service to humanity.

Three

Scholar-in-Residence

*That is happiness; to be dissolved
in something complete and great.*

—WILLA CATHER

Desperate to avoid the draft, desperate to find something to believe in, Forrest Church was not alone. The same could be said of countless young men of the Vietnam era who followed those instincts into a seminary. Yet Forrest's immediate concerns need to be understood in an even larger context, for many of his attitudes toward religion mirror broader trends among his generation.

Sociologists define Baby Boomers as Americans born between 1946 and 1964. The oldest of them, who came of age during the sixties, though hardly monolithic, possessed a remarkable generational cohesiveness and sense of identity. As they approached adulthood, many questioned established values at every turn. The consequent debates, which raged over politics, civil rights, the environment, gender roles, abortion, and homosexuality, also extended into the realm of religion.

Whether they remained within the faiths of their youth, switched affiliations, dropped out, or stayed unaffiliated, older Boomers approached religion with the skeptical, free-wheeling attitudes born of their era. They tended to distrust institutions. They were given to experimentation, blending different religious traditions into a new syncretism, or switching easily from one denomination to another. Open to disparate paths to truth, they paid special heed to tolerance. Their sense of entitlement, nurtured by several decades of affluence and permissive parenting, led them to a subjective, deeply personal approach to religion. Hence they moved from an ethic of self-denial to one of self-fulfillment, shaped by modern psychotherapy. Authenticity, the touchstone of sixties culture, was revered; religious institutions thought to be without it were scorned as hypocritical or irrelevant. A majority of Boomers believed in God, but the concept proved increasingly elastic—God as life force, divine creative power, or sacred web of being. The more highly educated the Boomer, the more likely the abandonment of orthodox ideas of God altogether. Even among older Boomers who disdained churches and synagogues, interest in spirituality thrived. Some practiced ancient Asian meditative traditions (often modified for Westerners). Others were drawn to Native American or pagan, feminist-inspired rites that brought them in touch with nature and all of humanity. In any case, the spirit of the age proclaimed that one could be spiritual whether one was conventionally religious or not.[1]

Of course, not all older Boomers matched this profile. The best fit occurred with those most influenced by sixties countercultural values. Among those least influenced by these values or, indeed, put off by them, there was in fact a resurgence of traditional faith. They may have danced to rock music and worn the occasional tie-dyed T-shirt, but they abhorred any undermining of time-honored patriotism and gender roles. They may have agreed with other Boomers about the need for authenticity in religion and an ethic of self-fulfillment, but they refused to give up on God. Orthodoxy was their mighty fortress. Besieged by a popular culture they thought immoral and by a disdainful media and cultural-political establishment, they found shelter in their faith. In the loving arms of a personal God and the communal warmth of their churches, they could reaffirm their beliefs, gird their strength, and eventually return to society to battle for righteousness' sake.[2] By the eighties, many would join the powerful religious right. On the religious left, Forrest Church would take note. Armed with a blend of sixties skepticism, universalist tolerance, and his father's penchant for finding the middle ground, he would combat their efforts to claim sole possession of Bible, family, and country. The preparation for this great work came in seminary.

Pacific School of Religion was a small interdenominational institution situated in Berkeley, a block from the University of California. It was not one of the nation's premier theological schools, but it had a geographical advantage for the Church newlyweds: Forrest could begin his explorations of religion while Amy continued her undergraduate education at Cal. During his year at PSR, Forrest largely shut out the noise of nearby Berkeley. Composer John Adams, living in Berkeley in the same era, remembered a Telegraph Avenue lined with "burned-out street people," "adolescent runaways," and street vendors selling "hash pipes, tie-dyed T-shirts, and Vietcong flags that smelled of patchouli and verbena."[3] But Forrest was too involved in his studies to pay attention to such distractions. After Stanford's sophistication, he was initially put off by some of PSR's teaching styles. His Old Testament professor, for example, required heavy doses of memorization. But since Forrest had never read these books of the Bible, he soon grew intrigued by their stories, poetry, and proverbs. Another professor treated his students like middle-schoolers, forcing them to write a one-page summary of each book they read.

"You would have thought," Forrest recalled, "that I would have found this to be an insult to my intelligence. In fact, I was so hungry for the pure knowledge that was being imparted that I just absorbed the first year of seminary course work like a sponge. And, by the end of that year, I believed in believers, I believed in belief. I didn't yet believe in God. The whole idea of trying to get inside the heads of people who were trying to understand the meaning of life was for me a natural academic segue from my own existential condition. Everything I touched was meaning."[4]

In terms of curriculum, as opposed to teaching methods, PSR was more indulgent. It allowed Forrest to range freely into courses on thinkers such as Kierkegaard and Nietzsche, whose outsider skepticism he found appealing, plus the likes of "Satire and Utopia" and "Religious and Ethical Values in Shakespeare." All his grades were As. During this year, Forrest also was exposed to two giants in the field. He studied the sociology of religion with the distinguished Berkeley sociologist Robert Bellah (later the co-author of *Habits of the Heart*), and through Wayne Rood he met John C. Bennett, the ethicist who had just stepped down as president of Union Theological Seminary in New York.[5]

To say that Rood was Forrest's mentor in this period understates his impact. Yet at first glance, such a close relationship seems unlikely. Rood was reared among very conservative Seventh Day Baptists and served as a teenaged driver for the flamboyant Los Angeles evangelist Aimee Semple McPherson. But over the years his horizons expanded. During World War II, he declared himself a pacifist but nonetheless enlisted in the army as a chaplain. He later earned a doctorate in theology at PSR. With Forrest Church, he shared a loathing for the war in Vietnam and a keen interest in the arts. For many years, he wrote and directed plays on religious themes. "I still considered myself something of a poet, something of a literary character," Forrest said, "and he indulged those pretensions of mine." For one course with Rood, Forrest wrote a screenplay, the content of which he could not remember later in life.

No doubt Rood took pleasure in the company of such a bright, enthusiastic student. He opened his home to Forrest one evening a week for dinner and conversation, and for the young man in search of a vocation, Rood's acceptance seemed like grace itself. "He took me under his wing," Forrest said. "He championed me. He was the first professor I ever had who loved me, and I loved him in return. It was his love that gave me the confidence that I was called to teach religion."[6]

Alongside Forrest's newfound interest in religious studies, his passion for classical music continued unabated. He and Timothy Pfaff, a PSR student who would become a classical music critic, spent their off-hours listening to Mahler and attending concerts of the San Francisco Symphony. Pfaff, a frequent guest at the Church apartment, observed an Amy with poise and grace quite beyond her years.

"She never did anything to hide her keen intelligence, but neither did she flaunt it . . . She was a beguilingly beautiful young woman who also seemed to have a strong inner compass." When Pfaff once showed up at the Church home wearing clothes "that were in the worst taste imaginable . . . she disguised her horror and found this remarkable way of making me feel really fashionable while—almost without my noticing it—changing a thing or two to turn down the wattage of my garish outfit. It's the kind of personal touch no one could teach, and she had it in spades." As for the two buddies' highbrow discussions of music and books, Amy honored them without being overly impressed. "I think she found us amusing and a little preposterous—but without doing so in a condescending way."[7]

After a single transformative year at Pacific School of Religion, Forrest had found his way. Inspired by Rood, exhilarated by the content of his courses, he was granted "a sense of belonging and some bona fides that I'd never really had before." Fascinated by religion, but not conventionally religious, he set out to become a scholar in the field. His aims were the aims of youth. He did not wish to acquire mere knowledge; he hoped to discover life's deepest meanings, to find himself face to face with truth itself.[8]

But if Forrest expected to become a first-rate scholar, he would have to transfer to a first-rate theological school. And before that, he would need to study Latin and Greek and familiarize himself with the basics of Western philosophy. Once again Wayne Rood led the way. He arranged for Forrest to serve a year's internship as Davie Napier's assistant in the Stanford chaplaincy, while Amy returned to her original alma mater to complete her bachelor's degree. Duties would be light, allowing Forrest ample time for study.

In the meantime, Amy and Forrest spent the summer of 1971 on a Marcona Corporation supertanker, *Pathfinder*, circumnavigating the globe. Embarking from Portland, Maine, the ship sailed the Atlantic, passed through the Mediterranean Sea, into the Indian Ocean, and across the Pacific to El Segundo, California. The couple, at sea for sixty-three days, got ashore for only ten hours, in Bahrain. Initially, Forrest tried his hand at writing an autobiographical novel, but quickly gave that up. Fiction simply wasn't his metier. Instead, he immersed himself in reading dozens of books he'd avoided during his undergraduate education. (Four of the five suitcases he brought were stuffed with reading matter.) Amy studied French and read Chaucer. In the evenings, he read aloud to her from *The Odyssey, The Magic Mountain* by Thomas Mann, and other classics. No matter how many gorgeous sunsets graced the *Pathfinder*'s stern, sailing around the world for this bookish couple was more Great Books course than romantic adventure.[9]

Back home, Forrest dove into his passions with uncommon exuberance. Having discovered Mahler, he could not get enough of the music. Encountering Thomas Mann, he devoured all of the master's works. The downside was that he sometimes neglected his wife. Benign, oblivious absorption in a subject could stray into noxious self-absorption. As a consequence, Forrest believed, the marriage suffered even early on:

"We would have friends over for dinner, she would cook, and afterwards I would play a Mahler symphony and not let people leave until they heard me recite [Milton's] 'Lycidas.' When I think back on what that must have been like, it's terrifying to imagine. What I was doing was sharing my love for these things with people I loved. I just couldn't help but assume that this would be as exciting to them as it was to me. So I really felt I was giving them all a great gift. It was imperious and insensitive, [but] it was animated by my own delight. I was an evangelist for everything that I discovered.

"I certainly didn't give [Amy] much space . . . I sucked the oxygen out of the room, and I regret that, but I was utterly unconscious of it at the time."[10]

Tim Pfaff, a keen observer of the couple, considered Forrest overly severe in his self-judgments, but he conceded that the young husband did have a bad habit of wounding Amy by making important decisions without consulting her. When they returned from their voyage, they seemed to Pfaff like a different couple: "There was an Ingmar Bergman–like silence and gravity to them. Their enthusiasm about the future seemed to mask a certain lack of zest about the present."[11]

At Stanford's Memorial Church, Forrest "counseled" students and conducted programs for them. One can envision sprightly discussions speculating on the existence of God, but the internship's primary, if unintended, function was to allow him to go his own way. Indeed, he was so negligent that his mentor threatened to fire him. He was busy taking introductory courses in Latin and classical Greek. On his own, he plowed through Greek philosophy, from the pre-Socratics through Plato and Aristotle, and onward to early modern thinkers such as Hobbes, Descartes, and Spinoza. Eager to get to his studies, he was up at five in the morning. He ate little, but drank lots of lapsang souchong tea. His weight plunged to 140 pounds, far too little for his six-foot, two-inch frame. Finally, heart palpitations sent him to the university infirmary. "There's nothing wrong with you," a doctor informed him, "that a little more sleep and lot less tea won't cure."[12]

Soon after, Forrest the ascetic was transformed briefly into Forrest the mystic. To his physical problems, anxiety was now added. He was agonizing over his upcoming first sermon, on the central Christian doctrine of resurrection. In search of help in making sense of a concept he found impenetrable, he ransacked contemporary theological works. In the midst of this turmoil, he became so sleep-deprived that he started hallucinating. Over a two-week period, on ten separate occasions, he felt the strong presence of his onetime girlfriend Kathy Kiilsgaard, whom he hadn't seen for several years. Then he dreamed about her: He was once again living in the basement pad in Boise when she arrived with a pack of Hells Angels goons, trying to force him to reconnect with her. In response, Forrest turned on the charm and invited them in for a beer. While all the men had a jolly time, Kathy felt neglected and soon left. In the wake of the dream, Forrest no longer felt her presence everywhere. Now that she was banished, he could go ahead and preach that debut sermon. He did so, and as he was greeting departing churchgoers, most of them politely praising what he considered a shoddy piece of sophistry, there she was. At that moment, Kathy Kiilsgaard was not a figment of his imagination.

Newly arrived on campus with her husband, an engineering student, she had noticed that Forrest was scheduled to speak and decided to show up.

Forrest's hallucinations may have been brought on by his meager diet, but their content had no medical explanation. To an outside observer, one aspect of this narrative jumps out for comment. The onetime girlfriend seems to be a stand-in for his wife—Amy feeling neglected and hoping for greater connection with her indifferent husband. Forrest never saw the experience that way. Nevertheless, he found it "completely authentic and very real." If it increased his respect for the great mystical traditions, however, it did not make a mystic of him. He was not one to sit for hours in meditation or to take orders from some authoritarian guru.[13]

Unlike some older Boomers, Forrest was never drawn to Eastern forms of meditation such as Zen or yoga or to homegrown exotica like Werner Erhard's est. "I had sort of a built-in allergy to all those things," he said. "There's not one of the pop religions that came through when I was at college and shortly thereafter that had the least amount of allure [for] me. It all had a kind of a medicine-show quality to it. I was at that point, remember, more of a skeptic. I was not coming from a traditional religious background, in which case I might have been drawn to these. I was from an ethical-humanist home. My skepticism [about] the church itself was probably less deep than my skepticism [about] the Zen ashrams and things like that . . . [They] all struck me as being quite shallow and very self-absorbed . . .

"I was not drawn away from the old, dead white [thinkers of the West]. I felt a need to have my grounding in them. In part before I rejected them, I really did want to know the foundations of Western religion and culture and philosophy . . . [Zen] was a discipline to empty yourself, not to fill yourself. And I was trying to fill my emptiness." Changing the metaphor, he concluded: "I needed to sharpen my blade, not to sort of follow the pixies into the mist."[14]

Harvard Divinity School would be the sharpener. While at Stanford, Forrest had queried visiting Reformation scholar Heiko Oberman about theological schools that were especially strong in church history. Should he go to Harvard or Yale? Oberman urged him to choose Harvard, primarily because of George Hunston Williams, whom he regarded as "the most engaging and passionate church historian" in the country. (Ironically, only later did Forrest learn that Oberman had previously been on the Harvard faculty with Williams, and that the rivalry between the two men had been so intense that Oberman had felt compelled to leave.) And so, in the fall of 1972, he and Amy enrolled at Harvard. She would pursue the new master's of theological studies (MTS), intended for those not expecting to enter the ministry or a doctoral program. He would take a master's of divinity (MDiv), followed by a doctorate. Because of its renown and rigor, he viewed Harvard as "the Everest that I needed to climb in order to do what I needed to do."[15]

Although Harvard University was founded in 1636 in large part for the instruction of a "learned ministry," the divinity school was not established as a separate graduate school until 1816. Initially, its students were predominantly Unitarians, inspired by such thinkers as Ralph Waldo Emerson and William Ellery Channing in the schism with the Congregationalists over the doctrine of the Trinity. By the beginning of the twentieth century, Harvard Divinity School had emerged as one of the most respected centers of interdenominational Protestant scholarship in the world. But by the end of World War II, the school had lost its luster. Its reputation was fading, its student body dwindling, and Harvard's president, James B. Conant, was no ally. In the view of Professor Williams, acting dean in the early fifties, Conant, a former chemistry professor, dismissed theology as "something like advanced alchemy." There was even talk of closing down the divinity school and having the faculty join forces with Meadville or another theological school in Chicago.[16]

Revival came under the leadership of Nathan M. Pusey. Taking over the university's presidency in 1953, this classicist and ardent Episcopalian spearheaded a campaign that would yield more than $3.5 million for the moribund divinity school. In his first major address, Pusey pronounced an "almost desperate urgency" for religious education and went on to criticize an "almost idolatrous preoccupation with the secular order." Given this impetus, a host of distinguished scholars flocked to Harvard. The biggest coup was Paul Tillich, the great systematic theologian who had fled Nazi Germany, lured away from Union Theological Seminary in New York in 1955. (Seven years later, he would be successfully wooed, in turn, by the University of Chicago.) Others soon followed him to Harvard. In New Testament studies, Krister Stendahl arrived from Sweden, Helmut Koester from Germany. Prominent Old Testament scholars included Frank Moore Cross and G. Ernest Wright. George Hunston Williams anchored the church history program. By the late fifties, the school established the Center for the Study of World Religions, attracting scholars in Islam, Buddhism, and Indian religions. By the sixties, Harvard Divinity School (HDS) unquestionably had regained its status as one of America's premier theological schools.[17]

Like Stanford, Harvard University had undergone enormous upheaval during the late sixties. Its divinity school was not immune to the era's shocks. The Vietnam War unleashed a wave of protest, based on theological concepts of just and unjust wars. Students marched against the war and demanded an end to the draft. They were active participants in Clergy and Laymen Concerned about Vietnam. They counseled Harvard undergraduates about conscientious objection. George Hunston Williams, who would be Forrest's mentor, delivered an eloquent speech at the historic anti-draft rally at Boston's Arlington Street Church on October 16, 1967, at which hundreds of men turned in their draft cards. In April 1969, after Harvard students were arrested for illegally occupying University Hall, HDS students planted the red flag of revolution atop Andover Hall, the main divinity school building. The challenge to the political status quo spilled over into religious thought. Liberation theology and feminist theology were newcomers born of the spirit of the age. The former, with its close identification with "the wretched of the earth," linked Christian doctrine to radical politics. The latter rejected traditional patriarchal concepts of God and encouraged women to enter the ministry. For some students, a syncretism of Christian beliefs with, say, Zen Buddhist practices offered an appealing alternative spirituality.[18]

By the time Forrest and Amy arrived, in the fall of 1972, most of the storms had passed. Throngs of angry, chanting students were but a memory. What remained, however, was the indictment that HDS was too white and too male. Krister Stendahl, dean since 1968 and a longtime advocate of the ordination of women, was committed to changing the demographics. He was far more successful at increasing the number of women students and faculty than at attracting African-Americans. Of the 281 students enrolled in 1972–73, 68 were women and 20 were black. In the following year, 87 were women and 21 were black out of a total of 296. Dean Stendahl lamented that only a quarter of the scholarship funds set aside that year for African-Americans had been used. As the number of women and minority students rose, so did their presence on the faculty, however slowly. In 1971, an African-American man was appointed to a tenured position. As for the women, untenured and visiting scholars served until 1983, when the first female professor finally received tenure. In the meantime, the Women's Caucus invented ingenious ways of making itself heard. In one of Professor Harvey Cox's classes, kazoos were handed out to be blown at any eruption of politically incorrect gender-exclusive language. By 1981, kazoos were hardly needed. From that point onward, women students outnumbered men at HDS.[19]

Most likely, Dean Stendahl had his campaign for diversity in mind when he appointed the very young Amy Furth Church as the divinity school's acting dean of students in the spring of 1975. She was a woman, and she possessed a calm demeanor that would serve her well. As a newly minted master's graduate, she was also in touch with the current student mood. "Everybody was at everybody else's throat in those days," said Rev. Peter Gomes, who presided over Harvard's Memorial Church, "and she had a very sound and reasonable and reassuring voice. She was not an ardent feminist in the sense of somebody who appeared to be ideologically driven and brittle." At the end of her eighteen-month term, in June 1976, the dean saluted her in terms that underscored her diplomatic skills: She combined a sense of justice, he reported, with common sense and sensitivity to the varied needs of an increasingly diverse student body.[20]

Amy often played the diplomat within the Church-Furth household, too. According to Robert A. Oden, Jr., then a doctoral student and later president of Carleton College, "Things did not rattle Amy. Her response was to be calm and think about it in a balanced way." But in this realm, her diplomacy could be more direct and down to earth. She was good, Oden said, at keeping Forrest's ego in check. "She was perfectly willing to say, 'Forrest, pick up after yourself,' or 'Stop talking about yourself in that way.'" In the blunt words of Holland Hendrix, another Ph.D. student and later president of Union Theological Seminary: "The thing about Amy is, she just put up with none of his bullshit—both in private and in public."[21]

Dennis R. MacDonald, who also entered HDS in 1972, said that Amy and Forrest cut quite a swath at the divinity school. "Between the two of them, they were really *formidable* [French pronunciation]. They were kind of the couple to emulate. She was very affable, outgoing, pleasant. And Forrest, of course, the son of a senator with a winsome smile, tall and unusual-looking, also the epitome of self-confidence." Rev. Gomes recalled: "People admired them. They both were smart and ready and charming people. There was a sense that they were going places. They were a model of a modern-thinking progressive religious couple."

Forrest's confidence was so huge, MacDonald and others thought, that he could seem overbearing and full of himself. "Frankly," Hendrix said, "it was an environment [in] which you're almost encouraged to cultivate and exert a strong ego, because we were being trained as the group that was going to influence scholarship for the next generation. So there was a certain . . . arrogance about your expectations."[22]

Initially, Forrest was more humbled than full of himself. In his first semester, he signed up for a course on "intertestamental literature." The term is used for ancient Hebrew wisdom writings, including the so-called Apocrypha, excluded from the canon of the Hebrew Bible and some versions of the Christian Old Testament. The course was taught by John

Strugnell, a brilliant English linguist and an editor of the Dead Sea Scrolls. He was also a notoriously troubled man, burdened with manic depression and alcoholism. (In 1990, in the wake of an anti-Semitic remark in an interview with a Tel Aviv newspaper, he was forced out of both the editing job and his Harvard professorship.) Belatedly, Forrest learned that he was the only nondoctoral student in the class. Apparently other MDiv students had heard that it was too daunting. Strugnell began the course with the book of Tobit, and by the end of the term, his scrupulous line-by-line textual analysis had covered only a single chapter. "I didn't have the faintest idea what was going on," Forrest confessed. "This in Aramaic, this in Syriac."

In the long run, though, grappling with the intricacies of intertestamental literature was worth the effort, making other courses seem less onerous. The B+ he received (along with another in medieval Greek) was his only deviation at Harvard from an otherwise flawless record of As. For the next two years, his course work concentrated on theology, church history, and languages (including Greek and Coptic).[23]

The boy so indifferent to his schoolwork had evolved into a young man on fire with learning. He was studying harder than ever before. If the work was demanding, the intellectual rewards were immense. "I'd go in [to the divinity school library] at nine o'clock in the morning, and I would work until eleven o'clock at night," Forrest said. "I was consumed by my passion for that particular form of learning. Part of it was driven by my ambition, but most of it was simply a desire to suck as much of the marrow out of those bones as I possibly could." Looking ahead to a career in academia, Forrest was also motivated by the new competition he could expect for faculty jobs. Since universities were now eager, even desperate, to add women to their faculties, many openings were at least tacitly reserved for them. In this environment, Forrest believed, a male applicant had to be truly exceptional. (Of course, many women believed just the opposite, with men continuing to hold the dominant role.)[24]

Forrest was blessed with qualities that made him an extraordinary student: superior intelligence, boyish enthusiasm, and boundless curiosity.

What's more—springing from a psychology formed in his earliest years—he was incapable of anything but independent thinking. Despite academia's claims to value the uninhibited pursuit of truth, that last trait could be hazardous. Some professors are so enamored of their pet theories that they expect students to march in lockstep with them. As Oden noted, "It's really easy in graduate school to figure out what mentors think and imitate that" and "be politically sensible in all the right ways."[25] Forrest, on the other hand, was very willing to say what he thought, not based on someone else's views, but on his own considered judgment. He was an intellectual risk taker.

In George Hunston Williams, he was also blessed. As Hollis Professor of Divinity, Williams occupied the oldest endowed chair in American higher education. Here was a mentor in no need of true-believing disciples. He, too, went his own, very idiosyncratic way.

Williams resisted easy categorization. He was a lifelong Unitarian somehow comfortable with the doctrine of the Trinity and a great admirer of Pope John Paul II (who later tapped him for the Knighthood of St. Gregory the Great). Williams opposed abortion just as ardently as he opposed the Vietnam War. He was a prodigious scholar who, in an age of specialization, refused to specialize. The subjects of his books ranged from American Universalism to the thought of John Paul II to the scholasticism of Anselm of Canterbury. In the estimate of his fellow HDS scholar Helmut Koester, Williams was "the last great general church historian." His landmark 1,500-page history, *Radical Reformation*, was not only a classic in Reformation studies, but it displayed Williams's steadfast commitment to the separation of church and state, a theme that would be central to Forrest Church's life's work.[26]

Williams's views were always nuanced and carefully reasoned. Consider that famous anti-draft rally in 1967 at Boston's Arlington Street Church, a historic Unitarian congregation served in the nineteenth century by William Ellery Channing. Yale's chaplain William Sloane Coffin and Dr. Benjamin Spock were the more famous speakers that day. But Williams's speech elicited the most dramatic moment. Coffin's memoir evokes Williams standing in the pulpit: "Suddenly I heard his voice rise. I saw an excited finger shaking in the direction of the single candle on the table below. 'There,' he shouted in words I recall as follows, 'there is Channing's own candlestick, the one he used night after night to illumine the progress of his writing. I am certain that were he also here for this occasion, its flame, illuminating as it does the faces of you resisters, would seem to him almost pentecostal. For you, gentlemen, are the very pillar of fire this nation needs to lead it out of the darkness now covering its people.'" To his horror, Williams's words unwittingly prompted some of the resisters to file up to the candle and burn their draft cards in full view of the TV cameras. In fact, he opposed such a gesture, preferring that they be sent to the Pentagon in protest. Because of the echoes of Nazi book burnings and libraries burned by tyrants, he deplored the burning of draft cards. "The manner of dissociation from this unjust war," he warned in the same speech, "should be solemn and not impetuous, anguished but not disorderly, respectful but resolute."[27]

Reason was the template that kept Williams's professional life in place. Perhaps it compensated for an anguished and disorderly personal life. Helmut Koester summed up Williams as "one of the most complicated persons that ever walked the face of this earth." He kept firing research assistants who could not meet his demanding standards. In departmental committee meetings, he quibbled endlessly over the wording of minutes. He discerned slights in the most innocent of gestures. Unable to drive a car, he was always cadging rides off students and faculty members. Once, when Williams was spending one of his occasional stints in a psychiatric ward, Forrest cleaned up his mentor's office, ridding it of hundreds of decades-old publishers' catalogs. The student thought he was doing the professor a favor; the professor was appalled. The chaos of Williams's office made perfectly good sense to him.

At home, there was little beyond mess. Williams's eldest son emigrated to Australia and was never heard from again. Another committed suicide. One winter, a granddaughter and son-in-law were drowned when their sled broke through the ice and plunged into a lake. Williams's wife left him. When she returned, she was soon diagnosed with Alzheimer's disease. Williams kept most of this misery to himself. Intensely private, he fortified his loneliness.[28]

There was no way Williams could match Wayne Rood's warm embrace, but that did not prohibit bonding on a professional level. As the ultimate generalist, Williams in effect gave Forrest Church permission to range broadly. "He made everything connect to everything else, and so my own sort of synthetic approach to scholarship was a gift from him," Forrest said. "I was the least specialized graduate student at Harvard, even after I went into my doctoral work." Despite Williams's sponsorship, Forrest had no blank check of approval. The professor remained as intimidating as ever; he didn't understand that other people might not know as much as he did. So Forrest churned out one learned paper after another, hoping not to disappoint George Williams, hoping to make his mark as a scholar on the rise.[29]

Forrest's maiden effort at scholarly publishing, in the august *Harvard Theological Review*, unabashedly hammered away at political correctness. "Sex and Salvation in Tertullian" sought to rescue the early Church Father from charges of misogyny brought by such feminist theologians as Mary Daly. In Forrest's reading, Tertullian's much-quoted invoking of the curse of Eve ("You are the devil's gateway") had been taken out of context, ignoring a written record far more egalitarian for both sexes on the means of salvation. Another paper drew on classical Greek and Roman rhetorical devices for a close textual analysis of St. Paul's New Testament Letter to Philemon. If the first was controversial, the second was straightforward academic fare. Both relied on rigorous logic and expertise in French, German, Latin, and Greek. Both were signed with the pen name he would use for many years. "F. Forrester Church" had a professorial ring to it, and it clearly set him off from his famous father.[30]

All the same, another part of Forrest's early scholarship was rooted in his family's devotion to politics. One piece analyzed the Korean minister Sun Myung Moon, the self-proclaimed second incarnation of Christ, and his American "Moonie" followers in light of earlier millenarian movements. In conclusion, Forrest allowed himself the observation that Moon had managed to "co-opt democracy, Christianity, and even the family, tapping American values and exploiting them for his own purposes." His effectiveness in gaining thousands of adherents, Forrest reflected, in a theme he would later make his own, underscored "our own failure to define our values in a convincing manner."[31]

Forrest's master's thesis sprang directly from his father's long-ago legacy, the so-called Jefferson Bible. Oddly enough, "The Gospel According to Thomas Jefferson" could have been written for a degree in U.S. history. In tracing the evolution of Jefferson's editing of a New Testament text compatible with his unorthodox thinking about Jesus, Forrest relies on earlier Jefferson scholarship and his own reading of Jefferson's extensive correspondence with luminaries such as John Adams and Joseph Priestly, the English scientist and Unitarian. Conventional theological students might not have been drawn to this subject. Forrest, however, clearly identified with Jefferson's firm commitment to a separation of church and state. He was equally comfortable with the Virginian's advice to a nephew: "Read the bible [sic] then, as you would read Livy or Tacitus . . . Your reason is the only oracle given you by heaven." Following his own counsel, Jefferson had extracted the essence of Jesus's teaching—"as easily distinguishable," he wrote, "as diamonds in a dunghill"—to reveal "the most sublime and benevolent code of morals which has ever been offered to man." Jefferson's loyalty lay with Jesus, not Christian churches and their apologists, which he believed had corrupted his message. Jefferson's conclusions were not precisely Forrest's. Ultimately, Forrest wrote, the president had reduced Jesus "to the dimensions of a rational eighteenth century man . . . Jefferson's was a search not so much for the *historical*, as for the *intelligible* Jesus." Forrest's thesis is notable not only for its intelligence and research. Here, for the first time, his skills as a writer come to the fore. (This was not a skill learned from his mentor, George Williams, whose dry-as-dust prose was marked by long sentences groaning under the weight of subordinate clauses.) Without sacrificing the scholar's bent for intellectual nuance, Forrest occasionally showcases an elegant style: "Adams was to take over from [Benjamin] Rush and Priestly their respective roles of trusted friend and learned teacher. What for ten years had lain dormant, Adams would rekindle. What had been feelings, he would urge into thoughts."[32]

The political realm, it turned out, was even closer at hand than the writing of a master's thesis. Not long after winning reelection in 1974, Senator Frank Church considered a run for the presidency that would take place two years later. His decision would matter greatly to his son. Forrest had evolved from the angst-ridden, angry young man of '68 to an enthusiastic backer of his father's principled liberalism. His success in graduate school had energized and emboldened his confidence. Because he was no longer groping for an authentic self, he no longer had to distance himself from his father. For several years now, he had been his father's ally, nothing like the "time bomb" of old. Eschewing absolutist idealism, he could appreciate the give-and-take of real-world politics and the superiority of liberal incrementalism over pie-in-the-sky radicalism. In the summer of 1974, Forrest had flown back to Idaho to work the hustings on behalf of his father. Despite his highbrow Harvard studies, he seemed like a natural. He was not only good at ancient languages and early church history but at shaking hands and working a crowd.[33]

By December of that year, Forrest was already urging his father to take the plunge into presidential politics. In a closely reasoned letter exhibiting remarkable political savvy, Forrest explained why. If the senator worried that he lacked name recognition, tossing his hat into the ring would quickly change that. Second, the campaign would only enhance his prestige and his ability to pursue a progressive political agenda. Third, it might lead to the consolation prize of the vice presidency. Fourth, he had little to lose and would have "a great adventure." Sounding more like a father than a son, he concluded: "If you choose not to run, I will obviously respect your decision. I recognize what an immense task it is to take this burden on."[34]

Forrest urged his father not to delay a decision, but the senator's integrity forced him to do just that. By mid-1975, Senator Church was virtually a household name. He was now the headline-making chairman of the Senate Select Committee on Intelligence. Informally known as the Church Committee, its investigations led to stunning exposés of FBI spying on U.S. citizens and CIA plots to assassinate Cuba's Fidel Castro and the Belgian Congo's Patrice Lumumba. While detractors accused Church of crippling U.S. intelligence agencies, Church insisted that America's honor lay squarely with a government that refused to engage in murder. "The United States must not adopt the tactics of the enemy," he proclaimed. "Means are as important as ends." Similarly, Church's sub-committee on multinational corporations laid bare an endemic culture of bribery abroad that could easily metamorphose into corruption at home.

Republicans claiming that these investigations were mere launching pads for a presidential run got it exactly wrong. In fact, by insisting on first completing this essential Senate business, Church sabotaged any chance of victory. As he deliberated, others jumped into the race, certain that the Watergate scandal had rendered the Republicans vulnerable. From the right of the party came Senator "Scoop" Jackson of Washington and Governor Jimmy Carter of Georgia. On the left was Congressman Morris Udall of Arizona, while Alabama's governor, George Wallace, in his final presidential bid, appealed to the white, blue-collar backlash against blacks and their white liberal allies.[35]

Near the end of 1975, Church and his aides finally resolved to set up a campaign organization. But because of his Senate responsibilities, he delayed announcing his candidacy until March 18, 1976. Forrest was eager to join the team but uncertain how this would affect his studies. According to the head of Harvard's doctoral program in religion, leaves of absence for students were out of the question. If Forrest took the semester off, he would have to reapply for admission upon his return. Abetting his father's career might jeopardize his own. But after Professor Williams and others took up Forrest's cause, the rules were waived and he was granted permission. After spending the opening months of the year at campaign headquarters in Washington, Forrest was dispatched to Nebraska, a Western state with demographics similar to Idaho's and thus

perhaps winnable. He would be his father's twenty-seven-year-old surrogate.[36]

The Nebraska campaign was bare-bones. It had little money and a
skeleton staff. What's more, the senator himself could not spend much
time in the state. While lacking in resources, the campaign countered
with an enthusiastic army of volunteers generated by a principled candidate. And it boasted a secret weapon. The senator's son was surprisingly
good on the campaign trail.

Nebraska's voters are bunched together in Omaha and the state capital
of Lincoln, and then spread thinly over dozens of sprawling rural coun-
ties. In Omaha, Church allied with labor unions and a young congressional candidate, John Cavanaugh. Meanwhile, Joe McCarter, a cattle rancher
who was chairman of Idaho's Democratic Party and head of the Church
forces in Nebraska, directed the senator's son in Lincoln and the west. Forrest's roles were multiple—as folksy kibitzer, smart interpreter of his father's views, and eloquent speaker. Though reared and educated among
the best and brightest, he could mingle easily among those who were not.
Before heading to college, for example, Forrest had taken a summer job
as a laborer at a Boise lumber mill with his friend Chris Burke. Forrest's
openness and sense of humor, according to Burke, led to an "instant rapport" with the crew of mostly high school dropouts. So now it was no
great stretch to drink beer alongside Nebraskan farmers and ranchers while
discussing agricultural price supports or water policy. "He reads people
beautifully, and I mean that in a good sense," said Church's advance man
Andy Litsky. "He was just completely and utterly disarming. He's got that
beaming smile and extraordinary warmth." In interviews with radio and
TV stations or newspaper editorial boards, he could expound his father's
positions with a sensitivity to local issues. "If you do advance," Litsky
said, "you have to tell the person what they're getting into, what the lay of
the land is. Forrest needed very little study."[37]

Forrest had grown up in the household of an outstanding public
speaker. Frank Church's speeches were exemplars of lucid prose, but his
style sometimes veered into a mannered, old-fashioned grandiloquence

that made him appear pompous. On the stump, though, his approach was more direct and plainspoken. For Forrest, speech-making had been an integral part of his experience as a student politician. More recently, he had given a few sermons in Boston, but clearly these did not prepare him well for Nebraska. After hearing one of the earliest, in 1972, Senator Church wrote his son that while the sermon was "beautifully written," it must have baffled the congregation. It was too much "like a treatise, each sentence of which needed to be read and pondered. I doubt that the spoken word can sink in that fast."

Once in Nebraska, however, Forrest readily adapted to the demands of the spoken word, mimicking his father's stump style. He avoided polysyllabic words; his sentences were short and punchy. His gestures were his father's. Like the senator, he would hold his arms outward from his chest, and then chop them downward to make a point. Both father and son spoke in a pleasant baritone. In the admiring eyes of Joe McCarter's wife, Mercedes, "He was absolutely channeling his father." The result, according to Litsky, was that he was "just phenomenal on the stump."[38]

After starting out at the bottom of the Democratic polls in Nebraska, Frank Church triumphed in the primary, edging national front-runner Jimmy Carter by 39 to 38 percent. "I was absolutely jazzed with being my father's surrogate," Forrest said. The win may have gone to his head. When he went on to the Oregon and California primaries, staffers there grumbled that he was "a bit of a busybody" whose pronouncements about how to run a campaign prompted more rolling of eyes than respectful attention. In any case, the Church train was fatally derailed when Governor Jerry Brown of California entered the race, snatching away liberal votes that might have gone to Church. Though the senator won five primaries that eventful year, he finished far behind the eventual nominee, Jimmy Carter.[39]

Nebraska lingered in Forrest's mind all the same. As Forrest told the story, Lieutenant Governor Gerald T. Whelan tried to entice him into relocating to the state, with the idea that he would be groomed to run for Congress in the First District, based in Lincoln. "I was given an opportunity to take the elevator to the fourteenth floor," he wrote in *Father and*

Son. Forrest was torn, one day finding the offer appealing, the next day thinking his rightful place was back at Harvard. Whether such an "offer" amounted to much remains an open question. Whelan died in 1993, and his two chief aides have no memory of it. "If there was anything serious, I would have known about it," Bill Hoppner said. "My guess is, it was an offhand comment." W. Don Nelson agreed. Otherwise, he said, Whelan "would have put me and Bill on the case." Will-o'-the-wisp or not, Forrest did take the matter seriously, and it was the talk of Church staffers in Nebraska.

In the end, Forrest decided to return to Harvard. The Nebraska scenario was nothing if not a long shot, and he would have faced charges of being a carpetbagger. If he really wanted a political career, Idaho would have been a likelier bet. What's more, according to Forrest, Amy would not have agreed to settling in Nebraska. Just completing her job as acting dean of students, she was poised for a very different future. Her next administrative position was as a financial aid officer at Harvard's Graduate School of Education. Ironically, it was Senator Church who weighed in with the decisive argument. He urged Forrest to finish what he'd started; he should complete his Ph.D., and Forrest finally agreed. He would continue on his own path, not his father's.[40]

The Ph.D. dissertation that awaited Forrest's attention at Harvard could hardly have been further removed from the gritty world of politics. To research "The Secret to the Gospel of Thomas," he had to first master Coptic, an ancient Egyptian language. The thesis itself was narrowly focused on a close analysis of one small portion of the Gospel of Thomas, a seminal Gnostic text. Testifying to the breadth of Forrest's language studies, it cited scriptures in Coptic and ancient Greek, and scholarly works primarily in English, German, and French, but also in Italian and Spanish.

The Gospel of Thomas is one of fifty-two papyrus texts discovered in 1945 in caves near the Egyptian village of Nag Hammadi. Written in Coptic, during the fourth century CE, they are translations of second-century Greek texts. Their primary interest to scholars is to illuminate the unsettled conditions surrounding the new religion inspired by Jesus of Nazareth, as various claims about his teachings and authority jostled for primacy. Because the Nag Hammadi texts took issue with the doctrines of virgin birth and bodily resurrection, the earliest Christian bishops denounced them as heresy. But it was precisely this element of controversy that drew Church to them. Like Jefferson's redacted Bible, the Gospel of Thomas was beyond the pale of orthodoxy. "I was finding my faith outside of the perimeters of accepted Christianity," Forrest said. "In each case, it's something right outside of the canon, but close enough that there is commerce between them." As an aspiring academic, he was also drawn to the study of Gnosticism, a field chockablock with exciting new work, some of it taking place at Harvard. HDS scholars Helmut Koester and George MacRae, a Jesuit priest, were part of a distinguished international team translating and interpreting the Nag Hammadi texts. While George Williams remained Forrest's official mentor, these two men served as his primary research guides for the dissertation.[41]

The term *Gnosticism*, as Elaine Pagels points out in *The Gnostic Gospels*, derives from the Greek word *gnosis*, usually translated as "knowledge," but better understood as "insight." Gnostics believed that they had unique access to intuited self-knowledge, and thus into human nature and destiny. In the Gospel of Thomas, Pagels notes, Jesus's sayings can seem "as cryptic and compelling as Zen koans." While similar to many of his sayings in the canonical gospels, they sometimes convey strikingly different ideas. This was clearly part of the intellectual exhilaration for Forrest, who detected in the Gospel "all the makings of a good mystery." Was it first and foremost "a roadmap [*sic*] to self-knowledge, devoted to the revelation of arcane wisdom and cosmic secrets," or "an ascetic handbook showing the way to salvation"? In other words, was its thrust primarily theological or ethical? After much close textual analysis and weighing of scholarly opinion, he concluded that it was the former.[42]

Was this sort of theological hair-splitting, this immersion in arcane scholarship, to be Forrest Church's future? Certainly, his quick and nimble mind made him adept at it. He had the confident backing of his

professors. And he had published a number of papers even before completing graduate study. Yet without intending to do so, George Williams
had already set Forrest off in a different direction.

As part of his MDiv program, Forrest was required to serve an internship. So Williams had directed him to his cousin, Rev. Rhys Williams,
who presided over historic First and Second Church in Boston. This was
the oldest Unitarian congregation in the city. At that point, Forrest's connections to this denomination had been minimal. Although Peter Fenn, his
closest friend since adolescence, was a Unitarian, he had never tried to
proselytize. (Even so, Forrest had spent many hours in the William Wallace
Fenn Room at HDS, named for Peter's great-grandfather, the Unitarian
dean of the divinity school early in the twentieth century.) During five
and a half years at Harvard, Forrest took no courses on Unitarianism, not
from Conrad Wright, the denomination's foremost historian. The great
Unitarian ethicist James Luther Adams had retired. Ralph Lazzaro, a Unitarian on the faculty, instructed Forrest only in languages. As for Williams,
whose father had been a Unitarian minister in Rochester, New York, he
followed a religious practice so idiosyncratic that it proved an unlikely
model for Forrest. The professor showed him the way to creative, wide-
ranging research, but not to a faith. In the classifications of divinity school
students, Forrest remained among the "unaffiliated."

What would Forrest do at First and Second Church? After the divinity student explained his scholarly ambitions, Rhys Williams assigned
him the unusual role of "church historian." From its founding, shortly
after John Winthrop and company stepped off the *Arabella* in 1630, the
church had employed both a minister and a teacher. Forrest, in effect,
would be that teacher. His main job was to research a history for the institution's 350th anniversary, coming up in 1980. Several times a year he
would also deliver a sermon. Forrest took the post in 1973. Two years later,
Williams persuaded him to accept ordination from the church. "That sly
old fox led by indirection," Forrest explained. "He never sat me down
and said, 'This is what you need to do.' He accepted my version of the
future. I was going to get a Ph.D., I was going to teach. But what he did,

in the most generous-hearted way, was to seduce me into the parish ministry."

On April 13, 1975, Forrest Church was ordained at First and Second Church. Taking part in the ceremony were the Unitarian Universalist scholars Conrad Wright and George Hunston Williams as well as Peter Fenn's grandfather, Rev. Dan Huntington Fenn. Though ordained by an individual church, he had not been officially "fellowshipped" into the Unitarian Universalist ministry, a process involving familiarity with UU texts, pastoral counseling experience, psychological interviews, and so on. Unaware of this lacuna, because of his aspirations to teach, he nevertheless wasn't playing by UU rules. Ordination was supposed to be the final step in fellowshipping.

In slow motion, but with a force that ultimately would prove irresistible, Forrest was being drawn into the orbit of Unitarian Universalism. It was the only denomination that could have accommodated his theological unorthodoxy and independent temperament.[43]

Four

Unitarians and Universalists

For most of us, our faith did not choose us, we chose it.
—FORREST CHURCH

It is easy to misunderstand Unitarian Universalism, to find it baffling and confusing, even incomprehensible. Some outsiders mistakenly believe that it is a religion in which "you can believe anything you want." Some see it as a Chinese restaurant menu of religion, where you pick a belief from Column A, Christianity, say, and a practice from Column B, Buddhism. To others, it seems more like a vehicle for the discussion of ethics and the promotion of liberal political causes than anything they would label a real religion. Religious ultraconservatives tend to deride it, if they pay attention at all, and humorists love to make sport of it. So the jokes keep piling up.

What do you get when you cross a Jehovah's Witness with a Unitarian Universalist? Someone who knocks on your door and asks what *you* believe.

How do you drive a Unitarian Universalist out of town? Burn a question mark on his front lawn.

Why are UUs the worst hymn singers? Because they're always reading ahead to see if they agree with the words.

Who answers Unitarian Universalist prayers? To Whom It May Concern.

Since Unitarians themselves usually write these jokes, no one could accuse them of lacking a sense of humor. Beneath all the wisecracks, however, lie some important truths. UUs are, indeed, open-minded about all sorts of religion (except close-minded varieties). They are full of questions; they don't accept arbitrary authorities telling them what to think; and most of them reject traditional ideas about God. All of these qualities are virtues. They point to a religion that respects the intellect and acknowledges the role of science in explaining the material universe, yet celebrates the communion of human connection and nurtures the search for profound spiritual truths. Missing from the jokes, yet vital to UU faith, is a bedrock feeling of awe and wonder before the everyday miracle of human life.

Above all, UUs are seekers, part of a long line of spiritual pilgrims deeply expressive of a shape-shifting American religious ethos. They believe in the value of searching as opposed to settling comfortably into any final destination. For them, the religious frontier always beckons. William Ellery Channing and Ralph Waldo Emerson led the nineteenth-century American vanguard, showing the way for a host of distinguished companions, including Herman Melville, journalist Horace Greeley, educator Horace Mann, Red Cross founder Clara Barton, author Margaret Fuller, novelist Louisa May Alcott, feminist Susan B. Anthony, and "Battle Hymn of the Republic" lyricist Julia Ward Howe. President William Howard Taft, two-time presidential candidate Adlai Stevenson, and Supreme Court Justice William O. Douglas were all Unitarians. More recently, Kurt Vonnegut, Christopher Reeve, William Schulz, president of Amnesty International, and World Wide Web inventor Tim Berners-Lee have been affiliated with the movement.

To understand what this religion means and where it comes from, one needs first to reach back to the earliest days of Christendom. Two strains of thought from this period eventually developed into the separate movements known as Unitarianism and Universalism. (Although they sometimes moved in parallel paths, especially during the twentieth century, they did not join forces until 1961.) The great irony, which Forrest Church loved to invoke, is that what is now a religion devoid of doctrine is named for two of them.

In the several centuries after the death of Jesus, as discussed in connection with Forrest's dissertation, his followers were widely diverse, his teachings and nature the subject of prolonged debate. Was he but the latest in a long line of Hebrew prophets? What was his relation to God? What precisely was his message? There was no central authority, no commonly accepted scripture, and no orthodox theology to resolve these and many other questions. The issues were not officially settled until the fourth century, when Constantine, eager to unify his fractious Roman Empire, convened the Council of Nicea. Discussions went on for two years. Finally, the supporters of Athanasius, who declared Jesus equal with God, won out over the camp of Arius, who believed Jesus was somehow more than human but not part of the deity. The triumphant Athanasian point of view would later be codified in the doctrine of the Trinity: the tripartite God of Father, Son, and Holy Spirit. Arianism survived, but only as a heresy on the fringes of the established Christian church. This idea of a single, unified God resurfaced much later under the name of Unitarianism. Meanwhile, the strand that would become Universalism arose out of the teachings of another Church Father, Origen of Alexandria, who argued that a just God would eventually grant salvation to all people, not just to a favored few. His views, too, were condemned as heresy.

Unitarians may not trouble themselves with saints, but among their ranks they count at least two martyrs. Michael Servetus grew up in sixteenth-century Spain in the era of the Inquisition. This was not a propitious time to question the Spanish church. Nonetheless, going well beyond the ideas of the Lutheran reformers who had inspired him, Servetus published *On the Errors of the Trinity*, calling it "a sterile doctrine which confuses the head and fails to warm the heart." After the Inquisition's inevitable order for his arrest, he fled to France, where under a pseudonym he became a distinguished physician. Later his religious doubts led him to write an even more inflammatory book, contending that the Trinity was invented by Satan to confuse people. He was captured, but then escaped to Geneva, hoping to find safety among John Calvin's followers. Instead, this Protestant reformer agreed with Catholics that Servetus had gone too far. In 1553, Servetus was tried, convicted of heresy, and burned at the stake.

Francis David's fate, though bad enough, wasn't quite as horrific. Originally a Catholic priest in Transylvania, David was propelled by Reformation thought into the Lutheran ministry, and then to Calvin's Reformed Church. Meanwhile, Transylvania's king, John Sigismund, a wise ruler mindful of all the conflicting religious currents swirling around him, issued several extraordinary edicts of religious toleration. In 1568, the king ordered a series of great debates between a Trinitarian and David as Unitarian spokesman. After another set of debates the next year, the king ordered that Unitarians and other freethinkers should be free to worship as they pleased. What's more, in a historic first, he and most of his countrymen declared themselves Unitarians. (Unlike Servetus, a dissident thinker, David was also a doer who established Unitarian churches.) But following Sigismund's death, all these gains were lost. A Catholic assumed the throne and imposed restrictions on Unitarian churches. Instead of conforming, David issued even more dangerous opinions, concluding that the Lord's Supper was not a sacrament and questioning whether it was appropriate to worship Jesus. He was tried for theological "innovation" and died in prison in 1579. Nonetheless, some Unitarians managed to hang on in Transylvania and continue there to this day. In the wake of the Reformation, other Unitarian groups also sprang up in Poland, the Netherlands, and England.[1]

If Arius and Origen, Servetus and David were ideological precursors of American Unitarians and Universalists, they were only distant cousins. For the most part, the American churches that eventually assumed these names were homegrown, emanating from New World theological controversies that erupted in the late eighteenth and early nineteenth centuries. Although both Unitarians and Universalists revolted against strict American Calvinism, they had very different theological emphases. Unitarians stressed the importance of individual conscience and personal piety over the Calvinist notion of innate depravity and individual powerlessness. Their rejection of the Trinity was a product of rational analysis; they could find no basis for it in scripture. Propelled by these beliefs, a number of Congregational churches in New England began to shift allegiance to the Unitarian camp in the late 1700s. As for the Universalists, the idea of an endless Hell was simply incompatible with their faith in a loving God.

Aside from theology, socioeconomic class also helped keep the two strands apart. Unitarians tended to be better educated, more prosperous, and more urban than Universalists. Their ministers were Harvard-trained; Universalists filled pulpits by a kind of apprentice system, not demanding a college education. Unitarian worship style, unlike that of the Universalists, favored restraint over emotional display. For all these reasons, Unitarians regarded Universalists "not as allies in a liberal crusade against Calvinism but as part of a chaotic and threatening group of rabble-rousers who simply preached an odd version of the emotional religion they opposed."[2]

Several key issues framed the debates and clarified the differences between Unitarians and Universalists: What is the nature of religious authority? How are we to regard the Bible? How do we define God? For Universalists especially, how does salvation work? By the latter half of the nineteenth century, however, thinkers in both denominations began to wonder whether these questions mattered much, whether a nontheist perspective corresponded better to science-based understandings of the world. "Deeds not creeds" became the great unifying standard. But the coexistence forged between theists and humanists could be as fragile and tenuous as that between early Unitarians and Universalists.

The first great manifesto of the American movement was William Ellery Channing's "Unitarian Christianity," transforming what had been an epithet, "Unitarian," into a proudly displayed calling card. This widely publicized 1819 sermon denounced the Calvinist notion of innate moral depravity and concluded that the doctrine of the Trinity was "irrational and unscriptural." Drawing on new schools of German biblical criticism, Channing declared the Bible "a book written for men, in the language of men" whose meaning should be sought "in the same manner of other books." Still, it contained the word of God, revealing a kind and benevolent deity who sent his son Jesus to save humanity from its failings. A rebuttal to Calvinist harshness and a plea for a more compassionate faith, the sermon was said to have had a larger circulation than any other American publication up to that time except Thomas Paine's *Common Sense*.[3]

Although clearly on Protestantism's left wing, Unitarians were nonetheless regarded as respectable Christians. Too much so, in the view of Ralph Waldo Emerson, in his speech to Harvard Divinity School's graduating class of 1838. Emerson, who had only recently left the Unitarian ministry to embark on a career as a lecturer and writer, felt his compatriots had settled into an unbecoming complacence. If the meaning of his poetic, oracular prose was not always clear, one thing was: His assertion of the individual's direct, unmediated intuition of the divine and his denial of Christian miracles put him well outside the Unitarian mainstream. As for the institutional church, he dismissed it as lifeless and cold, in thrall to rational thinking. Little wonder, then, that Harvard's Professor Andrews Norton later pronounced the great lecturer in the company of "infidels."[4]

Emerson, like scores of other influential Unitarians of the mid nineteenth century, represented a branch of Idealist philosophy that came to be called Transcendentalism. The relationship between Transcendentalism and Unitarianism was an uneasy one. Scholar Philip F. Gura reminds us that of the Unitarian ministers who identified with the philosophy, some "remained in the ministry as Unitarians; others redefined the nature of the churches they led . . . while still others left the church altogether." This was true not only because Transcendentalism encompassed myriad views, but also because its principles could be applied in different ways. One wing emphasized the perfection of the individual, anticipating the "self-actualization" of the 1970s. Channing once chided these folk for mistaking "their individualities for the Transcendent." On the other hand, the wing that claimed his allegiance looked outward to improve society, ranging from educational and prison reform to women's rights, utopian communities such as Brook Farm, and the battle against slavery. Transcendentalist Theodore Parker, for instance, whose theological independence earned him ostracism from fellow Unitarian ministers in Boston, became one of the most ardent champions of abolitionism.[5]

Not all Unitarians were willing to go that far. In the long view of history, we tend to adore rebels like these and ignore the middle-of-the-roaders who soldiered on. One leading light of the latter sort was Henry Whitney Bellows. As minister of the New York City church that Forrest Church would later inherit, Bellows made his mark not as a visionary thinker but as a tireless organizer and denominational diplomat. During the Civil War, he organized and led the U.S. Sanitary Commission, precursor to the American Red Cross. Given effective organization, he believed, liberal Christianity could supplant evangelical Protestantism as the dominant religious force in the country. Thus he spearheaded a movement to strengthen the American Unitarian Association, founded in 1825 as a loose association of individuals. His efforts reached fruition in 1865, with the establishment of the National Conference of Unitarian Churches. A theological moderate, Bellows lobbied hard to keep the phrase "Lord Jesus Christ" in the constitution preamble. His goal was inclusiveness. "We want to describe a large eno' circle to take in all who really belong with us . . . provided . . . the *fixed* leg of the compasses is in the heart of Jesus Christ, I care very little how wide & far it wanders."[6]

As the century wore on, the old split between Transcendentalists and non-Transcendentalists faded in importance. The new conflict lay between Unitarians who identified themselves as Christians and the "free spirits in the denomination who refused to acknowledge for Christianity any special rank among the religious traditions of mankind, on grounds either of its supernatural origin, or its exalted doctrine, or its beneficial consequences." Many of these gadflies and dissenters banded together in the Free Religious Association, which attracted not only Unitarians but also non-Unitarians, such as Felix Adler, founder of the Ethical Culture movement. They were influenced, in nearly equal measure, by evolutionary thought and a newfound respect for non-Western religions. Octavius Brooks Frothingham, for example, an illustrious New York City preacher, was a graduate of Harvard Divinity School like so many of his predecessors. Yet his views demonstrated just how far he had left them behind. Evolution, he contended, was not the enemy of religion, but the proper way of understanding it. Thus social life evolved just as flora and fauna did. As the title of his 1873 book implied, religion was morphing into "The Religion of Humanity." Frothingham remained a theist, even if wary of how to define God, the "Unsearchable One." He did assert this much: Deity was not expressed in a personality. As the organizing principle of the universe, it worked "in and through human nature."[7]

A more straightforward, unapologetic humanism—that is, a religion not based on any belief in God but instead on a faith in humanity—began to assert itself in early-twentieth-century Unitarianism. Not necessarily atheism, this viewpoint generally regarded "the God question" as irrelevant; the more pertinent question was how to live the good life, the ethical life. Nonetheless, the opposing viewpoint, what the Unitarian leader Samuel Eliot termed "lyrical theism," remained predominant. It affirmed "an ordered universe governed by a benign deity who acted through nature, law, and spirit upon the souls of men." By the 1920s, several high-profile, intradenominational debates underscored this ideological divide.[8]

The new humanist paradigm reached its fullest expression in the Humanist Manifesto of 1933. Grounded in the goodness of humanity and in the power for good of humanity's greatest tool, science, it expressed an optimistic faith in progress. At its heart were these assertions: Belief in a creator is unnecessary. Man is a part of nature and a product of evolution. Immortality is implicitly denied. Science is sufficient to explain the material universe. Humans must create their own values. Religion must be reshaped to accommodate these truths. In retrospect, the manifesto's audacious confidence seems not only misplaced but downright wrongheaded, for it failed to take into account the persistence of evil, soon manifest in the Holocaust and the atomic bomb. The document's thirty-four signers were primarily scholars and ministers. Fifteen were prominent Unitarians, including Rev. David Rhys Williams, the father of Forrest Church's Harvard mentor George Hunston Williams. One, Rev. Clinton Lee Scott, was a Universalist.[9]

Unitarianism proved an accommodating home for many religious humanists. Despite its American heritage in liberal Protestantism, it had long ago abandoned any doctrinal test for ministers and members. And its congregational polity meant that each church hired its own ministers and determined its own spiritual direction. So a humanist uncomfortable in a theistic-oriented church might find a more welcoming one on the other side of town. By the 1950s, self-identified humanists had grown to nearly half of the denomination's membership. Like the principle of coexistence that stabilized U.S.-Soviet relations during the Cold War, coexistence among Unitarian theists and humanists rested on the twin principles of creedlessness and toleration.

Universalists have a storied history of their own, though today's Unitarian Universalists may find it hard to identify with some of it. Theology, for one thing, seems to have propelled the early Universalists down some strange rabbit holes. Committed to a God with the attributes of a loving father, they found unimaginable any arbitrary sentences to Hell. A just and loving God might indeed punish his wayward creatures, but not in that horrific fashion. Consequently, they constructed elaborate rationales for the salvation of everyone.

John Murray, the great champion of early American Universalism, landed on these shores in search of a second chance. His arrival was not auspicious. He had fled England in 1770 following a series of tragedies—excommunication from the Methodist Church, the deaths of his wife and son, and a term in debtor's prison. Nearing the coast of New Jersey, his ship ran aground. He was saved and spent the rest of his life proclaiming a theology of universal salvation. Not an original thinker, his views were based on those of James Relly, who had converted him to

Universalism in London. Simply put, Relly held that "Jesus Christ had so thoroughly identified himself with humankind that he became completely tainted with humanity's sins, and that, through his death on the cross, he had atoned for both his own sins and the sins of all humankind, past, present, and future." However, only true believers would go to Heaven immediately; nonbelievers would temporarily abide in Hell, undergoing a period of purification. Advocates of this idea would come to be called Restorationists.[10]

Hosea Ballou, early Universalism's foremost theologian, took a different view. He and his supporters would be known as Ultra-Universalists. Largely self-educated and a bit rough-hewn in manner, Ballou could not have been more different from his Unitarian counterparts at Harvard. Yet his *Treatise on Atonement* of 1805 displayed a mind perfectly adapted to arcane theological speculation. His case for universal salvation begins with the assumption of an all-benevolent God, proceeds through various logical bends in the road, and concludes with the impossibility of God's creating "a being that would experience more misery than happiness." Ballou paid little attention to the question of future punishment, but it lingered among Universalist circles for years. By 1817, in a widely publicized debate, Ballou had threaded his way to the Ultraist position, arguing that "carnal nature, inclined to sinfulness, is destroyed by death, while the spiritual nature, committed to moral goodness, survives." Thus, there would be no rationale for punishment after death. Although both Restorationists and Ultra-Universalists had their adherents, by 1852, when Ballou died, his opponents were clearly in the majority.[11]

It is hard to imagine their Unitarian counterparts bothering with such angels-dancing-on-the-head-of-a-pin disputation. As one Universalist historian notes, "The chasm between the two groups is illustrated by the fact that Ballou and William Ellery Channing, the leaders of the two denominations, were not personally acquainted with each other even though they lived and ministered in the same city [Boston] for a quarter of a century!" It was true that most Universalists had jettisoned the Trinity, but the doctrinal divide remained huge. Thomas Starr King, a mid-nineteenth-century minister credentialed in both denominations, summed up the differences in a famous jest: Universalists think God is too good to damn them forever, while Unitarians think they are too good to be damned. This was wit in the service of accurate observation. For the Universalists, if not for the Unitarians, the precise disposition of sin remained firmly fixed at the top of the theological agenda.[12]

All the same, Universalists shared with Unitarians a passion for social reform. They, too, plunged into the temperance and antislavery movements. Their faith in salvation for all, including criminals, led them to fight for more humane prisons. Adin Ballou, a distant cousin of Hosea, founded Hopedale, an overtly Christian version of the Brook Farm utopian community. In the realm of women's rights, Universalists clearly outshone the Unitarians. Women had taken to their pulpits before 1863, but with the ordination of Olympia Brown in that year, they could claim the first woman officially sanctioned as a minister by an American church.[13]

In the latter third of the nineteenth century, while Unitarianism was being liberalized under the impact of evolutionary thought, Universalist theology seemed frozen in time. Universalists still adhered to a statement of faith written in 1803. When Herman Bisbee preached to his St. Paul congregation in 1872 that religion was "the effort which man makes to perfect himself, not the effort God makes to perfect him," he was booted out of the denomination. Gradually, however, more progressive voices began to prevail, energized in part by the World's Parliament of Religions, held in Chicago in 1893 in connection with the World's Columbian Exposition. In such a global context, the word *Universalist*, as generally understood, seemed all too parochial. As a denominational leader, J. M. Pullman, exhorted his colleagues a few years later: "You Universalists have squatted on the biggest word in the English language. Now the world is beginning to want that big word, and you Universalists must either improve the property or get off the premises!"[14]

No one was more responsible for improving the property than Clarence R. Skinner. A lifelong Universalist, Skinner was educated at one Universalist institution, St. Lawrence University, and later taught at another, the

Crane Theological School at Tufts University. Yet his book *The Social Implications of Universalism* (1915) charted a bold new path for the denomination. He advocated a "cosmic religion . . . founded upon a twentieth century psychology and theology." Its goal was "no longer to escape from earthly existence, but to make earthly existence as abundant and happy as it can be made." The Jesus he believed in, therefore, was Jesus as liberator, as champion of social justice. The Kingdom of God wasn't so much a heavenly home that awaited true believers after death as the just society here and now. This was the Social Gospel whose ranks included liberals of many stripes, from Baptists to Methodists to Unitarians. Skinner's beliefs pushed him into socialism and pacifism as well. Along with Rev. John Haynes Holmes, the onetime New York Unitarian who had moved beyond narrow ecclesiastical boundaries, he founded the Community Church of Boston in 1920. Nondenominational, the church required of its members only a "bond of union" calling for mutual assistance and the promotion of "truth, righteousness and love in the world."[15]

By 1943, General Superintendent Robert Cummins expanded the denomination's boundaries to an extent unimaginable fifty years earlier. Addressing the annual General Assembly, he pleaded that it "cannot be limited to Protestantism or to Christianity, not without denying its name. Ours is a world fellowship, not just a Christian sect. For so long as Universalism is universalism and not partialism, the fellowship bearing its name must succeed in making it unmistakably clear that *all* are welcome: theist and humanist, unitarian and trinitarian, colored and colorless. A circumscribed Universalism is unthinkable." Not all Universalists agreed with Cummins's broad embrace, but many Unitarians could. The stage was set for unity.[16]

Despite test probes about a merger launched every few decades by both denominations, nothing substantial had come of them. There were Unitarians who still regarded Universalists as too conservative theologically and too emotional in their worship style. By the same token, some Universalists found Unitarians cold and snobbish. More to the point, they feared that the Unitarians' larger numbers meant that unity would submerge the Universalist heritage. But by the postwar era, ideological differences had become minimized, and both sides were eager to pool resources in the service of liberal religion. Tentative cooperative steps begun in 1947 eventually resulted in full-blown consolidation in 1961. The Universalist Church of America and the American Unitarian Association were no more, replaced by the Unitarian Universalist Association (UUA).

In the parliamentary battles to write a set of Principles (in lieu of a rigid creed) for the new association, it was clear that theological questions still mattered. There were, according to one historian, essentially three factions: "the traditional theists, who wanted a reference not only to God but to our Christian heritage; the 'universalist' theists, who preferred acknowledging the 'great prophets and teachers of humanity in every age and tradition'; and the humanists, who would just as soon do without reference to any deity." In the final compromise wording, the second (and most important) of the six Principles read as follows: "To cherish and spread the universal truths taught by the great prophets and teachers of humanity in every age and tradition, immemorially summarized in the Judeo-Christian heritage as love to God and love to man." The earlier phrasing, "in *our* Judeo-Christian heritage," was deftly changed to accommodate humanists. Also struck from the final document was the phrase in the old Unitarian bylaws following "Judeo-Christian heritage"— "which Jesus taught as love to God and love to man." Forrest Church's predecessor at All Souls Church in New York City, Rev. Walter Kring, was at first incensed; this deletion, he charged, amounted to "anathemizing Jesus." Given the local control of individual churches and the long-standing tradition of "freedom of the pulpit," Kring had nothing to fear in the long run. He could continue to preach as he wished. So, too, could humanists and other varieties of liberals drawn to this tolerant and open-minded faith.[17]

This was the religion that Forrest Church embraced, at first tentatively and then with great gusto. It would shape him as much as he shaped it. Both would be vitalized and enlarged in the encounter.

By the late 1970s, when Forrest began his ministry, the Principles of

1961 were undergoing revision, and after several years of debate and compromise, a new formulation was officially approved in 1985. This would be the template for his defense of liberal religion. A big tent, it permitted—better yet, encouraged—variety, experimentation, individualism, soul-searching. It avoided proscription, creedal tests of membership, lists of thou-shalt-nots. You could be a follower of Jesus. You could combine your love of yoga with techniques of prayer. You might call yourself a Christian Unitarian, a Jewish Universalist, an agnostic, or an atheist. You were on the journey, though rarely sure of the destination. You just had to honor your neighbor's spiritual path as well as your own. Religion wasn't something you inherited; it was something you constructed out of study and experience and contemplation, and made your own. This was a chosen faith.

"We, the member congregations of the Unitarian Universalist Association," the Principles read, "covenant to affirm and promote:

- The inherent dignity and worth of every person;
- Justice, equity and compassion in human relations;
- Acceptance of one another and encouragement to spiritual growth in our congregations;
- A free and responsible search for truth and meaning;
- The right of conscience and the use of the democratic process within our congregations and in society at large;
- The goal of world community with peace, liberty and justice for all;
- Respect for the interdependent web of all existence of which we are a part.

The living tradition which we share draws from many sources:

- Direct experience of that transcending mystery and wonder, affirmed in all cultures, which moves us to a renewal of the spirit and an openness to the forces which create and uphold life;

- Words and deeds of prophetic women and men which challenge us to confront powers and structures of evil with justice, compassion and the transforming power of love;
- Wisdom from the world's religions which inspires us in our ethical and spiritual life;
- Jewish and Christian teachings which call us to respond to God's love by loving our neighbors as ourselves;
- Humanist teachings which counsel us to heed the guidance of reason and the results of science, and warn us against idolatries of the mind and spirit."

In 1995, a sixth source was added:

- "Spiritual teachings of Earth-centered traditions which celebrate the sacred circle of life and instruct us to live in harmony with the rhythms of nature."[18]

In contrast to creed-bound religions, these Principles opened the door to enormous diversity. In practice, of course, within this capacious, open-ended framework, an individual church or member generally pursued a narrower focus. Under the impact of tradition or a strong minister, churches tended to have distinctive personalities. Some were identifiably humanist, others clearly theist. Worship varied, too, from more formal approaches to freer, looser styles. Congregations used different terms to refer to themselves—church, society, fellowship. In some congregations, you felt decidedly New Age vibes; in others, liberal Protestants would feel right at home. Couples in religious "mixed marriages" often turned to Unitarian Universalism for common ground and a neutral place to instruct children in their religious heritage. Refugees from doctrines they found insulting to their intellect gravitated to the UUA fold. It was a way to keep in touch with religious questions while sorting through the answers. Liberals living in ultraconservative communities found the local Unitarian church a safe harbor where their commitment to social justice would be respected.

A survey of UU members published in 1973 documented the kind of pluralism later expressed in the Principles. Asked to explain their definition of God, only 2.9 percent responded "a supernatural being." Twenty-eight percent thought the question "irrelevant," and 1.8 percent actually found the God concept "harmful." Twenty-three percent cited Paul Tillich's formulation, "the ground of all being." The largest number of respondents, 44.2 percent, thought the word *God* might be "appropriately used as a name for some natural processes within the universe, such as love or creative evolution."

UU members were further asked about institutional affiliation. Only 11.2 percent preferred that the UUA move closer to "liberal Protestantism" or "the ecumenical movement within Christianity." Nearly 37 percent preferred a movement toward "an emerging universal religion," while a majority, 52 percent, wanted Unitarian Universalism to be considered a "distinctive humanistic religion."[19]

In the continuum that defined the wide range of UU congregations, the Unitarian Church of All Souls in New York City lay on the right. In the words of its historian, "Radical theological trends within the denomination have never had much of a place in the All Souls picture."[20] It was clearly theistic. Its ministers had no reservations about invoking God or the use of prayer. Its liturgy had a liberal Protestant feel. True, the UUA hymnal in use often substituted humanist or vaguely theistic lyrics for traditional Christian ones. But the choir director routinely drew on a classical-music literature replete with unapologetic references to God and Jesus. In other UU churches, this was the sort of provocation that might stir up congregational wrath.

The building itself, completed in 1932 in the Georgian-Colonial style, projects a tasteful dignity suggesting Unitarianism's New England roots. Set on the corner of Lexington Avenue and Eightieth Street on New York's tony Upper East Side, it was completed in the midst of the Great Depression largely due to the generosity of a wealthy member, George F. Baker, founder of a bank that grew into Citibank. The ivy-covered exterior is made of red Hudson River brick trimmed with Texas limestone. Inside, the sanctuary functions as a six-story-tall white space inviting quiet contemplation. High beige walls are flanked by Ionic columns separating the main seating area from side aisles. A towering, old-fashioned high pulpit—right out of the opening pages of *Moby-Dick*—stands at the front of the church. (Except for ceremonial occasions, such as Christmas Eve, it is no longer used for sermons; instead, the minister speaks from a lower pulpit much closer to the congregation.) Organ and choir are located at the rear of the sanctuary in a loft. Large simple chandeliers and white pews with mahogany trim add a soft, restful feel. Unlike many churches, this one is a paragon of crisp, clean lines, bare of ornamentation. There is no stained glass. A series of large, clear windows lend an airy, open feeling, as if to say, refresh yourself in the calm of this place but do not ignore the needs of the world outside.[21]

All Souls' past is on its walls. No memorials to disciples or saints, these are the plaques honoring the leaders who have made this particular church a denominational flagship. They underscore a heritage of continuity and longevity. Forrest Church had only eight predecessors, and all but two of them were educated at Harvard and/or its divinity school.

William Ellery Channing is here. Though never an All Souls minister, he served as inspiration for its founders. While traveling from Boston to Baltimore in 1819 to deliver the famous "Unitarian Christianity" sermon, he stopped in New York to visit his sister, Lucy Channing Russell. His ideas caught fire with a diverse group of religious liberals who soon established a congregation outside the boundaries of convention. Describing her fellow congregants in 1823, novelist Catherine Sedgwick wrote: "They are strangers here from inland and outland, English radicals & daughters of Erin, Germans and Hollanders, philosophic gentiles and unbelieving

Jews ... In this our ass'n [association] ... there is at least one of every sort."[22]

Here, too, is William Ware, the congregation's first minister, son of Henry Ware, whose elevation to the Hollis Chair of Divinity in 1805 marked the triumph of Unitarianism over Calvinism at Harvard College. Young Ware, more at home at his writing desk than in the pulpit, resigned after thirteen years to devote himself to what he loved most, the writing of historical novels set in the ancient Middle East.[23]

Here, of course, is Henry Whitney Bellows, whose forty-three-year tenure (1839–1882) was the church's longest by far. He is commemorated in the largest and most commanding of memorials: a larger-than-life-size bas-relief sculpted by Augustus Saint-Gaudens. Bellows's skill as an organizer, of the denomination and of the U.S. Sanitary Commission, have already been mentioned. He was also the consummate middle-of-the-roader. While other Unitarian visionaries were setting up short-lived utopian communities, the ever-pragmatic Bellows was collaborating with the economic elite and the Lincoln administration to deliver much-needed aid to the victims of the Civil War. When Unitarian abolitionists called for the immediate eradication of slavery, Bellows sided with the Free Soilers, who advocated containing slavery within the South rather than ending it altogether. When other Unitarians called for a religion that extended beyond Christianity, he adhered to a Christ-centric fixed pole. In setting up the National Conference, he even tried, and failed, to establish some kind of Unitarian creed. Nonetheless, as a prominent member of the so-called Broad Church group, he had no desire to be exclusive, to push those who disagreed with him out of the denomination. Indeed, one of his best qualities, according to his biographer, was his reluctance to take a position on any issue until he had thoroughly analyzed it from every angle.[24]

Here on the walls of All Souls is also the most unusual of these ministerial ghosts. William Laurence Sullivan, who presided from 1916 through 1922, not only grew up Roman Catholic but became a Paulist priest and a professor of theology at Catholic University in Washington, D.C. Disillusioned by the proclamation of papal infallibility in 1907 and Rome's unwillingness to come to terms with the modern world, he left the priest-hood and eventually made his way to Unitarianism and its ministry. Sullivan is best known for his attacks in the 1920s on the growing humanist movement within Unitarianism. Having found his home, after a harrowing spiritual journey, among traditional, God-fearing Unitarians, he was not about to have it gutted from within. Atheists were bad enough, he wrote in the denominational magazine, but believers in what he called "Half-God," or the God of evolutionary process, one who "blunders and flounders and experimentally struggles," were perhaps worse. In a later speech at a national Unitarian conference, he mocked believers in such a "bundle of gas" and suggested that they had no place in the church. Even for All Souls, this position was impolitic and extreme. But it highlights the congregation's consistently moderate-to-conservative stance within the denomination.[25]

Here, too, is Walter Donald Kring. Forrest Church's immediate pre-decessor presided over All Souls for twenty-three years, from 1955 to 1978. Kring was known for his pottery as much as for his preaching. His pots were displayed at the Metropolitan Museum of Art, among other museums, and at the American Pavilion of the 1958 World's Fair in Brussels. In theology, he was a vigorous defender of theism. He was the man who feared that the UUA's founding principles amounted to "anathemizing Jesus." He hoped that the new denomination would avoid forging a new religious syncretism and remain steadfast to its roots in a simple, creedless Christianity. An internationalist, he was an avid supporter of the United Nations. On domestic social issues, he ignored the siren call of sixties liberal chic. In particular, he took issue with Black Power advocates who demanded money for separatist projects and set off several years of morale-destroying discord within the denomination.[26]

Overall, Kring was a caretaker. He had no desire to shift All Souls from its accustomed course of "High-Church Unitarianism." His respect for this heritage is reflected on every page of the three volumes he wrote chronicling its history. In an era and a denomination unusually given to change, he was prone to resisting it. In a period of steep declines in membership and attendance among mainline Protestant churches, All Souls struggled, too. Its membership was aging and declining. Attendance at Sunday services had dwindled to a few hundred. When Reverend Kring announced in 1977 that he was ready to retire, church lay leaders resolved to recruit a leader who could revitalize, if not radicalize, this historic institution.

Five

Bright Lights, Big City

*Commuters give [New York] its tidal restlessness, natives give it solidity
and continuity, but the settlers give it passion.*

—E. B. WHITE

Rev. Rhys Williams, that "sly old fox," had a plan for Forrest
Church. He believed that his protégé had the makings of an outstanding minister. When he learned, in 1977, via the Unitarian
grapevine, that All Souls Church in New York was about to replace the
retiring Walter Kring, he went to work. Two years earlier, he had persuaded Forrest to be ordained at his First and Second Church in Boston.
That was the first step in nudging the would-be scholar into the parish
ministry. Over time, Forrest was encouraged to try on various ministerial tasks—primarily the occasional summer sermon—while completing
his doctoral studies at Harvard in church history.[1]

Now Williams had to move fast. All Souls, with its storied past, its
New York City allure, was a magnet that inevitably would draw the denomination's best and brightest.

First, he alerted Bert Zippel, the Hunter College psychology professor who chaired the All Souls search committee. Despite Forrest's youth
(he was only twenty-eight in the summer of 1977) and apparent future
in academia, Williams suggested, here was a young man well worth a
look. Next, he came down to All Souls to preach and talk up this future

denominational "dynamo." Then he arranged for Forrest himself to preach at All Souls in August, when services were held in a tiny chapel off the main sanctuary. Despite the customary small attendance, Forrest's impact was large. Search committee members who heard him were impressed by his intelligence and eloquence. Forrest, in turn, was impressed by their postservice response, when some challenged him about a sermon metaphor he'd inadvertently confused. Here was a congregation of smart, thoughtful New Yorkers unafraid to speak their minds. Williams's seed was planted.[2]

By this time, the committee's work was well under way. It had received nearly fifty résumés from interested ministers and interviewed half of them. It had traveled throughout the New York metropolitan area and to the denomination's annual General Assembly, held that summer in Ithaca, New York. This was a discreet process designed to hear ministers preach and get a sense of the possible fit between these "pre-candidates" and All Souls. Some of these men were surprised to learn that All Souls was not as conservative, politically and theologically, as they had imagined. One insisted that he was a good liberal, indeed, but not as far left as Americans for Democratic Action, for heaven's sake! John French, a courtly corporate lawyer on the committee, tartly responded that his wife, Eleanor Clark French, had in fact once been national president of that liberal advocacy organization. Brought up on Philadelphia's Main Line, she was an active Democratic partisan who ran unsuccessfully against John Lindsay in the Upper East Side's "Silk Stocking" congressional district. She was the type of liberal who was insulted that her husband had made it onto President Richard Nixon's infamous "Enemies List," and she hadn't. In the All Souls way, Ellie French combined good breeding with progressive politics and liberal religion.[3]

Not all All Souls members, of course, were Democrats, let alone liberals. The search committee, however, did mirror the rather narrow socioeconomic spectrum of the late-seventies congregation. Aside from Zippel and French, the committee included another attorney at a white-shoe law firm, a marketing executive, an advertising firm research director, a teacher at an exclusive private school, and a housewife who had married well. For the most part, they agreed in desiring a minister who could lift All Souls out of its doldrums without disturbing its basic ethos. "We were aware that we needed a few kicks in the pants," recalled one member. The right candidate would be neither "New Age flaky" nor "stick-in-the-mud."[4]

By October 1977, the committee invited six finalists to New York for further scrutiny. Much to his surprise, Forrest Church was among them. His initial response was a polite no. He was busy finishing his Ph.D. and headed toward academia, thank you very much. A cunningly nonchalant Williams suggested that he at least keep his options open. Why not go down and enjoy a free weekend in New York? No doubt he phoned Zippel and encouraged a second call to the reluctant Forrest. When the call came, as Williams knew it would, Forrest changed his mind and agreed to meet with the committee.

The first question, from Stephens Dietz, one of New York's most prominent advertising executives, got right to the point. "Young man, I understand you're not interested in this position. So why are you wasting our time?"

"I don't have the faintest memory of how I answered," Forrest said years later. "I was thrown back on my heels from the very beginning. My natural competitive juices, I'm sure, began to kick in, but, more important, about halfway through that [three-hour] interview, I was smitten."

Even as his passion for his own studies was ebbing, he found himself face-to-face with a fascinating group of people passionate about revitalizing a historic liberal church in New York City. The combination of people, place, and opportunity was electrifying. And it might never come again.

Just a year before, on the campaign trail in Nebraska, Forrest had felt a similar thrill, the possibility of a life of public speaking and public service. And although it was never a conscious part of the decision, somewhere in his psyche the specter of paternal approval loomed large. According to Forrest, his father had "greater sympathy for the life of public service in the church than he would for an elitist academic career. I would send him my articles, and he would say, 'I'm sure it's very impressive, but I didn't understand a word.' I could just imagine the alien quality of the endeavor, trying to determine what the rhetorical structure and design of Paul's letter to Philemon was, while my father was trying to reform the CIA."

In a shot, Forrest's frame of mind jumped from reluctance to wary enquiry to enthusiasm. If All Souls would have him, he would be their man.

The other finalists were middle-aged men, for whom All Souls would be a reward for past service, a career capstone. Given the choice between track record, age, and experience and promise, youth, and energy, the committee opted for the latter. "The gamble was enormous," Forrest said. "It was a pure roll of the dice."[5]

Not surprisingly, the recommendations from Forrest's Harvard mentors were uniformly glowing. Any lingering insecurity from Zippel, that Forrest was too young to have left "a tangible trail of error and misjudgments," they stressed, was unwarranted. From the great Unitarian ethicist James Luther Adams came an unsolicited letter predicting that Forrest was "destined to become a leader . . . in American religious life in general." All Souls, he added, would be fortunate to have Amy Furth Church by his side:

"She is a person of independent judgment as well as of poise and charm. My wife, Mrs. Adams, used to say that the heaviest disadvantage burdening a clergyman is a wife who thinks he is perfect. Amy Church . . . will not be a burden of that sort to her husband or to the parish."[6]

Only one step remained. Forrest and Amy would have to undergo "candidating week" during the first week of February. In addition to meeting constituent groups within the church, Forrest would give a sermon at the beginning of the week and at the end. The first fell flat. It was too scholarly, hardly the sort of message likely to lift spirits or revitalize a congregation. He was being too cautious, trying to appear older than his years. Forrest's partisans took him aside and advised a more down-to-earth approach. His second sermon proved far more appealing. That success, and his obvious charm and wit, sealed the deal. At the congregational meeting of February 13, 1978, Forrest Church was officially "called" to lead the Unitarian Church of All Souls. Most ministers facing such a vote count on a minimum approval of 80 percent. All Souls welcomed him with open arms: 130 to 2. Youth and promise had won the day. He would mark his first month on the job, in September, with his thirtieth birthday.[7]

The New York that became home to Forrest Church was still America's largest city (with a population just over seven million) and its financial and cultural capital. Here were Wall Street and international investment banks. Here were the great art museums, publishing houses, and television, magazine, and advertising empires. The city was Mecca for writers, artists, journalists, actors, lawyers, business executives, and bankers— anyone who hoped to cut a swath on the national stage. The twin towers of the World Trade Center, the world's tallest at 110 stories, seemed a brash embodiment of Frank Sinatra's signature hit about making it, "New York, New York."

New York meant excitement, opportunity, the constant churn of change. You never knew what might turn up around the next corner. Gays were coming out and acting up. Disco was king, unless you preferred the punk rock at CBGB. If your musical taste ran to classical, you could catch the new maestro at the New York Philharmonic, Zubin Mehta, just arrived from Los Angeles. At the New York City Ballet, George Balanchine and Jerome Robbins orchestrated one masterwork after another.

New York also meant trouble. Its litany of urban horrors—high crime rates, widespread drug abuse, deteriorating public schools, homeless people adrift on the streets—went on and on. One of every seven residents was on welfare. The South Bronx was losing ten square blocks a year to arson fires. Wits mocked pornography-ridden Times Square as the city's "erogenous zone." Olmsted and Vaux's onetime crown jewel was reduced to a late-night Johnny Carson punch line: "Martians landed in Central Park today . . . and were mugged."

As if all this weren't enough, the city suffered through a year terrorized by a serial killer who dubbed himself "Son of Sam." Roaming the city, David Berkowitz, a young postal clerk, killed six victims and wounded seven others with a .44-caliber pistol, all the while taunting the police to catch him. He was not apprehended until August 1977, when Forrest first visited All Souls.

During that same summer, on the night of July 13, electricity was accidentally cut off in all the city's boroughs. In the ensuing twenty-five-hour blackout, neighborhoods from Brooklyn to Queens, from the Bronx to Manhattan's Upper West Side, were ripped apart by looting and arson. Police and firefighters—pummeled by stones and chairs and worse—were initially powerless to stop the violence. Ultimately, 3,776 New Yorkers were rounded up in the largest mass arrests in the city's history. Commentators were aghast. "Is New York City, after all," the *Times* editorialized, "a failed ultra-urban experiment in which people eventually crack, social order eventually collapses, and reason ultimately yields to despair?"[8]

The nation's wealthiest zip code, 10021—a serene haven of stately town houses, apartment buildings, and All Souls Church—remained relatively unscathed during the Great Blackout of '77. It was not, however, immune to violence. On the week Forrest Church began his ministry in 1978, "Love and Death on the Upper East Side" was the lead story of that trendy Gotham chronicler, *New York* magazine. This was a lurid tale of a once-famous thoroughbred horse trainer, Buddy Jacobson; his ex-girlfriend, cover girl Melanie Cain; and the man who took his place in Cain's heart, Jack Tupper. Jacobson had murdered Tupper in an apartment building on East Eighty-fourth Street; the bullet-riddled body was later found in a Bronx garbage heap.[9]

The new minister and his wife had just moved into a three-story walkup on Lexington Avenue across from the church, a few blocks away from the murder. But at this moment, with an exciting new life awaiting them, perhaps nothing could dampen their spirits. While Forrest plunged into his duties with the usual exuberance, Amy gave birth to their first child. Frank Forrester Church V was born on September 20. Like his father, he would be known as Twig.

For All Souls Church, it's hard to exaggerate the symbolic power of this fresh-faced couple with a newborn in their arms. This was an institution badly in need of rebirth. The median age of members was fifty-five. Membership fell from 858 in 1976 to 388 in 1979, and the latter figure was probably inflated. Attendance at Sunday services, before Church's arrival, averaged an anemic hundred or so.[10]

Forrest Church was not just another young professional eager to make his mark in the big city. Like most of his predecessors at All Souls, he bore the Harvard pedigree. More telling, he arrived with the aura of political celebrity. Few names of that era had greater cachet among liberals than Frank Church. His leadership of Senate exposés of CIA treachery and corporate bribery had vaulted him into national prominence. It wasn't the officially titled Select Committee on Intelligence that grabbed the headlines of the mid-seventies. It was the "Church Committee."

Church didn't need to flaunt his background. Everyone knew it. And it wasn't his style anyway. In place of Reverend Kring's fifties-era starchy reserve, he projected the casual openness and warmth of his generation. To parishioners, it was always "Dr. Kring," though his doctorate was merely honorary. Dr. Church, with an earned doctorate, insisted early on that people call him Forrest. Figuratively and literally, he approached his congregation with open arms.

Before the opening of Sunday services, a former parish assistant remembered, Church would stand on the sidewalk, greeting people. "He was like this great big Saint Bernard that would sort of galumph up to people with delight and joy that they were there. He could be charming and he could, like all of us, make mistakes—call people by the wrong name. Nobody really cared because you had the sense that it was all coming from his heart."

If you brought a complaint about church business to him, one board member said, he was "tremendously disarming, so incredibly outgoing and likable that your objections melted away."[11]

One enticement All Souls offered was a green light for Church to continue his writing. He was encouraged to shape his ministry in the mold of William Ellery Channing, Theodore Parker, and Henry Whitney Bellows. The All Souls pulpit could be a bully pulpit to reach out far beyond the building's confines. This vision appealed to Forrest's gregarious personality and literary ambitions. "I am daily becoming more committed to the ministerial calling," he wrote to a colleague just two months into the job. "In fact, I cannot imagine going back to the airy confines of academia, having tasted now of the active life."[12]

Charm and good intentions would take him only so far. He had much to learn. He chose to study A. Powell Davies and Harry Emerson Fosdick, two of the nation's most influential liberal clergymen earlier in the twentieth century, as templates for a successful ministry. Davies, the son of Welsh Methodists, immigrated to the United States in 1928 and soon transferred his allegiance to the noncreedal Unitarians. At All Souls Church in Washington, D.C., he became the leading Unitarian spokesman of the 1940s and early '50s. His book topics ranged from the Dead Sea Scrolls to the evils of McCarthyism. He was an outspoken opponent of racial discrimination and the use of nuclear weapons, a defender of the United Nations and Planned Parenthood. At his death in 1957, a *Washington Post* editorial declared him "the most controversial of clergymen in the Nation's Capital." Davies would have considered that phrase an honor.[13]

Fosdick's politics were less predictably liberal than those of Davies. Yet in one respect, he was far more controversial, as part of a tiny minority of American pacifists during World War II. Though a committed Christian, Fosdick resisted creedal and denominational straitjackets. He believed neither in the Virgin Birth nor in a bodily resurrection of Christ. Hell, in his view, was a kind of "disorder of the self." Though a Baptist, he served at New York's First Presbyterian Church, until a nationwide movement of fundamentalists—some of whom derided him as a "Unitarian cuckoo"—drove him out in 1925. John D. Rockefeller Jr. soon lured him to the Park Avenue Baptist Church, with the promise of taking the helm of Riverside Church, the interdenominational cathedral he was building on Morningside Heights near Union Theological Seminary and Columbia University. Fosdick grew famous at Riverside as the nation's leading Protestant preacher and as an advocate for making modern psychology essential to the pastoral counseling tool kit. The two, he argued, were inextricably linked.[14]

For Forrest Church, Fosdick's example was most decisive in the art of preaching. The Riverside pastor's concept of a sermon—as "personal counseling on a group scale" or as "an animated conversation with an audience"[15]—comes close to describing what the mature Forrest eventually achieved. At his best, he brilliantly paired intellectual substance with emotional resonance. The latter emerged from daily encounters with parishioners in the privacy of his study. To the litany of their fears, failings, and foibles, he added his own, inevitably breaking down the barrier between pulpit and pew. Sermons were not simply lectures on topical subjects, not merely expositions of theological ideas. Their aim was to inspire and console, above all, to connect.

The pastor's duty, according to conventional wisdom, was to comfort the afflicted and afflict the comfortable. Yet Church recognized the difficulty of discerning just who was in which camp. "Very early on in my ministry," he said, "I discovered that everybody was in some way afflicted and needed comfort, and in some way comfortable and needed afflicting. Being pastoral included challenging a privileged group of Upper East Siders to put their faith into action. But it never was in place of dealing with their individual crises, dilemmas, insecurities, fears.

"I remember doing a service once where we were talking about the prisons. A couple of prisoners spoke, and I spoke about the need to reform the prisons. I remember a woman [in the pews] who was crying. About halfway through my sermon, she got up and left, and I never saw her again. I realized there was not a single thing in that entire service that could have given comfort to a person who was giving one more chance to religion, who was at her wit's end and looking for a lifeline. She came looking for bread, and we threw stones at her."[16]

The apprentice minister may not have thrown stones, but what he offered in the first year wasn't especially nourishing. Toward the end of it, the president of the All Souls board of trustees, Maxine Beshers, advised him to "work a little more on the sermons." As it was, Church already had been devoting nearly twenty hours a week to the task. To do more would have demanded that he abandon all other ministerial duties. Beshers's point, all the same, was that he was instructing his listeners more than moving them.[17]

To be sure, Church's scholarly impulse remained strong. All Souls congregants were tutored in the theology of the early Christian philosopher Origen, the mysteries of Hinduism's Rig Veda, and America's "first amnesty debate" after the Revolution. (Many of these topics were the subject of journal articles he was publishing.) They were reminded of their Unitarian heritage, with its emphasis on reason, freedom of thought, and tolerance.[18]

The older Church tended to laugh at his youthful homiletic ineptitude. Yet no matter what their subject was, these sermons were nearly always marked by intelligence and grace. On several occasions, they were remarkably touching. The birth of his son prompted reflections on the wonder and preciousness of life that went against the grain of seventies Me Decade self-absorption. Defining the individual as invariably bound up and nurtured in a web of interdependence, he proclaimed: "Rather than the world owing us a living, we owe our living to the world." In another sermon, he coined the phrase that infused "seize the day" with a bright new clarity. Instead of "pining over a past that is no more or longing for a future that may never be," he suggested the spiritual exercise of "nostalgia for the present."[19]

From the start, Church employed self-deprecating humor to close the distance between himself and parishioners. While informing them that he had completed his Ph.D. thesis, for instance, he made light of the accomplishment. "The good news for the rest of you is, first, that none will be forced to read it, and second, that I could not wring a sermon topic out of it if I tried."

Near the end of his first year, he demonstrated that Maxine Beshers's admonition had hit home. "You Are Not Alone" was his most intimate and confessional sermon yet. While weighing whether to accept the All

Souls post the year before, he revealed, he had sought advice from the experts at UUA headquarters in Boston. He was asked to consider whether he had experienced enough "real failure and pain to minister in depth to those who had." At the time, he didn't know how to reply. And, yes, he had been blessed with a loving family, excellent schooling, material comfort, and a generally sunny disposition. But from the pulpit Church admitted that he had, indeed, "many dark nights of the soul" when he felt his life was "a fraud and my accomplishments more superficial than sincere.

"I do not make it a practice to preach from a confessional stance," he cautioned. "Self-indulgence too often is the result." Yet it's no cause for shame, he went on, to open our hearts to one another in this church; rather, it is an opportunity to heal and grow. Over the years, this open-hearted approach would become, unashamedly, Church's signature homiletic style. It would become a tool, not for self-indulgence, but for probing the depths.[20]

Church ascended to the All Souls post without a seasoning elsewhere. His "promise" carried high expectations, but with mediocre performance, it could turn into a cudgel to beat him. He had rushed to complete his Ph.D. dissertation the summer before he arrived. And once there, he had to adjust to fatherhood and an unfamiliar city. On any measure of stress, he was off the charts. The people of All Souls could afford to give him time to find his way. What could not be postponed was the debate about the cross.

In the chancel at the front of the sanctuary, above the high pulpit, hung a large brass cross. This central symbol of Christianity, a visual representation of Christ as savior, is a fixture in Christian churches. In Unitarian churches, however, it was an anomaly, and outside of New England and pockets of the Northeast, it was rarely found. Before the 1961 union with Unitarians, Universalist churches employed the symbol of a circle with a small, off-center cross within it, implying that Christianity was one valid religion but not necessarily superior to others. Wherever a cross remained, it served as a reminder of denominational roots, not as an expression of current belief. UUs might revere Jesus as an inspiring moral teacher, but it was the rare one who accepted his deity as Christians do.[21]

In the waning years of his ministry, Walter Kring had slowly and subtly nudged his congregation toward removing All Souls' cross. It was an anachronism that did not accurately portray the spirit of the church. So he set in motion a series of meetings and committees to discuss the issue. Parishioners debated whether a different symbol—perhaps a representation of Earth floating in space—might be more appropriate given the denomination's universalist leanings. Opinon was fairly evenly divided, and tempers sometimes flared. Some members who defined themselves as "Unitarian Christians" saw no reason to change. Bert Zippel, chairman of the committee that brought Forrest to All Souls, was adamantly opposed to retaining the cross. What it said, loudly and clearly, he asserted, was "No Jews wanted." This despite the fact that, according to Kring, it was Jewish members themselves, at the outset of World War II, who had requested that the cross be installed. (It had been created for the previous All Souls edifice, and not used when the Lexington Avenue building was first opened.) Assimilated and eager to fit in, they wanted to be identified with a "Christian" institution. In any event, it was not until June 1978 that the congregation finally voted to remove the cross. But they did so on the condition that it would be reinstalled if there were no agreement on what to put in its place by February 1, 1979. Despite Kring's best efforts, resolution of the issue was Challenge Number One for the untested Forrest Church.[22]

Nurtured in a political household, Church drew on superb political instincts. He had "a sense of the room," in the same way that Bill Bradley had, in John McPhee's phrase, "a sense of where you are" on the basketball court. He could quickly grasp who the players were, what they wanted, and what was needed to get things done. In this case, he understood that he should remain neutral. He was the newcomer. What mattered most, he emphasized in several sermons, was civility, tolerance, and democratic decision-making. In the end, all those qualities triumphed. The congregation voted for what amounted to a split decision—to commission an original artwork that would be cross-like, if not a cross itself.[23]

A committee chaired by Schuyler Chapin, dean of Columbia University's School of the Arts and former general manager of the Metropolitan Opera, would pick the artist. Whomever they chose, it was clear, would have class. Sue Fuller met that standard. A student of the abstract painters Hans Hofmann and Josef Albers, she had exhibited string sculptures at the Museum of Modern Art, the Guggenheim, and London's Tate Gallery. The piece she finished for All Souls—sixty thousand feet of gold-colored fluorocarbon monofilament in two intersecting bars—looked like a cross tilted slightly rightward. Or it was something else—an airplane propeller, according to All Souls wags. In truth, it was a religious Rorschach test. If you needed to see a cross, it was there. If it seemed more like an abstract expression of the cosmos, that was there, too.[24]

"It worked," said Harris Riordan, parish assistant during that period. "Forrest was really good at arranging the conditions such that people come up with a decision that suits everyone. But he didn't do it with a heavy hand. He did it in a way that the congregation was also strengthened."

Church was earning their trust, establishing his leadership, learning when to push and when to hold back. But he had bigger plans for the church and for himself. Just five months into the job, he informed parishioners that he envisioned All Souls as "the flagship for religious liberals across the country." He would pick up the baton of Henry Whitney Bellows.[25]

To make that happen, Church would have to find ways to spread his message. The first step came a year later when he was asked to deliver the A. Powell Davies Memorial Address at All Souls Church in Washington, D.C. This was a distinguished lecture series inaugurated by Adlai Stevenson in 1959. Next, in August 1981, Forrest was invited to be theme speaker at the Southwest Unitarian Universalist Summer Institute, at Lake Texoma, on the Texas-Oklahoma border.

In these early lectures, the themes that would become central to

Forrest's ministry are sharply etched. He challenged Unitarians, so eager to dismiss orthodoxy elsewhere, to avoid getting stuck in orthodoxies of their own. And he encouraged them to emphasize what they believed rather than what beliefs they had discarded. Rightly understood, religion ought to be a positive, joyous experience. Without that, Unitarian Universalism would wither and die.

Freedom from superstition and dogma, that UU hallmark, was not enough. The age-old religious questions could not be ignored. What is the good life? What is the good person? What is my responsibility to my brothers and sisters? What is my relation to death? If the answers from other religions did not satisfy, that hardly negated the importance of the questions.

Even allegedly outdated concepts like "sin" and "salvation," Church contended, remained not only useful but essential. However narrowly defined by the Jerry Falwells of the world, these words spoke to human truths. The unbounded faith in human nature proclaimed by twentieth-century Unitarianism had been destroyed forever by the horrors of war and the Holocaust. The timeless demons within us—of greed, pride, and so on—too often overpowered our better angels. For a clearer understanding of "salvation," Church looked to the word's roots in health and wholeness. Besides finding meaning in old ideas reenvisioned, he found inspiration in Jesus. But this wasn't Falwell's Jesus. The Apostles' Creed cited Jesus's miraculous birth and resurrection but said nothing at all about Jesus's life. It was the life that mattered—"the power of his love, the penetrating simplicity of his teachings, the force of his example of service on behalf of the disenfranchised and downtrodden."

Here, too, Church introduced his evocative and original definition of religion: "our human response to the dual reality of being alive and having to die." Thus humans are the only religious animals, aware of their own mortality. This awareness gives to life an extraordinary intensity and piquancy. Our love gains in meaning precisely because it will one day be snatched away. "In facing death," he wrote, "one challenge above all others remains, to live in such a way that our lives will prove to have been worth dying for."

Drawing on sources as diverse as D. H. Lawrence, Emerson, Thoreau, Blake, and the Buddha, Church hailed life as an "undeserved, unexpected gift, holy, awesome and mysterious." Starting with the miracle of birth, the miraculous lay in the commonplace, in what was at hand every day, if only we would look with open eyes. The Buddha denied being a god, prophet, or saint. He was merely one who was truly "awake." Awakening, Church suggested, was the Unitarian Universalist version of conversion, "not so much changing who we are, but rather discovering who we are." In so doing, we are truly born again.[26]

These lectures were privately published in paperback and widely distributed. Bearing the catchy title of *Born Again Unitarian Universalism*, the book's intent was clear. Church was unabashedly comfortable with ideas well outside the usual UU parameters. This was passionate stuff, not the bloodless Unitarianism of the mid twentieth century. To most UUs, the very idea of being "born again" was off-putting, smacking of Bible Belt rubes. Church chose instead to expand the terms of debate, to see how a Unitarian perspective might be enlarged. In so doing, he hoped to move liberal religion from the margins to take its place at the larger American religious table.

One Neighbor at a Time

*The true preacher can be known by this, that he deals out
to the people his life . . . passed through the fire of thought.*

—RALPH WALDO EMERSON

Before Forrest Church could reach out to the nation, he had to solidify and revitalize his base. However influential its past, the present-day All Souls Church was badly in need of adrenaline. It was too small, too sleepy, too insular to have any impact beyond its own little world. Yet Forrest would have to bide his time. Moving too fast might be counterproductive. His parishioners were older than he and more set in their ways. He would first have to absorb the All Souls ethos and then shift it, ever so gently, toward more ambitious goals. He would have to be, like Rhys Williams, a sly fox.

What was this All Souls ethos? Call it "high-church Unitarianism." In an age when many UU societies eschewed using the word *God*, All Souls was clearly and unabashedly theistic. Its choir sang the works of the great European composers, including excerpts of masses and chorales in the Christian tradition. Its liturgy had a decidedly Protestant tone. *The Hymn and Service Book*, which All Souls had published on its own in 1957, was still in use. All of the readings included were texts from the Bible; all of the prayers would have been perfectly suitable in mainline Protestant denominations. There were five suggested Orders of Service. The

Lord's Prayer—"Our Father, who art in heaven, hallowed be thy name . . ."—stood at the center of each of them.

The UU protocol of "freedom of the pulpit" gave Forrest wide latitude over the form of Sunday services. So he gradually alternated between using this liturgy and one that was less traditional and less Christian in tone. Within a few years, the "red hymnal" was abandoned altogether, and the church began to use one published by the denomination. With this move, All Souls took a giant step from the 1950s into the '80s. "We seek to move beyond gender in the language of our worship," the preface of the new hymnal noted. "If religious language perpetuates views of the divine or the human in purely masculine forms, it runs contrary to our best understanding." Consequently, all words like *Lord*, from the Lord's Prayer, were banished from hymns. *Brotherhood, men,* and so on were transformed into more inclusive substitutes. Symbolically, the shift from the red hymnal to the new green hymnal of 1982 could not have been more striking.[1]

Within the denomination, the All Souls ethos was also conservative in terms of social activism. In the preceding two decades, many UU churches joined the struggle to end the Vietnam War, promote racial equality, and combat discrimination based on gender or sexual orientation. They took up the mantle of reform where Theodore Parker, Olympia Brown, and countless others had left off. But too many of them became, in Forrest's words, "social-action clearing houses." This was all well and good, up to a point. But people initially drawn to these churches because of their political tilt may have grown disappointed by a lack of spiritual sustenance. Unitarians, Church believed, ought to offer more depth than the standard answers supplied by the National Organization for Women or the American Civil Liberties Union.

Rev. Kring, "anti-antiwar, anti-protester," had stood on the establishment side of the Vietnam-era divide. He had also resisted what he saw as the radical chic of UU "Black Power" politics. Aside from a spirited advocacy of internationalism and the United Nations, social issues had remained low on the Kring agenda. The All Souls of his tenure kept largely aloof from the social problems roiling the nation and festering just outside its doors. Forrest Church tried to steer a middle way. Although he had no use for the church as a mere "social-action clearing house," he sought to ignite a spirit of compassion for New York City's poor.

"As the church became more politically, socially, ethically engaged, it became more spiritual at the same time," Forrest Church said. "We cut against the cliché of, is this a religious church or a political church?"[2]

As Church grew into his role, he was not shy about speaking out on such issues as the nuclear arms race, racism, or sexism, but he rarely evangelized on behalf of his own pet projects. In general, he believed that social action at All Souls should emerge from the ground up, not be imposed from the pulpit. (This had been Fosdick's view, too, at Riverside Church.) Hence Church's pragmatic policy of let-a-hundred-flowers-bloom reformism. For example, at one point All Souls hosted two competing groups dealing with animals, one objecting to any use in scientific experiments and another, desperate for cures for AIDS, taking the opposite view. Projects that proved their worthiness, Church knew, would flourish and endure. Some would thrive for a while, only to wither away when they'd outlived their usefulness. Some might die a quick death. Yet the assumption was that each would emerge from a base of congregational enthusiasm that might ultimately sustain it. The only restriction was that each social-action group be understood to speak only for itself, not for All Souls as a whole. "That's where you run into problems in a large congregation," Church said, "where you end up alienating members who feel that the church no longer speaks for them."[3]

Two and a half years into Church's ministry, it was time to speak out. It was adrenaline time. He took a page from philosopher Henri Bergson on static and dynamic religion. "Ours is a healthy church," he declared in a March 1981 sermon. "It is a comfortable church to be in and worship in. It is a friendly church . . . But is it, by Bergson's definition, a dynamic church? I would have to concede that in large measure it is not." Startled, the congregation responded by calling a special meeting that very afternoon. There members vowed to work in "lay ministry" with neighborhood organizations to improve the lot of the poor.[4]

When the Yorkville Emergency Alliance came calling, in the fall of that year, Forrest Church led by example. Yorkville, essentially the eastern and nonaffluent half of the Upper East Side, had historically been home to working-class families of German, Irish, Czech, Polish, Hungarian, and Jewish descent. By the eighties, the neighborhood was reeling under the effects of Reagan administration cuts in social services. Nearly five thousand residents subsisted on welfare. Paradoxically, the area's low crime rate also made it a natural sanctuary for homeless people from other parts of the city. "The likelihood of a homeless person being rolled on the Upper East Side was less than in other neighborhoods," said Rev. Hays Rockwell of St. James Episcopal Church, "so they would come and sleep in our [church] doorways."

Sparked by Rev. Alanson B. Houghton Jr. of the Church of the Heavenly Rest (Episcopal), Upper East Side clergy organized the Alliance as a means of raising money that would be funneled to cash-starved community agencies. The energetic, thirty-three-year-old Forrest Church was elected president. A grants committee was set up, chaired by Gay Vance, wife of the recently retired secretary of state, Cyrus Vance. The Alliance aided existing neighborhood agencies targeting youth, the poor, and the elderly. It also identified gaps in services, helping create the Neighborhood Coalition for Shelter, which cared for battered women, and the Yorkville Common Pantry, a soup kitchen serving a thousand needy residents at various churches and synagogues.

Oddly enough, the Reagan White House decided to give the Alliance a national award for being an example of how the trickle-down world of reduced government funding was going to shine brighter. To their dismay, Alliance board members learned that Reagan's "coordination office" in the executive branch had no intention of trying to replicate similar projects or to advocate for public-private partnerships, but was merely running "a PR shill to show how sloughing off [public] funding was proving a great success," Church said. "We, of course, happily turned them down."[5]

At All Souls itself, Church employed the stick of conscience and the carrot of his effervescent personality. In a November 1982 sermon, he quoted Fosdick on Unitarians as a prod. "The breeze of a mild good will fills their sails . . . But they soon land . . . They mean well but they mean well feebly." Next he quoted a slogan from a Poor People's Campaign rally in New Mexico: "I was hungry / and you formed a humanities club / and discussed my hunger." The better model, Church said, was Jesus of Nazareth, who actually fed the hungry. "Love in the abstract," he charged, "is a fraud."[6]

In that spirit, All Souls established "Monday Night Hospitality" in co-operation with other Upper East Side churches to provide dinner for the poor every day of the week. In the spring of 1983, the "Friday Soup Kitchen" followed suit. All Souls volunteers, including Amy Church, served dozens of neighbors a hot lunch every Friday in Fellowship Hall in the church basement. To avoid the taint of *noblesse oblige*, those being fed were always referred to as "guests." Social workers were on hand to help them gain access to social services, and sometimes a pianist dropped by to provide mealtime music. Unfortunately, the need to feed the hungry long outlasted both the Yorkville Emergency Alliance and the age of Reagan. In the first decade of the twenty-first century, these programs were larger than ever: 265 were being fed on Monday nights and 250 on Fridays.[7]

Another approach to aiding the poor was to focus on the next generation. In 1987, the economist and author Sylvia Ann Hewlett made the case for an All Souls Children's Task Force. More than 40 percent of the city's children, she noted, were growing up below the poverty line, while indices of child welfare were deteriorating, from unaffordable child care to rising school dropout rates to the number of crack babies abandoned in hospitals. Meanwhile, the "pro-family" slogan had become synonymous with right-wing polemics against abortion and gays, even as it avoided the everyday desperation of poor families. Liberals ought to take up the cause of dispossessed children, thus challenging the terms of who really was pro-family. In the meantime, there were a host of practical things that the people of All Souls could do. "You do not need to be a left-wing activist," Hewlett wrote, "to be concerned about babies being 'warehoused' in city hospitals."[8]

All Souls awakened even more. Volunteers visited hospitals, fed the hungry, tutored students at PS 151 in East Harlem, discovering myriad ways to relieve suffering and inspire children to achieve a better life. This was social service on the local level, if not activism aimed at changing social structures. This was about changing the world, in Forrest's phrase, "one neighbor at a time."

One vehicle for reaching kids was a time-tested one, the Boy Scouts and Girl Scouts. Members of the Children's Task Force had already established programs at the Prince George, a squalid welfare hotel on East Twenty-eighth Street riddled with drug dealing, when they learned about Scoutreach, a Scout program aimed at inner-city boys. Troop 103 was organized at the hotel with All Souls member Armando Mejia-Gallardo as scoutmaster. Soon the boys were hiking, camping, attending summer camp, visiting the nation's capital. The troop's first outing, on the Delaware River, was "crazy!" according to Mejia-Gallardo. "I didn't know how to handle these kids. The first day there were endless fights, not just with each other but with me. But after two days, I established my authority by putting them to bed and waking them up at a certain hour and just living a schedule. Soon they were just regular kids." Over time, the habits of setting goals, of working together, and of honoring good values paid off. For many of these boys—and their sisters in All Souls–sponsored Girl Scout troops—the results were higher grades, better family relations, and improved self-respect.[9]

Exhibit A was Jamel Oeser-Sweat. Though hardly typical, this Eagle Scout nonetheless represented that talent, if given a little guidance, could emerge from the lowest depths. Jamel's family life was precarious. His father had died when the boy was young, and his mother was hospitalized for a time for mental illness. Little wonder that his school attendance was spotty. But the experience with Troop 103 imbued him with new confidence, and after excelling in science, he was guided to a research program at Mount Sinai Hospital. The microbiology project he pursued there, on the spread of bacteria via hospital sponges, made him a tenth-place winner in the renowned Westinghouse Science Talent Search, usually dominated by students from the nation's top high schools. All the media attention that followed, he said, was "like being Cinderella. You wear your suit and go [to an awards event], and you have to go back to the projects by midnight." In the end, this Cinderella escaped the projects. He was awarded a full scholarship to New York University and later became an attorney.[10]

Meanwhile, Upper East Side clergymen formed an alliance with their counterparts in East Harlem, north of Ninety-sixth Street. Crossing 96th Street, as the organization was called, was designed to bridge the gaps between white haves and black have-nots. Though each group had much to learn from the other, it was the Upper East Siders who could provide educational expertise and money to the less privileged.

Through this organization, Forrest Church got to know the redoubtable Rev. Leroy Ricksy, pastor of the Church of the Resurrection. Ricksy's path to the ministry was as different from Forrest's as possible. Born in rural Virginia, Ricksy had spent much of his childhood in four foster families. He had dropped out of his segregated school—located, literally, in a chicken coop—in fifth grade to work on a farm. After drifting through years of drug addiction, homelessness, jail time, and a near-fatal stabbing, he had found a way out of hopelessness in Christianity and had eventually worked his way into the Congregational ministry.

Like many others, Forrest was moved and inspired by this unlikely journey. In the spirit of interracial amity, the two men resolved to form a "sister church" relationship between All Souls and Resurrection. The pastors preached in each other's pulpit, and parishioners held dinners in one another's homes. Ricksy had opened his church basement for kids with nowhere else to go after school. Soon he was calling his burgeoning operation the Booker T. Washington Learning Center, in honor of the pioneering African-American educator and self-help advocate. The kids' mothers and grandmothers helped out when they could, but Ricksy needed more volunteers, a lot more. Enter Mary-Ella Holst, a witty, energetic activist who had been All Souls' director of religious education. Holst was the first manager of what in time evolved into a steady All Souls pipeline. Volunteers tutored students, taught arts and computing skills, organized field trips to the local library and museums, donated books, hosted Christmas parties. And they raised tens of thousands of dollars, so that beneficiaries of the center's programs eventually ranged from preschoolers to adults studying for high-school equivalency degrees. To the people of the Booker T. Washington Center, "one neighbor at a time" became more than a well-meaning slogan.[11]

As All Souls began reaching out to its neighbors, the city was grappling with a mysterious, nameless menace, a new disease that seemed to single out Haitians, drug users, hemophiliacs, and gay men. By mid-1982, even if its causes remained unknown, the malady had been given a scientific name: acquired immune deficiency syndrome, or AIDS. For this gruesome, harrowing ravager, there was no cure. And because it was initially little understood, it scared everyone. Could you be contaminated by kissing, by using a public toilet seat, even by shaking the wrong person's hand? Never mind that none of these fears was warranted. Landlords evicted gay people; morticians refused to deal with AIDS-infected bodies. When Ryan White, a hemophiliac with AIDS, was expelled from his Indiana middle school, he became the poster child for a mindless fear that blamed the victim. Reactionary Bible thumpers upped the ante. Already condemning the morality of homosexuality, they hailed AIDS as God's scourge. Gay men, went the not-so-subtle message, deserved to die.

The people of All Souls disagreed, and Chuck Weiss strongly disagreed. A gay public-relations man, Weiss hoped that his church would lead the way. It could minister directly to AIDS patients, alleviate the psychological toll on their loved ones, educate the public, and encourage tolerance. Weiss found in Forrest Church a steadfast ally who grasped that this was one of the defining issues of his time, just as Vietnam had been in his college years. He vowed to be out in front on this one.

"AIDS: A Religious Response," Church's sermon of September 29, 1985, called for equal parts contrition, compassion, and action. Like many people, he confessed, he grew up with "a glib and thoughtless prejudice against homosexuals." Not until his first year of seminary, when he learned that his best friend there (Timothy Pfaff) was gay, did that prejudice begin to dissipate. They shared passions for music and poetry, and "every hour I spent with him, I learned something new about the power and possibilities of human expression." And despite having gay friends later, and even officiating at several funerals for AIDS victims, his response to the AIDS crisis had been tepid. "The proper word for this is *sin*. Every failure of moral imagination is a sin of omission." He then invoked Camus's *The Plague*, in which Father Paneloux interprets the disease's attack on his town in traditional terms as "the flail of God," just as the contemporary religious right was using AIDS as a hammer to beat gays. "But I believe in a different God than Jerry Falwell does," Church said. "I believe in a God of mercy, a God of infinite compassion. I believe in a God who inspired Jesus to reach out to the poor and the dispossessed, to prostitutes and prodigal children, to humble folk and outcasts, not only to reach out to them but to hold them in humble esteem." AIDS was being used as an excuse to act out age-old prejudices. "Give bigotry a pretext, and it will spread like cancer. Bigotry is far more virulent a virus than is AIDS . . . There is such a thing as Hell on earth, and it is populated for the most part by people who fear so deeply that they cannot love." To demonstrate All Souls' spirit of love, Church announced a forum on AIDS for that afternoon, with speakers from Gay Men's Health Crisis and the AIDS Medical Foundation. Members would be invited to form a Task Force on AIDS.[12]

Not only was the task force set up, but ministers from around the nation who had heard the news, which was broadcast on CNN, wrote and telephoned Church to inquire about replicating it. Led by Chuck Weiss and staffed by an army of volunteers, gay and straight, the task force plunged into the work. Face-to-face with a plague without a cure, their responsibilities seemed endless: individual counseling and support groups for AIDS patients, male and female; support groups for parents of adult children with AIDS; expert-staffed workshops to spread accurate information about the disease; financial support for PWA's (People with AIDS) *Coalition Newsletter* and for pediatric AIDS programs; weekend meals for home-bound AIDS patients through God's Love We Deliver; lobbying public officials for adequate funding for AIDS research and nondiscriminatory treatment of AIDS patients.[13]

For its members, the task force proved to be an energizing alternative to hand-wringing. Barbara Hosein, a biologist at the New York Blood Center, knew that the disease could not be transmitted by casual contact. So she brought her son to task-force meetings, and the nine-year-old became the group's de facto mascot. Inez Miller, a nurse, had witnessed up close the agonies of AIDS patients. Author Barbara Lazear Ascher had lost her brother to the disease and wrote a memoir about the experience, *Landscape Without Gravity*. Together, they added a quietly fierce determination to enlighten the public about the scourge.[14]

But what was the best way to do that? Margaret Blagg suggested an ad campaign in the city's subways and buses. If the task force could place public-service placards alongside those for breast cancer or asthma, AIDS might be domesticated. It would be less of a horror show, just another disease. People might begin to think rationally about it. Fear and loathing might be transformed into compassion. A friend of Blagg's, adman Richard Solomon, wrote the copy without pay. His art director, Katherine Ippoliti, drew pencil sketches of the faces of a man, a woman, and a child, one for each of three posters. The implication was clear: the disease could infect anyone, not just gay men. The messages were kept deliberately low-key and nonthreatening:

"AIDS is a human disease. It requires a humane response."

"AIDS. The more you understand, the more understanding you'll be."

"Treat people with AIDS with kindness. It won't kill you."

Below the slogan was the phone number for a national AIDS hotline, operated by the Centers for Disease Control. And below that, the name and address of the ad's sponsor, All Souls Church.[15]

There is no way to assess the campaign's effectiveness, though it did attract its share of media attention, including positive front-page coverage in *The Wall Street Journal.* And in 1991, the task force received the award for Outstanding AIDS Ministries from the AIDS National Interfaith Network. But for a month or so in 1987—that was all the time the church and its task force could afford—New York City residents were put on notice that there was a church that refused to bow to prejudice, that embraced gay people as worthy members of the human family.[16]

Bill Bechman certainly noticed. In 1980 he had moved to New York from Washington, D.C., to direct the human resources department for a nonprofit. As thrilled as he was to be in New York, he was anxious about this strange new disease targeting gay men like him. At the Baptist church in Washington where he served as organist, the minister had declared the disease God's punishment for sin. So when he saw the All Souls signs on the subway in 1987, he was taken aback and then intrigued and heartened. "People have that yearning to be pronounced good," he remembered feeling. He visited the church, felt immediately welcomed, and started volunteering with the AIDS Task Force. Within a few years, he was its president. A few years after that, he rose to the presidency of the church's board of trustees. As clearly as anyone, Bechman represented the path of compassion and service fostered by Forrest Church's leadership.[17]

In 1984, most of these programs were still in their infancy. Some had not even been imagined. All Souls was but one of many churches, in New York and elsewhere, whose collective conscience had been stirred to action. Reaching out to the less fortunate in its community hardly made it unique. Eventually, the scale of activity became impressive, indeed, but it was not yet there in 1984.

What did set it off was its minister. More precisely, in terms of the outside world's perspective, it was the minister's father. By the late seventies, Frank Church had finally achieved his lifelong dream of chairing the prestigious Senate Foreign Relations Committee. But his triumph was short-lived, and the power often illusory, as this liberal was forced to maneuver between a cautious President Carter and a newly powerful, virulently conservative right wing. Church's support for the 1978 treaties that returned the Panama Canal to the Panamanians cost him dearly. In the 1980 election, ultraconservative Congressman Steve Symms accused Church of "giving away" the canal and won the Senate seat for the Republicans. Even so, his margin of victory was only 4,262 votes, a mere 1 percent of the total.

After four illustrious terms in office, the former "boy senator" was still in his fifties. Life beyond the Senate beckoned, offering attractive opportunities. Hired by a big law firm, Whitman and Ransom, he earned a substantial income for the first time in his life. Given leeway to lecture and write about politics, he remained a liberal icon.[18]

And then he got sick. In the weeks before Christmas 1983, a weakened Church appeared gaunt and jaundiced. In January, he was admitted to Memorial Sloan-Kettering Cancer Center in New York for tests and a surgical procedure. Once again, as in his early manhood, the news was awful. His surgeons discovered an inoperable cancer of the pancreas that had spread to the liver. When a *New York Times* reporter requested an interview with the young minister about how he was coping with his father's illness, Forrest invited him instead to attend a Sunday church service. His pulpit tribute underlined the transformative impact of his father's bout with cancer thirty-five years before:

"Ever since my father's illness, my parents have lived on borrowed time. Fully aware of life's fragility, they have not been afraid to risk and give of themselves fully. Life for them is not a given, but a gift. It is a gift with a price attached. That price is death. . . . Death is the ultimate mystery. But there is a way to counter this fear. We can live in such a way that our lives prove worth dying for."[19]

Despite the grave diagnosis, the senior Church retained a sense of humor. Reading the *Times* account of the sermon in the hospital, he remarked to his son, "Well, Forrest, it looks like that is the last thing I'm going to be able to do to advance your career."[20]

Toward the end of the month, Frank Church left the hospital to spend his last months at home in Bethesda. He lingered until April 7, surrounded at his death by family and friends. He was fifty-nine years old. A memorial service in Washington's National Cathedral—with Ted Kennedy, George McGovern, and Forrest Church among the eulogists—was followed by another service at the Cathedral of the Rockies in Boise. There, Church continued the homage:

"Because my father was not afraid to die, he was not afraid to live. He did not spend his life, as so many of us do, little by little until he was gone. He gave it away to others . . . In his life, my father was a bit like the day star, rising early to prominence, brilliant in the dusk and against the darkness, showing other stars the way. When it came time for him to go, when his precious flame flickered, he was ready. Peacefully, naturally, with serenity and grace, he returned his light unto the eternal horizon. Like the day star, my father went out with the dawn."[21]

Forrest Church had been nurtured on Frank Church's legacy as a youth, rebelled against it as a college student, then returned to the fold to embrace it as a young man. Now, in the wake of his father's death, it was catapulting him onto the national stage.

The *Times* coverage of Forrest's sermon during his father's treatment at Sloan-Kettering was not the first time it had taken note of the young cleric. His arrival at All Souls in 1978 was the subject of a brief item, as was the dedication (the Unitarian term for christening) of his infant son, Frank, complete with a photo including the Idaho senator. In those halcyon days for the paper of record, the definition of "all the news that's fit to print" could be stretched almost infinitely.

By 1984 the media hive that is Manhattan began to stir. Following the *Times's* lead, *Esquire* jumped in. That year's December issue cited Church in its annual list of "The Best of the New Generation." In six categories— Science and Technology, Arts and Letters, Education and Social Service, Business and Industry, Entertainment, Sports and Style, and Politics and Law—*Esquire* toted up the rising stars under forty. Here were Bill Gates, Meryl Streep, Henry Louis Gates, John Adams, David Mamet, Thomas

L. Friedman, David Lynch, Sally Ride, Bill and Hillary Clinton—and Forrest Church.

"Church is the son of the late U.S. senator Frank Church," the citation began, "but his accomplishments go far beyond the coincidence of his birth." After praising the All Souls social-outreach programs, Forrest Church had encouraged, the magazine noted that the young minister had "taken his activism to the international level as one of the newest members of the Council on Economic Priorities, whose concerns are corporate responsibility and the arms race." According to George Rupp, then dean of Harvard Divinity School and later president of Rice and Columbia universities, Church was "a very promising leader in American religion and thought. He's one of the few preachers whose sermons I read."[22]

In fact, Church, a member of the divinity school's alumni council, had delivered a series of lectures there that fall, and Rupp also remembered Amy Furth Church as a well-regarded dean of students. How did he have access to Forrest's sermons in the pre-Internet age? "He sent them to me," Rupp reported years later. "He was a very good self-promoter. I don't say that critically—it was one of the ways he was effective."[23]

Next to jump on the bandwagon was *Avenue*, a Manhattan monthly catering to the affluent and influential. This admiring profile paid little attention to All Souls' social programs. "A Senator's Son Shuns Politics for the Pulpit" was all about personality and pedigree. It portrayed Forrest as a quietly eloquent preacher, gifted "spiritual provocateur," and dutiful son. Despite the worries of some parishioners that he harbored political ambitions, Forrest denied any such plans: "I can't imagine any other life that would give me the combination of opportunities for reflection and for service that this one does."

Of all these opportunities, the most attractive by far was to write books. His first, he announced, was scheduled for publication in the fall of 1985. The project had its origin in a conversation a few months after Senator Church's death. Over lunch at the Century Association, the venerable Manhattan club for authors, artists, and "amateurs of letters and the fine arts," with Schuyler Chapin and *NBC Nightly News* anchor John Chancellor, Church had discussed a recent *USA Today* article in which he was quoted on American taboos about death and dying in connection with his father's passing. The article had generated unprecedented reader response. Chapin and Chancellor suggested that he take advantage of that outpouring of interest to shape his ideas and experience into a book. So in July 1984, during his customary summer vacation, he encamped to Rhys Williams's home near Boston Common—Williams summered in Maine—and began to write. A month later, he had completed a 350-page manuscript. Tentatively titled "My Father's Footsteps," the book would meld biography and autobiography. It would be about both Frank and Forrest Church.[24]

Father and Son begins and ends with cancer. The disease shapes Frank Church's young manhood and, later, cuts his life short. So the book is inevitably about the arts of living and dying. It is also a story of conflict and reconciliation between two brilliant, ambitious men. As it chronicles the senator's rise to power and acclaim, it simultaneously analyzes his son's struggle for identity. "It is as if [an adolescent] is not free to become himself," Forrest writes, "until he is tested against his father in some field of judgment. Yet even then, the object is not simply to best his father and establish his independence, but also to win his father's blessing. Accordingly, the goal of such a contest is twofold: at once to vanquish and to be blessed."[25] As the narrative moves from Idaho to the pivot point of Stanford to New York, it's clear that Forrest never vanquishes Frank Church. He lacks the power and, finally, the desire. But what he yearns for, and eventually receives, is the blessing. What he bestows on his father, in turn, is grateful homage for a legacy of intellect, integrity, political passion, and paternal love.

Since *Father and Son* deals with death and dying, it must, according to the author's own definition, deal with religion. So the book concludes with reflections on his unorthodox beliefs about deity: "For me, God is the genius of the life force, that which is greater than all and yet present in each . . . God is not God's name. God is our name for the spirit that animates and impels and finally infolds our lives unto its own . . . We are part of something larger, something ongoing and eternal, inscrutable perhaps even unto itself."[26]

As memoirs go, this one was an unusual mix of the self-serving and the self-deprecatory. Church could make fun of his youthful follies even as he hitched his wagon to his father's star. To kick off the book's publication, Washington's liberal establishment gathered for a party hosted by Senator Claiborne Pell of Rhode Island. Former senators Edmund Muskie, Gaylord Nelson, and Albert Gore Sr. mingled with incumbent senators Alan Cranston, Howard Metzenbaum, and Gary Hart. Among the Democratic elite, Forrest Church was right at home. Later, appearing on NBC's *Today Show*, he offered sound bites with a politician's ease.[27]

The reviews were almost uniformly positive. Memoirs about parents are "often savage or saccharine, whining or windy," Washington journalist David Murray pointed out in a short notice in *The New York Times Book Review*. *Father and Son* was none of the above. Its author was "clearly a person of determination and insight . . . If Frank Church has a monument, it is that he made his son think his father was a great and good man. In these days, that is an accomplishment." In *The Washington Post*, veteran political observer Chalmers Roberts groused that the memoirist was "not a felicitous writer" but, overall, applauded his honest soul-searching. In Forrest's hometown *Idaho Statesman*, Rod Gramer, who would later cowrite a fine biography of Senator Church, neatly captured the book's strengths: it was "gracefully written, often humorous and profoundly humane."[28]

"Tempo," the *Chicago Tribune*'s features section, edited by former All Souls member Tom Stites, published an excerpt about the senator's final days. Likewise, *The Boston Globe* opted for an interview over a review. Trying to highlight in a catchy epigram the differences between his father's mission and his own, Forrest overstated them: "My father was interested in changing the country's political leanings. I am interested in changing what's in people's hearts." But the son was hardly above the political fray. Sermon after sermon in this period actively challenged conservative views on welfare, race, homosexuality, women, and the arms race.[29]

If nothing else, memoirs showcase personality. The astute book editor of the Fort Lauderdale *News/Sun-Sentinel* pinpointed one aspect of Church's. He "wouldn't be his father's son if he weren't a little in love with the sound of his own voice." Or, one might say with less bite, he wouldn't be a preacher. Similarly, UUA president William Schulz, professing that Senator Church was a political idol of his and Forrest one of his "dearest friends," informed readers of *Unitarian Universalist World*, the official voice of the denomination, that, along with "polish, charm, eloquence," his friend had inherited his father's "penchant for publicity." Church must have been slack-jawed. Even if accurate—and it was—why was this observation necessary in these circumstances? No matter. Schulz later proved to be a true friend when Church desperately needed one.[30]

In the meantime, Forrest had a friend in Bernice Kanner. An advertising columnist and feature writer for *New York*, Kanner had become an enthusiast while attending All Souls and had, in fact, encouraged him to write *Father and Son*. In the lax magazine world where she operated, the stringent rules banning conflicts of interest that keep newspaper reporters in line were often honored in the breach. Kanner's piece in *New York*, "The Church Revival: Packing 'Em In on the Upper East Side," was a love fest posing as a profile. Appearing in early November 1985, just as *Father and Son* was being published, it seemed a well-oiled cog in the book's marketing machine.

"A religious revival of sorts is under way in that bastion of secularism, the Upper East Side," Kanner swooned. "Propounding an eighties version of the liberal sixties theology of love, peace and activism . . . the son of the late senator Frank Church has brought a touch of old-fashioned prairie populism to the corner of 80th and Lexington." It's hard to sort out the clichés and downright inaccuracies in this flow of gush. Forrest wasn't a populist in politics or theology; Idaho is a mountain state west of the prairies; his "love, peace and activism" had almost nothing to do with the sixties.

"With his toothy aw-shucks smile and penchant for self-promotion," she continued, "Church has also become something of a media personality." With the memoir just out, a Larry King interview on CNN was about to follow his *Today Show* appearance. A second book, *The Devil and Dr. Church*, was coming out next May. And he was hosting a cable TV show, *Unitarian Universalist Discussions*.

All Souls membership, Kanner noted, had nearly doubled since Forrest assumed its pulpit. Admirers lined up to explain why. "Forrest Church is theater," Schuyler Chapin said, "not in the thunderous, hypnotic, show-biz way of Norman Vincent Peale or Fulton Sheen. He is theater that moves and touches, that humanizes religion." George Rupp, now president of Rice University, cited sermons with "a knack for putting complex ideas into elegant and catchy prose that paints pictures. Too often, liberal religious preachers fall into the trap of being exclusively intellectual. Forrest livens things up." Hays Rockwell, Forrest's colleague from the Yorkville Emergency Alliance, pointed to an infectious personality: "Forrest is exactly what he seems to be—candid, bright, warm, accepting. There are no facades . . . It's easy for him to say to a man or a woman, 'I love you' and 'Bless your heart.' It seems so out of place to hear it in New York, but then, incongruity is all part of Forrest's charm."

Part of the charm, too, was the way this minister fashioned sermons out of the dross of his own life—his son's questions about God or the death of his best friend in college. The confessional tack, Forrest explained, was "a way to ward off discovery. Being open means being less vulnerable to being exposed." It was also a kind of therapy. "My greatest fault has always been self-indulgence, narcissism, staring at my own reflection. When I preach, it's as much to myself as to others."

After summarizing the long march from senator's son to Unitarian minister, Kanner quoted the beaming Harvard mentor George Hunston Williams on his protégé: "Here is a man who could have taught in a seminary, gone into politics, or become the dean of a school, but he chose to become a parish minister. He savors life from aesthetics to athletics"—giving Kanner the opening to add that Church was a huge Mets fan.[31]

From the pages of *New York*, Forrest Church emerges as not only a luminous intellect, a persuasive speaker, the soul of caring and decency, but also a regular guy who likes to go to ball games. Aside from the reference to self-promotion and Forrest's eye-opening revelation of narcissism, it's hard to imagine a more glowing profile.

At All Souls, Forrest Church had developed a solid institutional base. In Harper and Row, he had found a publisher committed to nourishing and publicizing his talent. He had brains and ambition in spades. In liberal circles at least, the Church name retained a certain magic. The media eagerly embraced his photogenic smile and affable personality. Given this entrée, this flashing, welcoming green light, what was he going to do next?

Unlike some sons of famous men, who languish in self-indulgence or squander their opportunities, Forrest Church made good use of them. On one success, he built another, then another. With one momentous exception, he transcended any self-destructive impulses and made something of himself, something quite different from his father, and utterly valuable for Americans concerned about the relations between religion and politics.

Seven

Liberal Evangelist

Where are the Beechers, Abbotts, Coffins, and
Fosdicks of yesteryear?
—EDWIN SCOTT GAUSTAD, 1983

N ot since the 1920s," proclaimed *Time* magazine in 1985, "have political Fundamentalists been as well financed, visible, organized and effective. Deeply committed believers, working long and zealously, get tavern hours trimmed in Anchorage; disrupt school-board meetings in Hillsboro, Mo., as they demand to control the curriculum; force doctors to stop performing abortions in Virginia Beach, Va.; march in San Antonio streets to protest sex channels on cable TV. The shelves of religious bookstores are filled with their social protests, in which the buzz words 'secular humanism' are used to cover anything and everything the authors disapprove of."[1]

For Forrest Church and his allies among religious liberals, what did this flurry of fundamentalist activism mean? As America entered the eighties, how dramatically had the religious scene changed? Why had voices gotten louder, and the willingness to live and let live dimmed? What had disrupted the classic postwar status quo of Protestant, Catholic, and Jew, all valuing a tolerant American pluralism? Why did the occasional cultural clash now seem fated to escalate into perpetual cultural war?

The religious landscape that Forrest Church surveyed from All Souls Church had been turned upside down in recent decades. More than ever, during the 1970s and '80s, Americans viewed religion as a matter of personal choice or preference. The autonomous individual on a spiritual quest replaced the norm of obediently following the religion of one's family or ethnicity. According to one mid-eighties poll, one in three church members had switched from the denomination of their birth. Eastern religions such as Zen, no longer mere fads, took hold with new vigor. Catholics and Mormons asserted themselves with new confidence. America remained the most churchgoing of industrial nations, but the ecclesiastical landscape had been redesigned, in sociologist Andrew Greeley's phrase, into "a mosaic with permeable boundaries."[2]

Within this mosaic, mainline Protestants no longer held sway. Churches that historically had dominated the culture and defined its reigning values—Episcopalians, Methodists, Presbyterians, and Congregationalists—were losing members at alarming rates, while Southern Baptists and various evangelical and pentecostalist denominations and independent "megachurches" were adding to their rolls in record numbers. Birth rates account for some of this tidal shift. They were declining for the former, accelerating for the latter. Mainline denominations were also aging and having a harder time retaining their young; they started fewer new churches, which tend to draw larger numbers, while being chained to big, downtown edifices as the population swarmed to the suburbs; and they failed to attract newer immigrants.[3]

The losers in this numbers game tended to be liberal or moderate in theology; they read the Bible with a critical eye, through the lenses of symbol and myth. For the winners, the Old and New Testaments embodied truth itself. But who were these true believers and how had they managed to vault into such prominence in the eighties?

Contrary to common opinion, the terms *fundamentalist* and *evangelical* are not interchangeable. *Time* magazine's politically active "fundamentalists" no doubt included many people who preferred to be called evangelicals. All fundamentalists are evangelicals, but not all evangelicals, even if theologically conservative, are fundamentalists.

The National Association of Evangelicals was formed in 1942 to distinguish itself from both the liberal Federal Council of Churches (later known as the National Council of Churches) and from the more old-school fundamentalists defined by images of uneducated, backwoods preachers hollering to overwrought churchgoers. By and large, evangelicals stood on these essential points: the final authority of the Bible, its historical accuracy, salvation only through Jesus Christ, the importance of evangelism, and the spiritually charged daily life. While fundamentalists agree with all of these propositions, they add to them a degree of greater strictness, like biblical inerrancy. The Bible's story of the creation of the world in six days, for example, is taken as literal truth. Not all evangelicals would agree. For both, *born again* is a common term for the experience of a rapture-filled dedication to Jesus Christ as savior.[4]

Until the 1970s, both groups kept this world, as opposed to the heavenly realm they expect to enter after death, at arm's length. Since the world was corrupt and sin-ridden, there was little incentive to try to reform it. Besides, if the End Times and Jesus's Second Coming were imminent, what was the point? Early in the twentieth century, the evangelist Dwight Moody offered a nautical metaphor for the course believers should follow: God has given us a lifeboat upon a sea of sin and commanded us to save all we can.

Nancy Ammerman, a prominent sociologist of religion, neatly summarizes the subtle transformation of this idea: "The idea was simply, 'This world is doomed. There's nothing we can do about it. The only thing you can do is preach the Gospel and hope more souls will be saved.' From the mid-twenties until the mid-seventies, that was the dominant way evangelicals thought about politics, that it would of necessity mean compromising their standards, cooperating with people they didn't agree with . . .

"But Jerry Falwell and others could articulate the same theology, but with a little twist and nuance. 'Yes, Jesus is coming again. Yes, the world as we know it will disappear. But in the meantime, there is a space in history in which Christians are supposed to do all they can to actually make a difference in the world. If our primary job is to preach the Gospel, then we want to eliminate any possible barriers to doing that and maximize all of the possible ways of doing it.'

"So you want to get rid of communism because communism's a barrier. You want to be nice to Israel because Israel plays a role in the End Times. You want an American government that in every way possible makes it easy for Christians to do what they want to do, and that highlights the kind of moral character this nation needs in order to be an example to the world."[5]

Parallel to this ideological turning ran a surge of self-confidence and institutional strength. Not only were fundamentalists and evangelicals gaining numbers through higher birth rates, but more evangelicals were attending college, finding careers in business and the professions, becoming more urbanized, and adapting their Southern-rooted religious culture to the rest of the country. In short, they were joining the middle class. Their places of worship could no longer be dismissed as "churches of the disinherited." As sociologist James Davison Hunter notes, "With higher education, there is a sense of greater agency in the world, a sense of greater control over one's environment. These kinds of sensibilities and values tend to lead to political engagement."

Alongside churches, fundamentalists and evangelicals established an astonishing array of colleges and seminaries, publishing houses and television empires. Television, in particular, was fashioned into a powerful tool to spread not only the Gospel but ultraconservative political views. Unlike the mainline denominations, they embraced the "electronic church" with gusto. Willing to pay for airtime—funded through on-air pitches— they took to the medium like bees to flowers. Their emotion-laden, narrative-rich, musically appealing services made for good TV. By contrast, the very nature of liberal religion—nuanced, open-minded, and open to doubt—limited its opportunities on television. With the advent of cable networks in the 1980s, conservative voices extended and consolidated their nationwide reach.[6]

But what was their message? It was not simply spreading the Word of God, nor ranting against the evils of abortion, pornography, homosexuality, feminism, and evolution. It amounted to a declaration of war. On their side, in battle array, were the forces of righteousness; on the other, the forces of "secular humanism," which they equated with the very Devil.

The clash, as James Davison Hunter has observed, cut to the bone, making the 1980s and '90s an unceasing polemical battleground. No matter that most Americans stood somewhere in the middle. Two distinct visions of moral authority and national identity—"orthodox" and "progressive" in Hunter's phrasing—jousted for supremacy. The orthodox based moral authority on an omnipotent, transcendent God and His divinely revealed texts. From these sources flowed purpose, value, goodness, and identity. Moral judgments were founded on timeless standards beyond compromise. In the orthodox map of the world, America uniquely embodied providential wisdom. This was a Christian nation, its political-economic foundation built on an unchanging Constitution and unbridled "free enterprise." Progressives, on the other hand, rejected orthodox faiths as outmoded. They resymbolized them in light of reason and modern science. As education spread, they believed that cultural primitives such as religious fundamentalists would simply fade away. Moral and spiritual truths were conditional and relative. A pragmatic sense of context determined ethical choices and the good life. America, according to the progressive vision, was not God-inspired but a secular state with a Constitution adaptable to changing times. Progressive ideas of freedom focused more on the social and political rights of individuals than on an unfettered economy. Each side of this yawning cultural divide defined the other as dangerous and extremist. Each vied to discredit the enemy as beyond the pale of legitimate national discourse. Each employed the vocabulary of war.[7]

The most prominent warrior emerging from the religious right was Rev. Jerry Falwell. He was, in many ways, the anti–Forrest Church—son of a fundamentalist mother and alcoholic small businessman, graduate of an obscure Bible college, a homophobic, antifeminist Southern Republican, and a born-again rabble-rouser of a preacher. The Thomas Road Baptist Church in Lynchburg, Virginia, served as Falwell's base camp. Next came Liberty College (later named Liberty University), founded to infuse the business and professional mainstream with fundamentalist values. Via the *Old-Time Gospel Hour*, millions of television viewers and radio listeners were exposed to his standard sermon-stump speech, "The Spiritual Renaissance of America," a jeremiad that "laments the moral condition of a people, foresees cataclysmic consequences, and calls for dramatic moral reform and revival." And in 1979, in a direct march into the political arena, he and conservative allies founded the Moral Majority, implicitly declaring their refusal to be stigmatized and marginalized. It was, in the words of Falwell's most astute interpreter, Susan Friend Harding, "a kind of born-again Christian cultural diaspora, a movement out of exile and into the world."[8]

This dramatically reshaped religious landscape bewildered and infuriated religious liberals. After all, the likes of Jerry Falwell were supposed to have gone the way of the dodo. They weren't expected to exist near the end of the twentieth century, let alone thrive. To make matters worse, they swarmed into view as this era's equivalent of sixties antiwar demonstrators. Noisy and energetic, fueled by deep conviction, eager to make their presence felt, they monopolized media coverage.

Like his liberal colleagues, Forrest Church was appalled by the worldview, politics, and self-righteousness of the religious right. The language of End Times and "born again" stood as far from Unitarian thinking as possible. He could no more stomach their politics than his father could. The suggestion that the liberal values of tolerance and open-mindedness had opened the floodgates to libertinism he found insulting.

Yet Church chose not to be a warrior like Falwell. Jeremiads were not his style. Conciliation was his default mode. Denouncing the religious right, by itself, would do little good. That was only preaching to the liberal choir. Although he never expected his ideological opponents to change their minds, he nonetheless felt the need to listen to them. Aware of their pain and assaults on their dignity, he discerned a humanity worth honoring. And within his own camp, he perceived weaknesses not readily acknowledged.

Church's approach, evident from early in his career, never wavered from the even-handed conditional. "The Problem with Being Right," a 1981 sermon, exemplifies his inclination to turn a subject around to examine it from unexpected angles. Falwell had been quoted that, since he had the ear of God, he never doubted that he was right. Church considered the self-righteousness on display "staggering." It was simply impossible to know the will of God on anything, let alone on politics. Yet religious liberals ought to avoid a similar trap of assuming that their ideas could not be misguided. In this regard, he cited a bumper sticker then popular among Unitarians: "The Moral Majority Is Neither." Church deemed this message wrong on two counts. Its tone was as smug as that of its opponents. And Unitarians, a tiny band of freethinkers, should be careful not to earn the label of "immoral minority."[9]

Likewise, in another sermon, discussing the Nuclear Freeze movement, which sought to halt the arms race between the United States and the Soviet Union, Church warned proponents not to disparage the motives of people who disagreed with them. He agreed that "with each escalation the balance of terror becomes more precarious and the world less secure." But name-calling—one side "naifs," the other "fellow travelers"—wouldn't prevent the slide to nuclear Armageddon. "The only real hope," he wrote, "lies in our ability to hear one another out, fairly and openly and patiently."[10]

On the eve of the presidential election of 1984, Falwell provoked Church's ire again. The evangelist had anointed Ronald Reagan and George Bush "God's instruments in rebuilding America." Reagan, taking the cue, declared anti-abortion and pro-school-prayer positions as litmus tests for religious integrity. As for the Democratic nominee, Walter Mondale, he ignored the recent history of Vietnam and civil rights by suggesting that politics and religion shouldn't mix. In Church's view, both sides were "profoundly un-American and unbelievably short-sighted." His quarrel with the Republicans was obvious. But Mondale's viewpoint clouded a fundamental distinction: "To separate our religious values from our political convictions is impossible . . . The wall of separation is between religion and law, not between religion and politics."[11]

To a nuanced thinker like Church, a thorny issue like abortion required even more untangling. The brawl between "baby killers" and "right-wing fanatics," he wrote in *The Christian Century*, badly needed less heat and more light. Each side harangued the other from a posture of outmoded individualism. Even the less emotional terms used in the debate obscured realities. "The 'pro-life' position is actually not pro-life, but pro-birth," Church wrote. "Beyond birth, most 'pro-life' partisans pay precious little attention to the quality of life, to the interdependent web of lives which *is* life." Politicians who support a constitutional amendment prohibiting abortion usually balk at expanding prenatal care, child nutrition, or welfare programs. "On the other hand, at its most extreme, the 'pro-choice' position, while more aptly named, is buttressed by rhetoric which contrasts the value of the mother, who can choose, with that of the prospective child, who cannot." This view was nearly as blind as the other.

Abortion, Church asserted, was in fact killing, but with a difference. "Viewing ourselves in terms of the whole, we see that when a fetus is aborted, a part of us is killed. And by the same token, a part of us dies when an unwanted, soon-to-be-uncared-for child is brought into this world. When making life-and-death choices, we should ask not whether we should be allowed to kill, or what constitutes killing. We should ask whether our actions will enhance life more than they diminish it."

To clarify, Church invoked the theory of the just war, central to the Christian tradition since Augustine. As horrible as war was, it was sometimes necessary and appropriate in the name of a larger good, say, the defense of Western democracies against fascism. Aborting a fetus—that is, killing a potential person—was sometimes equally necessary. "By not mincing words here," he concluded, we "take into account their profound

moral gravity." On the one hand, the elegance and subtlety of the reason-
ing is powerful. On the other, this was a position likely to unsettle both
Planned Parenthood and the Moral Majority.[12]

During his divinity school days at Harvard, Forrest had boasted to a
Stanford chum that someday he might be hailed as "the next William
Sloan Coffin." That was not to be. Privately, Forrest may have known it
even then. A man "born sunny side up," a man who loathed confrontation,
a man intellectually prone to reject either/or points of view was not cut out
to wear the prophet's robe. "By nature," he informed his congregation in
1984, "I do not have a prophetic temperament. Perhaps that is why I so
often turn to humor to soften . . . what I have to say." The zeitgeist had
changed since the sixties as well. Aside from the occasional Nuclear Freeze
demonstration, liberals weren't marching much anymore. The Age of
Reagan had put them on the defensive. By the eighties, Democratic politicians were beginning to call themselves "progressives." The word *liberal*
had become more epithet than accolade.[13]

Still, Church could thunder when necessary, especially in reaction to
President Reagan's foreign-policy outrages. In the spring of 1985, Reagan
asked Congress to fund the contra guerrillas in a war against Nicaragua's
elected Sandinista government. In the same week, at Bitburg, Germany,
the president seemed to equate the SS officers buried there with victims
of the Holocaust. That Sunday, Forrest's sermon expressed "shame" for
his country. A year later, he erupted with indignation at Reagan's decision to bomb Libya in reprisal for a Libyan terrorist bombing of a German nightclub that killed a single GI. "When we resort to terrorism with
bombs of our own, killing innocent civilians and even children, we too
become terrorists." Such an ill-conceived response is not only politically
counterproductive, inspiring yet more terrorists, but denies us the moral
high ground. He gave his father the last words: "The United States must
not adopt the tactics of the enemy. Means are as important as ends . . . Each
time the means we use are wrong . . . the strength that makes us free is
lessened."[14]

On the domestic front, few public issues attracted as much of Church's attention as the separation of church and state. This was not usually a concern in New York, but in 1986 he decided to challenge the state legislature's business as usual. He returned an unsolicited grant of $10,000 designated for All Souls social outreach programs, one of the "member items" distributed by legislators to groups in their districts—similar to "earmarks" on the federal level. Decrying the system as "pork-barrel potluck," Church said the distribution of grants was inherently unfair: some deserving groups received money, while others were passed over. Worse, the money might be used, unconstitutionally, for religious purposes. An editorial in *The New York Times* condemned the sleazy practice and cheered on the shepherd of All Souls: "The pastor is right to look this gift horse in the mouth."[15]

Church clearly thrived under this kind of spotlight. Media attention such as this would have been unlikely had he chosen the professional route he originally planned, academia. Yet that option, lingering like the teasing smile of a beautiful woman, never completely left his mind.

A year before, in 1985, Harvard Divinity School was searching for a new dean. George Rupp was leaving to assume the presidency at Rice University. Was Church interested in being considered? Why not think about the matter, he told himself, why reject it out of hand? And so he apparently made the short list. Invited to Cambridge to a luncheon at the home of Derek Bok, the university's president, he was seated among divinity school professors, many of whom he knew, and divinity school donors, whom he didn't. But before the meal began, he was called away to take an urgent long-distance phone call. Bert Zippel, chairman of the committee that had lured him to All Souls and husband of Mary-Ella Holst, the church's religious education director, had just died. Excusing himself, he left the luncheon and flew home to New York to arrange a memorial service. "Dean Rupp was extremely agitated," Church remembered, "because he had me seated between two major givers." Soon thereafter, Church withdrew from consideration for the Harvard post.

His chances would have been slim at best anyway. He lacked the record of scholarly achievement that the board expected for such an appointment. And, to put it bluntly, he would have made an awful dean. He had a fierce dislike for committee work; he liked to go his own way, and he had little patience for cajoling prickly personalities. The title would have been grand; the everyday reality, for someone with Church's temperament, humdrum. He had a more suitable match back in New York.

"My calling was at All Souls," Church said. "My calling was not to sit between the two big donors in the president's house at Harvard raising more money for the divinity school and to deal with a brilliant but somewhat adolescent faculty."[16]

The steward of All Souls didn't need Harvard any more than Harvard needed him. He was making his own way. Despite the aversion to committees, he joined a few: the boards at Union Theological Seminary in New York, the UU-related Starr King School for the Ministry in Berkeley, the American/Israel Interfaith Committee, and Pro-Choice Citizens Action Council, among others.[17] And the media couldn't get enough of Forrest Church.

Nineteen eighty-six was a banner year for press coverage. In May, he was escorted into celebrity heaven. An upbeat profile in *People Weekly*, complete with photos of Amy and their children—Twig now had a sister, Nina Wynne Church, born on March 21, 1981—pronounced him "an inspiring new voice for liberal religion." The story highlighted the preacher's famous father, All Souls' good works, and Church's liberal take on religion: "I don't come thundering out of the pulpit with the quote-unquote truth. I am involved in a search and all of my conclusions are tentative." The article's final sentence saluted its subject with an enthusiastic amen: "Indeed, for many of his parishioners, there is more faith in Church's honest doubts than in others' pious certitudes."[18]

Next came Bernice Kanner, whose *New York* magazine profile in the previous year had vaulted Forrest into local prominence. In a long story in the magazine on the greed-driven business world, "What Price Ethics: The Morality of the Eighties," she allowed her minister at All Souls to speak his piece on the subject:

"We are living in a society of confused values, where people have lost a sense of confidence about right and wrong. When materialistic values become dominant, our heroes become superstars who value notoriety regardless of how they get it . . . There is a fascination with evil and abject behavior that is usually checked by society's strong condemnation of it. But that's not what is happening now."[19]

Also lining up were magazines catering to Middle America. *Parents* offered its readers a short item in which Forrest reprised the story of his estrangement from his father and their later reconciliation. The strangest media moment may have occurred when *Redbook* included him and Amy in a roundup of "5 Heartwarming Christmas Memories," written by the wives of famous clergymen. There, perhaps to their astonishment, were Forrest and Amy pictured alongside Norman Vincent Peale, the maestro of Main Street "positive thinking," and three fundamentalist evangelists, Rex Humbard, Oral Roberts, and Jerry Falwell himself. The Churches were clearly the token liberals. Amy's anecdote recalled a family gathering in New York that had had to be canceled by Frank Church's weakening condition due to cancer. Instead, she and Forrest traveled to Washington to spend time with him. It was the last Christmas they spent together. Amy clearly revered her father-in-law, "such a special man—funny, warm, and extraordinarily thoughtful."[20]

Church was also busy making news in ways that mattered. His own church was thriving. Under his leadership, All Souls had grown from 388 members in 1979 to 842 in 1986, 910 in 1987, and 1,023 the following year. But the denomination was struggling. After reaching a high of 282,307 adherents in 1968, membership plummeted to 131,844 by 1982. From that low, it climbed slowly upward. Still, it remained a small denomination at the margins of American religious life. Consider, for example, comparative figures for 1980. The Unitarian Universalist Association, with some 154,000 members, was only slightly larger than the Society of Friends (Quakers), with roughly 130,000 members, and not quite twice the size of the Old Order Amish, which counted 84,000 devotees. The behemoths were the Roman Catholics (47 million), the Southern Baptist Convention (16.2 million), and the United Methodist Church (11.5 million).[21]

Despite the conservative tide, UU leaders saw opportunities for growth. If Americans were increasingly mixing and matching religious beliefs and practices, if ties to the religious institutions of their birth had unraveled, if they found new strains of spirituality appealing, they might well gravitate toward the openness and tolerance of Unitarian Universalism. Conservatives owned a substantial amount of the available religious turf, certainly, but millions still refused to set foot on it. During the 1980s and '90s, a yearning for "spirituality" seemed palpable. Whether meditating, believing in angels, or reviving ancient pagan rites, devotees discovered a new sense of wholeness, direct connection with a realm that could not be understood within normal, everyday existence. Some of this interest was ephemeral, of course, mere dabbling, and some spiritual seekers defined their quest as an alternative to churchgoing. This was spirituality, they insisted, not religion. For UUs, however, boundaries between the two were porous and unimportant.

At the same time, national opinion polls continued to show that virtually all Americans believed in some concept of God. Even though, in one Gallup survey, 94 percent of Americans said they believed in a God or a universal spirit, 5 percent of that group conceived of God as "an idea but not a being," 2 percent as "an impersonal Creator who cannot be reached by our prayers," and 3 percent said they did not know the nature of God. According to the same poll, only 11 percent of college graduates believed in biblical inerrancy, and 10 percent regarded the Bible as "an ancient book of fables, legends, history, and moral precepts." The holders of these ideas, however small a portion of the population, represented a window of opportunity for liberal religion. What's more, the mid-century humanist domination of the UUA that would have been a brake on expansion was now fading. Eighty-five percent of new recruits to Unitarianism, UUA president William Schulz estimated, were "comfortable with the use of the term 'God' and would understand 'God' as the source of all blessings unbidden." And the theists, he told a reporter in 1987, now had a new champion, a "bona fide celebrity clergyman" in Forrest Church.[22]

Five years earlier, in an essay titled "Did the Fundamentalists Win?," eminent church historian Edwin Scott Gaustad had plaintively asked, "Where are the Beechers, Abbotts, Coffins, and Fosdicks of yesteryear?"[23] Perhaps now their heir had arrived. The Word according to Dr. Church would come packaged in two forms, spoken and printed. In speeches, Church delighted in the role of "liberal evangelist." In print, his popular weekly column in the *Chicago Tribune* would offer gentle moral observations, making a national readership provided by syndication seem imminent.

As he traveled the country, often on tours to promote one of his books, Church's charm and diplomatic skills gave him the air of the proverbial reasonable man. "If you put Forrester Church, who once protested American involvement in Vietnam, in the same room with Jerry Falwell," an account in the *Houston Chronicle* began, "surely there would be a debate. But when the rhetoric cooled, chances are Church would shake hands with his opponent . . . American liberal religion would seem to need a leader like Church."

Church didn't present himself solely as antidote to the religious right. He was equally critical of some liberals. "I call them fundamentalists of the left and fundamentalists of the right," he said. "Both have no sense of mystery, no sense of poetry. They're literalists . . . Both, to my mind, are idolaters. They trivialize religion. They worship the Bible or worship themselves instead of worshipping God."

Still, his critique in the *Houston Chronicle* cut more sharply against right-wing fundamentalists. They ignored the "built-in bias" of Jesus's teachings in favor of the poor over the rich, and their purchase on "family values" was equally flawed. Pat Robertson's agenda, for example, was, in fact, "radically anti-family because today's family is often a single mother with three or four children . . . struggling to support those children." Yet Robertson was unwilling to advocate the kind of day care and government support required to sustain that family.[24]

In Atlanta, Church adapted agreeably to Bible Belt tradition. He presided over what was dubbed a "UU revival," an evening of preaching, singing, socializing, and dancing organized by local UU churches. In Minneapolis, he asserted that the potential for UU growth was "staggering. For every person in our churches who has found a spiritual home, there are dozens like them in the community who are still seeking, and all those people need to know that such a church as ours exists." But he warned that "we do not offer a heavenly insurance policy or a religious security blanket." And in Seattle, he cautioned against the siren call of New Age mumbo-jumbo. It seemed "a rather empty response to the deep sense of emptiness and hollowness in many people's lives. There's a tremendous religious vacuum to be filled." But New Age practices, he said, too often slipped into a self-absorption that ignored the needs of others. His approach to religious seekers, while generous and open-armed, had its limits.[25]

By this time, Church had become an eloquent preacher and an exacting wordsmith. But aside from several op-ed pieces for New York City dailies, he had never written for newspapers. In 1986, while visiting Chicago to promote *Father and Son*, he had lunch with Tom Stites, a former All Souls parishioner who had been an editor at the *Times* and now edited the *Tribune*'s features section. After Stites published an excerpt of the book, one of his bosses raved, "This guy is spectacular. What a talent!" So the next step was hardly surprising. During lunch, Forrest mused that the newspaper world could use a column that brought a moral perspective to people's everyday problems, much like Harry Stein's popular column in *Esquire* magazine. Stites invited Forrest to give it a go for his newspaper. After a brief audition, substituting for a vacationing columnist, he was offered a regular slot on Sundays. With a wink and a nod, the column, begun in October 1986, was called "Fundamentals."[26]

The writing style was conversational, the tone wry and charming. For the 700-word format, Church shaped little stories, with clear-cut beginnings, development, and an ending that finished with a snap. Like his sermons, the columns often made light of his own failings. His children showed up occasionally as questioning philosophers, while Amy was portrayed as sensible straight man to Forrest's bumbling comedian. Part Erma Bombeck, part Robert Fulghum, Church offered gentle fables for modern times. These weren't sermons, of course, but tidbits of wry, sometimes counterintuitive wisdom from a man well acquainted with human frailty.

Church adapted easily to newspaper prose. His short, muscular sentences quickly grabbed a reader's attention. "I attended a formal dinner this past week," one column began. "You know the scene: Men dress up like waiters, women like tropical fish."[27] But as the subject matter darkened, as it often did, the tone shifted from funny to compassionate. In some pieces, he would take up the subject of punctuality or how to give compliments, then, having established a rapport with his readers, in other pieces he probed weightier matters such as AIDS or the death of a child.

"The [Im]perfect Primer" illustrates Church at his wittiest. It's a sermonette, without theology, about that devil, perfectionism. Here he tackles the way people sabotage their confidence by contrasting their weaknesses with other people's strengths. We envy a coworker's creativity, say, while overlooking that "she has just broken up with her seventh husband, has a coke habit and is on the edge of a nervous breakdown." Underlining the point with delicious ridicule, he concocts "Dr. Church's Primer on Perfection" and offers three Commandments: "Covet thy neighbor's strengths, but overlook his or her deficiencies . . . Overlook thine achievements . . . Stoutly remain fatalistic with respect to all flaws." It's the rare reader who failed to laugh and learn from columns like this.[28]

The reader response was so enthusiastic, according to Stites, that the newspaper's top editors decided to syndicate the column through Tribune Media Services. He would not have been the first clergyman to reach an immense audience via mainstream media. Billy Graham and Archbishop Fulton Sheen, a Catholic, had pioneered the way. He would represent the religious left to their religious right. But before a contract was signed, Church's agent raised questions about it, prolonging negotiations, and Stites was promoted. He was no longer in charge of the column. Unaccountably, the new features editor canceled it, after a year-and-a-half run, in August 1988. Since the syndicate required its columnists to be based at a home paper, Church was effectively orphaned.

"It was such a close call," Stites said. "That was one of the times that Forrest had the door opened to being a national voice, and then had it slammed—out of pure misalignment of the universe."[29]

Eight

Author, Author!

I kept hearing his name: Forrest Church,
Forrest Church, Forrest Church.

—BILL MOYERS

However adept as a columnist, Forrest Church would have to
cultivate a larger audience as an author. He could leverage the
success of *Father and Son*, which in 1985 had received substantial press coverage, into a devoted readership. Books would be his primary means of expanding the boundaries of liberal religion. He hoped
his words would reach beyond his denomination to "the unchurched,"
wary of institutional religion; to spiritual seekers unaware of Unitarian
Universalism's open door; to Christians alienated from the narrowness of
creeds; to Jews put off by outworn traditions; and to agnostics who
couldn't believe in a God he couldn't believe in, either, because it was
"too small." To all of these, he offered a message that respected the intellect and honored the heart.

Book ideas came easily to Church. Just as he never suffered from
writer's block, he never failed to have a book proposal warming on the
back burner. In the months before publication of *Father and Son*, he proposed a collection of sermons as a follow-up volume. Clayton Carlson,
the erudite publisher of Harper & Row's books on religion, countered
with a proposal of his own:

Why not write, from a liberal point of view, "a civilized little book on the *Devil*? . . . Now nothing turns on a publisher more than a taboo—and what is more of a taboo for liberals? . . . I have no doubt that the extremes of cultic religion are going to raise supernaturalism to a new respectability in the general culture in the coming years . . . So images of the Devil are going to be with us whether we like it or not."[1]

To Forrest Church, this was an irresistible proposition. Given his contrarian sensibility, the word *taboo* had the allure of raw meat to a leopard. The very idea of writing about a concept so linked in the public mind with conservative religion stimulated his intellectual juices. Since this was precisely a subject many Unitarian thinkers disdained, he would take it on, with relish.

The book that Harper & Row published in 1986, *The Devil & Dr. Church: A Guide to Hell for Atheists and True Believers*, was billed as a kind of *Screwtape Letters* for its time. If not quite false advertising, this was misleading. C. S. Lewis's 1942 classic epistolary novel, in which a senior demon instructs an acolyte in the proper ways of luring humans into the service of "Our Father Below," relied on biting satire. While making fun of religious shallowness, it made the case for a tough-minded Christianity. But Forrest Church was neither Christian apologist nor satirist. Uncomfortable with ridicule, he was compassionate where Lewis was sly. He brandished wit, to be sure, but the smile with which he greeted parishioners on Sunday mornings he also retained on the page. One final distinction between the two: Hell for Dr. Church existed in the here and now.

To be sure, *The Devil & Dr. Church* displays Church in a playful mode. "Orthodox and fundamentalist alike will find it blasphemous," he writes, "and my liberal friends will find it treasonous, ridden with superstition." Less C. S. Lewis than G. K. Chesterton—Chesterton's adage "Angels can fly because they take themselves lightly" appears in the preface—its style is witty and epigrammatic. Serious but never solemn, the book ranges widely over secular and religious literature to suggest this thesis: "The devil exists, by nature is a deceiver, and, accordingly, is manifest where we least expect to find him. In turn, the devil's greatest accomplishment is to lead us to believe that he does not exist; his most successful ruse is to cloak himself in virtue; and his favorite guises commend him in ways that impress us, such as patriotism, nationalism, freedom, tolerance, respectability, sophistication, and piety. The devil's true nature is evil disguised as good—which is to say he almost always appears in drag."

Invoking "the devil," of course, is Church's way of investigating the nature of evil. And what was evil but "a perversion of the good," just as the devil was a fallen angel? "There is no good," he writes, "that is not capable of being wrenched from its own context . . . This is what idolatry is all about, a part of the whole that is elevated into something disproportionate and therefore destructive."[2]

Idolatry rears its head when tolerance becomes a belief in nothing, when love is subverted into control over another, when sophistication slides into snobbery. These examples represent evil on a small scale. Far more alarming is the "cloak of piety" American conservatives throw around an out-of-control arms race. To some, like Hal Lindsey, author of the era's bestselling *The Late Great Planet Earth*, nuclear war followed by the Rapture, in which believers are taken up into heaven, isn't a catastrophe but the welcomed fulfillment of biblical prophecy. To Church, however, the devil himself could not have invented anything more diabolical.

Church's God, following process theology, is immanent and evolving, "co-creator with us, as together we move freely toward an undetermined destiny." The fundamentalist dualist vision errs by self-servingly separating the sheep from the goats: "Every theology that elevates one people or tribe over another . . . that posits the condemnation of others as a pledge in earnest for one's election, is a demonic theology."[3]

Irreligion is no better. Worshipping "the grubby little ego," the atheist is estranged from "any true sense of the intimate, awesome, mysterious connectedness, beyond knowing or naming." If this connectedness is hard to pin down, for Church it is best expressed in the Jesus of the Gospels who defies the devil's temptations and urges followers to lose their lives in order to find them. This Jesus stands in sharp contrast to the Christ of the idolaters. This sort of Jesus brings people together rather than divides them, preaches love not hate, sees the Good Samaritan, not the demon, in the gay man.

Ostensibly about evil, *The Devil & Dr. Church* does ramble. Given the author's propensity for skipping from here to there, it's not always easy to follow the argument. But his provocative intelligence and wit are evident on every page.

Although the mainstream press rarely pays much attention to religious books, this one received more than the usual share.[4] In light of the generally positive response, Church and Clayton Carlson decided to make a trilogy out of this "remythologizing" of hoary Christian ideas. The devil, or hell, book would be followed by one on heaven, then another on purgatory. But in the meantime, Church was eager to write a much more ambitious "Universalist manifesto" that would put his stamp on contemporary theology. Carlson, however, suggested that he first finish the trilogy:

"Take your time to do a book that will become a classic, fully rounded statement rather than a book of the moment. It should act as a counterpoint to what will obviously become your image with the short books—as 'the great communicator' (I shudder even to use the phrase)—and should demonstrate that there is careful, genuine substance behind all the glitter . . . Add on to the role of the man of practical action (viz the 'Grease in Albany' [a reference to All Souls' refusal to accept state funds for outreach programs]) and there will be no end to the overall impact that can be made."[5]

This was both compliment and caution. Hadn't *The Devil & Dr. Church* exhibited *both* substance and glitter? In any event, Carlson was committed to doing what a good publisher does: to position a writer in the best possible media spotlight and to comprehend the place of the current book within the long arc of his career. It was also clear that Church restlessly anticipated that next leap forward.

The second book in the trilogy, *Entertaining Angels: A Guide to Heaven for Atheists and True Believers,* published in 1987, placed a tricky bet. It hoped to capitalize on the era's fascination with angels while challenging both Christian orthodoxy and New Age faddishness. (According to Church's preface, even his wife was fond of angel replicas, having collected two of them every Christmas since she was a girl.) Not supernatural celestial beings equipped with wings but angels as messengers of God, as symbolic intermediaries between this world and the divine, were Church's subject. To a reporter from New York's *Daily News*, he made clear his impatience with claptrap like channeling and past-life regression, popularized by movie star Shirley MacLaine. "There's so much fraud in this," he said. As for reincarnation, a lot of these new gurus were probably "the latest incarnation of P. T. Barnum." Still, he understood the hunger for "metaphysical connectedness." In *Entertaining Angels*, he proposed a more substantial, more intellectually respectable way to achieve it.[6]

In spite of the publisher's counsel to postpone any large-scale Universalist manifesto, Church managed to smuggle most of his Universalism into *Entertaining Angels*. That the book was just over a hundred pages long could not mask its large ambitions. Ostensibly narrowly focused on angels and heaven, the book widened into an entire religious philosophy expressed in the language of metaphor. It bears a closer look.

"My thesis is a simple one," he begins. "If angels came in packages we'd almost always pick the wrong one. Even as the devil is evil disguised, angels are goodness disguised . . . Jesus discovered the realm of God in a mustard seed, the smallest and least portentous of all seeds. Mustard seeds and angels have this in common. They are little epiphanies of the divine amidst the ordinary."

Church finds a germ of evil—a good thing gone wrong—even within his own tradition. Since the Reformation, he writes, theological liberalism has been conducting a "search-and-destroy mission . . . to strip away the trappings of religion, the mystagogy and priestcraft, in an attempt to restore to faith its intellectual and ethical integrity." Despite its achievements, this was "a little like trying to find the seed of an onion by peeling away its layers. Eventually nothing is left but our tears."

Rationality by itself, he says, cannot "come even close to understanding the mystery of being alive and having to die . . . Our most profound encounters lead inexorably from the rational to the trans-rational realm. Yet myth, parable, and paradox—our only tools for enlightenment here— liberals have seen fit to lock away."

Church's self-definition extracts what he regards as the best from several theological worlds. He calls himself a Christian Universalist, his Universalism modified by Christianity, not, he emphasizes, the other way around. The paradoxes of Jesus's life and thought anchor his Universalism. To explain his position, he draws on his familiar metaphor of a cathedral as a place of many windows, one light:

"Universalism can be perverted in two ways. One is to elevate one truth into a universal truth ('My church is the one true church'); the other is to reduce distinctive truths to a lowest common denominator ('All religion is merely a set of variations upon the golden rule'). The Universalism I embrace does neither. It holds that the same light shines through all our windows, but each window is different. The windows modify the light, even as Christianity does my Universalism . . .

"Fundamentalists, whatever their persuasion, claim that the light shines through their window only. Skeptics draw the opposite conclusion. Seeing the bewildering variety of windows and observing the folly of the worshipers, they conclude that there is no light. But the windows are not the light. The whole light—God, Truth—is beyond our perceiving."[7]

Following this overview, Church relies on rhetorical tropes about angels—"being on the side of angels," say, or "the angel of death"—to sort out and title his chapters. Thus he opts for the essayist's liberty to roam at will over the theologian's imperative to make a closely reasoned argument.

Church draws on Chesterton again to attack perfectionism, a habit that angels know to shun. After all, "angels can fly because they take themselves lightly." Taking oneself lightly means forgiving oneself and making allowances for everyday human frailty. "If practiced to perfection," Church writes, "any virtue can become a vice." Honesty can be cruel; justice can be perverted into heartlessness; temperance can slip into aridity.[8]

The certainty of "being on the side of the angels" can surely be the most dangerous of "virtues." Nowhere, Church asserts, is this more evident than in foolish rhetoric justifying the arms race. And where today do we encounter "angels unawares"? Why not, he suggests, look into the eyes of a gay man dying of AIDS, for, according to the New Testament, the persecuted are especially beloved of God?

Church declines to read his Bible literally. The most refreshing thing about it, he says, is that it is "about sinners sinning and being saved. It's full of surprises designed to awaken us from smugness."[9] He approaches the subject of prayer from a similarly liberal perspective. Prayers of confession require an honest and healing confrontation with the self; prayers about others can lead to reconciliation with them; and prayers of gratitude refuse to take life for granted. Prayers, in short, pave the way to wholeness, the only heaven we will ever know.

To be born again, in Church's parlance, is to accept the undeserved gift of life "consciously, reverentially, with humility and thanksgiving . . . In return for this gift, we understand that the world doesn't owe us a living. It is we who owe the world a living: our own."[10] His sense of awe and wonder here is rooted in the transcendentalism of Emerson and Thoreau or the mystical visions of William Blake, who found "a world in a grain of sand, and heaven in a wildflower." Heaven is not an eternity in time, but an eternity in depth, available at our fingertips every day, if we would only seize the opportunity.

It is hard to see what additional insight readers of these first two books could find in *The Seven Deadly Virtues: A Guide to Purgatory for Atheists and True Believers* (1988). Church seems here to be merely going through the motions; once committed to a trilogy, he had to finish it. Since the notion of purgatory itself is suspect, a Catholic idea that Church acknowledges has no basis in the Bible, he tacks hither and yon trying to create a cohesive narrative out of a notion. The need to fit his thoughts into a theological category makes him obviously labor.

Something we can call purgatory, Church insists, exists in this life. And unlike the misconception that it's a place of punishment, it's "that place of purification where those being saved do not begrudge but rather welcome their pains as emblems of their reunion with God."[11] What he actually means by this is hard to say. When he turns his attention to the philosophical virtues (prudence and justice, temperance and fortitude) and the theological virtues (faith, hope, and love), we can at least comprehend him. His argument is that virtues become vices when they are overdone to a fault. But he's already played that theme in the previous book.

Oliver North, the Marine Corps officer in President Reagan's National Security Council involved in the illicit Iran-Contra scandal, for example, serves as poster boy for the hubris of superpatriotism. "Here we have the perfect recipe for deadly virtue," Church writes. "Take any set of actions, however half-baked or rancid, dress them with a liberal helping of God and family, add a bit of individual spiciness, wrap the whole dish in the American flag, and give it a name like 'Project Democracy.'"[12]

As for Dickens's Scrooge, he upholds the virtue of prudence, with its sights set rigidly on security. The result is a prison of invulnerability, where one is walled off from other people. Few texts, Church writes, are better than *A Christmas Carol* at depicting "the workings of purgatory." Scrooge "enters fires that both illumine and purify" and "emerges stripped of selfish self-regard and clothed with communal goodwill."[13]

Indeed, community lies at the heart of Church's theology. We exist, he asserts, only in a framework created and shared by other people. As individuals, we cannot live without love, nor should we die without giving out all the love we can. The privatism espoused by both right-wing political philosophy and the culture of narcissism has the calculus exactly backward. In the age of possible nuclear and eco-annihilation, "the vision of community here and now on earth, a shared humanity in which all God's children must find their way haltingly, but hand in hand, toward peace" is nothing less than imperative.[14]

Despite the reduced impact of *Entertaining Angels* and *The Seven Deadly Virtues*, neither of which received much review attention, the trilogy as a whole introduced Forrest Church to a much larger public. Unitarians, it was clear from the many letters he received, swelled with pride as one of their own emerged as a respected national voice. Religious liberals beyond

Unitarian Universalists were also taking notice, admiring the overall thrust of his endeavor while sometimes demurring on specific ideas.[15]

As an author, Church was a restless multitasker. Even while writing for a broad popular audience, he followed his intellectual curiosity into several editing projects with more limited appeal. During the "summer vacations" spent in Laguna Niguel, California, at the home of Amy's parents, he often churned out not one but several books. While busy writing one, he would edit another. One reason he was so prolific was a laserlike focus on work all day. In fact, when the rush of ideas would not let him sleep, he worked more efficiently during the night. The other reason is that Church had help from research assistants.

Terrence J. Mulry, an All Souls parishioner who had been raised a Catholic, was the first. Mulry connected Forrest directly to the publishing world. Formerly director of planning and administration at the large publishing house of Macmillan, he decided, in his thirties, to enroll in Harvard Divinity School. After Mulry did spadework for *The Seven Deadly Virtues*, he introduced Church to Macmillan executives, who signed him up for a series of theological reference books for the backlist, where books with perennial appeal are expected to sell year after year. As work on the books proceeded, queries and answers would shuttle back and forth by overnight mail between Church at All Souls and Mulry at Harvard. For Church, publishing these books allowed him to keep a hand in the scholarly world, at least minimally, and to encourage his fellow Unitarians to be as open to Christian influences as they were to more trendy spiritualities coursing through the denomination.[16]

The Essential Tillich (1987) was intended as an introduction to one of twentieth-century Protestantism's greatest thinkers. Born in Germany, Paul Tillich immigrated in 1933 to the United States, where he taught at Union Theological Seminary, Harvard, and the University of Chicago. He died in 1965, well before Church arrived at Harvard, but the young seminary student was drawn to the German's expression of a "mature and thoughtful version of my incipient theology." Still, after sampling a bit of the Tillich corpus, he put off diving into the rest, so that he could forge a way of thinking about ultimate questions that would be his own.

Years later, when Church accepted Macmillan publisher Charles Scribner III's invitation to compile an anthology, it was an utterly audacious act. Not a Tillich scholar at all, he was but an amateur admirer. In a way, the endeavor typified Forrest Church as much as any task he ever took on. Here his quintessential qualities stood out in bold relief—boundless enthusiasm, brash confidence, a willingness to plunge into what was for him unexplored territory, a defiance of established academic boundaries, a fascination with religion's deepest probings. "Goodness knows," he said later, "from the scholarly eye, it was as irresponsible an act as could be imagined." In the end, perhaps miraculously, he won the imprimatur of Tillich's widow and daughter by stitching together excerpts from Tillich's systematic theology and more general writings, to make the formidable German's ideas more accessible and comprehensible to lay readers. According to a scholar's review in the *Newsletter of the North American Paul Tillich Society*, which called the book "an excellent introduction" to the subject, well-suited for undergraduate and seminary instruction, he had succeeded.[17] The volume was republished by the University of Chicago Press in 1999 and is still in print.

Since he was not a Christian, Church was drawn to the Universalist and existentialist aspects of Tillich's theology. "Being religious," Tillich wrote, in a mode that Church found sympathetic, "means asking passionately the question of the meaning of our existence and being willing to receive answers, even if the answers hurt. Such an idea . . . does not describe religion as the belief in the existence of gods or one God, and as a set of activities and institutions for the sake of relating to these beings." As for God, Tillich saw it as "the name for that which concerns man ultimately. This does not mean that there is a being called God and then the demand that man should be ultimately concerned about him. It means that whatever concerns a man ultimately becomes god for him."[18]

For Church, Tillich remained more necessary than ever, a corrective to the era's dogmas of right and left, of believers and nonbelievers: "In a time of growing tribalism, Tillich was a religious diplomat at large, respectful of differences, chary of absolutes, devout and yet skeptical, mindful of the limits of all theology, including his own."[19] With good reason, Forrest Church could have used the same words to define himself.

In short order, Church followed this anthology with another trilogy drawing on his interest in early Christianity. From this point, Mulry, who was doing yeoman work compiling materials from the libraries of Harvard University, shared co-authorship for each book, while Church wrote short introductions. *The Macmillan Book of Earliest Christian Prayers* and *The Macmillan Book of Earliest Christian Hymns* came out in 1988, followed by *The Macmillan Book of Earliest Christian Meditations* in 1989. Though these anthologies drew on sometimes esoteric sources, they were not laden with scholarly apparatus and were intended, according to Church's introduction to *Prayers*, as "daily devotional refreshment" for lay readers. Moreover, they eschewed orthodoxy, weaving "a quilt of many traditions" out of the Apocrypha, the Gnostic gospels, and the Greek and Coptic Christian traditions, among others. (Tucked in between these books came *Everyday Miracles*, a collection of Church's *Chicago Tribune* columns published by Harper & Row in 1988.)

Church and Mulry collaborated on one more project that united a prayer book with the twelve steps of the burgeoning addiction-recovery movement. Alcoholics Anonymous was but the best known of a host of organizations dedicated to giving new life to the victims of alcohol and drug abuse. The key to these groups' success, according to the co-authors, lay in a "simple but profound set of spiritual principles," beginning with a recognition of the individual's powerlessness in the face of addiction and the need for reliance on a "higher power" to combat it. *One Prayer at a Time: A Twelve-Step Anthology for Those in Recovery and All Who Seek a Deeper Faith* (1989) hoped to comfort people no matter how they defined this "higher power." Each of its twelve chapters begins with a Psalm, followed by devotions from a more expansive religious base than the Christian prayer books. Here are not only Protestant and Catholic prayers but also selections from Jewish, Buddhist, Muslim, and Unitarian faiths.[20]

In the publication of this little paperback lay a hidden irony. Already a heavy drinker, Church was not yet ready to admit that perhaps he fell into the category of those his book sought to help. That acknowledgment would arrive much later, forced upon him, as it is for so many in similar straits, in the wake of crisis.

Prolific writers can make their mark even on people who haven't read their books. Book lovers sort through reviews and pick up tips from friends about what's worth reading. So even if they are not exactly a known quantity, these writers are in the air, part of the scene. By the late eighties, Church's numerous books, sermons, and newspaper pieces were beginning to have that kind of impact.

"He was on the radar to anybody who followed New York life, particularly New York religious life," Bill Moyers recalled. "I kept hearing his name: Forrest Church, Forrest Church, Forrest Church. Friends of mine belonged to the church, and they would say, 'It's a great sermon by Forrest Church. You should go hear him' . . . He was somebody who was taken seriously in this city by thinking people, whether they were religious or not."

Moyers, a liberal Baptist, had read one of Forrest's books and found in this Unitarian a kindred spirit, steeped in the Social Gospel and willing to push back against the harshness and rigidity of the religious right. So when he put together an interview series with diverse "public thinkers," he invited Forrest Church. Of the interview subjects included in the PBS series *A World of Ideas*, which aired in 1988 and was edited into a book the following year, Church was one of the youngest and perhaps the least known to the general public. Here were notables from many walks of life, including historian Henry Steele Commager, novelist E. L. Doctorow, playwright August Wilson, physicist Steven Weinberg, historian Barbara Tuchman, and management consultant Peter Drucker. Their common bond, according to Moyers, was a belief that "the life of the mind and the life of the republic are inseparable."[21]

Though Moyers questions Church about familiar issues—church-state separation, Jerry Falwell, patriotism, Forrest's relationship with his father— the answers are rarely predictable. Though both men share similar world- views, this is less a dance than a boxing match, requiring toughness and agility. When Moyers jabs, Church parries. Moyers keeps pushing, and Church has to defend himself. In the end, it's clear that he sparkled at ex- temporaneous debate as well as in the pulpit and on the printed page.

The most spirited give-and-take arises over moral issues. After Church sanctions abortion as justified killing, using his just-war analogy, Moyers says, "So I hear you saying that a society may be moral that al- lows immoral choices." Forrest responds:

"In this day, particularly, if we don't endure quite a bit of ambiguity, we will become rigid and potentially dangerous and tyrannical. The am- biguity here is that we never can finally know what a right decision is. The people who frighten me the most are the ones who are a hundred percent sure of what's right, and who are hellbent to enforce that on everyone."

On the issue of pornography, Moyers's sense of repugnance faces off against Church's fears of censorship:

Moyers: "The government can rid the society of pornography."
Church: "And does so in the Soviet Union. Is there no middle
         ground?"
Moyers: "On Times Square, there's no middle ground. The por-
         nographers have won."
Church: "Well, to a degree. However, one can draw the line and
         start making basic choices. [We should not tolerate tele-
         phone porn] because a child can get access to it . . . Who
         is going to define pornography? We've seen it all over
         this country, in local ordinances and local school sys-
         tems. They're defining Anne Frank as pornography.
         They'll soon be defining *Snow White and the Seven Dwarfs*
         as pornography."

Summing up his views of morality, Church says, "We must move from judgmental morality to compassionate, respectful, and cooperative morality . . . We're sinners. I'm one liberal who doesn't have any trouble with the notion of sin. As long as we're open about sins and confess them as well and honestly as we can, and forgive other people theirs, then we can begin to live together as sinners who are also gifted with a tremendous potential for good in this world."

Having read *The Seven Deadly Virtues*, Moyers asks Church what are his own deadly virtues. His first answer feels entirely genuine. "Oh, probably self-deprecating humor," he says, "which everyone celebrates me for, so that I now use it as a device to gain fans rather than letting it be something that comes spinning out of me." Humor could be a means of disguise, it seems, as well as revelation. By contrast, his other answers, citing tolerance, reason, and freedom, are a stock response right out of the book.

Insights like this into Church's psyche pop up only twice. The other one occurs at the conclusion of the interview, when he is asked about a reference in *The Seven Deadly Sins* to tragedies that throw us up against life's limits. "I have not had the privilege of a life-changing failure," he replies, "but my life isn't over yet." This son of a U.S. senator, scion of Stanford and Harvard, steward of a flagship Unitarian congregation, this man with multiple advantages did not anticipate that he might yet face such a failure, and struggle to overcome it.[22]

As the Moyers interview demonstrated, religion and politics remained Church's passions. He enjoyed thinking about each separately, as well as the dilemmas of their intersection. Few figures in American history shared the same interests more than Thomas Jefferson—U.S. president, author of Virginia's religious freedom law, a Unitarian in spirit, and an admirer of the teachings of Jesus. Jefferson's claim that "there is not a young man now living in the U.S. who will not die an [sic] Unitarian"[23] made him all the more sympathetic, if an unreliable prophet. In 1989, Church persuaded Beacon Press to issue *The Jefferson Bible: The Life and Morals of Jesus of Nazareth*, the tiny spark that had set him on his religious journey many years before. With the exception of an expensive scholarly

edition and a gift-shop pocket book sold at Monticello, the book had
been out of print for years. For the Beacon edition, Church supplied an
introduction—in effect, a brief summary of his master's thesis, which
explained the origin of the text—and Jaroslav Pelikan, a distinguished
biblical scholar at Yale, wrote an afterword on other Enlightenment-
influenced thinkers with a similar rationalist approach to the Jesus story.
In print since its publication, the little volume has sold more than 95,000
copies—testimony to the timeless appeal of Jefferson and his subject.

In the same year, Church briefly resumed a newspaper column. "Words
for Sunday" had a three-month spring run in the *New York Post*, the conservative tabloid. Light, genial, and accessible, the essays took up where his
Tribune column had left off. Rather than preach, they tried to cast light on
living a good life. Church wrote about people who'd turned their lives
around, like a ninety-six-year-old woman whose poetry looked bad news
in the eye and laughed it aside; the wrongs done to animals by humans; the
coming-of-age of his Boomer Generation. It's not clear whether the column was cut short by the paper or by its writer, who had more pressing
business. Certainly, several important books were percolating by then.
However short-lived, "Words for Sunday" served as one more platform
enabling Church to reach beyond his usual constituency.[24]

Public ministry, in its many varieties, was Church's calling. From the
beginning of his tenure at All Souls, lay leaders assumed that he would be
writing books and articles, speaking to non-Unitarian audiences, fulfilling
the role of scholar-preacher. His ability to do this, however, required that
he not be overwhelmed by responsibilities at the church itself. A year after
his arrival, in the fall of 1979, he hired a part-time assistant minister, Richard Leonard, to take on various parish duties. But Leonard, despite a rich
bass voice and a wry sense of humor, did not like to preach. (He did enjoy
officiating at weddings, and, by the eighties, his ceremonies for Japanese
couples drawn to the thrill of nuptials in New York City became a significant revenue source for the church.) Given All Souls' growing membership, Church needed additional help. By 1986, he was eager to hire a
full-time colleague who would assist in preaching and administration.

In some ways, John A. Buehrens, minister of First Unitarian Church in Dallas, mirrored Forrest Church. He was a brilliant, articulate graduate of Harvard (where he served as an undergraduate research assistant to Church's mentor, George Hunston Williams) and its divinity school. He, too, was driven by ego and ambition. Both shared a common vision of Unitarian Universalism: that it ought to expand its horizons beyond a "lowest common denominator" of liberal social activism. By reclaiming its history and paying closer attention to theology, they believed, UU spirituality would be enriched and deepened.

Under Buehrens's leadership, the Dallas church had grown into the eighth largest in the denomination, but he was increasingly restless and bored—and alienated by Texas conservatism. His wife, Gwen Langdoc Buehrens, who had just been ordained the first female Episcopal priest in the diocese, was subjected to a flurry of hate mail and bomb threats. Even her would-be colleagues let her down. "Half of the priests in the diocese wouldn't speak to her or acknowledge her presence," Buehrens said.

Under the circumstances, New York seemed infinitely more inviting. Though technically hired as an assistant minister, Buehrens was paid at a higher rate and often referred to as co-minister. "I was giving up being the senior minister in a fairly large church. For my own professional dignity," he said, "I certainly didn't want to be understood as somebody's assistant." Within Episcopal circles, however, he did become known as the spouse of the associate rector at the Church of the Holy Trinity, for Gwen Buehrens had landed this job, with its rectory apartment, within walking distance of All Souls.[25]

With the arrival of Buehrens, in January 1987, All Souls began a new era of shared leadership. Despite the finessing of the new minister's title, this was not a leadership of equals. Church remained the CEO, the final decision-maker and the public voice of All Souls. He delivered 60 percent of the sermons, retained responsibility for fund-raising, and represented the church at most public forums and media appearances. Both ministers handled some basic counseling, but any serious matters were referred to professional psychologists. Buehrens did his share of the preaching, supervised the staff, and coordinated volunteer programs. He was no longer bored.

"We were taking in over two hundred members a year," he said. "I remember one Christmas Eve when the place was so packed that the then-president of Yale University couldn't get a seat—Benno Schmidt . . . At its peak, the social-ministry programs had as many as eight hundred volunteers. There were weeks when we had four hundred people attending adult religious growth and learning opportunities of one sort or another. Lively doesn't quite cover it."[26]

Few ministers excel at everything expected of them. In a perfect world, they would be equally good in the roles of preacher, counselor, administrator, fund-raiser, visionary, and institution builder. The new leadership structure implicitly acknowledged that administrative ability eluded Church. It also freed him up. In his view, it "brought ballast into our hold. It kept us from being personality-driven. We had a ministerial core as opposed to a ministerial star . . . Now, it was enlightened self-interest, because it also gave me much more time to write, much more time to carry out my civic involvement, my national involvement. It was absolutely win-win for me."[27]

The arrangement was not always win-win for Buehrens. While he busied himself with the daily chores that the senior minister shunned, Church received most of the public acclaim. "I found it harder to be number two than I thought it would be," Buehrens said. His resentment built up especially during the senior minister's five months, from April through August 1989, as a Montgomery Fellow at Dartmouth College. In this prestigious appointment, Church followed in the footsteps of Toni Morrison, Gerald Ford, Dean Rusk, Saul Bellow, and John Updike. While he taught a seminar on religion and politics in American history, delivered public lectures, and worked on another book, Buehrens struggled to keep the All Souls mother ship afloat. Meanwhile, Church collected mash notes from admirers at Dartmouth. The emeritus dean of the college libraries complimented him for a "stunningly fine talk." After the same speech, the head of University Press of New England reported that his wife "sighed and wondered" if Church would consider running for president of the United States. No doubt it was hard not to let this sort of flummery go to one's head.[28]

One joint venture, however, took Buehrens forever out of the shadows. The two ministers co-wrote a book that became a bestselling primer on Unitarian Universalism. It's typical of these men that each claimed to have conceived the idea for *Our Chosen Faith* and then invited the other to join in the project. What's clear is that Beacon Press, which is affiliated with the UUA, initially had so little confidence in the project that it paid an advance of only five hundred dollars to each man. Despite that pessimism, the book has sold more than 80,000 copies since publication in 1989.[29]

Our Chosen Faith hoped to fill a gap. Jack Mendelsohn, a prominent UU minister and biographer of William Ellery Channing, had published *Why I Am a Unitarian* in 1960. In the 1964 edition, Mendelsohn renamed the volume *Why I Am a Unitarian Universalist*, reflecting the 1961 union of the two denominations, and in 1985 revised it slightly and gave it yet another title, *Being Liberal in an Illiberal Age*. It had been a serviceable introduction for its era, and Mendelsohn even tipped his hat to Church's *Born Again Unitarian Universalism* as "a delightful volume." But, in the view of Buehrens and Church, the times called for a new approach, organized around the UUA's then-current "five sources of belief." In five pairs of alternating chapters, each co-author wrote about a single source. By having the two men bat the same idea back and forth, like tennis players, the book would illustrate the essential point that, in Buehrens's words, UUs "don't speak with a single voice."[30]

The volume's foreword, by UUA president William Schulz, reflected the denomination's progressive role in society. Schulz takes pride in the swelling numbers of female ministers (25 percent and growing) and leadership in the fight against homophobia but laments that the UUA has not expanded beyond its overwhelmingly white, upper-middle-class base. In theological trends, while reason remains a central "watchword," alongside freedom and tolerance, today's UUs recognize that "there are some angles from which the Spirit cannot be glimpsed by even the sharpest analytical eye." Schulz introduces Church, "perpetually bedecked in a New York Mets cap," as a man who "conveys warmth and confidence wherever he goes . . . the master of bonhomie and bon mot." As for Buehrens, he possesses "as agile a theological mind as any Unitarian Universalist."[31]

The opening sentence of Church's preface sets the tone: "All theology is autobiography." What we believe, he suggests, reflects what our parents believe and how we react to that, followed by contemplation of our later experience. Ideas are born, inevitably, from specific histories. In the case of Unitarian Universalists, this observation rings especially true, because "our faith did not choose us, we chose it." This is as true of UUs who grew up in other faiths as it is of UU youth, who are encouraged to explore religious options with an open mind.[32]

Despite the format of alternating chapters, the co-authors forgo debate for complementary narratives. The tone is conversational, dotted with personal anecdote and UU history. Church's challenge is to ground his customary themes within UU tradition. His commentary on the first "source"—"Direct experience of that transcending mystery and wonder, affirmed in all cultures, which moves us to a renewal of the spirit and an openness to the forces which create and uphold life"—draws heavily on his *Born Again* book. He translates the idea of direct experience as a series of "awakenings," a deepened and renewed appreciation for, in D. H. Lawrence's phrase, "the low, vast murmur of life." He summons Emerson on "the miraculous in the common." Out of recognition of this gift comes not only awe and wonder but gratitude.[33]

Church's chapter on the second source—"Words and deeds of prophetic women and men which challenge us to confront powers and structures of evil with justice, compassion, and the transforming power of love"—cites Unitarian luminaries from the nineteenth century (Bellows and Parker) and the twentieth (A. Powell Davies, James Reeb, a UU minister martyred in the civil rights struggle in Selma, Alabama, and Whitney Young, head of the Urban League). Titling his chapter "Deeds Not Creeds," he recalls the great achievements of Unitarianism and Universalism to banish ideas of hell and original sin from their theologies, while cautioning that the legacy has an implicit downside. "The problem," he writes, "is that even as a theology based upon evil and sinfulness tends to stint on goodness, one based upon goodness may be equally obtuse when it comes to evil and sin." And sin lay not just with the enemies of Parker and Reeb, but within everyone.[34]

Church's "cathedral of the world" fits neatly within the third source, "Wisdom from the world's religions." His Universalist metaphor, he notes, follows a long line of predecessors, including James Freeman Clarke, a pioneer in the comparative study of religion, and Jenkin Lloyd Jones, an organizer of the Parliament of Religions at the 1893 Columbian Exhibition in Chicago. All of the worshippers in this cathedral gaze upward at the windows, standing in the light they all share, even as they interpret the light in their own fashion. (In the follow-up chapter, Buehrens offers his only demurral: "Within the cathedral, no one seems to be talking to anyone else." For him, dialogue is essential to religious growth; in discussion with people of different views, one's own are clarified and deepened.)[35]

Church's comfort level with the fourth source, Jewish and Christian teachings, is as obvious as is his uneasiness with the fifth, humanist teachings. His version of Unitarian Universalism unabashedly embraces Jesus of Nazareth as a worthy guide. He finds comfort and wisdom throughout the Bible, but in none of the creeds created in Jesus's name. As concrete manuals for right living, however, this collection of human-made books is spectacularly uneven, "the most sublime sentiments" existing alongside "theological and ethical barbarisms." In conclusion, he offers a breathtaking rewording of the Beatitudes that could come only from someone inspired by Christian tradition. "Blessed are the poor in spirit," it begins, "for they know the unutterable beauty of simple things."[36]

Church approaches humanism gingerly. After bending over backward to praise the Humanist Manifesto of 1933 as a "profoundly spiritual document" that properly validates science as our authority on the nature of the physical world, he warns of the dangers of humanist "idolatry." "Are we liberals who happen to gather in churches," he asks, "or religious people who practice our religion according to liberal principles?" In this context, the Unitarian Universalist watchwords of reason, freedom, and tolerance, while valuable guidelines, should not be elevated into modern idols. In a rare departure from his diplomatic equilibrium, the author unleashes harsh words for the unbridled individualism of "free spirits" who join UU churches and make a mockery of freedom. They "know how to do one thing when they find themselves in any institution. They know how to savage it . . . We need to invest a little of our precious freedom, and bond ourselves to others in redemptive community." (We can only assume that Church is reacting here to egregious examples of ecclesiastical disruption.) Furthermore, a mind-set rigidly deferential to reason often mistakes the "trans-rational" realm for the irrational. On this issue, contemporary science—from cell biology to astrophysics—promotes nothing if not an attitude of awe and wonder. Within this framework, he concludes, theists and humanists can find ample common ground.[37]

On all these issues, Church knew exactly where he stood, and he could articulate his viewpoint with unusual clarity and eloquence. But he had been reared in a household where everyone knew how to play the political game. He understood when to reach across the aisle, to forge alliances and, if necessary, soften his rhetoric. This lifetime of experience also meshed well with his personality. Averse to confrontation, eager to please, optimistic in spirit, he followed the Dale Carnegie school of diplomacy, forever striving to "win friends and influence people." Not fake, not put on for the occasion, this was his quintessential self. These qualities would come to the fore in his next book, which yoked his passions for religion and politics.

Throughout the eighties, with Ronald Reagan in the White House and Republicans dominating the legislative agenda, liberals spent much of the time in a defensive crouch. Conservatives had successfully, if inaccurately, portrayed them as halfhearted patriots, secularists hostile to religion, saboteurs of family life. By doing so, conservatives had won over the blue-collar white vote and destroyed the New Deal coalition. Liberals might be persuasive on economic issues vital to working people, but when the

Frank and Bethine Church: A legacy of liberalism. CHURCH FAMILY

Cowboy buddies: Jimmy Bruce and Forrest, Boise, Idaho.
CHURCH FAMILY

A teenaged Forrest at his grandparents' Robinson Bar Ranch, Idaho.

Forrest campaigns for his father in Nebraska's Democratic presidential primary, 1976.

Young man in search of an
identity: Forrest, circa 1968.

Changing of the guard: A baby-faced Rev. Forrest Church, not quite thirty, succeeds Rev. Walter Kring, right, at All Souls Church, 1978. ALL SOULS CHURCH

Rev. Forrest Church in front of historic
All Souls Church. All Souls Church

Father and son: Forrest with his son, Frank. CHURCH FAMILY

Church at Monticello: Thomas Jefferson's views on religion were an early inspiration.
STEPHANIE GROSS

Forrest Church and Carolyn Buck Luce, 2006: They called each other "soul mates."
CHURCH-BUCK LUCE FAMILY

In the pulpit: A blend of intellectual substance and emotional resonance.

Near the end: Still reading, still asking the big questions.

focus shifted to moral issues, liberal political columnist E. J. Dionne Jr. observed, they had little to say. "Their admirable devotion to social tolerance made many liberals uneasy with talk about virtue." While defending the welfare state, they couldn't articulate "what moral values the welfare state should promote."[38]

But Forrest Church, with his unsurpassed credentials and authority, could. Steeped in the liberal tradition and respected as author and pastor, he could command a national platform for his views. While other liberals disavowed the term itself, redefining themselves as "neoliberals" or "progressives," he chose to embrace it. Rather than run away from "the L word," he sought to link liberalism with treasured American values. It wasn't an albatross but a badge of honor. He would take back flag, Bible, and family from the religious right.

In the spring of 1989, Simon and Schuster signed up Church for a book that would eventually bear the provocative title *God and Other Famous Liberals: Reclaiming the Politics of America*. His advance was $50,000, a substantial sum for the time, especially for a book on religion, underscoring the publisher's high hopes for the project. Church began working on it, with the aid of a student researcher, while at Dartmouth that summer. By the following summer, however, he was clearly struggling. None of his other books, often spun quickly out of sermons, had demanded so much of him. "I have never spent more than six weeks writing a book," he wrote to his editor, boasting as much as complaining. Now he was bogged down in detail, losing his sense of direction. Believing it to be his most important book yet, however, he kept at it, and by that fall, as he neared completion of the manuscript, his confidence had soared. In talks with Simon and Schuster, he was given the impression that the book would be published in the fall of 1991, the timing auspicious as presidential primary campaigns heated up in early 1992. A two-week publicity tour would give the book wings, and excerpts would be shopped to *Harper's* and *The Atlantic Monthly*.[39]

God and Other Famous Liberals, finally published in January 1992, is a fascinating pastiche—part theology, part political manifesto, part history lesson. Church sculpts his versions of God and Jesus, Washington and Jefferson, Lincoln and FDR into a resplendent liberal pantheon. Written in an engaging, sprightly style emerging from his preaching and newspaper writing, the book is dotted with quotable sentences: "God, the most famous liberal of all, has a bleeding heart that never stops . . . Any religion so weak that its survival depends on the support of government is unworthy of the name."[40] Opinion expressed with such pith and vigor, of course, could inflame liberalism's enemies as much as energize its defenders. One thing is certain. Just such a clarion call for liberal awakening is precisely what E. J. Dionne Jr. had in mind.

"I gave up on Bible, family, and flag twenty-five years ago," the opening sentence declares. Part of the generation of anti–Vietnam War rebels, Church rejected liberalism as inadequate to meet the radical challenges of the day. Patriotism, the traditional family, and orthodox religion all seemed outmoded, doomed to history's scrap heap. Having grown up, and now secure in his roles of minister, family man, and patriot, he knows better. Interpreted within a liberal framework, that triumvirate can be not only reclaimed but proclaimed. "The fundamentalists don't own Jesus and the prophets any more than the Vietnam hawks owned the flag."[41]

Church's case for a rejuvenated liberalism rests on close inspection of its dictionary definitions. For him, it's "not a fixed set of doctrines but a temper, a public spirit of openness and generosity." To be liberal is to be bountiful, generous, openhearted; to be free from bigotry and prejudice; to be open to new ideas; to lean toward freedom and democracy. American political liberalism of the 1960s and '70s, however, fell victim to a pendulum swing in political mood and to its own excesses. "When the rights of criminals are more vigorously protected than those of their victims, or when freedom of speech extends to racial, religious, or sexual defamation, liberalism becomes an easy target, a self-caricature." So, too, when the generosity of Lyndon Johnson's Great Society programs spilled over into profligacy. If this seems heresy to rigid liberals, so be it. Nor would all of them follow Church as he turns to the nation's founding. While the advent of democracy in Europe was decidedly secular, our nation's founding, he emphasizes, was inspired by "people of faith." What they did not establish, however, was a Christian nation.[42]

In reclaiming the Bible, Church interprets God and Jesus within a liberal theological framework. "Every word I can conjure for God is a synonym for liberal," he writes. "God is munificent and openhanded . . . As the ground of our being, God is ample and plenteous. As healer and comforter, God is charitable and benevolent. As our redeemer, God is generous and forgiving." His Jesus, anything but a biblical literalist, prizes deeds over creeds. This Nazarene breaks the Sabbath and consorts with despised prostitutes and tax collectors. If Jesus were alive today, his parable would tell the story of the Good Homosexual instead of the Good Samaritan.

This Jesus disdains religious show and believes prayer should not be an act of public piety. In this light, the religious right's insistence on the right to pray in public schools seems peculiarly misguided. "Reduced to a mechanical and perfunctory act," Church writes, "prayer is trivialized." As for broader church-state relations, he invokes the Jesus who advises us to "render unto Caesar the things that are Caesar's, and to God what are God's." History makes a similar point, ignored by the right wing. Granting a church an official status and financial support does not guarantee a thriving religion. On the contrary, the European experience confirms the opposite conclusion. In Britain and Sweden, for example, religious support is dwindling, while it thrives, despite suppression, behind the Iron Curtain. In the United States, insisting on keeping church and state separate is hardly an antireligious act. It has produced a religious culture of unprecedented vitality, and its inventors and defenders are some of the most honored icons of American history.[43]

Roger Williams, a Baptist, pioneered the way before the Revolution. Jefferson and Madison co-authored Virginia's path-breaking Declaration of Rights, which enshrined "the free exercise of religion" as a right, not a privilege. George Washington continually reassured Catholics, Jews, and Protestant sects of their right to practice religion as they saw fit without government interference. The Founders held to different religious beliefs. Some were Christians, and some were deists who rarely set foot in church. Few were outright atheists. But nearly all believed that religious vitality rested on two pillars: keeping government out of religion, and keeping religion out of government. In this spirit, Lincoln defied the National Reform Association, a sort of proto–Moral Majority of its time that advocated a constitutional amendment declaring the United States a Christian nation. Finally, FDR joins the Church pantheon as author of the Four Freedoms, including unlimited freedom of worship.

"Those who dismiss the spiritual foundations of the republic," Church writes, "cannot be relied on to ensure and protect the principles upon which this nation was founded: biblical teachings concerning equity, justice, mercy, and humility; and the broader religious conviction that all are created equal and endowed by their creator with certain inalienable rights . . . On the other hand, those who impose a doctrinal understanding of Christianity on the Declaration of Independence and the Constitution misread and subvert the intentions of our nation's architects."[44]

The implications for today call for balance. Unlike the most ardent of civil libertarians, for example, Church does not advocate the elimination of the word *God* from our currency or the Pledge of Allegiance. The motto "In God We Trust" underscores our faith in a power higher than the almighty dollar. That the nation remains "*under* God" in the pledge emphasizes that declaring a United States *over* God would amount to idolatry. Seen in this light, these phrases add up not to a holy alliance of church and state, but to a wise recognition of the state's limitations.[45]

On family issues, Church constructs a moral rationale in defense of the welfare state. Underlying each policy position is a benevolent God exemplified by the life and teachings of Jesus. The welfare state's safety net, from unemployment insurance to food stamps to child-care assistance, he argues, does tend to keep families together. Bans on abortion, on the other hand, tend to produce unwanted children who end up on the public dole. On an economic basis, too, refusing to bail out poor families only ensures that they will cost taxpayers more in the long run. Additionally, Church's liberal views of morality require him to support feminists and homosexuals in defiance of the religious right. Here there is no room for compromise. He does acknowledge, however, that government cannot bear the burden of lifting up the disadvantaged by itself. Private associations, including churches like All Souls, must also do their neighborly part.[46]

Church's call for "neighborliness" is very much in keeping with the communitarianism championed by many of the era's Jewish and Christian thinkers. *Commonweal* and *Tikkun*, one a Catholic magazine, the other Jewish, were prime exemplars of this point of view. Like them, Forrest continually fought for balance between individual rights and the needs of community. The definition of community that began with family and neighborhood stretched to nation and world. However defined, it acted as buffer against the relentless assaults of business-oriented privatism and fundamentalist-inspired corporatism. The former tried to dismantle government oversight so that business could do what it pleased. This was the tyranny of Mammon. The latter tried to impose its religious beliefs on everyone. This was the idolatry of theocracy. *God and Other Famous Liberals* proposed a radically different view of American public life. Would America listen?

Nine

Church of the Heavenly Unrest

I have not had the privilege of a life-changing failure
but my life isn't over yet.

—FORREST CHURCH, 1988

O n February 11, 1991, a brief letter arrived in the mailboxes of
the members of All Souls Church.

Dear Friends,

We are writing with sad news. After twenty years together, we have decided to end our marriage.

Please know that we have searched our hearts long and hard before arriving at this decision. We have sought professional counseling. We have struggled deeply with the possible consequences for our children. If we did not both believe that this is the right course, however difficult for all of us, we would not embark on it.

Ours is neither more nor less sad than the end of any marriage, but we do feel an extra burden of responsibility for the disappointment this will bring to a community we both cherish. Over the past thirteen years we have been sustained by your love and support. Now we ask also for your compassion and understanding.[1]

The letter was signed by Forrest Church and Amy Furth Church.

Mary-Ella Holst, vice president of the All Souls board of trustees, wrote in her journal the next day: "Camelot is over . . . We cannot help but lose our innocence."[2]

When Rev. Church next assumed the pulpit, on February 24, his sermon was titled "Confessions." It was remarkable both for what was confessed and what was left unsaid. The point of any confessional preaching, he said, is to illuminate not the preacher's life, but the listener's life. "There is a trick to this . . . One's confessions from the pulpit must seem more personal than they actually are. Were I to confess anything truly personal and intimate, it would only distract you from pondering your own life." And the danger is this: "When something deeply personal happens in my life, something that I can't help but reveal to you, you may be shocked, amazed, angered; you may even feel betrayed."

In the previous week's sermon, John Buehrens had prepared the way for this message, comparing ministers to skaters on the public ice. "So much of who we must appear to be dazzles on the surface," Church paraphrased, "so much of who we really are is buried hidden in the waters below."

Things can be hidden, Church said, not only from the public but from the minister as well. "I have tried not to elevate myself to a higher moral order, or even to hold myself to impossible standards simply because of my office. But I have felt myself immune to certain things, such as the possibility of divorce . . . It was too frightening to contemplate, the possible vulnerability; I just couldn't accept it. I would spoil the skater's flourish and grace and ease that I had practiced for so long, and to such applause, that they had become second nature to me."

Through psychotherapy, Church said, he had learned that his lack of introspection, his refusal to acknowledge feelings of anger and emptiness, had destroyed the possibility of intimacy. "I have poured my entire life into my work and my writings, into uncomplicated, wonderful friendships, and into escape. This hiding, this conflict avoidance, has had a subtle, slow, but ultimately devastating effect on my life, especially my marriage . . .

"I am guilty not only of many sins of omission, but also sins of commission. I want you to know that, but I am not today, nor ever, going to go any further than this into the details of my private life. All I can say is, what I have shared with you about the failure of my marriage is far more important than anything I have not."

In closing, Church asked for forgiveness, as hard as that might be to give, and assured the congregation that the experience had schooled him in a lesson he had often preached, that of humility. He hoped it would make him a better minister.[3]

During the next few weeks, the subjects of Church's sermons shifted dramatically from the personal to the political. He talked about the AIDS crisis, the founding of Mother's Day in 1872 by Unitarian Julia Ward Howe as a day of resistance to war, and about the nation's central preoccupation, the Persian Gulf War. In response to Iraq's invasion of Kuwait, Operation Desert Storm launched against Saddam Hussein's hapless forces a high-tech lightning war. After weeks of precision bombing, the Iraqi army was crushed by U.S. and Allied armies in a matter of days.

The opening salvos of the war at All Souls had not yet begun, but this was a conflict that would last far longer than the short-lived Gulf War. What Church had not mentioned, neither to the congregation nor even to his wife, was the other woman.

Carolyn Buck Luce was a thirty-eight-year-old beauty, a high-powered businesswoman, a married mother of two young children, and a parishioner of All Souls. During the previous year, she had served as chair of the church's Annual Giving campaign.

Buck Luce was raised in an upper-middle-class, secular Jewish household in Syracuse. Earl and Minna Buck met in the late forties at the University of Chicago Law School, where she was one of only two female students in her class. Earl, along with a brother, chose to run a family-owned commercial cleaning business rather than practice law. After rearing three children, Minna became a government lawyer and later a family court judge. Carolyn was the middle child, bright but not always diligent at her studies, emerging during adolescence, in her mother's words, as "a social butterfly," and in her own, as "a huge rebel." While Forrest Church engaged in cerebral forms of protest at Stanford University, Carolyn, six years younger, actually protested, traveling to Washington, D.C., to march in an anti-Vietnam rally, and, back home, organizing a strike and teach-in at Nottingham High School. For this youthful exuberance, she was temporarily suspended. Within the Buck family constellation, Carolyn felt stranded between a "Miss Perfect" older sister with straight As and a younger brother, "the only boy, who thus could do no wrong." Getting suspended and getting mediocre grades was what a "black sheep" like her did. Not surprisingly, every college to which she applied turned her down.[4]

As an eight-year-old in 1960, a John Kennedy–inspired Carolyn had dreamed of being "a world leader." That aspiration now looked not only beyond reach but positively silly. But this strong-willed young woman managed to get accepted at Ohio State in the middle of the year, earned her own set of straight As, and within a year transferred to Georgetown, the first-choice school that had initially rejected her. By the time she graduated with a double major in Russian studies and business, she had been tapped for Phi Beta Kappa honors. "When she set her mind on something," her mother said, "there was no stopping her."

After a brief stint as a U.S. Foreign Service officer in the Soviet Union, Buck realized that government work was not a good fit for her "more action-oriented, risk-taking" style. After earning an MBA at Columbia, she entered the New York banking world, hoping to "make an impact on the world faster." Very quickly, she did. She was often the only woman in the room. This distinction cut two ways: She had to perform very well, perhaps better than her male rivals, and, if she did, she would stand out in the crowd.

"If I hadn't pushed, I wouldn't have been in the room," she said. "I remember I was five years into my career at Citi [Citibank in New York], and they were having clients come in and I wasn't invited to the meeting. I went to the vice president, and I said, 'I want to be in that meeting. I've never been to a meeting where I haven't added value. If I don't add value, don't invite me to any more meetings.'" She began to add such good value that she shot up the executive ladder, propelled by the merger-and-acquisition scrambles of the eighties.[5]

"I've always liked business because it's a human drama," she said. "You're competing, and it's intellectually stimulating. Then when you add to that doing transactions, that's a real high. It's like skiing down a black diamond, very intense. It requires a lot of strategy, a lot of technical knowledge, a lot of personal dynamics."

Within two years, between 1986 and 1988, Buck Luce made two giant career leaps. First, she was put in charge of the Citibank team that secured financing for Canadian real-estate magnate Robert Campeau's acquisition of the Allied family of clothing-store chains, including Brooks Brothers and Ann Taylor. Few people imagined that Campeau, a flamboyant maverick, could pull off such a deal, since Allied's market value was ten times that of his own firm. Flush with this success, Buck Luce was hired away from Citi by the banking firm of First Boston. There she was in the midst of financing Campeau's even more complicated, more spectacular deal, a takeover of Federated Department Stores (Bloomingdale's, Bullock's, Rich's, Filene's, and others), when Campeau lured her to join him as one of his top three advisers.

"It was a huge opportunity for me," she said. "I knew he was crazy, but he was brilliant. And he had a very interesting team around him of really good people . . . Almost all the jobs I've had, I've created. They didn't exist. I'm a good strategist because I don't have a little voice in me saying, 'You can't do that.'"[6]

Unquestionably, Buck Luce thrived on taking risks, but this one proved to be more volatile than she had anticipated. She continually found herself caught between her mercurial boss and the lenders she had courted. In the spring of 1989, frustrated by Campeau's increasingly erratic business judgments, she quit. Nine months later, Federated and Allied Stores made dubious history, filing for the largest bankruptcy ever recorded in retailing. For Buck Luce, it was a time to regroup and rethink her career. For two years she and another former Campeau executive, James Roddy, managed their own boutique firm. But in the summer of 1991, she signed on as a senior partner with Ernst & Young. Despite its different set of challenges, the accounting giant proved to be a relatively safe haven. As Minna Buck put it, it was "free of the Campeau taint."[7]

Early in her Citibank career, Carolyn Buck had met another rising young star named Michael D. Luce, who later became an executive at Bear Stearns, the now-defunct investment bank and securities brokerage. They married and had two sons, Jacob and Nathan. In February 1991, when Forrest and Amy Church announced the breakup of their marriage, Jacob was six, and Nathan four. Frank Church, then twelve, was poised on the cusp of adolescence. His sister, Nina, was about to turn ten.

According to Church, his marriage had been shaky for a long time. Not tempestuous, the relationship instead fell victim to a slow, quiet unraveling. He and Amy rarely quarreled, though they did disagree about how to deal with their son's emerging difficulties at school. (Eventually, this very bright boy was diagnosed with Klinefelter syndrome, a genetic defect that causes learning disabilities and growth deficiencies during puberty and prevents most men who have it from fathering children.) The warmth gradually ebbed from the Church marriage, replaced by a cool, formal distance. Church buried his uneasiness, his discontent, his reluctance to face his demons in the writing of books. Writing, of course, had its own rewards. It allowed him to hone his intellectual gifts and earn kudos in the marketplace of ideas. But Amy resented the time it took away from family and deplored Forrest's ignoring of her needs and his injudicious use of family anecdotes in sermons and books. Her resentment was so great, she told John Buehrens, that she refused to read her husband's books.

"I did three books one summer [in the late eighties]," Church said, "and after I finished the third one I thought we were going out to celebrate.

That's when she asked me for a divorce. I was completely blind-sided. In retrospect, I can understand it completely.

"We were living in her parents' home in Laguna Niguel, California. I would get up about six and work until midnight. I would come out for meals, swim with the kids a little bit, do occasional things, but I was locked in the zone. I just emotionally didn't notice.

"We drifted very far apart. She was aware of that. I have nothing but regret for my ignoring of her emotional needs during that time. I don't know whether I was self-absorbed, but I become a vehicle for whatever it is I'm working on, and it absorbs me. I was on a high the whole time, and I just didn't notice what was going on around me."[8]

This was but one of several times, according to Church, that his wife had suggested divorce. It's not clear whether these occasions were set off by his infidelities or whether Amy was even aware of them. In 1976, while campaigning for his father in the Nebraska presidential primary, Forrest had a brief sexual liaison. Later, he had sexual relationships with several women, not All Souls members, who were highly placed in Unitarian Universalist circles. He declined to characterize these as "affairs":

"There were a couple of women," he said, "with whom I built a friendship that had a sexual dimension. It was not the center part of the relationships. They were short-lived and had long before become friendships by the time I met Carolyn. The first encounter that actually presented any kind of danger to my marriage whatsoever was Carolyn."[9]

By 1990, his marriage now loveless, Church found himself irresistibly drawn to Carolyn Buck Luce, no matter that she was married. She was beautiful and brilliant, warm and gracious, immensely successful. "Initially, it was an obsession," he said. "I would look out on the congregation and everybody would be in black and white, and she'd be in color. It was frightening to me. Every encounter I had with her was like a magical encounter. I simply lost my balance. And so I went for help."[10]

Initially, he sought advice from John Buehrens and from his closest confidant among New York clergy, Rev. Stephen Bauman, of Christ Church, Methodist. The revelation that his colleague was attracted to a married parishioner alarmed Buehrens. Above all, he disapproved on moral grounds, but he also warned Church of jeopardizing his All Souls post and his role as a prominent spokesman for liberal religion. Bauman and his family often socialized with the Churches; they had children of roughly the same age. He also enjoyed with Forrest the all-male fellowship of a poker group that met on the occasional evening at the Union Theological Seminary apartment of Holland Hendrix, Forrest's graduate school friend who was now the seminary's president. Here was "a peer group that we could take our politically incorrect laments to and spend some good time whining," Hendrix said. "It was a wonderful support group, and we just had a blast."[11]

It was to Bauman that Church brought the news that his marriage was in tatters and that Carolyn Buck Luce haunted his dreams. Taking in the story, Bauman was struck by his friend's emotional naïveté, in stark contrast with his intellectual prowess. "I don't think he had a coherent sense of himself emotionally," Bauman said. "I was always sort of thunderstruck by the set of discoveries he was having about himself. It was a childlike quality in some ways. All the new emotional information was just discovery after discovery after discovery . . . His need to talk and debrief it was a way for him to figure out what he was actually feeling." It was as though his friend had never experienced real love.[12]

The conversations with Bauman and Buehrens helped Forrest realize that his marriage was, indeed, dead. In the meantime, Buehrens urged Forrest to consult with Dr. David M. Kelley, who directed a psychotherapy reference service used by All Souls and many other New York churches. The psychologist suggested to Forrest that he could test whether his attraction to Carolyn was in fact an obsession, a mere fantasy that would be destroyed by actual knowledge of the person, as opposed to genuine feelings that might lead to love. To do that, he would have to spend a lot of time with her. So Forrest and Carolyn began to lunch together. They spilled out their life stories, their disappointments with their marriages, their aspirations. And they fell in love.

"I was not thinking about divorce and remarriage. I was not thinking," Church said. "I was like a moth to flame. I knew we were soul mates."[13]

The pair began to spend more and more time together. Bauman real-ized later that Forrest's requests to borrow his apartment, so that he could "get away from the family and concentrate on his work," were covers for assignations with Buck Luce. During the summer of 1990, Valerie Am-sterdam, a member of All Souls' board of trustees and its president in 1991, served as the couple's unknowing beard when Forrest would sug-gest that she and Carolyn attend Mets games with him. Invariably, Amy was said to be not interested or too busy to join them.[14]

A few All Souls leaders sensed that Church's marriage seemed a bit worse for wear, but apparently no one at All Souls, aside from Buehrens, knew about the burgeoning romance with Buck Luce. The February 11 letter announcing the divorce provoked more sadness and disappointment than dismay or shock, testimony to the fact that Forrest and Amy were both very well liked. In the nineties, nearly everyone agreed, divorces happened, they were tough on the kids, but life somehow went on. And for a while, life at the church did go on as usual. Authors Kurt Vonnegut and Dan Wakefield appeared at an All Souls–sponsored peace vigil. Church hosted the monthly World of Ideas series in March, in conversa-tion with Harvard theologian Harvey Cox. In a typical week, the Femi-nist Women's Group, the AIDS Task Force, the Prayer and Meditation Circle, and the Women's Reading Group all met; on Monday evening and at noon on Friday, the homeless were served their meals.[15]

In retrospect, Church acknowledged that he made two mistakes dur-ing this period. He should never have urged Amy to co-sign the Febru-ary 11 letter. That was blatantly unfair and hypocritical, even cynical. By using his wife to help cover up his affair, he was lying to her. He should have been forthright about falling in love with Carolyn and then sought a divorce.

To this sin of omission, he unaccountably added one of commission, equally reckless. Knowing that Michael Luce's marriage was in trouble, he signed his name to a letter routinely sent to parishioners under duress: He offered to counsel the man he had cuckolded. (He never actually counseled Luce, a fact later lost on his opponents.)[16] In any event, sending such a letter was blind hubris and sheer madness, the stuff of soap opera run amok. Blinded by love, Forrest Church was not thinking. And when people eventually found out about this letter, it drove them into a fury.

The announcement that Forrest and Amy's marriage was ending, of course, provoked no end of gossip and rumor. Was another woman waiting in the wings for Forrest? If so, who could it be? But by this time, Forrest and Carolyn could not seem to contain or delay their romance. On several occasions they were spotted being amorous in public. Perhaps in need of further confession, Church confided to one of his best friends at All Souls, Robert G. Cox. Cox's wife then tossed the grenade that shattered the illusion of an amicable separation. She reported the affair to Amy, Amy confronted Forrest, he confessed, and she threw him out of their apartment. For several weeks he bunked with friends, until he found a small basement apartment near the church. When his children would come to visit, they dubbed it "the mouse house" because of the dead mice littering the stoop.[17]

Though living apart, Forrest and Amy could not avoid each other. Since the fall of 1987, Amy had been director of religious education at All Souls. Bright, hardworking, and restless at home, she needed to put her talents to work. She had been hired despite the objections of some pillars of the church who believed that having Forrest as Amy's boss was a recipe for disaster. So now, in 1991, she not only supervised the children's Sunday classes, but during the first of two Sunday services, delivered a little homily to the children gathered around her at the front of the church sanctuary, with her estranged husband seated a few feet away.

Church always beamed in the presence of All Souls children. He adored dedications, the Unitarian equivalent of christenings, where he would pinch the baby's cheeks because, as he said, "they're so cute." His smile was a tighter one now.

In public, Amy had always radiated a quiet, rather formal elegance. She liked things kept orderly. Her persona was cool, calm, even-keeled. All this stood in stark contrast to her husband's style. Now, however, humiliated by the revelation that her husband had deceived her, she lost some of her self-control. At one dinner party, she blurted out that she had "made Forrest what he is, and now look what he's done to me!" At a religious education committee meeting, she complained that, in light of her husband's infidelity, she would have to be tested for AIDS. To the board of trustees, Amy insisted that her husband ought to be forced to take a leave of absence. Hearing this demand, Church shouted to Buehrens that someone had to "control that woman."[18]

While Amy Church supervised the church school, John Buehrens presided over an extensive adult education program that took place on Sunday mornings in Fellowship Hall in the church basement. In the fall of 1989, with Church's consent, he arranged to hire an old acquaintance, Dr. Louis Pojman, to a two-year term as the church's first "scholar-in-residence." They had met when Buehrens led First Unitarian Church of Dallas, and Pojman taught at the University of Texas branch in the city. Ordained in the Reformed Church of America, Pojman later abandoned that conservative faith while earning a Ph.D. in ethics at Union Theological Seminary. Next, he added a doctorate in philosophy from Oxford. Now on leave from the philosophy and religion department at the University of Mississippi and living in New York, Pojman was invited to lecture at All Souls.[19]

During the first months of 1991, Pojman's lecture series "Moral Dilemmas: Matters of Life and Death" covered death and dying, suicide and euthanasia, abortion, and other familiar topics. This was followed by the series "Environmental Ethics." He was a stimulating thinker who won distinguished teaching awards wherever he taught, and his following in Fellowship Hall was large and enthusiastic. Now learning of an ethical dilemma closer to home, Pojman interrupted this schedule to deliver, on March 24, "Moral Guilt, Shame and Forgiveness." This was unmistakably a shot over the bow directed at All Souls' senior minister, preaching at the same time upstairs. Pojman noted that Unitarians prided themselves on debating controversial issues and taking unconventional stands. Creedlessness implied a certain fearlessness. But did they dare confront so flammable an issue? How, the professor demanded, could church members discuss ethics in the abstract, while ignoring ethical questions directly in front of them?

Not surprisingly, Pojman became a polarizing force. Some praised his courage, his ability to cut to the heart of the matter, his refusal to silence himself because of his status as the church's invited guest. Others despised him as a cheeky interloper, a provocateur, a "snake in the grass." The first group began to raise the ultimate question: whether Forrest Church deserved to remain at the helm of All Souls. Without excusing his moral failings, the other group nonetheless considered him the institution's keystone, largely responsible for its past success and essential to its future. To send him packing would be unthinkable. Each side came to believe that the other threatened the stability and integrity of All Souls.[20]

In response to these rumblings from the basement, David Kelley was enlisted to give a talk on "When Clergy Divorce" as an adult education class. In the monthly church bulletin, Richard Leonard, the part-time assistant minister, reminded parishioners that he, too, had been divorced after a seventeen-year marriage and that many people emerge from this painful experience "certainly wiser, perhaps sadder, maybe even considerably happier than they were before."[21]

John Buehrens, however, was ensnared in a thicket of entangling relationships. Both Church and Pojman were his friends. And he not only liked and admired Amy, but his wife, Gwen, had become one of Amy's best friends and her fiercely loyal advocate. Working with Forrest during the day and going home to Gwen at night, Buehrens said, made "the triangulations just incredible." Trying to remain neutral, he caught flak from both sides. While Church's detractors believed he should lead the charge on their behalf, his supporters came to define neutrality as a form of betrayal.[22]

If Buehrens's position at All Souls was inherently fraught, it was complicated even more by national Unitarian politics. By the spring of 1991, he was a candidate for the presidency of the Unitarian Universalist Association. Though the election did not take place until 1993, the campaign, much like a U.S. presidential run, required a two-year criss-crossing of the country to raise money and win support. Everywhere he went, he was forced to fend off gossip about Forrest—some of it true, some false, all of it handicapping his chances. "I was just libeled by a good many people for association with Forrest," Buehrens said.

Ultimately, Church believed, Buehrens's ambition trumped loyalty to his friend: "The moment I became controversial," he said, "he distanced himself from me. I began hearing things that he was saying to others, both on the campaign trail and in the church, that were derogatory.

"I called him in and I said, 'No one was more supportive of my decision to get a divorce and get remarried. And yet, I'm hearing all sorts of backstabbing, and I just don't understand it.' He cried. At the end of crying he said, 'Forrest, you and I just have a different set of morals.' That's the way that he had worked it out. It did chill my affections for him."[23]

Among the All Souls board of trustees, opinion about their senior minister was divided. None of them thought Forrest had handled the breakup of his marriage well, and they told him so with some heat. "At one point," remembered board member Schuyler Chapin, "I just held up my hand and said, 'Let's not make this a kangaroo court.' This was just a perfect example of whipping up emotions on no substantial evidence in a kind of modern-day Salem witchcraft trial." But in public, board members presented a united front. In a May 2 statement, they unanimously affirmed Church's leadership and urged parishioners to let him and his wife "resolve their differences privately."

A few days later, Pojman fired back, lecturing directly on the subject of ministerial ethics. He passed out copies of the Unitarian Universalist Ministers Association guidelines, which stated in part, "As a sexual being, I will recognize the power that ministry gives me and refrain from practices which are harmful to others and which endanger my integrity or my professional effectiveness." The code specifically prohibited sexual activity with a child, an unwilling adult, a counselee, or a spouse or partner of a person in the congregation. Aside from violation of this code, Pojman's argument, here and in letters to church members and denominational officials, emphasized four points:

Forrest failed to tell the truth to his wife and congregation.

He asked others to be "nonjudgmental," but, in fact, sought to avoid being held accountable for his misdeeds.

Forgiveness is appropriate after remorse. But Forrest had shown no genuine remorse.

While Forrest contended that he had never put himself on a pedestal, pretending to be morally superior to his flock, Pojman argued that moral standards must, indeed, be higher for clergy. They must lead exemplary lives.

In the discussion that followed Pojman's talk, the church's fault lines could not have been clearer. On one side stood Robert Miness, who called the board's statement of support for Forrest "a whitewash" and demanded that he resign. But, asked a member on the other side, didn't Jesus himself forgive sinners? "What do you want Forrest to do? Get down on his hands and knees?"[24]

Earlier, Amy Church hoped that she might be able to retain her position as religious education director, but the board's affirmation of her estranged husband made that option untenable. So on May 19, during the traditional graduation service for the church school, she was given a farewell with speeches and a quilt designed and sewn by church women. "Very emotional for me, for all," Mary-Ella Holst wrote in her journal. "But Amy's goodbye was carried off with grace . . . She seemed to appreciate the quilt very much . . . When I got home I felt an emptiness, a gap. Partly Amy, her leaving being more real, and also partly [board president Valerie Amsterdam] and I at lunch talking about how many hours and hours we had spent on our hope that it is over for us. And what a misuse of time it seems. Private matter played out in public at the cost of our time."[25]

(The board of trustees also voted to award Amy three thousand dollars toward her tuition at New York Theological Seminary. After earning an MDiv degree there, she worked in the city as a hospital chaplain.[26])

It was not until June 9 that Church met with parishioners face-to-face at a tense meeting after the Sunday service to answer questions. Once again, he apologized for his lapses and for disappointing the congregation. And, for the first time, he admitted publicly to an affair, though without naming Carolyn Buck Luce, who was now divorced. But if he thought this admission would put an end to things, he was wrong. Pojman fought back the next evening, insisting at the All Souls board meeting, to which he had been invited, that Church's only honorable course was resignation. The board disagreed. But in the June/Summer edition of the church bulletin, an increasingly wary Church sounded a penitential note: "I am very sorry for the hurt, anger, and confusion that many of you feel. Things haven't been handled perfectly by any of us, and I take my full measure of responsibility for that . . . Next year, one important agenda is to establish a full measure of trust. Pedestals are out."[27]

Every summer, Unitarian Universalists from the United States and Canada gather in a General Assembly. They worship, listen to speeches, attend workshops, elect their leaders, meet old friends, and invigorate their sense of identity and mission. One of the highlights is the Service of the Living Tradition, which pays homage to newly ordained ministers and those who are retiring or have died during the past year. Well before Church's affair roiled the waters at All Souls, his friend and UUA president William Schulz had tapped him to deliver the sermon in June. Now, speaking before an audience of several thousand in Hollywood, Florida, Church drew on the God-and-flag themes from his forthcoming book, *God and Other Famous Liberals*.

But the real news was made outside the auditorium. Knots of protestors, many of them women, chanted anti-Church slogans and held up signs denouncing his selection as speaker. Even if their numbers were small, the demonstration amounted to an unusual rebuke to the most prominent spokesman for their faith. Word filtered down to Unitarian teenagers in attendance as well. Alison Miller, then a member of All Souls' teen group and later an assistant minister at the church, remembered having to defend her minister against peers who jeered, "Oh, you're from *that* congregation. I can't believe what your minister's done!"[28]

During the summer, while All Souls slumbered in semi-vacation mode, Church and the board of trustees were lulled into believing that the crisis was over. Charged up by Pojman's articulate attacks and their own sense of outrage, however, the minister's opponents were just beginning to organize. They were led by two high-profile couples, Alexander and Jeannette Watson Sanger and Robert and Barbara Lazear Ascher, and by Sean Connor.

The Sangers bore distinguished pedigrees. Alex was the grandson of birth-control pioneer Margaret Sanger. Jeannette's father, Thomas J. Watson Jr., had been chairman of IBM. A former Wall Street lawyer, Alex now ran Planned Parenthood of New York. His wife operated a bookstore adjacent to the Whitney Museum, Books & Co., that showcased her exquisite taste in books and had become a gathering spot for the literati. Robert Ascher was a highly regarded psychiatrist. Barbara, the author of several nonfiction books, had for a time written the "Hers" column in *The New York Times*. Sean Connor, Alex's roommate at Princeton, had moved to Rhode Island, but the former All Souls board president was so offended by Church's misbehavior that he returned occasionally to New York to aid in the campaign.[29]

Recruited to All Souls by Sean Connor, the Sangers had grown to love the sermons, the music, and Amy Church's programs for their children. For Alex, the church's appeal was "a combination of being intellectual and nondogmatic, asking the right questions, and saying there's no one answer. I've spent my career fighting against people who think they have all the right answers." As for Jeannette, she found Forrest "so charismatic and, probably like a lot of women in the congregation, I had a little crush on him. He was good-looking, dynamic, so smart and funny." Only after they started attending did they realize that the attractive young couple across the hallway of their Upper East Side apartment building at 7 Gracie Square was their minister and his wife.[30]

While the Sangers shared similar mainline Protestant roots, Barbara and Robert Ascher typified couples who came to All Souls from divergent religious backgrounds. Barbara was raised in the Episcopal church; Robert's family was culturally Jewish and fervently nonreligious, but he was drawn to the timeless questions about meaning by his Catholic nannies and by reading Paul Tillich while an undergraduate at Columbia. Both were seekers in need of a spiritual home.

Barbara introduced Bob to All Souls in the late eighties. "He just fell in love with it," she said. "The day we joined, we felt we should go out dancing on the streets. Oh my goodness, my husband was devoted! I think Bob loved Forrest like a son. He saw Forrest for all his strengths and for his boyish nonstrengths and loved him for all of it."[31] But Church's affair and subsequent attempts to justify his actions fatally tore that bond.

Like the Sangers and Aschers, people come to church for spiritual guidance, but they also project their yearnings and hopes, their aspirations for wholeness and sustenance, onto the clergy. The relationship is always a matter of the heart. Taken to extremes, this can evolve into what Forrest disparaged as the *Wizard of Oz* model for ministry, in which the minister is viewed as a larger-than-life miracle worker. As much as he tried to avoid that through self-deprecating humor, Forrest said, "The harder I tried, the more I got elevated. It was the only thing I knew how to do to knock this pedestal down." Ironically, self-abnegation from the pulpit made him even more beloved.[32]

Barbara Ascher's explanation for her disillusionment is a variation on this theme: "Charismatic leaders are never fully aware of their power, and therefore not respectful enough of their power. So Forrest had this power, and it was a power of love, and there is not a soul who doesn't want to be loved. [The congregation was] revolving around this center, for better or worse. We had become a family. We had all found a place where it's safe to have a voice, where there's a sense of deep trust. So when that dream—and, of course, it was a dream—was swept away, the responses were perhaps overwrought. It felt the way it would feel if your parents are getting divorced. I remember feeling homeless. I had lost something very dear to me. So it felt desperately, desperately sad."[33]

Roslyn Will was a participant if not a leader in the anti-Church faction. Her sadness was rooted in a special relationship with her minister. Though he was some twenty years younger, she saw him as her mentor. After her children were grown and she was looking for something to do, he encouraged her to get involved in church activities. "I was really just dying to start doing things again," she said. They would meet every week or so to discuss her involvement in social-outreach programs. "Maybe because I didn't go to college, I went from not being able to say two words to people, especially if I thought they were in different social strata, to being able to talk to anybody, being able to lead meetings. I felt like the church was almost like a college."

So Church's fall from grace struck with enormous force. "I had for a long time idolized him as what a minister should be," she said. "And he was so young that it felt almost like he was a son."[34]

In the face of such shattered dreams, reasoned argument was impossible. Nonetheless, when All Souls resumed its full schedule of services and activities in September, Church hoped that a conciliatory spirit would fend off trouble. His pastoral letter in the monthly bulletin proclaimed a set of early "New Year's" resolutions. He vowed to "redress the balance" between his public and pastoral ministries and spend more time attending to the parish. He would balance his personal and professional lives "more thoughtfully" so that he spent more time with his children. He would take a hiatus from writing books. And he asked church members to "shame me into keeping them."

In a sermon too glibly titled "What I Did on My Summer Vacation," Church expanded on these themes. Unlike Christian ministers, who preached "the Word of God" as expressed in the Bible, he said, those in the liberal religious tradition were forced to rely on themselves, to turn their own experience "into knowledge, perhaps even truth . . . We can't cite chapter and verse. We can't tell you to look it up . . . Instead we are constrained to work from the limitations of our own being, drawing from imperfect lives and imperfect understandings." Imperfection, indeed, was his theme. He admitted that his sermons had been too shallow, that he had been inattentive to his children, that he had not come to grips with the pain that he had caused.

"We'll never be pure," he concluded. "We'll never be perfect . . . I am not nor do I pretend to be any better than you. If you need me to be, I will probably disappoint you. I am not a book, not a scripture, not a possessor of the one true word. I am a human being . . ."[35]

For his opponents, statements like this never went far enough. Rather than mollified, they were now determined to force Forrest Church out of his post. On Sunday mornings, Alex Sanger, Sean Connor, and Robert Ascher stood outside the church handing out leaflets denouncing Church and petitions demanding his resignation. Some parishioners read them and agreed. Others called them "trash" and tossed them into the gutter. Tempers flared, friends broke into arguments, people stopped talking to each other. All this turmoil in a normally tranquil safe haven pushed some parishioners temporarily out the door. They didn't come to church to fight, so they stopped coming.[36]

If Church would not resign, his opponents resolved to kick him out. According to All Souls bylaws, only ten members' signatures were required to force a recall vote. By September 26, the board of trustees, aware of petitions already circulating, reluctantly decided to face the inevitable. Despite their efforts since spring to dampen congregational anger and declare their minister's marital woes an off-limits private matter, All Souls would end up voting whether to retain their leader of fourteen years. They scheduled a vote for Sunday, October 13 (later pushed back to the fifteenth, to avoid the Columbus Day weekend). Voters would be given only two choices: to affirm or to remove Forrest Church.[37]

In the meantime, opponents chose to wield another weapon, the press. This was a dubious strategy, for it made them look unseemly, airing dirty laundry in public, especially when they claimed to care so much about Amy and the children. If Amy already felt humiliated by the exposure of Forrest's affair at All Souls, how would she feel if all of New York knew about it? And why possibly subject the children to their classmates' taunts? Opponents went ahead anyway, planting stories in the tabloids.

By early October, the *Daily News* jumped into the fray, first with an item in the "Apple Sauce" gossip column, followed by a longer news article in which none of those involved came off looking very good. Jeannette Sanger said she knew people whose weddings took place at All Souls who now felt as though they were no longer married. "Things would be different," according to Valerie Amsterdam, if the affair were with "a 16-year-old girl in an alley, and all, as opposed to a woman he plans to marry." And why was Amy telling a reporter that "it's extremely painful that it's become such a public thing"?[38]

Newspapers are drawn to controversy like sharks to blood, but given this level of journalism, nuance never had a chance. The *New York Post* yoked the sensational with the unfair and unbalanced. Its headline: RANDY REV. FACES CHURCH VOTE. Its story: Three quotes from Forrest foes and none from his supporters.[39]

The New York Times, always more circumspect than the tabloids, nonetheless felt compelled to join the fray because word was out that *New York* magazine was about to cover the story. Peter Steinfels, the *Times's* national religion correspondent, remembered the paper's internal debate. "On one side was the feeling that this is a matter of personal struggles, failings. It's not usually the kind of thing that the *Times* does. The other side of it was, if this were a Southern conservative televangelist, we wouldn't hesitate for a moment to cover it. We would consider it quite relevant because it did speak to the question of the fit or lack of fit between what a person was preaching and what he was practicing."[40]

Not surprisingly, Steinfels's piece was remarkably evenhanded, quoting generously from partisans on both sides. Although the reporter characterized Church as "one of Manhattan's most admired clergymen," he also quoted one dissident comparing his minister to a famously sinning televangelist: he was but "a Jimmy Swaggart in tweeds."

In the battle for All Souls, Church's opponents wrapped themselves in the cloak of righteousness. They presented themselves as upholders of truth and morality. Because he unquestionably had erred, they seemed to occupy the moral high ground. His supporters, unable to defend Forrest's misbehavior unequivocally, had to speak the language of institutionalism, of protecting the church's stability. Thus they could seem unfeeling and legalistic. In the *Times* article, Amsterdam sounded too much like the criminal defense lawyer she was: "Do Unitarians look to the Ten Commandments as something literal and written in stone? We don't have a set of absolute rules as do some other churches." Mary-Ella Holst's sound bite of "there's right, there's wrong, and there's real" may have sounded as though she was immune to ethical nuance, when, in fact, nuance was precisely her point. Ethical rules should not be set in stone, indeed, but take into account life's messy, muddy entanglements.[41]

New York's piece, "Church of the Heavenly Unrest," appeared a few days before the All Souls vote. Its author, freelance writer Rusty Unger, had learned about the controversy at a dinner party given by Robert and Barbara Ascher. Though Unger wrote that the All Souls situation was very different from the sex scandals currently roiling fundamentalist waters—"There are no hookers, pederasts, bimbos, or felons here"—her piece emphasized the theme of the woman scorned, the open displays of affection between Church and Buck Luce, and Pojman's claim that Church had admitted past adulteries to him (he had never publicly admitted them). It falsely claimed that the minister's customary benediction of "I love you" was a product of his recent love affair. In fact, it had been his signature for years. Quoting opponents at length, while allotting far fewer words to supporters, the article made little attempt to disguise its bias. Especially disturbing to Unitarians everywhere was the inclusion of jokes implying that they had no ethical bearings whatsoever. This view was given explicit expression by a Duke University ethics professor Unger cited, who commented that "they have firm moral convictions that people shouldn't have firm moral convictions, and that's why they're just stupid." It's hard to imagine the magazine tolerating that level of denigration of any other religion.[42]

If John Buehrens sought to maintain his neutrality, he probably should not have told Unger some parishioner's observation that "Forrest was the mind and the soul of this place, but Amy was the heart." It was just the sort of comment to expose his exceedingly mixed feelings. As the day of the vote approached, Church's opponents kept pressuring Buehrens to denounce his colleague, or to resign as a gesture of disapproval. He wouldn't do either one. And to keep the other side at bay, Buehrens made it clear that he was not hankering for Forrest's job. He would leave All Souls in 1993, whether or not he won the UUA presidency that year. (In fact, he did win.)

"There is a tendency, under circumstances like this, for people to look for the Associate Minister either as rescuer or co-conspirator," he wrote to Jeannette Sanger. "I am neither." As for his campaign to lead the UUA, "the controversy at All Souls has already made [it] more complicated. If I am made to hang in someone else's tree, I will find that unfair, but not surprising."[43]

Meantime, the question of whether Forrest Church would hang was about to be settled. As the day of the vote approached, he made two final pleas for forgiveness and support. In a letter to church members, he made three points. The first clarified facts that the opposition had muddied. He had never taken sexual advantage of any parishioner. He and Carolyn fell in love in the context of their faltering marriages, and they planned to marry next summer. "Surely," he wrote, "we would rewrite a few pages of history to make them cleaner if we could, but we cannot." He never counseled Carolyn or Michael Luce, but he granted that the letter to Luce "should not have been sent out with my signature." Second, he rejected the notion in the New York article impugning the Unitarian faith. "That we are not dogmatic or narrowly moralistic does not mean that we are not ethical and moral in our communal faith, vision, and action." Finally, he counseled church members to "be kind to one another. There are no devils here. Not me. Not the people who are attacking me. We are all human beings who struggle with what it means to be alive and have to die."

Church's sermon two days before the vote took its theme and title from the Sondheim musical *Into the Woods*, which he had just seen on public television. In this fairy tale, each of the characters is searching for something missing in their lives: money, love, beauty, power. To find them, they must pluck up their courage and enter the woods, the great unknown. By the end of the first act, they do find what they want there. In the second, however, things go very wrong. A giant crushes their houses, and they are cast back into the woods. They blame one another, point fingers at scapegoats, and lose all hope—until they find ways to cooperate for the common good.

In Church's reading, the show is an allegory of the tensions between individual and community. Instead of drawing parallels with the tumult at All Souls, he merely suggested them. "What finally redeems this apparently tragic vision," he said, "is the recognition of universal kinship, which when acknowledged, brings us together, wiser, more humble, and better equipped to enter the woods again." As for liberal ministers, sometimes they are good guides, sometimes not. "But we are not, nor do we claim to be, in possession of the one true map. We do not preach follow me, but walk alongside of me should you so wish. We try to help you forgive yourself when you fail . . . We also ask the same of you."[44]

In its long and distinguished history, All Souls had never had to deal with a situation so messy, so embarrassing, so potentially destructive of its reputation and mission. To keep reporters and ineligible voters out of the church sanctuary during the vote, the board of trustees hired several guards to man the doors. After meeting with dissident leaders, the board agreed on the meeting's ground rules. Church members would pick up ballots in the basement Fellowship Hall and then show them to monitors to enter the sanctuary. As in all congregational meetings, eligible voters had to meet three criteria: to be sixteen or older and to have signed the church register, to have made a financial contribution in the past year, and to have attended at least four services. To ensure that as many people as possible could vote, the voting guidelines would be interpreted liberally. Each side would be allotted ten minutes for an opening statement or statements, followed by two-minute statements by members of the congregation lined up at two separate microphones. To chair the meeting, the board and dissidents settled on Paul Frank. A respected attorney and former board president, he was a man of even-tempered disposition who saw merit in both sides of this issue.[45]

Despite fears that things might get out of hand, the meeting itself went surprisingly smoothly. The guards probably weren't necessary. For one thing, dissidents knew they didn't have the votes to win. For another, emotions had been running so high for so long that people on both sides felt absolutely exhausted.

Neither Church nor his wife was there. Ever the diplomat, John Buehrens went out to dinner with Forrest while his wife dined with Amy. The Buehrens' daughter Erica babysat Twig and Nina. A courageous Carolyn Buck Luce, who had stayed away from the church for months, chose to attend. "I needed to be there," she said later, "to let people know that I totally understood their anger and hurt and betrayal."[46]

Paul Frank's opening statement set the tone. He encouraged an attitude of respect for everyone's views so that, no matter how the vote went, the church community, for which all had a "deep and abiding affection," could move forward in a spirit of reconciliation.

A letter read on behalf of longtime member Marietta Moskin, who was out of town, ably summarized the argument in defense of her minister. "I remember the long discussions about the wisdom of calling an untested academic . . . without previous experience in the field. [But] Forrest arrived like a breath of fresh air and he endeared himself with his wit, his brilliant sermons, his unbridled enthusiasms." As the years went by, he brought "new life, growth, and prestige to the church." Recently, some new members have regarded him with "uncritical hero worship . . . But Unitarians do not worship idols or icons. Unitarian

ministers are not sacramental figures of authority to be raised above ordinary mortals."

What's more, Unitarians at All Souls affirm the teachings of Jesus,
"who taught about forgiveness . . . about seeing the beam in one's own
eye before pointing out the mote in the eye of another." She alluded to
other religious and political leaders marred by less than perfect personal
lives whose message and effectiveness carried on with undiminished authority. Finally, she predicted that the current "trials and tribulations"
would "add new dimensions to Forrest's future ministry."[47]

Alexander Sanger delivered the opening statement for the opposition.
Despite the general tone of civility, this pro-choice advocate later said, "For
me, the atmosphere was like addressing the National Right to Life Convention. I've never felt such hostility." Speaking fast in order to deliver his entire speech, he soon realized that he wouldn't finish it; he would have to
abandon a paragraph here, another there. It was his final opportunity to lay
out the prosecution in a case he knew he could not win.

As spiritual leader, Sanger said, Church had not set the proper example:
"To live a moral life. To tell the truth. To be a man of character." He rejected the notion that a Unitarian minister is "merely a peer . . . He stands
above us in a pulpit. He was graduated from divinity school. He has rules
he must obey—a Ministerial Code of Ethics. And he has the moral and
ethical traditions of our Judeo-Christian heritage . . . to live by . . . To require this is not to demand, however, that Forrest go to hell or that he be
permanently defrocked, or that he not marry the woman he now loves."
Still, his actions, his hypocrisy, and his deceit had degraded the ministry
and been destructive to All Souls life. And what would happen to All
Souls if Church were forced out? It wouldn't be reduced to "a hovel," as
he had recently claimed in the press. Who knew, perhaps they would
find another bright young minister, like the very young Forrest Church.
The All Souls community, he concluded, was far bigger, far more important than its head minister.[48]

After two and a half hours, after forty-six other church members
stepped to the microphones and had their say, and after the secret ballot

was tallied, the ayes had it. Forrest Church had been affirmed by 73 percent, 370 votes to 136.[49]

The next day's tabloids swatted him one more time. SEX-FLAP PASTOR IS RETAINED, blared the *Daily News*, while the *Post* upped the ante with WIFE-CHEATING PREACHER KEEPS HIS JOB. But now, after nearly a year, the tumult was over. Forrest Church and All Souls could get back to business, if not quite business as usual. It was a time to hunker down.

Ten

Return to Grace

We should not feel embarrassed by our difficulties,
only by our failure to grow anything beautiful from them.

—ALAIN DE BOTTON

Since September 1991, Forrest Church had been living with Carolyn Buck Luce and her young sons in their Upper East Side apartment, a few blocks from All Souls Church. The new couple planned
to marry as soon as possible. She was now divorced, and his divorce proceedings would be completed early in the following year.

Although Buck Luce was tough and savvy in an unforgiving, male-
dominated business world, she exuded very different qualities at home.
Overflowing with warmth, generosity, and social graces, she expected her
husband-to-be to learn something he had not yet fully grasped: the daily
give-and-take between equal partners.

"I was for the first time in a full-bodied, full-barreled relationship
with another human being," Church said. "Carolyn taught me how to
include another completely in my life. She demanded full presence and
attention."[1]

This helps to explain why, while Church had apologized to his All
Souls parishioners for many things in the past year, he had never issued
an "I have sinned" statement. His reluctance to admit outright that the
extramarital affair had been wrong surely stemmed from pride and ego,

and it ignored Amy Church's pain and public humiliation. But it was also deeply rooted in his conviction that the love he discovered with Buck Luce possessed an intensity, depth, and wholeness that he had never before experienced. For Forrest Church, there was no need to apologize for finding his soul mate.

Throughout the ordeal at All Souls, she had been his rock. "If it had not been for Carolyn," he said years later, "I would have had a hard time surviving. I'm by nature conflict-averse. I would skirt flames rather than walk through them, and Carolyn disciplined me to walk through the flames.

"I was always preternaturally beloved, and all of a sudden that image crumbled. In some ways, I'd been the Wizard of Oz. The curtain had been pulled out, and I was the little man with the machine and the red ball of fire. I felt very exposed. I'm not a bad man, but I'm a bad wizard.

"I did not want the pain. I wanted to run. I wanted to start a new life. I might have returned to the academic world. That would have been extremely destructive to the church if I had done that, if I'd acted on my selfish desire to just escape. The board of trustees was forthright with me, insisting that I stay the course and not let the church down. They wanted me to stay; it would divide the church more if I left. By staying, we would weather this."[2]

Five days after the climactic vote of October 15, All Souls went back to business. At a Sunday service focused on the ordination of its ministerial intern, Marie deYoung, Forrest Church gave a sermon entitled "Ministry." Notably, it reasserted his judgment that Unitarian ministers should not be held to higher ethical standards than their congregations. "We are earthen vessels, not china or porcelain," he said. "We have feet of clay as does everyone else. By accepting a ministerial call, our failures become public, not private failures. With this comes a responsibility that we will not always bear as well as we would like. But it is equally important that we avoid moralistic presumption. Our ongoing charge is to do our earthly best to be openly and fully ourselves, not to pretend that knowledge always spells wisdom, or that the study of religion makes one holy, because neither is necessarily true."

If this sermon lacked the contrition some parishioners expected, Church's message in the November monthly bulletin retreated slightly from his posture of self-justification: "Had there been a third line on the ballot reading 'affirm with reservations' many who voted both for and against me would have found this a more palatable alternative. Accordingly, while I rejoice that my ministry has been so strongly affirmed, I still accept the vote as a reprimand."[3]

Reprimand or not, Forrest Church put behind him what came to be called The Troubles with relative ease. "I did not obsess on or even spend much time reflecting on what I coulda, shoulda, woulda done if everything had been right," Church said. "It's just not the way my mind works."[4] But for church members, even his most fervent backers, this period seemed to require a pause for grieving—for their lost innocence, for the formerly unquestioned bond with their minister. Some wondered whether he should have taken a leave of absence, as a kind of penance. But such a leave never occurred to him. Nor did the board of trustees consider that an appropriate course.

"Forrest had to live through [all the emotions his parishioners were experiencing]," board member Christina Bellamy said. "To take a break from it would have been a mistake. Now that you've had this vote and people have basically said, 'Okay, we're going to forgive you for this and we want to go on. But you need to be here with us and struggle with us in our pain.' That was the best form of penance that he could have had."

The paradoxical power at the heart of Forrest Church's ministry was on full display during these months. Unquestionably, he was an inspiring, charismatic leader, but his leadership style intentionally and assertively promoted an outpouring of congregational activity that was beyond his sway, that had a life of its own. He was not leading the AIDS Task Force, the Children's Task Force, the Boy Scouts, or the programs that fed the poor; All Souls members were. In their activity and busyness and mutual support, Church's parishioners were healing themselves.

Bellamy again: "It's like anything that happens in a family. You work

together and cry together and do things together until eventually the
pain of it begins to dissipate, and slowly but surely you become whole
again. But it would not have happened if Forrest had not allowed this
church to develop that foundation from the bottom up."[5]

For his part, Church set up dozens of private meetings with disgruntled
parishioners. The primary aim was not to defend himself but simply to
listen. For Roslyn Will, who had invested so much of herself in the church,
the encounter proved so painful that she could barely talk: "Every time I
wanted to, I started to cry. I was that upset."[6]

Several hundred parishioners, it's estimated, were upset enough to
withdraw their membership from All Souls. For a while, small groups of
them, including Roslyn and David Will, met in one another's apartments
for makeshift Sunday services, like the early Christians. The Sangers led a
group across the hall from Amy Church's apartment. Amy and her children would join them for a gathering that was part religious service, part
support group. One time they read aloud William Steig's picture book
Amos & Boris, a tale of friendship in which a whale rescues a mouse in the
ocean, and later the mouse is able to return the favor. "We all cried,"
Jeannette Sanger remembered. "We were in mourning for our church,"
said Barbara Ascher. When these informal services ran their course, after
a few months, people drifted off to the better-organized institutional life
of other churches, or to no church at all.[7]

Amy Church was not quite finished with All Souls. The trustees agreed
to let her attend the December 9 board meeting so that she could confront
them face-to-face. Forrest Church, who usually took part in these meetings, chose not to be there. She was not surprised, she said in her rebuke to
the board, because he could not bear to hear what she had to say. For the
issues were never about infidelity or divorce, she said, but his deception
and dishonesty. And while the board insisted that this was a purely private
matter, she had never been allowed her husband's privilege of privacy.
What's more, the board had attacked the motives and character of anyone
who believed that Forrest had forfeited any rightful claim to his job. While

defending him to a fault, she said, board members had treated her viciously. They had disgraced the church and broken her heart.[8]

The public attacks on Forrest Church were not over, either. Somehow the country's most notorious scandal sheet got wind of the story. In the next day's *National Enquirer*, the headline read PREACHER'S LOVE TRIANGLE SPARKS UNHOLY SCANDAL IN THE PULPIT. The story repeated previously reported details of the affair, while punching them up, *Enquirer*-style. The subhead: "He takes a parishioner as his mistress then offers help to her husband!" *Enquirer* reporters also managed to entice comment from an embittered Michael Luce. Calling Church "an evil man," Luce expressed shock that "the man who ruined my life is now living in my apartment and bringing up my children." Ever drawn to the outrageous, the *Enquirer* also highlighted in huge type a quote cherry-picked from the earlier *Times* piece: a parishioner dismissing Forrest as nothing more than "a Jimmy Swaggart in tweeds."[9]

Was he?

Forrest Church's fall from grace hardly took place in a vacuum. For several years before 1991, sex scandals involving men of the cloth had been the talk of the nation. But most of the headline-makers were Satan-denouncing fundamentalist shouters who embraced the Republican Party almost as fervently as the Bible. Outside the world of televangelism, Jim Bakker and Jimmy Swaggart remained little known until their indiscretions transformed them into clowns and hypocrites in the mainstream media.

The North Carolina–based Bakker had built his PTL (Praise the Lord) television network into an empire grossing $120 million a year. But in March 1987, the *Charlotte Observer* broke the story that this married Pentecostalist preacher had carried on an affair with a twenty-one-year-old church secretary eight years before and then paid her to remain silent. Although Bakker resigned his ministry, he refused to admit to any kind of moral transgression. His misfortunes, he claimed, were the fault of "treacherous former friends" who had lured him into a sexual encounter at a time of "great stress in my marital life." Not only widely pilloried

by the press, Bakker ended up spending five years in prison for defraud-
ing PTL supporters out of $158 million.

Swaggart was another Pentecostalist with an enormous television following. A year after the Bakker scandal, reporters from ABC's *Nightline*
caught Swaggart in a motel with a prostitute.

Pentecostalists are characterized by their charismatic worship practice
of "speaking in tongues," symbolizing the presence of the Holy Spirit.
Once their scandals were exposed, Bakker and Swaggart chose to speak
in starkly different tongues. Bakker stonewalled, admitting nothing,
while a chastened Swaggart readily confessed. Standing before his congregation and family in Baton Rouge, Louisiana, he told his wife that he
had sinned against her, and begged her forgiveness. Then he proceeded
to admit to sinning against his children, his church, his Bible college,
and his denomination (the Assemblies of God), and asked, in turn, for
their forgiveness. In contrast with Bakker, he survived the ordeal—despite
a denominational reprimand—because he honestly confronted his moral
failure and vowed not to repeat it. A year later, his TV programs still
reached an audience of 800,000. His period of grace, however, proved
short-lived. On October 15, 1991—the very day of All Souls' vote on
whether to retain Forrest Church—when Swaggart was arrested for a traffic
violation, another prostitute was with him in his car, and his ministry soon
crumbled.[10]

Clearly, Forrest Church was no Jimmy Swaggart in tweeds. He had
not been involved with a prostitute, but with another consenting adult
who was in the process of leaving an unhappy marriage. In one crucial
sense, Church had acted more like Bakker than Swaggart. His refusal to
issue a Swaggart-like "I have sinned" statement made him vulnerable, not
only to his critics but also to his supporters, who wished he had handled
things more directly and honestly. Instead of coming clean, he had danced
around questions of moral failure.

In short, Church had apologized but not confessed. Apology and confession are not the same, observes Susan Wise Bauer in *The Art of the Public Grovel: Sexual Sin and Public Confession in America*: "An apology is an

expression of regret: *I am sorry.* A confession is an admission of fault: *I am sorry because I did wrong. I sinned.*" In the age of ever-more-candid talk shows and ever more twelve-step programs, confession emerged as the clearest path to redemption in America. Talk shows were less forums for discussion than confession opened up for all to see; in twelve-step programs, an admission of guilt was the first step toward recovery.

After sincere contrition, Bauer argues, Americans will forgive almost any transgression. "As it evolved in the twentieth century," she writes, "the public confession . . . became a ceremonial laying down of power, made so that followers could pick that power up and hand it back . . . We both idolize and hate our leaders; we need and resent them; we want to submit, but only once we are reassured that the person to whom we submit is no better than we are." Seen in this light, Forrest Church was lucky to have survived. He had not laid down his power, but he was able to keep it anyway.[11]

Seeking to head off trouble, Church had notified officials at Unitarian headquarters in Boston early in 1991 of his affair with Buck Luce, and of his intentions to divorce and remarry. To UUA president William Schulz and David Pohl, director of the Department of Ministry, he admitted that he had broken the letter of the denomination's ethical code but, he felt, not its spirit, which was aimed at preventing abusive relationships between ministers and parishioners under their care. Above all, the code sought to protect the powerless from the powerful. But no one could accuse Forrest Church of taking advantage of Carolyn Buck Luce.[12]

The Unitarian Universalist Association, like many religious bodies, was struggling with how to deal with sexual abuse in an age of sexual freedom. The sexual revolution that had been part of Forrest Church's coming-of-age—from premarital sex and "open marriage" to higher divorce rates and greater acceptance of homosexuality—had swept through every level of society. Traditional norms of fidelity and lifelong commitment battled against a far more permissive outlook. Greater sexual freedom was hardly consonant with sexual abuse. But, all too often, revered pastors, priests, and rabbis were exposed as predators, preying on those who came to them for advice and comfort.

In the early eighties, the Pacific Northwest chapter of the UU Ministerial Association hired one of the foremost experts in the field, Rev. Marie Fortune, as a consultant to deal with an erring clergyman. A minister of the United Church of Christ and author of the pathbreaking *Is Nothing Sacred? The Story of a Pastor, the Women He Sexually Abused, and the Congregation He Nearly Destroyed*, Fortune had advised many Protestant denominations on this issue. Out of her recommendations and a great deal of debate, Unitarians revised and tightened their ethical code, which she then declared the clearest of any she had studied. Still, the number of cases that came to the attention of the denomination kept rising. The increase was due, in part, to more stringent enforcement, which was partly due, in turn, to the rising number of women among Unitarian clergy. Between 1957 and 1978, only nine ministers were female, and none were senior parish ministers. But by the eighties, the UUA was ordaining more females than males, and women were emerging as national leaders.[13]

One of them, Rev. Carolyn Owen-Towle of San Diego, now chaired the national UU Ministerial Association. Speaking of clergy sexual abuse, she said, "For many years, the old boys used to look the other way." Now that was going to stop.[14]

Whatever happened to Forrest Church, the shadow of Tony Perrino would loom large over him. Between 1978 and 1990, Anthony Freiss Perrino served as the highly regarded minister of the Unitarian Society of Santa Barbara, and a local magazine named this charismatic charmer one of the city's ten most influential citizens. While there, he also wrote two devotional books, one of which was published by the UUA. As he was about to take over leadership of Cleveland's First Unitarian Church in 1990, however, it was alleged that he had been sexually involved with nearly two dozen women from his Santa Barbara church. Before the Cleveland church elders could take action, he resigned, and David Pohl's UU Ministerial Committee promptly "removed him from fellowship."

While not an official defrocking—one's ordination cannot be taken away—this act clearly rendered Perrino persona non grata to UU congregations for many years.[15]

Despite the fact that the circumstances were radically different, the case of Tony Perrino made it hard for the UUA to ignore that of Forrest Church. *Every* case would be carefully scrutinized. At stake was the denomination's reputation.

Someone at All Souls—it's not clear who—complained to the UU Metro New York Ministerial Association that Forrest Church had thus far avoided any disciplinary action. Was nothing going to be done? After intense discussion, and despite the October 15 affirmative vote at All Souls, the executive committee recommended to the national UU Ministerial Association that it investigate.[16]

The central issue, unquestionably, was ethics, but in the background lay an unspoken agenda of envy, according to Rev. Lee Barker, then minister of Unitarian Church of Montclair, New Jersey, who sat on the Metro New York executive committee and later served as president of the denomination's Meadville Lombard Theological School. Some of Church's colleagues felt that he had received the plum position of All Souls without paying his dues and on the coattails of his famous father. Resentment lingered, too, because he had been ordained years ago before he was properly "fellowshipped." This was a several-year process requiring an internship, study of Unitarian theology and history, and psychological testing, followed by ordination. After a belated chaplaincy internship at a Boston hospital in the mid-eighties, Church cheekily titled his All Souls sermon recounting the experience "What I Did on My Summer Vacation," a title foolishly reprinted in September of 1991.

What's more, Barker said, "Here was a guy who was not particularly collegial. He was doing his own thing." Church's attendance at the denomination's annual retreats for ministers of large congregations was spotty. "Plus, he had what may be perceived as a paternalistic view toward those who were not as accomplished as he. I don't think actually it was, but he made pronouncements, he's thinking at a different level than so many other people, and a lot of people had a hard time with that."[17]

What eventually took place had some of the trappings of a trial. The "jury" consisted of an ad hoc investigative committee of three clergy appointed by Rev. Leon Hopper, Owen-Towle's successor as president of the national UU Ministerial Association. Permitted to name one committee member, Church chose his old Boston mentor, Rev. Rhys Williams. Following telephone discussions with those involved, the "trial" took place on December 10, 1991, at a Marriott hotel near LaGuardia Airport in New York City. There the committee conducted a series of separate formal interviews with Amy Furth, Forrest Church, and several Metro New York ministers. The aim was to gather facts, hear opinions, and, later, to recommend any action to Hopper.

Church's "lawyer" during these proceedings was Barker. He was first interviewed alone and then together with Church. In the first interview, Barker noted that another UU minister in New Jersey had recently resigned over accusations of "multiple abuse of counselees" and that "just possibly some of the anger directed toward Forrester could be coming from this other situation." And he underscored that Church was in therapy and a much humbler man than he had been.

Privately, Barker had worried that his "client" would seem anything but humble during his interview. He needed to project that he had "learned his lesson." Barker's advice: "Don't defend what you did. Because he was kind of in that mood of 'Well, you know, it wasn't so bad.' I remember going to a restaurant before we went into the meeting and saying, 'I'm just going to kick you in the shins if you don't appear chastened enough.' He was able to pull it together, but I actually remember having to interrupt him [with kicks] a couple of times."[18]

To some extent, the kicks worked. The investigative committee's "verdict" was that Church, indeed, had violated UU ministerial ethics by carrying on a sexual affair with a married parishioner and had been dishonest with his wife and with Buck Luce's husband about the affair.

The situation, however, did not "compare in seriousness to the sexual abuse of a child, an unwilling adult, or a counselee." The committee left ultimate judgment to Hopper and his executive committee. In a dissenting addendum to the committee's report, Rhys Williams complained that the people of All Souls already had offered judgment by voting that Church remain their minister: "Are we interfering with the life of a congregation? Is this being done because of the publicity? Forrest's prominence? Jealousy from some of his colleagues?"[19]

In the end, Hopper and company opted for relative leniency. The executive committee issued a "reprimand" instead of a "sanction." This amounted to a slap on the wrist, an admonishment for wrongdoing; the more punitive sanction might have forced him out of the pulpit temporarily or even led to defellowshipping. Pulled in divergent directions by the Metro New York committee and the vote at All Souls, according to Hopper, the committee felt some punishment was in order but not the stark, career-threatening implications of defellowshipping. Forrest Church was not a Tony Perrino. News of the reprimand was conveyed to UU ministers in their next newsletter, but there was no announcement of it at All Souls.[20]

Although Forrest Church had informed his parishioners that he was going to leave off the writing of books for a while, he had some unfinished business in this regard. His *God and Other Famous Liberals*, which had the potential to be central to his public ministry, was due out soon. Its punchy title, provocative thesis, and quotable prose should have drawn a substantial audience on the eve of a presidential primary season. It was originally scheduled for fall 1991 publication, but was pushed back to mid-January of 1992, either because of the author's recent notoriety or more mundane publishing-world reasons. In terms of promotion, however, the damage had been done. No matter how glowing the reviews, it would have been difficult for Church to go out on the road speaking about "reclaiming God, Bible, and family" from the religious right. Too many had read or heard of the lurid headlines, and if they hadn't, right-wing believers would have made sure that they did. What's more, even the Unitarian base would have been hard to rally. The Troubles at All Souls had rendered him more lightning rod for controversy than Unitarian statesman. At any rate, what was to have been a two-week book tour was slashed to two days in the national capital. As a publicity campaign for a book with a $50,000 advance, this was a paltry effort. The publisher, it seemed, gave up on the book before it had a chance to go anywhere.[21]

In the long arc of Church's career, this was a major opportunity squandered. The timing for such a book was perfect. He had found a powerhouse mainstream publisher, Simon and Schuster. And because he had a talent for connecting with lay readers, he had built an audience with the potential, under these circumstances, to be expanded geometrically.

But, in a classic tradeoff, the moment was lost. Just at the hour that Forrest Church might have ascended to greater national prominence, love had swept him up in its whirlwind, and he was forced to lower his public profile. The next few years would be a time for reflection and self-evaluation, for discovering what this love really required of him.

For Amy Furth, this was a turning point as well. She was now a single mother. Not only did she feel that All Souls had treated her shamefully but, according to Dennis MacDonald, who later became her husband, "she felt isolated from her parents who at first blamed her for not keeping her man." The painful experience of the past year would keep Furth in therapy for years. Initially intent on moving back to her home state of California, she looked into schools and houses there but concluded that she ought not to deprive her children of contact with their father. "That was such a strong and brave thing for her to do," her daughter, Nina, said much later. For two years, Amy and her children lived in a railroad apartment on Manhattan's Upper West Side before moving into a larger three-bedroom, rent-stabilized apartment farther north near Columbia University.[22]

To make a living, Furth needed to supplement her Harvard master's in theology, a general degree rather than a vocational credential. So while raising two children, she enrolled in an MDiv program at New York

Theological Seminary. This was an innovative institution focused on nontraditional community ministries and nontraditional students, including many entering the field as a second career. With her degree and United Church of Christ ordination in hand, she found work as a chaplain at the Florence Nightingale nursing home, situated where the Upper East Side meets East Harlem, and not far from several All Souls–funded programs for the poor.

"She just worked so hard," Nina said. "We were like a team. If she wasn't coming home early, I was cooking dinner, and on Saturdays she and I would spend all day doing laundry and cleaning together. I remember going to IKEA with her, and we'd come home and we'd build furniture. Our whole house was from IKEA. She built a really strong, sturdy home for me.

"Being protective of my mom was the number-one feeling I can remember, because I knew that she was hurting. I just wanted to do anything in my power to make her feel better."

Nina was the classic "good kid" in a divorce, trying to soothe hurts and act the diplomat between warring factions. A sunny personality like her father, she fit the role naturally. She quickly grew fond of her younger stepbrothers. When visiting them, she fell into a routine of singing bedtime lullabies to them with her stepmother. "It was through loving the boys," she said, "that I was able to get close to Carolyn."

Nina also excelled at school. At PS 158 and at a private high school, Fieldston, "I was a star student and had a lot of friends and was really involved in extracurricular activities. My parents didn't have to worry about me. And it was the worst thing for Frank. Here I am a little Goody Two-Shoes who can't do any wrong, and he's just this kid who can't seem to pull himself together."[23]

"Man, I was a mess!" Frank remembered. "That was definitely the beginning of my spiral. I was nasty both to my father and mother, and everyone. I was just really full of bile."

Like Forrest Church, Frank had the burden of following a famous father. Yet his situation was far worse, compounded by divorce, the onset of puberty, and undiagnosed medical problems. The impact of all this was deeply painful. Throughout his adolescence, Frank said, he hated his father. He believed his father was "only a presence in my life when I screwed up. Tons of therapists said, 'You screwed up to get the attention of your father.' It took us a long time to break out of that system."

Continually angry, struggling with schoolwork, Frank had no clue why he was different from everyone else. The routines of everyday life seemed to baffle him. He was disorganized, neglecting to bring schoolbooks home, forgetting what homework he was supposed to do. For this very bright boy, something was clearly amiss. He could be delightfully funny or downright mean. You never knew what strange thing might pop out of his mouth. For years, his parents didn't know what to do. They tried school after school.

After three years at PS 158, Frank attended Churchill, a school for students with learning disabilities, until sixth grade, then Trevor Day School, which emphasized "experiential learning," followed by a couple of years at Millbrook, a prep school in rural Dutchess County north of New York. "Had some pretty nasty sort of depression," Frank said, "dropped out of there, went to Beekman [a self-described "tutoring school" in New York] for a couple of months. Then I went back to Trevor Day high school for about a year, and then I derailed. I tried to kill myself and was hospitalized."

Desperate to find answers, yet uncertain about remedies, Frank's parents enrolled him in what he called a "reform school." John Dewey Academy, in Great Barrington, Massachusetts, undertakes to educate "bright, troubled adolescents with a history of self-defeating or self-destructive choices." It's not clear whether Dewey, the founder of "progressive education," would have endorsed the academy's tough-love approach to its twenty to thirty-five students.

"It was a brutal program," Frank said. "Constant academics, summer school, group therapy three times a week. Confrontational, in-your-face breaking you down, kind of destroying your convoluted dishonesty, all your problems. Instead of just letting you work it out, they frickin' worked it out for you in front of twenty other people. It was ridiculous, awful. It was good at the same time, you know?"[24]

It was not until this period that Frank's Klinefelter syndrome was finally diagnosed. This explained a lot, since many of its victims also suffer from learning disabilities and behavioral problems. Some, like Frank, also have a higher rate of developing Type 1 diabetes. But neither the syndrome nor diabetes is curable; they have to be managed. So the young man who had trouble organizing his day was now expected to administer regular testosterone treatments and insulin injections. He did not have an easy time of it.[25]

Nina Church was the only one of the Church-Luce brood who navigated a relatively untroubled adolescence. When the very smart Jacob Luce reached high school, he grew so bored with his studies at the private Dalton School that he had to repeat a grade. His poor marks, he said, threw him into many a "knock-down, drag-out screaming fight" with his mother. Likewise, his brother, Nate, was sent off to a New Jersey boarding school, Blair Academy, because his parents told him he "needed structure."[26]

Once Frank and Nina graduated from high school, Amy Furth felt free to return to California, where her parents and sister still lived. Pursuing further graduate study at Claremont School of Theology, she encountered Dennis R. MacDonald, a New Testament scholar who had been a friend of hers and Forrest's while at Harvard. In the seventies, MacDonald had been married to another woman, but he thought then that Forrest was "the luckiest guy alive" to be married to the attractive, intelligent Amy. Now single, Furth and MacDonald began dating, and, in 2000, they were married.[27]

During the difficult days of 1991, several All Souls friends had welcomed Forrest and Carolyn to their summer homes on Shelter Island, situated in Gardiners Bay between eastern Long Island's North and South Forks. Unpretentious and quiet, with a small-town, time-out-of-time flavor, it had none of the chic and flash of the fabled Hamptons—

which was precisely what endeared it to year-round and summer residents alike. Church and Buck Luce were so taken with this tranquil place that, in October, after the decisive All Souls vote, they bought a large house there as a retreat from city pressures. From the back of the house, with a deck and a yard sloping down to the bay, the vistas seemed endless. Over time, the house became a treasured haven, furnished informally for relaxing with family and friends.

"It's that Wonderland escape, like going through the Looking Glass when you cross on the ferry over there," Church said. "It is the horizontal to New York's vertical. I look out with a hundred-and-eighty-degree view of the bay and get lost in eternity. It keeps my soul humming."

On July 25, 1992, a small group of guests gathered at the Ram's Head Inn on the island for the wedding of Forrest Church and Carolyn Buck Luce, and then adjourned to the new summer place on the bay for a reception. Rev. Richard Leonard, who had presided over countless weddings at All Souls Church, officiated.[28]

Seeing Church and Buck Luce together was to witness a rare kind of love. They delighted in each other's presence, respected each other's brains and professional achievements, consoled each other through the children's crises. They enjoyed traveling the world, or simply playing board games. He'd recommend a book he'd read, and she'd read it. Each was the other's best cheerleader. Buck Luce found his books and sermons inspiring; he was in awe of her ability to hold her own among Masters of the Universe. They were spirited debaters of social-political issues. At a dinner party, he once proclaimed what a pleasure it was to be married to a woman who was as smart as he. "You wish!" she countered, with a twinkle in her eye.[29]

They could be as tender as they were combative. Robert Oxnam, former president of the Asia Foundation and a family friend, recalled a visit to Shelter Island: "They were watching television or out on their deck, and each had one sock on. I asked what that was all about. 'Well, we rub each other's feet,' they said. You know, it was someplace between caring and kinky. It was very, very sweet."

More naturally social than her husband, Buck Luce balanced his innate shyness. Like his politician father, Church could mask that trait while
on the public stage, but he was most at home lying on his living room
couch absorbed in a book. But a flicker of uneasiness could surface in an
unscripted environment, like a cocktail party among strangers.

Buck Luce orchestrated their social occasions. "She is the family love
component on a kind of day-to-day operating basis," Oxnam said. "She
makes family gatherings welcoming and warm. She's completely comfortable in figuring out what is the right Christmas gift, or how to make
the most special kind of celebration." She also served as the family's emotional early-warning system. As Sylvia Ann Hewlett, an economist and
Buck Luce intimate, observed, "It's a pretty classic case that she has more
emotional intelligence than he does. She does a great job of paying attention and figuring out two steps ahead that [one of the children] is going
to need some special attention."[30]

In many ways, Forrest Church remained a work-in-progress. Both his
religious and personal lives tended to be matters more of the head than the
heart. All of us can believe the truth of things without deeply feeling it.
Sometimes life-changing events have to happen before we get there.
Church's ordeal of 1991 only began a process that would take years; his
wife would be the catalyst for real change. Rev. Bill Grimbol, a Presbyterian minister on Shelter Island who became close to the couple, witnessed
a gradual transformation over nearly two decades. "Carolyn really gave
Forrest back his heart. I don't know if Forrest felt deeply before that. What
I do know is that Carolyn became the lens through which he was able to
see more deeply and feel more deeply and become far more humane."[31]

Forrest Church, the pastor, could plumb some of the depths. Had it
been otherwise, he surely would not have survived the 1991 vote at All
Souls. Every week, his parishioners felt the embrace of his love, in sermons, counseling, and memorial services. Making "I love you" central
to his Sunday benediction wasn't fakery, but a heartfelt affirmation of
God's love for all humanity (*agape*, in Greek) and, by extension, his own
pastoral concern. He often said that he didn't begin to grasp what it

meant to be a minister until he had conducted his first funeral. Love, the great healer, and death, the great leveler, lay at the heart of his ministry.

Alison Miller: "When my father passed away, I remember Forrest coming over to our apartment and us creating the memorial service. Forrest asked me what my favorite hymn was. It was 'Joyful, Joyful,' but that didn't seem appropriate for a memorial service. He asked, 'Does that encapsulate how you feel about your father and what his life meant to you?' He walked us through that. So we wound up using 'Joyful, Joyful' and another very joyful song, 'Morning Has Broken,' which was my father's favorite hymn. I very much remember his paying attention to me, a mere fourteen-year-old, in terms of my needs."[32]

But a death wasn't necessary for Church to reach out with compassion to those in need.

Another parishioner: "April 30th, 2001, was supposed to be the last day of my life. I wouldn't die from illness, accident or disease. I wasn't that lucky. Rather, I planned to end my miserable existence that day by my own hand. My addictions to drugs and alcohol, and my own despair and sense of failure had brought me to the end of the road—or so I thought. Obviously, I failed—one last failure, I thought—and instead of awaking to the hell I was expecting, I awoke in Bellevue's emergency room.

"When I returned to the 8th floor psych ward [following a transfer to another hospital], I made a call that changed my life. I called All Souls. I told them that my ex-wife and I were members and that I had stopped going to church years before—that's all I could get out before I dissolved in sobs. I needed help.

"Barely an hour later, as I stood on line for 'meds,' I felt a hand on my shoulder. I turned suddenly—it was Forrest, with a big toothy grin. He hugged me, and asked the nurses to let us use a meeting room to talk. He vaguely remembered me from years ago—he was more familiar with my ex-wife. And we began to talk. I had lost my son, my home, my business, my self-respect. I had lost hope. I had lost faith. After letting me go on and on, Forrest finally said, 'Well, Steve, looks like we have a long road ahead of us—and we'll travel it together one step at a time—let's get started!' We talked for three hours about everything—but most importantly how to take that first step: learning to accept my powerlessness over alcohol and drugs, and learning to turn my life over to a power greater than myself when I couldn't do it by myself . . . Forrest left me that night with something I never thought I could ever have again—hope. And when he hugged me goodbye and said 'I love you' I felt safe. I was not alone.

"Over the months that followed, I spoke to Forrest day after day . . . and here was this wonderful, learned, busy, important man nodding his head in acknowledgement and understanding as if he knew, instead of shaking his head in judgment. We continued talking and meeting for years. Baby steps turned into days, weeks and months of sobriety and clarity and serenity and hope and faith."[33]

Nor did Church have to know the people he ministered to.

Rev. Victoria Weinstein, while a first-year student at Harvard Divinity School: "I was really at odds with the Unitarian Universalist students. They would talk about how irritating it was to have to deal with everything through the Christian lens. I was embarrassed by them because they were disdainful. It was really upsetting because I was a lifelong UU and never thought about claiming to be anything else, even though by the time I entered I was having strongly theistic and Christian leanings and exploring that. I was starting to wonder whether I was in the wrong denomination. So I really didn't know what to do. I didn't know who to talk to.

"I'd read a couple of Forrest's books, and I knew he was a very admired figure in our ministry. I found his [office telephone] number somehow. It was a hot summer night. I knew he wouldn't be there. I didn't want to find anybody there. I left this two-, three-minute message, very distraught, on his voice mail. I really did not expect a response, but at nine A.M. I got a call from him. He was just right there. His presence was so palpable and focused, and he had such care. I kept saying, 'Let me let you go. You must be very busy.' And he kept saying, 'No, I'm okay. Tell me about this and such, and what classes are you taking? What do you really love?' We talked about the Bible and how intensely I was coming to love it. He was so excited about that. And before we hung up, he said, 'I'm just so excited that I'm going to have you for a colleague.' It was such a gift."[34]

Nor did Church's "parishioners" have to be nearby.

Fulgence Ndagijimane, as reported by All Souls member Richard Ford: "Forrest's influence reached farther and deeper than many realized. A few years ago, a young Burundian [Ndagijimane] was in Nairobi completing his studies and preparing to take his vows as a Dominican priest. He planned to return to Burundi and spend his life in the priesthood. As he contemplated the vows he would soon be affirming, a few questions lingered. He sought opinions from faculty and fellow students, but without success.

"So he did what all modern Africans do; he turned to the Internet. Within a day he had found sites of Unitarian Universalist groups, including the Web site of All Souls NYC. A small phrase and tiny box caught his attention: 'For additional information, click here and send an e-mail to the minister.' Why not? Fulgence sent some questions. "The minister," of course, was Forrest, and within twenty-four hours Fulgence had a reply. Not only a reply but a set of suggested sermons he could find on the All Souls Web site and, to no one's surprise, a list of some of Forrest's books that would soon appear in the mail. And appear they did. The sermons whetted Fulgence's appetite. The books became the main course, and the dessert was his eventual decision not only to become a UU but to return to his home in Bujumbura and start a UU church."[35]

Gracious attention to anyone seeking help remained a constant in Church's career, as did his public ministry. Between the publication of *God and Other Famous Liberals* and his next book, there was a hiatus of four and a half years, an unusually long time for this prolific writer. But he had promised parishioners to pay closer attention to their needs, and he was exhausted from the emotional turmoil of 1991. More to the point, he was "working on his soul." This second marriage, he said, "required me to grow up. That's another thing about having been a 'free-range kid': You can give yourself a pass on growing up. There's a Peter Pan quality to it.

"I had always been the most demanding ego in the room and

delighted my friends with it. I mean, it was not an imperious ego; it was not a controlling ego, at least not in any destructive way. It was more of a galvanizing and entertaining ego. But it was, nonetheless, never balanced by a partnership that demanded my full attention and participation. The person most responsible for changing that was Carolyn."

The books he wrote now would reflect this greater emotional maturity. He would write in a more reflective, inward-looking mode, setting aside for a while commentary on the role of religion in the public square. As the spokesman for liberal religion retreated from view, the pastor took over.

In retrospect, Church felt that his early trilogy—the books on heaven, hell, and limbo—counted as mere juvenilia, marked by glib "intellectual pyrotechnics." One hardly needs to agree with such a harsh assessment to observe that the first book to emerge from this period, *Life Lines*, published in 1996, probed life's mysteries with far greater depth. "It's not surprising," Church said, "that I chose Ecclesiastes as my meditative model for it."[36]

Perhaps it was not surprising, but relying on a book from the Hebrew Bible as a narrative framework was not an obvious choice for a Unitarian minister. Given his lengthy interruption from book-writing, Church found the task harder than anticipated. *Life Lines* began as a sort of mea culpa, with his divorce and remarriage as entry point for constructing a more general meditation on the uses of adversity. But after a few years he abandoned that idea as unimportant to the reader and distracting from his primary argument. "My early drafts were quite bad," he confessed to his agent. "I thrashed about, and made only circular progress for a long time," until settling on Ecclesiastes as his guide. The book would also take aim at "the quick fix folks who offer bromides to an increasingly credulous (and dissatisfied) populace, the very people who are making 'spiritual books' best sellers, and then feeling bad about themselves for not 'getting it right.' "[37]

Life Lines evolved into a spiritual book devoid of the "quick fixes"

Church derided. Too wide-ranging to fit the self-help category, and not quite a book of meditations—though sections could be used for that purpose—it rightfully belongs on the shelf of wisdom literature alongside Ecclesiastes itself. One senses the weight of the author's recent experience on every page. "Failure strips our lives of pretense," he writes. "It forces us to realize that we are not in charge." Overall, the power of Church's epi-grammatic prose and skillful use of anecdotes propel the reader along an enlightening spiritual journey, however dark and troubled.

Ecclesiastes, our guide, never sugarcoats the overriding truth: life is dif-ficult, fragile, painful, and unpredictable. "Simply put," Church writes, "everyone suffers. That is a given. Suffering is a birthright far more in-alienable than happiness." However, it is not suffering but our response to it that defines who we are. "Over the years, my parishioners have taught me two lessons. When cast into the depths, to survive we must let go of things that will not save us. Then we must reach out for things that can . . . Unless we reach out to and for others, seeking meaning not in our own suffering but in our shared experience of the human condition, our life-lines will not hold."[38]

As Church surveys the many varieties of woe, he stretches beyond the wisdom of Ecclesiastes to Persian poet Rumi, Buddhist and Stoic thought, the Protestant Kierkegaard, and the Catholic Thomas Merton. From the ancient Jews, he admires the custom of crying into ceremonial "tear cups." To suffer, in such a case, is to feel. Your tears are precious because they show that you care. "A full cup of tears is proof that you have felt deeply, suffered, and survived."[39]

Church is aware of the tensions between the desire for individual freedom and the embrace of community, but the contemporary world wants us to pretend that we are wholly in charge, that suffering can be sidestepped, or that it is unreal. He dismisses the culture of self-help books for asserting that happiness is within easy grasp, that we are mas-ters of our fate. Happiness cannot be willed or sustained indefinitely, nor can freedom from difficulties be guaranteed. Similarly, Emerson's ethos of self-reliance, with its enormous impact on American culture, ignores the reality that we are social beings. Isolated, we wither; only in community do we thrive.

Church's most withering scorn is reserved for one stream of the New Age movement, cursed by the legacy of Nietzsche.

"One might sum up [its message] as follows: 'You are in pain. It is someone else's fault, especially society's. It is also your fault, because you have it in your power to escape it, first by naming (the knowledge piece), second by rejecting (the power piece), and finally by setting yourself free (the liberation piece). Then you will be everything you are not now: strong, vital, grounded, independent, wise, and—since you would not wish to forget the rest of us—nurturing, caring, sustaining, and loving, insofar as you are loved.' "

This is neo-Nietzschean nonsense, Church says, because most of its prophets hoped to lift adherents above "the sorry lot . . . the conventional limitations" of common humanity. "The human condition becomes something to escape as an act of human will, not to accept as a fact of human birth."[40] Always, Church tacks back to his definition of religion, with the human animal as the only animal living with the fateful knowledge that it must die.

The theme of suffering inevitably leads the author into the question of God's responsibility. Church's theology has no room for a capricious God "who would allow earthquakes and Auschwitz." Likewise, he rejects the vindictive Calvinist God who raises up believers to be saved, and consigns the rest to eternal damnation. If the God concept means anything to him, it is a God of loving-kindness, mercy, and compassion, expressed in the everyday activities of mortal humans. God is not transcendent and omnipotent, removed from all creation, but embedded in it. Whenever people suffer, so does God.

Why they suffer is not the right question. How they suffer is. And at this point, Church returns to the necessity of human connection. Without the love generated through interactions with other people, our suffering remains meaningless. With it, because it requires empathy with others who also suffer, it can be endured, even redeemed. Linked to others, we can open ourselves in awe and wonder to the mystery of being in this world.

This is no message for those in need of easy answers. It promises no glorious afterlife, no ultimate salvation from sorrow. But it grants a measure of peace in the real world where endings, like answers to philosophical questions, are often indeterminate. While writing this book, Church was reading Patrick O'Brian's series of Napoleonic-era maritime novels. After transporting readers across oceans, through thrilling battles and intellectual puzzles, the novelist ends the final volume *in medias res*, without a clear-cut conclusion. Plot lines are left suspended, ambiguities unresolved. For Church, this is as it should be. "When we die," he writes, "everyone else's story goes on, but we are not there to discover how they turn out . . . That's the way it is. Our lives stop in the middle."[41]

Eager to promote *Life Lines*, Church embarked on the kind of national tour he had expected for *God and Other Famous Liberals* in 1992. Arranged with the aid of his publisher, it was no doubt largely self-funded. The small Beacon Press couldn't afford such tours, but it did set up radio and television coverage when Church spoke at Unitarian churches in San Francisco, Boston, Washington, D.C., and elsewhere. This time around, he also received national coverage, with interviews on the *Today Show*, NBC's *Nightside*, *The Diane Rehm Show* on National Public Radio, and *This Is America* with Dennis Wholey on public television.[42]

Buoyed by the reception of *Life Lines*, Church set out to compose a sort of sequel. *Lifecraft: The Art of Meaning in the Everyday*, published by Beacon in 2000, begins with the presumption that there is no such thing as "the meaning of life." We don't so much discover meaning, the author says, as attach multiple meanings to different aspects of our lives. These meanings are self-created and continually evolving. They emerge from our experiences, our beliefs, and, especially, our encounters with others. Following the lead of British philosopher Bernard Williams, Church suggests that these meanings take shape as we pursue various "life projects." In Church's view, these projects range from growing up and developing love, and being a parent to finding a vocation and coming to terms with the idea of God.

Given multiple life projects, meaning is always under construction, "not a work in progress but a series of works in progress." To understand the process otherwise is to court despair. "As long as we think of ourselves in absolute terms as successful or unsuccessful, healthy or ill, victor or victim, saved or damned," Church writes, "the moment the world turns against us, as surely it will, we risk sacrificing all sense of meaning."[43]

With the opening words of the preface, Church opens his arms to wounded souls in search of meaning.

"Let me begin by telling you a little about yourself. To one extent or another the following is true:

"You are self-conscious about your appearance.

"You feel guilty about things you have done or failed to do.

"You sometimes have a hard time accepting yourself or forgiving others . . .

"You are a frustrated husband, wife, or partner, or you are frustrated not to be a husband, wife, or partner . . .

"However successful you are, you fail in ways that matter both to you and to your loved ones."

Having established this litany of worries and insecurities in his readers, Church exposes some of his own, including lying to his wife and children, and quelling his fears with alcohol.[44]

Throughout the book, autobiographical stories become central to Church's message that all of us, no matter how successful, fail. We create meaning by trying, failing, and trying again. By puncturing his own pomposity, he allows readers to identify with him. Thus he mentions the over-the-top, health-threatening asceticism he adopted during his stint as an assistant chaplain at Stanford, and his youthful romantic obsession with dying young. "I subconsciously determined that the best way to avoid competing with my very successful father was to check out before I had a chance to fail."[45]

Church's stories of his own "growing up project" are poignant and humorous, depicting the evolution of a sometimes foolish young man who grows into a thoughtful adult. Moving on to "the God project," he eschews humor to recount his early Christian tutoring at his grandmother's knee, followed by later skepticism and the eventual shaping of his Unitarian views. His most useful device for others to think about God is to suggest different types of seekers—Champion, Dreamer, Mystic, and so on—who hope to comprehend what is ultimately beyond understanding. Though somewhat arbitrary, these categories focus our attention on what it is we want "God" to be, and how a believer ought to act. The Champion, for instance, in expecting absolute justice from God, downplays the quality of divine mercy. The Mystic, exalting her own contemplation, often withdraws from efforts to heal this world's pain.[46]

An encounter with a Swiss cabbie prompts the author to consider "the prayer project." Profoundly distrustful of religious institutions and Christian orthodoxy, this man nonetheless prayed with conviction. Here the author is at his persuasive best, drawing in skeptics of this ancient practice, showing them how to meditate in a spirit of openness and humility, without expectation. Prayer, he suggests, is not about eliciting answers or asking favors. It is about embracing silence and becoming attuned with oneself and the cosmos, and thus attaining a wholeness embraced by many religious traditions. "You can have as free a spirit as my Swiss cabdriver," Church writes, "and still say your prayers."[47]

Clearly, Church was becoming more attuned with himself. In *Lifecraft,* he expressed a deeper spirituality than he had previously attained, but his journey still had miles to go. Troubling issues still lay below this calm, reassuring exterior. The man behind the author was still hiding, still wrestling, still not entirely honest with himself.

Between these two linked books, Church published three more. In 1993, he complained bitterly to his agent that *God and Other Famous Liberals* had been "orphaned" by Simon and Schuster. That the publisher had provided no significant editing or promotion was especially galling since he felt it was his best book to that point. "I haven't started going downhill (yet!)," he wrote. It wasn't until 1996 that Church persuaded

Walker & Company to bring out a paperback edition.[48] In 1998, Church again turned to Beacon to publish *Without Apology: Collected Meditations on Liberal Religion*, an anthology of excerpts from the sermons of A. Powell Davies.[49]

In that same year, Church and John Buehrens published an expanded version of *Our Chosen Faith*. Buehrens had suggested a new edition to reflect the Unitarian Universalist Association's decision to add "spiritual teachings of earth-centered traditions" to its five previous "sources of faith." Beacon Press publisher Helene Atwan welcomed the idea, while suggesting a name change, *A Chosen Faith*, so that the book would seem more inviting to readers who were not already UUs. Bestselling author and former UU minister Robert Fulghum signed on to write a brief and enticing foreword.[50]

On the face of it, the notion of "earth-centered traditions" might not seem to resonate with Church's more traditional, Jesus-based reading of Unitarianism, but he nonetheless rose to the occasion. His chapter in the new edition, "For the Beauty of the Earth," diplomatically connected biblical adoration for the creation, nineteenth-century Unitarian Transcendentalism, and twentieth-century Wiccans. Though the addition of this sixth faith source had prompted considerable debate at the UUA's General Assembly in 1995, Church reminded readers that the denomination stood, above all, for an open mind. What's more, a reverent attention to nature had characterized its Transcendentalist thinkers more than a century before, not to mention the ancient shapers of the Bible.

Never an outdoorsman, Church's encounters with nature were infrequent. But he recounts one awe-inspiring rafting trip with his family down the Middle Fork of Idaho's Salmon River—surrounded by mountains, shooting the rapids. "I was a part of, not apart from, the ground of our being. Its power was real, my own derivative and unimportant . . . I heard the cosmos sing and watched nature dance. This was religion."

We need not accept superstition or a naive animism, Church says, to appreciate "an intimate experience of the mystery of creation." Our commitment to rationalism should not rule out the existence of the trans-rational, since a huge range of our experience defies rational analysis.

To underscore the ability of Unitarian Universalism to accommodate seemingly divergent patterns of belief, Church cites a parishioner, Margot Adler, author, NPR correspondent, and a priestess of Wicca. "When I asked Margot why she chose All Souls, she told me that she loves the rit-ual. It creates a sacred space for her within which she can worship." De-spite their differences, Church writes, "I understand how she is able to translate from one sacred liturgy to another and find meaning in the uni-versals that connect them. It is important to remember this as we continue to develop from a faith that first took wings in the Protestant Reformation to one that encompasses an increasingly diverse complement of inspirational sources."[51]

Despite Church's broad-minded acceptance of the UUA's sixth source of faith, he had never been much of an environmentalist. Oddly enough, it was Rudolph Giuliani who, in a manner of speaking, converted him to the cause.

The flamboyant former U.S. attorney first ran for mayor of New York City in 1989, losing to David Dinkins, the low-keyed, tennis-playing Manhattan borough president who, as the city's first black mayor, pledged to promote racial healing. But Church grew disillusioned with Dinkins's ability to turn the city around from its slough of crime and drugs. Beyond that, Church had a terrible row with the mayor in 1993 when he ran for reelection, once more against Giuliani. One of Dinkins's campaign man-agers, former boxer Jose Torres, derided Giuliani on television as a candi-date whose election would empower "Ku Klux Klan types." As a member of the Partnership of Faith, a clergy group committed to keeping racial fears and hatreds out of the campaign, Church was outraged by Torres's wild charges and said so in an op-ed piece for the *New York Post*. In re-sponse, the mayor called in Church for a dressing-down of his own. "For me to be lecturing him about race," Church said, "was more than he was, perhaps rightfully, willing to accept. It was an explosive meeting."[52]

Meantime, Giuliani, no fool, came courting. Dennison Young Jr., who became Giuliani's chief counsel, had gotten to know Church when their daughters were attending the same school. According to Young, the future mayor was seeking to expand his political base, and a Democrat who presided over a prominent Upper East Side church and was the son of a former Democratic U.S. senator was just the sort of high-profile catch he desired. "The bottom line, though," Young said, "was that here was someone who was seriously concerned about the direction of the city." After meeting with Giuliani at his All Souls office, Church found the candidate's vision so persuasive that he agreed to introduce him to ministers he knew in East Harlem and to become a behind-the-scenes supporter. (In keeping with his strict views on church-state separation, he never endorsed any political candidates from the pulpit.)

Once Giuliani won the election, Church served on the transition team, led by Young, helping to staff various city posts. Eventually, he, too, was tapped to join the administration. After turning down a seat on the Landmarks Preservation Commission—it didn't suit his interests, he said—Church was appointed chairman of the Council on the Environment of New York City. He would serve from 1996 through 2006 (including a reappointment by Giuliani's successor, Michael Bloomberg).[53]

A public-private enterprise, with 10 to 20 percent of its funding provided by the city, the council had four main functions: to run the local greenmarkets, to assist community groups in creating and maintaining pocket parks and community gardens (often on city-owned vacant lots), to foster environmental awareness among schoolchildren, and to assist businesses and other institutions with recycling and environmental retrofitting.

"I wouldn't exactly call Forrest a staunch environmentalist when he started," said council executive director Lys McLaughlin. "He didn't know much about the Clean Air Act, and that sort of thing. It was a departure for him. But he was hugely supportive of our efforts, and he was an amusing speaker who would gather up people with his enthusiasm. He understood the importance of these gardens to their communities."

The council's good work was hardly controversial, but the fate of the gardens themselves became an issue during the late nineties when Mayor Giuliani decided that the city would be better served by selling off the lots, supposedly to erect affordable housing. Community leaders and advocates of a greener New York vehemently disagreed. The battle was not finally resolved until 1999, when most of the gardens were saved, after the lots were bought for more than $4 million by a coalition of Bette Midler's New York Restoration Project and the Trust for Public Land. Church and McLaughlin had to stay above the fray, given their public roles, but they clearly sided with the parks' saviors.[54]

Giuliani, Church believed, was "somewhat cavalier in dismissing the value of open-space greening. We had a map made of the entire city, mapping every open space. I was extremely interested in spreading the word and protecting each of these precious little thumbprints of property all over the city. They're tiny gardens, but exquisite."

The mayor had his blind spots, especially about race. But in Church's overall assessment, Giuliani was "probably *the* great mayor of New York of the twentieth century. He made the ungovernable city a model city."

Church cites as an example the transformation of 101st and 102nd Streets in East Harlem, where All Souls–generated funding supports the Booker T. Washington Learning Center and other programs. "There was a time that, whenever I went up there, I was scared. Now you go up there, and there are kids playing in the street and people sitting on the stoops, no prostitution, no drug pushing. It was a fabulous transformation, and Giuliani is first and foremost responsible for that.

"He's an operatic character, and he needs to be in the center of the stage, singing at full voice, with some of the scenery on fire. When he went in, that's exactly what we needed because, indeed, the scenery was on fire. He had two great years, his first and his last, and the last I consider accidental."[55]

Even if the Council on the Environment was a small, out-of-the-way operation with thirty employees, Church's part-time service there nonetheless satisfied a need for hands-on civic involvement never met before.

In 1976, he had been thrilled by the excitement of a political campaign, but chairing the council required different skills than oratory and media sound bites. An astute diplomat and listener, he built consensus among board members and supported the executive director when someone had to be fired.

Serving in a Republican administration was an anomaly for this life-long Democrat. But, like his father, Church appreciated the virtue of crossing party lines when it seemed prudent. Direct participation in the public arena was equally anomalous. Since 1976, he had never seriously considered running for office. Church's default setting was as observer-commentator, assessing events from the pulpit or the op-ed page.

On the national scene, Church generally welcomed the rise of Bill Clinton. A Democrat with a liberal approach to foreign policy, race, and health care, Clinton proved more conservative on deficit reduction and welfare reform. Not only the poster boy for centrist Democrats eager to move beyond sixties-era liberalism, he was also a master campaigner whose aw-shucks charm could convert eye-rolling skeptics into true believers.

Introduced to Clinton the presidential candidate during the 1992 campaign, Church shook hands again when the president visited New York's Riverside Church in February 1997. This was the onset of an ominous time. In April, Special Prosecutor Kenneth Starr persuaded a federal court to extend the life of his Whitewater grand jury investigating alleged Clinton misdeeds in Arkansas. Meanwhile, the case of Paula Jones, a former Arkansas state employee suing Clinton for sexual harassment while he was governor, had reached the U.S. Supreme Court. From afar, Church cheered on the president, writing that he had "dignified [his] office while wading through—I hope you don't mind me saying this—more thrown shit than any deserving President since Jefferson and Lincoln."[56]

By late next year, the shit was beginning to stick. With the help of Starr's investigations, it was only a few short steps from intern Monica Lewinsky's leaks about hanky-panky in the White House to presidential impeachment.

Forrest Church was appalled—by Clinton's squalid behavior, by Starr's needless public exposure of titillating sexual detail, and by congressional Republicans' determination to reap political benefit. Should the president resign? Did he deserve to be impeached? Church's sermon of September 13, 1998, waffled on the first question, and answered the second with a no. Clearly, Clinton was "a profoundly flawed man" and "a poster child for sexual addiction" who had used his power to take advantage of a young intern. But his moral failures, however reprehensible, hardly rose to the level of impeachable crimes against the state. "If we impeach President Clinton for the sex and lies that are the whole burden of the Starr report," Church said, "we might have to think about impeaching the entire presidency." After all, President Kennedy "had a Mafia moll in his bed," thus compromising national security. President Johnson lied about North Vietnamese attacks as phony justification for escalating the Vietnam War, thus ensuring thousands upon thousands more deaths. But now the nation faced an impeachment premised on moral zealotry run amok. Finally, Church hoped that Clinton's announced contrition was sincere, for only in this way could he achieve genuine repentance.

"I know this from personal experience," he concluded. "At the end of my marriage with Amy and before I married Carolyn six years ago, Carolyn and I engaged in an affair. We both regret that deeply. Not the end of our first marriages, not that we got married—which is a daily blessing—but the deception with which our marriages ended . . . We lied to our spouses and we were caught. We now are grateful for this, because to get away with a lie is almost always more corrosive to the soul than to get caught in one. In part this is because we can only receive forgiveness if we ask for it. For Carolyn and me, the forgiveness of our children and of this congregation were godsends. But they would not have been deserved . . . if we hadn't suffered personal embarrassment and hadn't continued to this very day following the long hard road from contrition to repentance."[57]

Clearly, Church's identification with Clinton was not only ideological and political. He sensed a kindred soul, a man of great aspirations and decent intentions but one who was flawed and in need of redemption. So he sent the sermon to the president and received a handwritten reply. The president had read the sermon, he wrote, "with appreciation and respect. I can only hope events of the last few days have caused you to question even more the wisdom of resignation, not for my value but for the value of our Constitution and all we've fought for.

"As for my contrition, it's deep and real. Repentance and change is a journey—I believe you would approve of the things I am doing to make it."

In the previous year, Church had sent the president a paperback edition of *God and Other Famous Liberals*, and Helene Atwan of the Beacon Press mailed him *Life Lines*. A voracious reader, Clinton may well have read them, even while in the White House. He replied with signed thank-you notes for both. And he was aware of Church's 1991 crisis. In closing, he added, "After reading your writings and your sermon, I'm glad you got to keep your job!"[58]

In an op-ed written for New York's *Daily News*, Church expanded on the theme of presidential imperfection. Clinton's prosecutors, he wrote, indulged in a very un-American assumption, the moral perfection of our leaders. This was silly and naive. "Our heroes don't embody virtue, they show character. They fail and then recover . . . [They] aren't pious, they're plucky. Some are sinners who repent and are saved. All are fighters who refuse to go down for the count." Pundits are wrong in taking "a two-dimensional view of public morality. To be a good leader private morals are almost always less important than a larger moral vision. We celebrate our great Presidents from Jefferson to Kennedy for public, not private, reasons." Of late, President Clinton had demonstrated true grit. "He's the boxer on the ropes who's knocked down twice, gets back up and wins the round. He's the drunk who quits the bottle just in time to save not only himself but also the city. We Americans love that . . . Who knows—if President Clinton manages to supplement his public character with a little private virtue, at the end of this one we may even be able to cheer."[59]

In December, just weeks before the House of Representatives voted to impeach the president, Church penned another op-ed, for *Newsday*, on the "inquisition" taking place in Washington. He found the self-righteous stance of conservative Christians especially galling. "I invite the Religious Right and their Republican servants to go back to the Bible. What makes their flawed heroes any different from our flawed president?" Then he recounted the stories of Abraham lying to the pharaoh (thus permitting the sovereign to have sex with his wife), Jacob lying to his father (thus stealing his birthright from his brother), and King David dispatching the husband of his mistress into battle (and to his death) so that he could marry her.

The piece was syndicated and picked up around the country, from Spokane to New Hampshire. Just after Christmas, Church mailed a copy to the president, along with a note: "I am so proud of you. Hang in there. Don't bend or break . . . Have a restful and private holiday. You deserve it!"[60]

On November 18, 2001, in a sermon titled "The God-Shaped Hole," Forrest Church stunned the people of All Souls with the news that he was a recovering alcoholic. After a decade of trying and failing to give up drinking, in the previous year he had finally succeeded. Most church leaders and parishioners were not aware that he had a problem. Like many of them, he seemed to be a convivial social drinker. Yes, he drank quite a lot on occasion, but they had never seen him drunk, never seen him incapable of delivering sermons or presiding over meetings and funerals. Drinking certainly had not prevented him from writing book after book.[61]

On one level, Church hid his drinking in plain sight. From early in his ministry, the subject showed up in numerous sermons and articles. Sometimes he flaunted his own boozing as mere foible and turned it into another vehicle for humor. If he took it very seriously when it afflicted others, in himself it amounted to a minor distraction, a gnat to be swatted away and be done with.

A 1982 sermon, "It's Never Too Late," for instance, spoke to the theme of taking charge of one's life, in spite of earlier failures. As a Cub Scout dropout in his boyhood, he had hopefully collected stories of youthful underachievers: Churchill having to repeat sixth grade, Einstein not speaking until he was four. As for Unitarian Universalists, as constructors of their own credos, they were predisposed to the conviction that they could reinvent themselves. In that spirit, Church offered several tips for change:

"First, do not confuse the difficult with the impossible. Second, accept failure, but do not resign yourself to it. Third, accept weakness, but look beyond it for some higher or greater power whose strength you can tap." In this connection, he singled out the dangers of alcohol. "Few habits are more overpowering or insidious than the addiction to alcohol . . . It can begin as your servant and end up making you its slave." But redemption is possible. He had witnessed that transformation time and again among parishioners. And then he returned to the Scouting theme. "So when I have been lost, blessedly not lost in the forest of alcoholism but lost in many other forests of bewilderment and distraction, I have looked for a stream that I might follow."

A month later in another sermon, Church announced his decision to give up drinking for Lent. The season demanded a substitution of habits for disciplines. But when Lent is over, he added, "I shall leap at the opportunity to drink again. I am not the stuff of which long distance martyrs are made."[62]

In his *Chicago Tribune* columns of the late eighties, Church's habit was to make light of his imbibing. Writing for an audience far away, he could describe with a smile the lunch scene at his favorite neighborhood bar-and-grill. "The great charm of this establishment is that most of the people I know wouldn't think of setting foot in there. Thus, I avoid my parishioners, particularly the blessed few who might be scandalized by clerical self-indulgence. ('Not to worry, madame. It's just a little quirk of mine; I happen to enjoy an olive or two with my ice water')." Another piece joked, "I tend to drink defensively at holiday parties: that is to say, too much." Drinking with Amy in this setting was a division of labor. "We drink gin and tonics: mine unadulterated by tonic, hers uncontaminated by gin."[63]

Although these columns originally were written for Chicagoans, they were collected into a book, *Everyday Miracles*, that could be read by anyone, including parishioners of All Souls. Because Church had not yet defined his drinking as a problem, he was not afraid of exposing it. In the language of twelve-step programs, he was in denial.

Oddly enough, he had even proposed writing a nationally syndicated column, "Day by Day," to be co-written by Dwight Lee Wolter, an All Souls member and author of several books on recovery. The column's target audience would be people in twelve-step programs, their families, and the countless others "simply struggling from day to day." In the spring of 1992, Church and Wolter pitched the idea to Tom Stites, Church's former editor at the *Chicago Tribune*, now at Universal Press Syndicate, suggesting a short, question-and-answer format in the manner of "Dear Abby." One of those momentary enthusiasms that flew out of Church now and then, it never got off the ground.[64]

Forrest Church grew up in a family where alcohol was a constant presence. His parents came of age in the forties, when the first question to any guest in many households was "Would you like a drink?" Although both Frank and Bethine Church drank a lot, they could hold their liquor and were not alcoholics. Until his final year of high school, Forrest rarely drank. His buddy Peter Fenn remembers driving into the District of Colombia, where the drinking age was eighteen instead of Maryland's twenty-one, for beers with their gang. Forrest's experience in college, where future alcoholics often indulge in binge drinking, departed from that norm. "I didn't drink to excess in college, ever," he said later. Certainly, he drank his share of beer and wine, but the intoxicant of choice for his generation was marijuana.[65]

Church's heavy drinking began in divinity school. After a long day of

study, he and his friend Holland Hendrix would head to the Harvard
Faculty Club and knock back three martinis each. Once at All Souls, he
fell into a more destructive pattern. He would start with scotch at noon,
sometimes as early as ten A.M., and continue steadily through the day and
evening. "At times I was drinking as much as a fifth of scotch a day," he
said. "There are twelve two-ounce drinks in a fifth, and from twelve
noon until twelve at night, I would have twelve drinks." Added to that,
if he was eating lunch out, was a martini or two. Given the freedom to
write at home, he could safely hide his addiction. At the office, this routine was harder to maintain, but he had a stash tucked away in a drawer.
With the door closed, to keep his pipe smoke from the rest of the church
offices, he could sneak the occasional nip.

So much alcohol would cripple most people, but not Church. "I never
got drunk," he said. "I never woke up in the morning with a hangover. I
never had a blackout. Drunkenness was not the goal. The goal, as I look
back on it, was to tamp down my feelings and keep them contained so
that I didn't fret overmuch. Many of my friendships were drinking friendships. They were very relaxed. I didn't get brooding or angry with my
drinking; I was just relaxed by it."[66]

Drinking was "very much part of his identity," reported Kathleen
(Kay) Montgomery, longtime executive vice president of the Unitarian
Universalist Association. Like the New York Mets baseball cap he would
often wear, "it was part of a persona—not quite good ol' boy, but it had
some elements of that."[67]

In his classic 1983 study of alcoholism, Harvard-based psychiatrist
Dr. George E. Vaillant underscored its "unstable, chameleon-like quality."
Both a disease and a behavior disorder, alcoholism can take many forms.
Someone with Church's symptoms is now called a "high-functioning alcoholic." According to the National Institute of Alcohol Abuse and Alcoholism, nearly 20 percent of all alcoholics fall into this category. Often
well-educated and very successful, these are people who appear on the
surface to be doing just fine. They defy the stereotypes. They hold stress-

ful jobs and earn the respect of their colleagues. Their social lives may be filled with marriage and children, friendships, and volunteer work in the community. But they are haunted by cravings for alcohol. And as the amount they can tolerate keeps rising, so does their secret shame and remorse. Until they hit the bottom, they refuse to consider themselves alcoholics.

In the words of Caroline Knapp, from her memoir *Drinking: A Love Story*, these are alcoholics who see no kinship with "the bum in the subway drinking from the bottle" or "the red-faced salesman slugging it down in a cheap hotel." No, they're "OK, safe, in sufficient control." Until, of course, they're not.[68]

Because Church counseled people with drinking problems, he knew that he was drinking too much. So from time to time, he would try to limit his drinking. "I would force myself to drink only after five o'clock. Do that for a couple of months. Or I would drink only two drinks a night. Or I would drink only wine—but that wouldn't last for very long.

"I was like a person saying, 'I have no real problem with stopping smoking. I've done it fifty times.'

"There were lots of times I just would stop for a week or two. Those would become very edgy times. I would become sort of white-knuckled. I was not myself. I would say, 'Geez, I have to get back to being who I am.' All through my first marriage, I was a heavy drinker."[69]

Once Church remarried, however, the pattern of abuse remained. Having never spent time around a heavy drinker, his wife didn't know what to make of this behavior. "I called him Dr. Jekyll and Mr. Hyde," Buck Luce said. "It became clearer and clearer to me that there was a mercurial nature to him that didn't make sense to me. At times he could really be irrational, afraid of things."

"When Carolyn would come home from work and I would be a little bit fuzzy or not completely focused," Church said, "she would jump on me and then I would get frightened. I would spin in fear of her, and she'd like that even less than my being slightly fuzzy."

"We would get into arguments," Buck Luce said, "and I just felt Forrest wasn't arguing with *me*. It was [about] all the things he didn't like about his mother. It was very surreal. I would say to him, 'You're acting out some kind of passion play that has nothing to do with me.'

"The bottom line was, I had gotten to a point in my life where I didn't want to have to hide my feelings. I didn't want to have to walk on eggshells. I wanted an adult relationship. Forrest was the love of my life, a soul mate, and I didn't want it to be ruined."

Buck Luce insisted that they go into counseling to try to sort things out. Their therapist quickly put his finger on the centerpiece of the puzzle, that Church was an alcoholic. "That was the first time we actually used that term," she said.[70]

Church decided to approach George Dorsey for advice. A retired insurance company executive and a member of All Souls' board of trustees, Dorsey had also served as president of Alcoholics Anonymous International. A man of wisdom and wit, he had been there himself and been sober for decades. But when Church first broached the subject with Dorsey, the AA veteran refused to put any label on his minister, wondering if he truly were an alcoholic. It was, in fact, a ruse to get Church to discover the truth for himself.

"That's something I do," Dorsey said, "to help people get rid of the last vestiges of denial. I never suggested he go to AA, ever. We had several conversations about his drinking, and I let him talk. He'd been counseling alcoholics for decades. So why should I counsel him? It would have been counterproductive, particularly with Forrest's personality. I'm not going to lecture him on alcoholism. He would just push back."[71]

Eventually, Church ended up going on his own to an AA group at St. Monica's Roman Catholic Church on East Seventy-ninth Street, a short walk from All Souls. As Dorsey predicted, it was hard for Church to grasp the depth of his affliction and the nature of the AA commitment. High-functioning alcoholics, accustomed to success, have trouble accepting AA's first step, admitting that they are in thrall to alcohol. So Church dutifully attended his AA meetings for three months, collected his three-month token of congratulations, said, "Well, I've taken care of that!" and went out and had a drink.

"It was very difficult to change the pattern," he said. "I was afraid that I was going to change into someone I would not like and the world would not like."

Finally, Buck Luce issued an ultimatum: "It was his choice whether I was a roommate or his wife. I wasn't going to be his wife if he had a mistress that was more important to him than me. And that got his attention." So Church returned to AA. This time he had been humbled enough to take his condition more seriously.

Most AA members link with a "sponsor" who acts as a lifeline when the urge to drink becomes overpowering. Bill Thompson, a regular at St. Monica's 7:15 A.M. meeting who sometimes attended All Souls, assumed that role for Church. Before alcoholism forced him out at Doubleday, he was a veteran editor famous for discovering Stephen King in the slush pile and for editing John Grisham. Church never called Thompson in need, never seemed to want help. What's more, in the sharing of experiences at AA meetings, the "round robin," Church seemed to be lecturing or sermonizing rather than digging into his psyche. "We never heard anything about Forrest," Thompson said. "He was an arm's-length sharer, very, very close to the vest.

"The whole persona that he projected was 'I hear what you're saying, but not only do I already know it, but I know it better.' He never articulated that, but that was what came across. He had this element of both ego and hubris."[72]

Church remembered his second stint at AA this way: "I knew the drill. I knew the philosophy. It was crucial assistance for about three months, very helpful for the next three months, kind of neutral for the last three months, like carrying coals to Newcastle."

In any event, sometime in 2000, after a year's exposure to AA, Church emerged sober and would never drink again. After a few more months of worry that he might slip, the specter lifted. "The temptation went away," he said. "My memory of what it was like to drink went away. Carolyn's hundred-percent intolerance was sufficient incentive for me not to slip. I very quickly realized that I had the same sense of humor, that I had just as much fun. Plus, I had an additional three hours in the day, it seemed, because I was alert, awake, and focused all the time."

Buck Luce was relieved and delighted: "I finally found the adult that I married, as opposed to the little boy who was either very high or very low, but never just right."

Why someone descends into alcoholism is a question without clear answers. Family background, genetics, and other factors may play a role. In Church's case, it's clear, the burden of having a famous father weighed on him.

"I realized how much, from my youngest days, I had been guided by fear of failure, fear of success, fear of my feelings," Church said. "I'm certain that part of it is this: You have such a dramatic model of such high achievement that I was never sure that I could compete with that. So I would almost intentionally not compete against it. Ambition was in my blood, yet I was also skittish about fame. I ran from my successes as quickly as I ran from my failures.

"If I had an opportunity to go to a party with every big name in the book because I'd just been on a [television] show, I would say yes, and then I would have a couple more drinks than usual and decide that I wouldn't go. I wouldn't put myself in the line of fire. Some part of me didn't want to test myself against my father, I expect."[73]

In this vein, Church's early publication history—two and sometimes three books a year—seems a frantic effort to make his mark in the world. In his own view, they amounted to surrogates for himself. If readers loved them, then he felt loved. "There's an insistent, self-deprecatory desire to be loved in that early outpouring of work," he said.[74]

Buck Luce also believed that her husband bore the scars of "benign neglect." Part of that fearful "little boy" that Buck Luce demanded grow up was a psychological response to being raised as a "free-range kid."

One result of being left to his own devices while his parents engaged in politics was a fierce sense of independence and a reluctance to play by the usual rules. Another was a feeling of abandonment. Both had long and complicated consequences.

"When Forrest and I first began a friendship," Buck Luce said, "his view of his world was he's had the best childhood that anyone could ever have. That was an alcohol-induced view of the world. He was the little boy who was, on the one hand, extremely positive, but also bearing an awful lot of hurt. Where all the self-medication came from was he wasn't comfortable feeling sadness and hurt."[75]

The man who may have lacked the requisite humility to appreciate the AA experience at its most profound nonetheless emerged from it with new maturity. It was another growth spurt, more powerful and complete than that produced by the trials of 1991.

Two of Church's confidants, witnesses to the man who drank and the man who had quit, testified to a remarkable transformation.

Rev. Stephen Bauman: Forrest had been "emotionally disconnected. Carolyn is the one who pushed him to find out who the hell he was. Authentic love actually does make us grow up. If you are in an authentically loving relationship, you end up evolving in healthy ways. There was a generative quality to their relationship.

"Forrest became a project for Carolyn in some way. Dressing him, putting him together, putting the Forrest Church package together. The drinking fits into that. In other words, 'Let's clean up this picture.' He didn't say it like this, but he was like a willing subject to be nurtured.

"There had always been an anxious presence, an agitated something going on. And I think that quieted down. That gave him greater access to authentic wisdom as opposed to cleverness and knowledge."[76]

Rev. Bill Grimbol on Shelter Island: "The biggest difference was that he became emotional. It wasn't just the intellect. Suddenly it was all there. There were times that I got so pissed off at him because he was too 'up.' I remember one time just saying, 'You sound like a frickin' Mousketeer, as happy as can be. Why don't you tell me where you're really at?' He looked at me, saying, 'That's where I'm really at.' That was the truth. He came to a point where he just felt his life was damn delightful. He felt blessed beyond measure."[77]

Eleven

A National Pulpit

By law, church and state are separate in America . . .
But by tradition, religion and politics are interdependent,
especially in times of crisis.

—FORREST CHURCH

On September 11, 2001, a handful of fanatics flying hijacked airplanes attacked America in the name of God. Their targets were the World Trade Center and the Pentagon, those twin emblems of American triumphalism, the belief that America is uniquely powerful, divinely favored, and invulnerable.

Stunned and frightened, Americans vowed revenge. They wept and they prayed. And Forrest Church's eloquent understanding of the tragedy vaulted him once again onto the national stage.

All Souls opened its doors for a service of prayer and remembrance on the evening of September 12. Hundreds of people came forward to light candles in honor of the dead and the missing. With the pews filled, Church reached out with compassion to his stunned, grieving listeners. He preached with the authority of a man freshly delivered from the grip of alcoholism, a man in touch as never before with the depths of his being. Having been given new life himself, he sought to offer solace in the face of so much death.

"How precious life is and how fragile," he said. "How profoundly we need one another, especially now, but more than just now . . .

"So let me begin simply by saying, 'I love you.' I love your tears and the depths from which they spring. I love how much you want to do something, anything, to make this all better. We all feel helpless right now; I know that. At times like these and today uniquely so, in the midst of our daily stroll through life reality leaps out from behind the bushes and mugs us. How I ache for those of you who have lost dear friends and loved ones to this senseless and barbaric act of terror. How I ache for all of us, who awakened this morning to a new skyline, not only here in New York, but all across America."

Church also issued a warning. Certainly, justice required that the United States respond to terrorism with force, but that force must always be proportionate to our goals, for our violence might be just as reprehensible as terrorist violence. "Our only hope lies in . . . how well we balance justice and mercy, retribution and compassion, the might of weapons and the power of love."

Finally, he suggested the possibility that out of such horrific events might come a measure of redemption. "Never forget the e-mail sent by a doomed employee in the World Trade Center, who, just before his life was over, wrote the words, 'Thank you for being such a great friend.' Never forget the man and woman holding hands as they leapt together to their death. Pay close attention to these and every other note of almost unbearable poignancy as it rings amidst the cacophony. Pay attention and then commit them to the memory of your heart. For though the future as we knew it is no longer, we now know that the very worst of which human beings are capable can bring out the very best."[1]

A few days later, Church told a *New York Times* reporter, "I have never had the privilege of participating in a more profound worship experience. The deep hunger to be together is palpable."[2]

If houses of worship brought together communities, television united the nation. After watching the tragedy unfold on live TV, Americans gathered before their sets in the following days to mourn, to try to make sense of what had happened, and to debate the political consequences.

Television suited Forrest Church. In previous appearances, Church had demonstrated a remarkable combination of intelligence, eloquence, and poise. He was a natural talking head, though his commentary was anything but glib. He had a knack for grappling with complex issues, viewing them from different angles, and offering a thoughtful, sometimes unpredictable, viewpoint. What's more, he spoke as a gentleman, as far removed as possible from cable TV's bare-knuckled brawlers.

Earlier that year, on public television's *News Hour* with Jim Lehrer, Church had made the case against government support of "faith-based" social programs. Like his opposition to New York State aid in the mid-eighties, his opposition to President Bush's initiative was based on a strict view of church-state separation. The wall between "saving souls and serving them," he warned, was permeable, and deciding which programs to fund usually elevated certain favored religious institutions over others.[3]

It was not surprising to see Forrest Church invited to appear on *Good Morning America* on September 14 with Diane Sawyer and Charlie Gibson, nor to see him later that day alongside Dan Rather as CBS covered the National Prayer Service at Washington's National Cathedral. Aside from being intelligent and articulate, he embodied a religious neutral zone as a Unitarian, neither Protestant nor Catholic, neither Muslim nor Jewish. From the perspective of national unity, he was a shrewd choice.

On PBS's *News Hour*, Church had been one of several commentators, but on the 14th he was the only one. To be singled out in this way was a singular honor, especially for a man who had been subjected to so much bad press a decade before. In the eyes of the mainstream media at least, he had been rehabilitated. More significant, these two national television appearances together represented, by a wide margin, his largest audience ever.

Not an occasion for proselytizing, this was a time to reflect on the nation's wounded spirit and the nature of the "war" ahead. On both networks, Church suggested that good might emerge out of such evil circumstances. (He put it succinctly to a *New York* magazine reporter the following month: "People seem to be taking their own spiritual temperature. They're reexamining their lives, their priorities, and in a strange way they're contemplating their own obituaries . . . contemplating what meaning they are bringing to life.") Second, he cited the adage to "choose your enemies carefully, for you will become like them." As he told Rather, "We must seek justice and not vengeance . . . If not, we will be answering hatred with hatred and we will be imitating those whom we so despise."

Many Americans wondered, Gibson asked, if we were now at war with Islam. "This is not a war between civilizations," Church replied. "This is a war between civilization and anarchy." Indeed, many Muslims were appalled that the name of their God had been "taken so savagely in vain. These are terrorists for God, [but] God has nothing to do with it."

But wasn't there an element of Islam that put a premium on martyrdom, Sawyer pushed him, and thus inevitably planted the seeds of fanaticism? "Every faith has this seed potentially," Church countered, "where everyone gives up on this world and invests wholly in an image of the afterlife." The fanatics responsible for September 11 were no more representative of Islam, he said, than an Aryan Nation Christian militia stood for the essence of Christianity.

Informed that Jerry Falwell had claimed the attacks to be in part God's retribution for America's abortionists, homosexuals, and feminists, an obviously astonished Church said, "I can't believe that," and urged Americans not to become as hate-filled as their enemies.

With Rather, Church's remarks preceded and followed two hours of solemn pageantry. The National Cathedral filled with the president and first lady, former presidents, the Cabinet, and other dignitaries. The U.S. Army orchestra played, soprano Denyce Graves sang. Billy Graham and other clergy—Protestant, Catholic, Jew, and Muslim—spoke and prayed. For Church, this wasn't a time for discussion or debate; his role was to add an additional grace note of dignity to Rather's newscaster style. Afterward, Church interpreted the service as a kind of national sacrament that knit us together in our grieving. He was particularly pleased by the presence of an imam, "whose God has been so desecrated." Observing that Graham had cited the "mystery and reality of evil," he hoped that the nation could also go forward inspired by the "mystery and reality of love."[4]

Although no one from All Souls perished on September 11, each of its members was no more than two degrees of separation from someone who had died. So during the following weeks Church's sermons reiterated his message of solace. At the same time, the sudden turn of events galvanized his pen. After a year of sobriety in which he looked at the world with renewed confidence, he said years later, "Everything shimmered with new vitality. Then 9/11 came, and basically it was a clarion call, in part because I was a religious leader in my movement, in part because I was in New York City, in part because of the way the whole event touched me. And all my energies were free."[5]

His next book was in stores by November 11. *Restoring Faith: America's Religious Leaders Answer Terror with Hope* was inspired by a telephone conversation several days after 9/11 with Tim Bent, an All Souls parishioner who was his editor at St. Martin's Press. Church was writing another book for Bent when the editor suggested that a sermon collection from diverse sources might help lift American spirits. Church quickly got to work, soliciting ideas from ministerial acquaintances and Gustav Niebuhr, then the national religion correspondent for *The New York Times*. Within days he had assembled a collection of voices representing a religious and geographical cross-section of America.

"He saw this as a healing opportunity," said George Gibson, publisher at Walker & Company, who promptly brought out the book in paperback.[6]

Church wrote an introduction and, with Bent's aid, shaped a book that remains surprisingly moving years after its publication. Opening with an invocation in the form of a poem by a Disciples of Christ minister, the little volume concludes with a benediction by a Presbyterian. In between are highlights from candle-lighting ceremonies of September 12, a Muslim prayer service of September 14, Christian services on Sunday, September 16, and Rosh Hashanah services on September 17 and 18. A Catholic priest whose brother was killed in the World Trade Center exhorts his parishioners not to fall prey to hate. An imam prays that all Muslims not be tarred by the terrorist brush. Contributors range from an evangelical Southern Baptist to the very liberal chaplain at Stanford University, from Rabbi Harold Kushner to theologian Harvey Cox.

To promote the book, Church appeared on NBC's *Today Show*, thus touching base at his third major network in the wake of 9/11. To host Ann Curry, he underscored a great irony—that the attacks meant to divide us had in fact brought us together. "We began to see our own tears in one another's eyes. It was as if the nation together had a loss in the family."

That the family was not entirely harmonious, however, is clear from this footnote about the making of *Restoring Faith*. In the course of editing the book, Church reached out to the imam of an imposing mosque on New York's Upper East Side. Three days after 9/11, Muhammad Gemeaha, leader of the Islamic Cultural Center of New York City, had delivered a sermon in English to an interfaith audience calling for peace, healing, and love among people of all religions. It seemed exactly right for Church's anthology, and the imam agreed to participate. But two weeks later, Gemeaha suddenly moved back to Cairo, and, in an interview on an Arabic Web site, reportedly blamed Jews for the terrorist attacks. An appalled Church had to turn elsewhere to find his moderate Muslim voice.[7]

In the aftermath of fear, mourning, and anger, 9/11 prompted a wave of national soul-searching not seen since the 1960s. Amid the confusion, Forrest Church saw a rare opportunity to redefine the meanings of American patriotism, themes he had begun exploring in *God and Other Famous Liberals*. But first, he had to complete the book he was writing for Tim Bent.

Bringing God Home, dedicated to Carolyn Buck Luce and to his AA guides George Dorsey and Bill Thompson, was the fruit of Church's triumph over alcoholism. The "God-shaped hole" in his life that drinking represented had to be filled with God, as newly experienced. It was not that sobriety reordered his theology, but that the God Church had previously intellectualized, he could now feel. "Yet what a world of difference: to feel, not merely know, what one believes." By chronicling his own journey, Church tries to point the way for others whose pathway to God is blocked by doubt, on the one hand, or rigid creed, on the other.[8]

"When we don't believe in God," he writes, "it's not that we believe in nothing; rather we believe in almost anything . . . Afraid of what I might discover if I delved too deeply into myself, I continued to find ways to subdue my consciousness. I accomplished this feat most effectively through the expedient of alcohol, which for years had served me as a kind of God substitute. As long as another power greater than myself presided over me, I could not bring God into my life."[9]

Church supplements an account of his own quest with contemporary stories of recovery from addiction and with classic spiritual journeys, from Homer's *Odyssey*, the Bible's Prodigal Son, and Augustine's *Confessions* to Bunyan's *Pilgrim's Progress* and Dickens's *A Christmas Carol*. In each case, he who was lost is found—by returning home and acknowledging its true value for the first time. Seen with mature eyes, the hidden treasures at home emerge from obscurity, blossoming into more beautiful versions of themselves.

The God that Church now embraces is neither the bearded old man in the sky of his childhood, nor the tidy intellectual constructs he used to admire from afar. "Today, in a sense," he writes, "I believe only in God. Only something as large as God encompasses the mystery and wonder of my being. To do justice to life as I experience it, everything else is far too small." In Church's interpretation, God is thus "*our name for a power that is greater than all and yet present in each*: the life force; the Holy; Being itself." To those who object that this definition is too fuzzy, Church insists that a measure of vagueness is necessary. Only poetic language can convey the idea's symbolic nuance and vitality, and anything more precise presumes a knowledge beyond human capacity.[10]

And what of an afterlife? Church takes into account the thought of Plato, Jesus, Thoreau, Twain, and Freud, before taking an agnostic position. In the end, the question hardly matters. "For me, to bring God

home right here and now is—as they say—to die and go to Heaven. It
may be all of Heaven we will ever know." Nothing, he suggests, could
be as amazing as life itself, which is not a given but a gift. "In return for
the gift, we understand that the world doesn't owe us a living. It is we
who owe the world a living: our own."

But then, unaccountably, Church gets swept up in maudlin, conventional Christian rhetoric. "I take some consolation," he writes, "in knowing death will bring us peace. We will join our departed loved ones. We
will be with Jesus. God will carry us home."[11] Reunited with loved ones
and nestled in the bosom of Jesus? After saying that we can know nothing about any postlife existence? One wonders how this bit of orthodoxy,
so alien to Church's thought, sneaked into these pages.

The anomaly seems especially puzzling since Church concludes with a
nod to the two unconventional visionaries most responsible for bringing
God home to him: Ralph Waldo Emerson and Sufi poet Rumi. "Poets
and storytellers," he writes, "touch me more than theologians do." Philosopher George Santayana had dismissed Emerson's Transcendentalism as
sentimental, his concepts of Spirit and Over-Soul incomprehensible because they were so vaguely defined. Yet this is precisely why Church admires this aspect of Emersonian thought. "All Emerson could do," he
writes, "was to mirror his awe and humility in childlike reverence for the
creation and his small yet consciousness-charged place in it." Rumi had no
truck with doctrine, either, but possessed the loving heart of a true universalist. "Every prophet, every saint," Rumi wrote, "has his path, but as they
return to God, all are one." Uniting the Transcendentalist seer and the
Muslim poet in holy alliance, this all-encompassing embrace embodied
the true spirit of Church's universalism.[12]

Church's wrestling with how to talk about God would have been
almost inconceivable for many Unitarians of the previous generation,
dominated by humanists. They would have felt more comfortable, however, with his second book published in 2002, *The American Creed*. However energized by the post-9/11 debate about American patriotism and
purpose, Church felt it lacked a proper historical perspective. The inter-

section of religion and politics had produced in America a distinctive and valuable legacy, misunderstood, he believed, by conservatives and liberals alike. If *God and Other Famous Liberals* had been a call to arms for contemporary liberals, *The American Creed* was a historical probe into the heart of American identity.

Tim Bent pared down Church's narrative into a brief, condensed primer. "He had this tendency toward the prolix because he wrote so easily," Bent explained, and because he was accustomed to writing for the spoken word where repetition is often necessary to clarify a point.

"I think the manic part of Forrest came out when he started to write a book. He would write all night, and you would make editing comments, and the next morning he would have a revised chapter for you to look at. I would tell him to slow down, to let it sit for a week or two.

"He got that real quickly. When you gave him an edited manuscript, he was just all over you with love: 'This is great!' And the harder you were on him, the greater he loved it. It showed him how seriously you were taking him, pushing him harder into doing something different and new."[13]

Imagine the chutzpah required for someone like Forrest Church to put together a book titled *The American Creed: A Spiritual and Patriotic Primer*. Neither academic historian nor theologian but a working pastor in charge of a large New York City church, he boldly offered a short course on American identity. Thus the book reflected not only Bent's crisp editing, but Church's confidence and daring. It was the work of an impassioned amateur.

Church's thesis is simple. Embodied in the Declaration of Independence, the American creed—of justice for all, because we are all created equal, and liberty for all, because we are "endowed by the Creator with certain inalienable rights"—was modified and expanded throughout the country's history. Often honored in the breach, it nonetheless remained the pole star of our collective ideals. As G. K. Chesterton once noted, "America is the only nation in the world that is founded on a creed," one set forth "with theological lucidity" in the Declaration. We were, he said, "a nation with the soul of a church."

Pursuing this theme, Church calls our unique polity "a union of faith and freedom, in which faith elevates freedom and freedom tempers faith." Thus he takes issue with advocates of a Christian or a secularist vision of the nation, both of whom "misread the script of our founders." Here, once again, are Church's fundamentalists of right and left. "Some call for a return to what they proclaim to be our founders' faith. They excoriate the nation for its loss of values, often persuasive in their critique but misguided in their understanding of the American way and of American history. Secularists on the left are equally wrongheaded. If ours is explicitly not a Christian nation, it is nonetheless built on a religious foundation. By law, church and state are separate in America, to the signal advantage of both. But by tradition, religion and politics are interdependent, especially in times of crisis."[14]

Consistent with this evenhanded approach, Church steers between the right wing's uncritical flag-waving and the America bashing at the left wing's fringes. As in *God and Other Famous Liberals*, he ushers out the usual liberal icons for admiration. Roger Williams is the great builder of the wall between church and state, Jefferson the Declaration's principal architect, Lincoln the champion of union under God, FDR the enunciator of the Four Freedoms, and Martin Luther King Jr. the apostle of racial justice. Whether conventionally religious or not—Jefferson and Lincoln certainly were not—all held to a bedrock belief that America was sustained and guided by divine inspiration. This did not mean that America was better than other nations. Far from it. On matters of race and imperialist overreach, in fact, it often faltered. But it meant that "In God We Trust" is a motto of real substance.

Along the way, Church offers spirited readings of our various national anthems and patriotic celebrations. He describes the march of democracy as incorporating the aspirations of immigrants, blacks, and women. And he extends a bipartisan hand to Presidents Eisenhower and George W. Bush, the former for alerting us to the dangers of the "military-industrial complex," and the latter for a speech urging authoritarian China to expand its political freedom. In the wake of 9/11, Church warns that the genius of America can never be summed up by its military and economic might. Nor are we the "amoral secularists" of terrorist caricature. As long as we hold fast to the ideals of the American Creed, our identity is secure.

Church's books were always blessed with blurbs from the famous. But when the 2003 paperback edition of *The American Creed*, newly subtitled "A Biography of the Declaration of Independence," was issued, it bore the imprimatur of a political Higher Power. "Forrest Church has given us a great gift," wrote Bill Clinton. "This book shows us why so many Americans for over two centuries have kept their faith in our fundamental principles."

A robust, uninhibited love of country was not always fashionable on the left, but it was dear to Church's heart. In part, this was due to his parents' influence. By mid-life, it was also nurtured by his affiliation with the Franklin and Eleanor Roosevelt Institute. Since 1987, he had served on the board of directors of this organization dedicated to preserving the legacy of these beacons of what historian Arthur Schlesinger Jr. once called "the vital center," between hidebound conservatism and radical collectivism. Institute liberals carried on a love affair with their country even when they feared it was veering dangerously off course. In FDR's Four Freedoms—freedom from fear, freedom from want, freedom of speech, and freedom of religion—Church found the substantive core of his liberal politics. Rooseveltian liberalism—open-ended, given to experimentation, anti-ideological—appealed to Church's skepticism toward rigid creeds, whether religious or political. What's more, its pragmatic approach to problem-solving resonated with his easygoing temperament. "He had a way of inviting you in to think about something in a fresh way," said Christopher Breiseth, the institute's former president. "That was one of his gifts."[15]

Sitting on the deck on Shelter Island, Forrest Church and Tim Bent batted around one book idea after another. In the wake of 9/11, they asked, what was the one thing on every American's mind? Fear, of course. At a time of enormous anxiety, could he think about self-help in a fresh way?

Given that he would be wandering far afield from his usual subjects, did he dare try? With Bent's aid, he took up the dare. The title of his book came straight from Franklin Roosevelt himself.

Published in 2004, *Freedom from Fear* bears all the markers of the self-help genre—short sentences, paragraphs, and chapters; case studies from real life; lots of lists with snappy titles. Five categories of fear (fright, worry, guilt, insecurity, and dread) and three types of courage (the courage to act, to love, and to be) are cataloged. At the end, a *Freedom from Fear* Book Club is appended, offering Church's glosses on classic novels and contemporary guidebooks. Holding up the entire edifice is an easily memorized mantra: "Do what you can. Want what you have. Be who you are."

To combat our fears, Church suggests ten "keys to freedom." Despite being wrapped in self-help code phrases, Church's advice is often identical with his pulpit wisdom. That it is wiser to practice "thoughtful wishing" than wishful thinking, for example, was a frequent sermon trope. Some of his admonitions—to break down a fear into its component parts so that each can be dealt with separately—are genuinely helpful. There are memorable lines: "Fear is more likely to move trouble from one burner to another than to turn down the flame." And on the necessity of courage in the face of fear: "At our finest, we are all actors. The well-lived life springs from the well-played role." But while Church summons up inspiring stories about brave parishioners, his default position is to cite one deep thinker after another: "Aristotle introduced the golden mean to Western philosophy 2,500 years ago." Nietzsche shows up two pages later. On the first page of one chapter, he cites a triumvirate of Descartes, Goethe, and Shakespeare. Throughout, his penchant for lecturing and sermonizing trumps his eagerness to offer a therapeutic helping hand. Clearly, Church isn't comfortable with the genre.[16]

In *Life Lines* and *Lifecraft,* Church had authored consoling, deeply affecting works of inspiration. But for self-help to work, a more practical, down-to-earth mode of operation is required. "You have to have a structure," Bent explained. "Here's Step A. This is what you do, and now we move to Step B, and so on. In the end, *Freedom from Fear* isn't convincing because it's more discursive and essayistic. That's just the way Forrest thought. We tried to reach out in a way that didn't quite succeed."[17]

Still, the book undeniably provided insight for some readers. And one has to admire the author's own willingness to take a chance on something well outside his usual comfort zone. In the book's acknowledgments, Church thanks Bent for "jauntily [proposing] that if Ralph Waldo Emerson were writing today, he would more than likely be considered a self-help author." Thus the All Souls pastor dared to follow in the footsteps of the author of "Self-Reliance" and "Heroism."[18]

Freedom from Fear mentions in passing "the liberation that comes with forgiveness," a theme that Church returned to again and again, in sermons and books. In *Life Lines*, he commends the idea of loving your enemies as "the most paradoxical of Jesus' teachings, something new in the canons of religious literature." In *Lifecraft*, he defines prayers of forgiveness as the hardest kind to say, but ultimately the most rewarding. "Picture in your mind," Church writes, "someone from whom you are estranged." While praying for her, you will discover that it is impossible, in the same breath, to hate her. Though you may not change her attitude toward you, you may change yourself. "It may lift at least some of the burden of resentment you carry in your own heart . . . When we reconcile ourselves with another, we ourselves are healed."[19]

Many people find forgiveness difficult, even impossible. One of life's most daunting challenges, it is most often honored in the breach. Instead of Jesus, Alexander Pope—"To err is human, to forgive divine"—sums up conventional wisdom. Yet Forrest Church sided with the carpenter over the poet. He practiced what he preached.

At All Souls, although the wounds from the 1991 Troubles healed slowly, what was remarkable was that, over time, so many of them did. People not only began to talk to each other again but they forgave each other.

Consider the case of Louis Pojman and Forrest Church. Pojman was the philosophy professor hired to direct All Souls' adult education programs, whose lectures on ethics gave intellectual ballast to those who wanted to oust Church from his post. He, as much as anyone, was responsible for bringing matters to a boil. He spoke directly to the question of Church's infidelity, took his concerns to the church board, and lobbied to require an up-or-down vote on Church's tenure.

By the late nineties, Pojman had left the faculty at the University of Mississippi and was teaching at West Point, just north of New York City. In the spring of 2000, a curious Pojman and his wife, Trudy, decided to attend a Sunday service at All Souls. While greeting parishioners afterward, Church spotted the Pojmans and, according to Trudy, "put out that right hand and in a booming voice said, 'Welcome back!' Well, that set everything level." Following a few amiable meetings soon afterward with the professor, Church resolved to invite him to give a series of lectures in the adult education program. When he announced the decision to All Souls lay leaders, they were outraged. Church defended Pojman, saying, "Look, we're into reconciliation. This is a perfect opportunity to do that. Plus, he's a very good teacher." But the board was adamantly opposed. "In their view," Church said, "he was the snake in Eden, the enemy of All Souls." So a sheepish Church had to rescind the invitation.

Fortunately, this incident did not end the relationship, and Church and Pojman remained in touch. When Church learned in 2005 that Pojman was dying of cancer, he visited him several times in New York Hospital. At Pojman's request, Church arranged for the memorial service to be held at All Souls and wrote a testimonial in his honor. "He was a very impressive guy. So focused, so valiant," Church said later. "At the end, our affection was complete and sealed."[20]

One by one, Church and other key opponents of 1991 found a way to forgive each other. Diana Cullen, born Jewish, tried other churches and a Reform synagogue and found them all wanting. As time passed, she said, "The events of '91 became much less important. I got something from him and the church that transcended his personal life . . . I remember feeling very nervous when I came back. But when he saw me [in a pew], he really looked pleased and reached down to shake my hand. I felt so relieved." After a few years, Alex and Jeannette Sanger, too, began to attend Christmas services and then others throughout the year. Meanwhile, as Barbara Ascher returned to the Episcopalian Christianity she was raised in, supplemented by Buddhist meditation, her husband, Robert, who had sorely missed the All Souls worship experience, returned to the fold. "Bob was very, very happy to be back," she said.

By early 2002, the seventy-seven-year-old Robert Ascher was dying. Barbara informed Church that her husband wanted him to preside over a memorial service at All Souls, and the pastor readily agreed. In the same conversation, she apologized for her passionate attacks against him in 1991. His response was forgiveness made flesh: "He just patted me on the back and said, 'Aw, that's old stuff.'" When Church visited Robert in the Ascher apartment, sometimes their friends the Sangers were there. "I just threw my arms around him," Jeannette remembered, "and he would give me a big hug." Two years later, Alex was invited to All Souls to give a talk on women's reproductive rights, and this time the board of trustees put up no barriers. Reconciliation was all but complete.[21]

Because he embodied love—in his smile, in his embrace, in the soothing balm of his words—Forrest Church was hard to resist. He took special pleasure in expressing his benevolence through mentoring the young, and its recipients were forever grateful.

After two years at Yale Divinity School, Ken Beldon arrived at All Souls "a broken person." His mother had died suddenly in her late forties, his college romance had ended, and he suffered from clinical depression. "When I heard that sermon, in beautiful Forrest language, that 'death takes love's measure'—wrestling as I was with my mom's untimely death—I remember crying during the service, and it felt like a safe place to do that." Church took Beldon under his wing and put him to work, co-leading a junior-high group and teaching a Bible study class.

"As many great mentors do," Beldon said, "he perceived something in me right away. At that point where my confidence in myself was ebbing, he gave me an opportunity to shine in some small ways. I felt very gently led but, even more, I felt given permission to share my gifts. Here was someone whose brilliance was unsurpassed, but who understood from his own life experience what it meant to be broken and what healing meant, too. This was an experience of grace."

Thus empowered, Beldon completed his education at Union Theological Seminary and entered the Unitarian ministry.[22]

For Marc Loustau, who was working for a liberal New York think tank but contemplating becoming a minister, the experience was more intellectual. As a self-described "very ambitious twenty-two-year-old," he informed Church of his desire to beef up his academic preparation for theological school. The minister's response, he said, was immediate and enthusiastic: "Great. We'll meet once a month and go over some of the books that I've read and found interesting over the years." So for the next three years the eager young man and the learned middle-aged man convened the equivalent of an Oxford tutorial. Loustau got the preparation he needed to succeed at Harvard Divinity School, and Church acquired a smart research assistant for several of his books. "It felt like I was doing what I was destined to do," Loustau said. "I fell in love with academia again." So much so that rather than enter the parish ministry, he decided to pursue a doctorate for an academic career. He would follow Forrest Church's road not taken.[23]

"He was a kind of father figure for a lot of us," UU minister Alison Miller said. "He delighted in giving everyone permission to be themselves to the fullest."[24]

To Robert Oxnam, Church gave permission to express a multitude of selves. Not a twenty-something but a man slightly older than Church, Oxnam first encountered the minister after attending a Christmas Eve service in 2003 with his wife, Vishakha Desai, who had succeeded him as president of the Asia Society. Oxnam was so taken with Church that he got in touch, and the two men made a lunch date. With every ensuing lunch, their mutual admiration grew. "I'd found a kindred spirit," Oxnam said. They could talk politics and history, China (Oxnam's field), religion and values. Oxnam learned that Frank Church, one of his heroes, was Forrest's father, while Church discovered that Robert was the grandson of a liberal icon of the forties and fifties, G. Bromley Oxnam, a

Methodist bishop, stalwart foe of McCarthyism, and president of the World Council of Churches. "We talked easily about both the joy and the burden of grappling with [famous] forebears," Oxnam said.

Indeed, they had more in common. Each had endured a difficult divorce, and each had given up the addictions of booze and cigarettes. "Both of us still chewed Nicorettes in a kind of secret way," Oxnam said. "He chewed two milligrams, and I chewed four milligrams. We found we could joke about it. He called me a bigger addict."

Before long, Oxnam confided as well about his dissociative identity disorder, formerly known as multiple personality disorder. Besides Robert, there were ten additional personalities taking turns inhabiting his head, and sometimes leading him into destructive behavior. Not only was Church not put off by this news, but he insisted that, in effect, everyone consisted of multiple identities, each of which holds sway under different circumstances. He refused to define his new friend as a freak; he was just a more complicated version of himself. Oxnam was struggling to write a memoir about his condition, but it wasn't working and he had nearly given up on it. But Church insisted that the story needed to be heard, in its own unique way. He advised his friend to rewrite the manuscript, not from a single perspective, but by giving voice to each of his separate personalities. Two weeks later, after receiving a fresh draft from Oxnam, Church put on his editor's hat. Here was the serial enthusiast at work. "For each of the drafts, over the next few months," Oxnam said, "he dropped no matter what else he was doing, and within a few hours, an edited version would come back to me." The book that emerged was called *A Fractured Mind*. By then the bond between the men was unbreakable.[25]

In October 2006, death confronted Forrest Church as swiftly and finally as had love when he encountered Carolyn Buck Luce in 1990. Doctors informed him that he had a form of inoperable esophageal cancer and that he could expect, at best, six more months of life. Religion, he had said repeatedly, was the human response to the dual reality of being alive and having to die. Now, face-to-face with that ultimate reality, how would he respond? What sources of sustenance could lift him up during this ordeal? What sort of man was he, after all?

When Church received the diagnosis by phone, Carolyn Buck Luce was about to head to the airport for a long-scheduled business trip to India. Since neither death nor any treatment was imminent, her husband insisted that she go ahead as planned. Next, he informed relatives and friends. Oxnam, who was at his vacation home on the North Fork of Long Island, immediately drove back to New York and stayed with his friend for four days. They watched football, "a way to release us," and talked and talked.

"We talked about his death," Oxnam said. "When it would happen. What the memorial service should look like. Where information for the obit could be found. How was he going to be able to face pain?

"I watched the guy telescope the stages of coping with death so that he went from shock to acceptance in a period of a few hours, or a few days, rather than over what it usually requires, which is weeks, months, and perhaps never. I watched something even more remarkable, the ultimate test in his theology, the dual reality of being alive and having to die. It changed from 'That's how one should live,' which is head-proven, to the reality of 'I've got to accept this for myself.'"[26]

Church's October 17 letter to the congregation conveyed the news with a mixture of stoic purpose and signature optimism. "The best thing you can do to bolster my already high spirits," he wrote, "is to carry on all of your good works, continue to expand our ministries during this critical period in the life of our nation and world, worship to a fare-thee-well, and keep the budget balanced! . . . As for my three mantras—do what you can, want what you have, and be who you are—I practice each every day, feeling myself blessed beyond measure."

A month later, he reported unexpected progress. His doctors had been able to operate, after all, and had removed the entire esophagus. To allow him to continue to eat, they had extracted parts of his stomach to create a feeding tube. "I now possess a promising, if not yet fully functional, 'estomagus,'" Church joked. For the next few months, he would have to be fed by a pump through a tube directly into the lower intestine. Additionally, the operation had paralyzed one of his vocal cords so that he could speak only with great difficulty. The disease, diagnosed as adenoid cystic carcinoma, progressed slowly, and survival rates, he asserted with more hope than accuracy, "seem promising indeed."

Church's next report was positively breezy. "All is terrific here. I'm up to about a mile's walk each day, and I sleep through much of my night 'feeding.' Being hooked up to a food pump for ten hours is no picnic, but neither is it particularly onerous . . . Oddly, in some ways, I feel better than ever. Not that the pleasures and utility of eating, drinking, and speaking are overrated—they aren't—but rather that we underrate life almost criminally every day we take it for granted!"

By December, Church could once again eat and drink normally, but his speaking voice had not fully returned. And the most pertinent news was dire. His cancer was not in fact adenoid carcinoma, but the more aggressive second-stage squamous-cell carcinoma. "The other news from the final pathology report is cheery: the tumor was small; the margins around the surgery were clear, and the lymph nodes negative. This should give me a fair shot at complete recovery."[27]

No one can say with certainty what causes a specific cancer, but the occurrence of this type of cancer was not surprising, given Church's previous lifestyle. He smoked a pipe and cigarettes (Salem Lights) for many years, and was an extremely heavy drinker for four decades. Church's longtime habits put him dangerously at risk for cancer. According to Memorial Sloan-Kettering Cancer Center, where Church was treated, "The combination of smoking with long-term and/or heavy use of alcohol is the most significant risk factor for esophageal squamous cell cancer." That finding is buttressed by a recent overview in *The New England Journal of Medicine*: "Substantial alcohol intake, especially in combination with smoking, greatly increases the risk of squamous-cell carcinoma . . . and may account for more than 90 percent of all cases of squamous-cell carcinoma of the esophagus in the developed world."[28]

When Church returned to the pulpit, in late January of 2007, after a three-and-a-half-month hiatus, his voice was pinched and smaller than before his surgery, but his spirits were high: "I know it's two weeks early, but do you know what I feel like right now, having emerged from my den, blinking in the light, mounting again this good pulpit—that's right, I feel like the proverbial groundhog. Punxsutawney Phil has nothing on me. I've emerged from my hole. I can't see my shadow. And I'm here to tell you that spring is right around the corner." No wonder that his listeners broke into applause.

Assuming he was healthy enough—and there was no need for radiation or chemotherapy now—he would continue to preach once a month. Still, he would be stepping aside from his leadership role as All Souls' senior minister, ceding that position to the associate minister, Rev. Galen Guengerich, whom he had been grooming as his eventual replacement. Church's new title, minister of public theology, simply codified what had always been his forte, spreading the message of liberal religion across the nation.

Guengerich had served as Church's right hand since 1993. While just a boy, he had seemed to find his calling as a Mennonite preacher, but later exposure to the intellectual rigors of Princeton Theological Seminary began to undermine his Christian faith. He nonetheless graduated at the top of his class, found his way to Unitarian Universalism, and eventually earned a doctorate in theology at the University of Chicago. If not a Harvard graduate, as so many of his predecessors had been, he certainly embodied the All Souls tradition of a learned ministry.

"Some of you," Church continued on that January Sunday, "may have read my book *Life Lines: Holding On (and Letting Go)*. So much of life consists in holding on to what we must and letting go for dear life when holding on would be grasping. In this proposed transition I hope to do both—at once to hold on and to let go, each in precisely the way I should."

When Church took to the pulpit in the following month, he expanded on the theme "Beating the Odds." Under the original diagnosis, his chances of survival had been 1 in 20; now, after surgery, they had increased to 1 in 4. Ever the optimist, he chose to regard this as good news. Never mind that a 25 percent chance of making it might bring others to tears.

"If there's a moral to this story—beyond the obvious one that I might usefully have quit drinking and smoking decades before I did some seven years ago—it doesn't lie on the surface of these shifting odds." Rather, it lay in the wondrous fact of having lived at all.

"So what did we do to deserve this, whatever 'this' might happen to be at any given moment in our life's unfolding saga? Please! The odds against our being here to ask that impertinent question beggar reckoning. Which is where the second element in the fundamental religious equation [after awe] kicks into play: Humility. You likely know my favorite etymology: *human, humane, humanitarian, humility, humble, humus.* Dust to dust and ashes to ashes. And in between, erupting into consciousness—into pain and hope and trust and fear and grief and love—the miracle of life."[29]

This wasn't spinning the truth. This was the truth, as Church had long understood it. The Earth doesn't owe us a living; we owe it, and we ought to savor as many years as we are lucky to have.

In the months to come, Church would regain his voice and resume preaching as he was able. But most of his strength was devoted to completing a magnum opus that he had been working on for several years, born out of the transforming fires of 9/11. In the broadest sense, the question that spurred him was this: What was the relationship between religion and the American polity? More narrowly put, the question became: Was this nation, as some conservatives asserted, conceived in liberty, then wrapped in the swaddling clothes of Christianity? Or, conversely, was a firm separation of church and state built into the national order from the very beginning? He had been grappling with these questions far earlier than 2001, of course, but the patriotic fervor sparked by the threat of terrorism made the issues all the more relevant.

In 2004, Church edited a little volume for Beacon Press that took up the thread begun with *God and Other Famous Liberals* and continued with *The American Creed. The Separation of Church and State: Writings on a Fundamental Freedom by America's Founders* gathered seminal works by such luminaries as Washington, Jefferson, Madison, and Samuel and John Adams, plus those of lesser-known religious figures, including the Baptist John Leland and the Presbyterian Caleb Wallace. The revolution that led to American religious liberty, Church wrote in an introduction, was "powered by two very different engines: one driven by eighteenth-century Enlightenment values, the other guided by Christian imperatives that grew out of the Great Awakening." The former stressed freedom *from* religion, while the latter demanded freedom *for* the practice of religion. "Together, these seemingly opposite world-views collaborated brilliantly and effectively to establish the separation of church and state in America."[30]

This thesis would be fully documented in the magisterial work that came next, *So Help Me God: The Founding Fathers and the First Great Battle Over Church and State* (2007). In Church's long publishing history, this work was the outlier. All of his previous books were relatively brief syntheses of his reading and reflection; only the edited works bore any hint of scholarly apparatus. By contrast, this was a 444-page tome based on deep research in original sources, fitted out with endnotes and bibliography. In fact, but for some astute editing that sharpened Church's argument and curtailed his penchant for telling one anecdote after another, it might have ended up far fatter. In the end, the author deftly added plenty of narrative honey to make its analytical medicine go down. This history was not only shrewdly argued but a delight to read.

Conceived amid contemporary America's culture wars, *So Help Me God* probed the nation's first such war for clues to our national political-religious identity. "Any diligent student of American history," Jerry Falwell once asserted, is forced to conclude that America "was founded by godly men upon godly principles to be a Christian nation." Aspiring to be the Republican nominee for president in 2008, Mitt Romney accused secularists of going well beyond separation of church and state by seeking to "remove from the public domain any acknowledgment of God." Ever the centrist liberal, Forrest Church took the middle ground. His book vehemently disagreed with the former and subtly agreed with the latter.

Was the young American Republic going to become a Commonwealth of God or an Empire of Liberty? *So Help Me God* traces the transition from the former view (grounded in Puritan New England) to the latter (based on Enlightenment thought). By Monroe's presidency, the balance had decisively tilted toward liberty. In the narrative, Church lays out four major themes. First, the United States was founded neither as a Christian nation nor as a totally secular one. Second, none of the first five presidents was a Christian by the standards of today's Evangelicals. Only John Adams was a church member, and all of them doubted the divinity of Christ. Third, the very disestablishment of religion paved the way for the remarkable vitality of American religious life. Fourth, in spite of the presidential leaning toward secularism, these early presidents endorsed unfettered religious expression as much as they opposed government sponsorship of religion.

Though far from uniform in their religious beliefs, none of the first presidents felt, as do most of today's presidential aspirants, a need to confess, or pretend to confess, to Christian orthodoxy. Washington, for instance, though reared in the Anglican faith, believed in a Deist God. This Great Watchmaker kept the universe running, but otherwise stayed aloof from the human fray. In many years of correspondence, public and private, Washington mentions Christ only once, in a letter composed by an aide to Delaware Indians. John Adams, though "theologically unitarian and skeptical toward almost every tenet of orthodox Christianity," worshipped without fail in a Congregational church. Jefferson, inspired by the French Enlightenment, was an even more ardent Deist than Washington, loathed the intrusion of clergy into politics, and charged that Christendom had made a sham of the great teachings of his "Jefferson Bible" Jesus. Madison, having distanced himself from the Anglicanism of his youth, served as the principal architect of church-state separation in Virginia and framer of the First Amendment. Monroe, because he was "secular to the bone . . . and not interested enough in religion to bother being disrespectful toward anyone's cherished beliefs," probably would have been disqualified from either major party's presidential ticket in our era.[31]

Just as Forrest Church's theology is built on paradox, his reading of history is thick with irony. "Did you know," he writes, "that George Washington was so opposed to religious lobbying that he cursed church interference in government affairs even when he *agreed* with those who were trying to reverse national policy? His successor, John Adams, deemed the church essential to government, even if Christian theology happened to be false (which he suspected it was). Thomas Jefferson, who built a famous 'wall of separation between church and state,' worshipped on Sundays at a chapel set up in the Capitol." And the most intriguing role reversal from today's perspective: "In the early Republic, even as most Baptists stood on the religious left as champions for church-state separation, an equal majority of Unitarians lined up on the religious right to demand a seat for God in government."[32]

Wedged uneasily between Washington's benign presidency and Monroe's "Era of Good Feeling," Jefferson's tenure was marked by a religious culture war far more virulent than anything witnessed in the time of Jerry Falwell and Forrest Church. Jefferson's Democratic Republicans, alleged Enlightenment atheists, squared off against Federalists, supposed harbingers of a return to aristocracy and established religion. Each side despised the other not merely as political enemy, but as destroyer of true religion. For Church, this history underscores the explosiveness of the combination. "Religious politics draw their ferocity from how *cosmic* the outcome seems . . . American electioneering is brutal to begin with; throw salvation into the mix and, if people aren't careful, it can become toxic." Nonetheless, he can't help finding a silver lining in religion's high profile: It acted as counterbalance in the national soul to the otherwise sovereign rule of unrestrained individualism.[33]

Forrest Church desperately wanted this book to be taken seriously as a work of significant scholarship. Its completion brought him full circle from his days as a budding academic at Harvard. He had poured three years of his life into its research, writing, and editing, and, given the cancer diagnosis, he did not know how many more years he had left. The manuscript he brought to editors Tim Bent and Katie Hall was voluminous. Its more than 400,000 words made it nearly ten times longer than most of his books. He regarded Bent as the finest editor he ever worked with, but the process of whittling it down put a momentary strain on the relationship.

"He was hungry for renown," Bent said, but "there was no cynicism to any of this. There was always, on both our parts, the belief that each project had something important and wonderful to contribute . . . Success meant getting the word out to a wider circle.

"That said, Forrest's hunger sometimes did exhaust me. At one point, *in extremis*—it involved whether *So Help Me God* should be published as three voluminous tomes—I reminded him that, come on, it was only a book, that there were more important things to life, that no book was truly a monument; let's just slow things down and temper expectations and ambitions. He snapped back, hard, that *this book* was the most important thing to him, ever, and I of all people should get that. It was not his finest moment, nor mine."[34]

For the most part, Church need not have worried. *So Help Me God* drew hosannas nearly everywhere attention was paid. On his syndicated public television show, the sometimes combative Tavis Smiley proved unusually deferential. *Kirkus*, the prepublication review that does not shy away from scorching appraisals, called the book "fascinating and subtle." Neither were its subtleties lost online in the *Daily Kos*, where Joan McCarter described it as "an engaging, beautifully crafted and meticulously researched history." The liberal blog also published McCarter's thorough and thoughtful e-mail interview with Church. While this assessment was hardly surprising—since the interviewer's father, Joe McCarter, had led the presidential primary campaign for Senator Frank Church in Nebraska in 1976—an equally deferential interview in the Mormon-operated *Deseret News* in Salt Lake City was.[35]

Church was disappointed by *The New York Times*'s lack of coverage. But it's easy to understand why he had not been reviewed there since *God and Other Famous Liberals* in 1992. His books after that one were so disparate that the newspaper's cultural arbiters must have been confused about what sort of writer Forrest Church actually was. Journalism loves categories. Following several inspirational books in the nineties, this full-time pastor had written a book on his reaffirmation of faith while overcoming alcoholism, a self-help book, and a "biography of the Declaration of Independence." Being so hard to pigeonhole made him seem like an amateur, however inspired or gifted. Just how credible a historian, they must have wondered, could he possibly be?

Fortunately for Church, this question did not seem to matter to the editors of *The New Yorker*, where his book was given respectful notice though not singled out among several similar books. In the pages of the august *New York Review of Books*, however, *So Help Me God* received the imprimatur of one of the deans of early American history. Gordon S. Wood of Brown University was a winner of the Pulitzer and Bancroft Prizes and author of *Empire of Liberty: A History of the Early Republic, 1789–1815*, in the esteemed Oxford University Press series of volumes on U.S. history. There could hardly be a more knowledgeable or discerning reviewer. Wood's assessment—that the book was "an illuminating and entertaining work of history, and the best account of the first five presidents and their relation to religion that we have"—fully validated Church as a historian of genuine gifts.[36]

Basking in the glow of such high-level recognition, Church hoped to follow this success with other volumes dealing with American presidents and religion. As he plunged into the research, reading legions of histories and biographies, his plan shifted course several times. In one scenario, the next book would encompass the entire sweep of the American presidency from the beginning through George W. Bush, with an emphasis on pivotal moments, such as wartime, that shifted the church-state balance.

But since President Lincoln proved as mesmerizing and enigmatic a figure for Church as he had for countless others, he recast his book proposal to focus on "the God of Abraham." Events of the early nineteenth century would be taken into account as mere prologue to the Civil War presidency that demolished Jefferson's wall of separation. Here was the great irony. Though Lincoln was a religious skeptic, "he united church and state in ways no president had done before." According to Church, three convictions drove him: that the union's survival rested on God's will, that the war was God's punishment for the people's collective sin, and that he was God's anointed agent to fashion a Christian republic. Church believed that this controversial thesis amounted to a real breakthrough in Lincoln studies. But he was not about to stop there. He imagined a series of five additional books that would take the story into the twenty-first century.[37]

This was not a preposterous goal. Church had found a subject compelling enough to harness and focus his enthusiasm for years. But the recurrence of ever more aggressive cancer forced him to put aside such a formidable project. He would be unable to further burnish his credentials as a historian.

Instead, in the short time he had left, he resolved to put together a short book on the great, resounding leitmotif of his life and thought: love and death. Always an unapologetic recycler of previously published materials and unpublished sermons, he now stitched them together with strands of autobiography to produce his most moving book. Learning, eloquence, and compassion—all are fused here into the deepest wisdom. Elegiac yet not maudlin, deeply personal yet universal in import, *Love and Death* is a masterly meditation on the art of dying, and living, well.

The book is structured around death's omnipresence in Church's life, from his father's brush with testicular cancer when Church was just a toddler to his own battle with esophageal cancer. He recalls the deaths of elderly relatives, when life's ending seemed utterly natural, and the premature passing of his college friend that shattered his youthful innocence. Before pneumonia took down Dalton Denton, Church had romanticized early death, as "the only way I could think of to compete with my famous father." Now, buried in grief, he realized how much he loved his friend: "Dalton proved that death is far more real and love far more essential than I had imagined either to be."[38]

Church's dying heroes, from his parish or from the World Trade Center towers, sense that their "immortality" lies in the love they give away. Those lucky enough to survive, like his father, learn to take life not as a given, but as a gift never to be taken for granted. Thus love and death are inextricably intertwined.

Far from downbeat, the book becomes an anthem in praise of the life well lived. Longevity is not the issue for the author; depth is. Life's trapdoors, he reminds us, can open at any time, curtailing or smashing our dreams. Yet if we fear to risk, we risk closing down altogether any chance of real living.

Just as every cliché carries a germ of truth, Church transforms the seemingly trite observation into the realm of the profound. Seen in this light, the mantras from his self-help book yield expansive insights beyond that of feel-good nostrums. Within a simple carapace, they convey a rare, transcendent beauty. They are Zen koans without the bafflement.

Want what you have. Do what you can. Be who you are.

"Wanting what we have mutes the pangs of desire, which visits from an imaginary future to cast a shadow on the present, which is real. Doing what we can focuses our minds on what is possible, no more, no less, thereby filling each moment with conscious, practicable endeavor. And being who we are helps us reject the fool's gold of self-delusion. It also demands integrity—being straight with ourselves and others."

Church then turns these words on his own condition.

"Those who know my mantra sometimes test me with it. 'So Forrest, do you really want cancer?' 'I want what I have,' I reply. 'To selectively eliminate all pain from our lives may work, for a brief time, for a drunkard or a drug addict, but we cannot wish away all that is wrong with us without including all that is right.' Each day that I am sick, I pray for the sun to come up, for people to love me, for manageable tasks that I can still accomplish, for a little extra courage . . . In short, I back away from the bedarkened pane of my health to gain a prospect of the whole window I am blessed to look through. The light then dances in my daughter,

Nina's, eyes. I laugh once more at my little foibles. My son, Frank, and I celebrate the Mets' acquisition of an all-star pitcher. I call my dear friends, Jack Watson and Peter Fenn, on the phone and talk for an hour about everything under the sun.

"Yes, I kvetch at unseemly waits at the chemo center (until I realize how many other folks have cancer and are waiting in line for their treatment also). I fall into a sour humor when my body wears down and cannot do what I want it to do (until I shift gears and tackle something that falls well within my powers, like a moderately difficult sudoku or one of Robin Hobbs's splendid fantasy novels, where almost every character is doing worse than I am). I even snap at my wife, Carolyn, when she tries too hard to fatten me up for the kill. But that, too, eventually is good for a laugh. So I do want what I have, even as I do what I can . . . Pray for the right things, and your prayers will be answered."[39]

Forrest Church was not praying to stay alive indefinitely. That wasn't the bargain. He was dying, but he was alive as never before—demonstrating for others how to live, fully and deeply, no matter how many years or months they had left.

For this irrepressible writer nearing the end, being alive meant gathering his strength and publishing one more book. If *Love and Death* put a capstone on Church's pastoral meditations, *The Cathedral of the World: A Universalist Theology* collected excerpts, sometimes reworked slightly, from books, sermons, and essays to produce a comprehensive overview of his theology. In the first half of the book, however—a miscellany of reflections drawn from *God and Other Famous Liberals*, *The American Creed*, and other sources—theology per se is often absent. Church attacks the war in Iraq as misguided nationalism run amok, laments the continuing danger of nuclear war, and warns against the false idolatry of turning churches into political institutions in disguise.

In the second half, Church's theology takes center stage. It begins in awe and humility before the grand spectacle of the universe and ends in the transforming power of love as antidote to death. It is shaped further by the twin strands of Unitarianism and Universalism. This legacy, in his familiar cathedral metaphor, translates into "one light, many windows." Furthermore, he urges rationalists to open up to the realm of the transrational, "powers so beyond our control and understanding as to be unimaginable," and to the possibility of God, however defined. As a Universalist, the only religious claims he discounts entirely are those that claim an exclusive path to truth or that fail the ethical test of good behavior.[40]

Always open-minded and intellectually grounded, Church's thinking about God evolved over time. As a student, he was more dispassionate outside observer than believer. Later he gravitated toward Tillich's concept of "the ground of our being." Eventually, he balanced this abstraction with an embrace of Emersonian transcendentalism. However misguided the "sovereign individualism" of "Self-Reliance," Emerson's theology of the interdependent web of existence is inspiring. For the essayist and poet, deity existed everywhere: "Heaven walks among us ordinarily muffled in such triple or tenfold disguises that the wisest are deceived and no one suspects the days to be gods." Echoing the Sage of Concord, Church writes, "Theologians are wise to close their learned tomes at times and reopen the book of nature."

Yet Church emerges as no wide-eyed sentimentalist. His transcendentalism coexists with a worldview rooted in the Christianity that gave rise to Unitarianism and Universalism. For one thing, he believes in the pervasive reality of evil: "If you don't like the word 'sin,' substitute another—'humankind's innate humanity,' perhaps—but don't underestimate the concept, or think that we are all born good and then somehow get destroyed or twisted by society . . . sin is bred in the human bone." Similarly, he is comfortable espousing what might be called an updated "soft trinitarianism"—"God above us, God within us, and God among us." Freely interpreted, like this, the ancient doctrine seems to him "more suggestive of God's possible nature" than "undifferentiated oneness." Finally, grounding his ethics in the wisdom teachings of Jesus, Church's blueprint for Christian Universalism is complete.[41]

On the back of the book, the writer's champions proclaimed his importance in our national life. According to Episcopalian Bishop John Shelby Spong, he was "one of America's most gifted clergymen." In the estimation of Princeton's Cornel West, he stood as "a towering public intellectual." Gary Dorrien, Reinhold Niebuhr professor of social ethics at Union Theological Seminary, pronounced him "the leading Unitarian Universalist theologian of our time."

Twelve

The Measure of a Man

He invented his own space. He tended his own garden
and he tended it very well.

—REV. PETER GOMES

orrest Church was a protean figure, inhabiting the roles of pastor, public intellectual, and theologian with uncommon ability. In the three decades from 1980 through 2010, there was no major American religious figure quite like him.

Consider the era's other popular writers on religion. He was not a professor, like Cornel West, Harvey Cox, or Elaine Pagels. His books plumbed the depths in ways that Robert Fulghum's never did. Unlike Peter Gomes at Harvard, he did not serve as a university chaplain. Unlike Jim Wallis, on the religious left, or Rick Warren, on the religious right, he was not an Evangelical. He was not Jewish, like Rabbi Harold S. Kushner. He declined to stir the pot à la Bishop Spong, notorious for contending that Jesus might have been married and Saint Paul gay. Like Garry Wills, he did write knowledgeably about religion, politics, and history. But Wills was no clergyman.

In truth, Forrest Church was one of a kind. "He invented his own space," Gomes observed. "He tended his own garden and he tended it very well."[1] This space, this garden was akin to that occupied by his nineteenth-century Unitarian forebears, in particular William Ellery Channing, the man who seeded the creation of All Souls Church in New York in 1819. A learned, bookish man, Channing stepped into the pulpit every Sunday to transform himself into the most eloquent of preachers. His gracious personality made him, in a biographer's phrase, "a superbly civilized controversialist." Only gradually, reluctantly, and against his moderate, even-handed temperament, did Channing shake off his proper Bostonian manner to emerge, in his last years, as a stirring moral champion of abolitionism. For doing so, he drew flak from both sides of the debate on slavery.[2]

The times would not permit Forrest Church to be the next William Sloan Coffin. Nor would his personality. Instead of manning the barricades, he wrote books and preached graceful sermons. These were his weapons of choice. Eight of those sermons and addresses were included in the annual anthology *Representative American Speeches*. A liberal in an overwhelmingly conservative era, he fought unceasingly to take back Bible and flag from the religious right and to ensure the separation of church and state. This was a daunting task, one that continues as membership in conservative Christian denominations rises, that of liberal denominations declines, and too many political liberals turn their backs on religion altogether. Still, Rabbi Kushner noted, "He made sure that everybody in America knew that the perspective of the Falwells and Pat Robertsons was not the only religious view."[3]

Church reinvented Channing's learned ministry for the age of electronic media. He was as sharp and poised under questioning by TV and radio interviewers as he was on the printed page. "Superbly civilized," he was the pastor who warned fellow liberals not to sneer at fundamentalists but to try to understand their underlying cultural anxieties.

There were many different writers named Forrest Church. Sermon writer, newspaper columnist, anthologist, essayist, author of inspirational books, self-help writer, theologian, and historian—he lived all of these roles. Some, of course, fit better than others. Chalk up self-help writer as a failure, but otherwise his versatile excellence amazed. Whatever the genre, the prose flowed with sinuous, enticing ease. He had a gift for the telling metaphor that clarified complex ideas, for the witty turn of phrase that drew in a reluctant reader. Much of the prose, as originally composed, was incredibly taut. Only occasionally did the preacher within— "phrases piled upon phrases" in "a cascading quality," noted *UU World*'s editor, Christopher Walton—have to be reined in.[4]

His gift for storytelling and lucid prose could well have translated into national recognition as a newspaper columnist. Had he lived longer, his skills as historian of the intersection of religion and politics in U.S. history would have cemented his prominence. As it was, his best books should have an enduring shelf life. *A Chosen Faith*, co-written with John Buehrens, remains the indispensable guide to Unitarian Universalism. Seminary students find their way into a great theologian via *The Essential Tillich*. Out of the author's real-life struggles, *Bringing God Home* creates an accessible and deeply felt liberal theology. *The American Creed* seizes the historically accurate high ground in our collective narrative, above the barrens of religious and secular obscurantism. *So Help Me God* is a landmark in its field, and the gems of his pastoral theology, *Life Lines* and *Love and Death*, take the dross of human suffering and transmute it into the gold of empathetic inspiration.

"He didn't know who he wanted to be," Tim Bent believed, while acknowledging Church's desire to excel at each of those genres. "I worried sometimes that he published too much," Bent said. "From the publishing point of view, a scarce commodity is not a bad thing."

"A lot of writers approach the task of writing a book with a little bit more fear," said Helene Atwan, publisher of the Beacon Press. "Forrest was totally fearless; nothing daunted him. He had a little touch of hypergraphia, you know, the disease of wanting to write all the time."[5]

He wrote fifteen books (not counting the early and privately published *Born Again Unitarian Universalism*) and edited ten more. If this was a manifestation of addictive behavior, every writing project nonetheless originated in response to a specific occasion. Forrest Church often quipped that he had never "committed a bestseller," as though to do so were a sin. But his friends and editors knew that he yearned for his books to break out of the pack, to make an indelible impact on the national conversation. That goal arose not only from personal ambition but also, as Bent observed, from Church's feeling that "he had a kind of mission" to make his views on liberal religion and church-state relations not only heard but widely accepted.[6]

Church's core constituency, of course, was among Unitarian Universalists. Whatever his stature in the larger national arena, he was unquestionably the leading UU voice of his generation. Taking the long view, he feared that his denomination had backed itself into a historical dead end, marginalized itself from the religious mainstream. His strategy, instead, was two-pronged. Toward his co-religionists, he exhorted a spirit of genuine openness toward people they might define as "Other." Try to fathom the insecurity that drives the fundamentalist Christian, he urged. Don't isolate yourselves, out of pride and self-righteousness, from other religious communities. And don't create a false idol out of progressive politics. The search for justice, he reminded UUs, ought to emerge from deeper religious-philosophical premises than those of the Democratic National Committee or *The Huffington Post*.

Second, Church spearheaded the movement to "remythologize" a Unitarian faith grown too cerebral and anti-theological. He was not the only leader in this regard, but his books and speeches were the most noteworthy expressions of the reaffirmation of God language in the denomination. "There's been no theological voice in Unitarian Universalism in the last twenty-five years or more," according to former UUA president John Buehrens, "who has done more to help push Unitarian Universalism in the direction of a deeper spirituality."

From the other side of the divide, humanists were in transition, too, absorbing an enriched sense of spirituality, often springing from a kind of deep ecology. A devotion to Mother Earth could well pave the way to some idea of Mother God. Humanists were increasingly willing to acknowledge that some things were simply ineffable and inestimable, and that they, too, were part of the religious experience. "Part of Forrest's genius," noted Buehrens's predecessor William Schulz, "is that it was very difficult to label him. He was an especially effective bridge builder among all the varieties of theology. He certainly was comfortable with 'God talk.' But at the same time his understanding of God and religion was far broader than any traditional theistic notions. He did so in a way that humanists, even outright atheists, could respond to, feel comfortable with, and translate in ways that are meaningful to them."[7]

Early on, Church developed an aphoristic style. Initially, it was employed in the service of wit. His bons mots poked holes in outdated ideas and enlivened newspaper columns. But the style took on greater substance when it memorably defined basic terms of theological engagement. "One of the great strengths of Christianity," he said, "is that if you ask a person what he believes, he says, 'I believe in Christ being crucified. I believe in the Father, Son, and Holy Spirit'—a whole series of mantras that give you definitions of your faith. For Unitarian Universalism or any kind of liberal religion, those mantras are missing, and if you can believe in anything you end up believing more often in nothing. And so part of my very self-conscious goal was to give people some touchstones by which to live."

And so he did:

"Religion is our human response to the dual reality of being alive and having to die."

"The goal of life is to live in such a way that our lives will prove worth dying for."

"God is not God's name. God is our name for that which is greater than all and yet present in each."

"Want what you have. Do what you can. Be who you are."

This was vibrant religion, more meaningful than systematic theology or metaphysical argument. It emerged from his intellect, but it was grounded in everyday involvement with a congregation. His parishioners' struggles and sorrows taught him as much as any book. And his affirmation of the transrational led him beyond mere reason. Since, as he wrote, "poets and storytellers touch me more than theologians do," he was inevitably drawn to metaphor to explain his sense of the divine.

If God was "that which is greater than all and yet present in each," he likened it to a three-dimensional hologram—laser recordings of images on a photo plate made of thousands of tiny lenses.

"This was Forrest's favorite analogy for divine reflexivity and transcendence," Gary Dorrien observed. "A single shard of a shattered photo plate contains the plate's entire image, just as each cell contains the full genetic coding for a person's entire being. The hologram suggests God's reflexive nature in a way that transforms our relationships with the divine and each other: 'Spun out of star-stuff, illumined by God, we participate in the miracle that we ponder.'"

Above all, Church linked an updated Emersonian transcendentalism with a tragic sense of life. The bounty of life was to be savored, precisely because it was finite and bounded by suffering. Human love, extended freely, gave expression to the God within, and, like God, would surely outlive us. Dorrien again: "Emerson had no doctrine, Forrest stressed; the deeper he got into something, the more metaphorical he became, to his credit. Emerson grasped that religious truth is like the truth of poetry, and he had a home in the universe 'because the universal God dwelled in his mind and heart.'"[8]

Despite his achievements, Forrest Church never quite reached the mountaintop of his aspirations. In another era, his talents might have carried him to greater renown. But he was fated to live at a time of conservative ascendancy, when his ideological opponents reigned over both church and state. For many Americans, the very word *liberal* was suspect. So this unabashed champion of liberal religion and liberal politics was continually forced to fight a rearguard action. What's more, his institutional base was a tiny denomination under the radar of his countrymen. Given a more prominent bully pulpit—say, New York City's Riverside Church or Harvard's Memorial Church—he might have enjoyed a higher profile. Perhaps, too, his dizzying number of disparate books confused readers and critics about his central mission, or his views were too nuanced. Extremists grab attention, even when they are wrong. Finally, his messy divorce rendered him suspect, at a crucial moment in his career, even within some liberal circles.

Just as his thinking about religion often turned on paradox, Forrest Church embodied paradox. A very public man, he was at bottom shy, a preacher most at home alone with a book. He took infinite care with things he cared about, like his writing, but was infinitely impatient with things that bored him, like administrative detail. (Thank God for church administrators and associate ministers!) People who did not know him well saw in him an enormous ego. Better put, he had an expansive ego, based on confidence in his outsized talents, yet balanced by shyness, kindness, good manners, and worry that his latest book wasn't quite good enough. He wrote thousands of thank-you notes by hand. Though he didn't suffer fools gladly, his disarming charm proved capable of keeping them at arm's length. Aware of his own great gifts, he appreciated and cultivated them in others. A great talker, he could spin out a topic for hours. Often, his dialogues amounted to monologues in disguise. He loved to tell stories that put him in the fool's garb, while delighted to be the story's object.

As a thinker, Robert Oxnam noted, he inhabited "that remarkable world that is self" while admitting into that world a whirlwind of ideas. Oxnam compared the process to hitting a ball against the walls of a squash court. "The idea hit this wall, then that wall and the next. He could make that linkage."[9] This was the serial enthusiast in microcosm, not simply jumping from one perception to another, but learning something from each and connecting them into a fresh, new idea.

Anyone who encountered Church was immediately struck by his exuberance. Radiating an endless stream of energy, optimism, and good cheer, he claimed that he was "born sunny-side up." There was a good deal of truth in this, but underneath lay a powerful undercurrent of anxiety, often unacknowledged and medicated for decades by heavy drinking. As the son of a well-known U.S. senator, he was born with a proverbial silver spoon in his mouth. He shamelessly trumpeted this fact throughout his life, dropping Frank Church's name into countless sermons and books. But being the son of a famous father can be as much burden as advantage. As Kurt Vonnegut's son, Mark, observed, "In general people don't wish the children of famous people well. It's somehow fitting that we screw up or come to tragic ends."[10] Far from screwing up, Forrest Church parlayed this head start into an outstanding career of his own. Yet in the final pages of *Love and Death*, we find these haunting words:

"To one who ranks humility first among all virtues, perhaps the best thing about having a famous father is that almost nothing I accomplished would ever, in the world's eye at least, measure up. As soon as I shifted my feet from my father's ground to my own, I stopped competing with him, but I certainly never ran the danger of surpassing him. That, blessedly I think, has made all my own successes seem modest ones. Yet, I don't in the least look back on a life somehow incomplete or unrealized. Be who you are, I remind myself. I was. And I am."[11]

Why bring this comparison up near his life's end? Because, despite the mantra, it still mattered. Forrest Church couldn't leave the tape measure in the drawer. The inner voice asserting "good enough" still battled the voice taunting "not enough." Despite all the books and scores of accolades, this central theme of his first book, *Father and Son*, remained as powerful as ever.

To his credit, Church belatedly realized that his son bore a similar burden and tried his best to ease it. As a young man, he admitted, he had been an inattentive father, his reading and writing often walling himself off from his wife and children. When Frank was young, he had trouble accepting the reality of his physical and emotional problems, and the alienation between father and son kept them at a distance for years. After the cancer diagnosis, however, Church bought season tickets to Mets games so that he and Frank could cheer on their favorite baseball team together. He took to reading the fantasy novels that Frank loved. He learned to listen to him. But he never stopped worrying about him.

Church and Rev. Bill Grimbol, whose son had developed a drinking problem after his mother died in middle age, often discussed the state of their troubled children. Rev. Grimbol, who ran a teen center on Shelter Island and had written books for adolescents, proved a wise counselor on the subject of parent-child relationships. Having gotten to know Frank reasonably well, he could act as Frank's interpreter to Church. Frank's message to his father, Grimbol deduced, was this: "Dad, I'm going to love you, not worship you. That love is going to include that you piss me off and you make me angry and you disappoint me. I don't have to agree with you on everything. I'm not carved in your image, nor do I want to be . . . Love me for exactly who I am." This message, of course, was similar to Church's own message to his father.

Even as Frank became an adult, their relationship continued to be defined by tension between love and anxiety. One summer, while Grimbol was at Church's home on the island, Frank, now well into his twenties, rowed a kayak far out into the bay, disappearing into the horizon. Suddenly, the air exploded with the rumble of thunder, and heavy winds churned up the water. "Within about ten minutes, the rain was becoming horizontal in sheets. Everyone was trying to stay calm," Grimbol remembered. "But Forrest became like a Canadian Mountie, pacing with these binoculars until he finally yelled out, 'I've found him!' He could see him. He never let that kid out of his sight until that kayak touched shore. I thought, that is what he feels: My job is to bring this kid home. That became his job, overall, with Frank."[12]

An imperfect father, Forrest Church grew into a good-enough one.

He was an extraordinary speaker and writer, an impassioned champion of liberal religion, an essential public intellectual, a man who gave love as freely as he needed it given to him.

But perhaps his most lasting legacy was to demonstrate how to die with grace and dignity.

Thirteen

Love and Death

To be blessed in death, we must learn to live.

—PHILIPPE DE MORNAY

On February 3, 2008, Forrest Church shocked his congregation. They had dared to hope that his cancer might be in permanent remission. But now it had returned and spread to his liver and lungs.

"There is no way to sugarcoat the news," his letter informed parishioners who may have missed his sermon of the same date. "I shall undergo a regimen of chemotherapy, more for palliative than curative reasons, but must face the certainty that my cancer is terminal and the great likelihood that my future will be measured in months not years.

"You have accompanied me on this journey from its beginning. What a comfort that has been. In matters of mortality, we are all companions (the word means 'break bread together'). From its very beginning, our repast has been a feast.

"In more than one respect, I feel very lucky. In the fall of 2006, my family had a dress rehearsal for the drama we now are entering in earnest. My wife, Carolyn, and our four children, Frank, Nina, Jacob, and Nathan, were able then to begin working through the complex feelings that always accompany the loss of a family member, especially a parent.

As for me, I have greeted every day since my reprieve (and shall the days to come) as gravy."[1]

Under the care of Dr. David Kelsen, chief of gastrointestinal oncology at Memorial Sloan-Kettering Cancer Center, Church began a weekly course of chemotherapy on February 12. He was enrolled in a clinical trial involving 250 patients nationwide, including 20 at Sloan-Kettering. They were given the experimental drug Erbitux manufactured by Im-Clone. "He is particularly pleased," Carolyn Buck Luce informed the congregation, "that he feels well enough to work on his book, read the bundles of wonderful notes and letters, play with the cats, and pass the time happily with our kids and close friends." Privately, Church also took a gleeful, ironic pleasure in noting that ImClone was the company where Martha Stewart's skulduggery had resulted in a prison sentence. She had been betting—he noted, as a way of forgiving her—on the very substance that was his current lifesaver.[2]

If he were as lucky as he hoped, however, life could be extended only nine to twelve months. Still, what person doesn't cherish a little more gravy? Aside from general weakness, which kept him lying down for hours, the major side effects of chemo were a sore mouth and neuropathy in the hands and feet (a lack of feeling caused by the dying of nerve endings). Eventually, the neuropathy would cause him to walk with a slight side-to-side wobble. His cheeks took on the bright hue of a fresh Macintosh apple. He was in no pain.

For maintaining his strength and minimizing the effects of chemo, Church relied on a secret weapon. "The steroids they give me to help me tolerate the chemo have me as strong and feisty as Roger Clemens," he e-mailed me after one of our interviews. "Up at two every morning writing. What a way to go!"[3]

As soon as Church received his fateful diagnosis, he resolved to write *Love and Death*. It was, of course, a book that he had been writing all his life. It not only braided together his past and present but beautifully encapsulated his pastoral theology. The process of writing organized his time and gave him purpose. A writer above all else, he would keep doing what he most loved until he could do it no longer. "I've got eighteen chapters polished into final draft form with only two to go!" he reported in the same e-mail. Just three weeks after beginning the project, he sent the finished manuscript to his publisher.

When Church was not writing, he read or listened to music. Since college days, classical music had plunged him into profundities beyond words, and it now provided consolation and buoyancy as he approached the mystery most defying human understanding.

"I'm a serial enthusiast," he said, "so one day I'll listen to all nine Bruckner symphonies, and one day all nine Mahler symphonies, and one day all seven Sibelius symphonies. I've got the complete Beethoven piano sonatas and string quartets. I'll go to Arvo Pärt and John Tavener when I want something meditative and just edgy enough to keep me alert. I have music on almost all the time. It's eighty percent background, twenty percent focused listening."[4]

Sometimes even steroids were no match for the draining effects of chemo. However sunny-side up his personality, his body told a different story. "Those days are just endured," he said. "I feel like I've been hit by a truck. I do my best to read."

For escape, Church turned to the fantasy novels recommended by his son, Frank, "The Wheel of Time" series by Robert Jordan and the epics of Robin Hobb and R. Scott Bakker. "I did it initially to relate to what he was interested in," he said. "Now I do it because I find it completely beguiling," with religious and philosophical themes encased in marvelous storytelling. Best of all, he said, "Everybody in the books is having a worse time than I am."[5]

In the spring, Michael Luce surprised Church with a letter warmly expressing his sympathy and commending him for being a good stepfather to his sons. "That was as generous as a person could be," Church said. "Mike is a very good man. I'm just deeply touched by this. It's part of this web of reconciliation that allows me to have no unfinished business as I face my death."[6]

Once a month, Church summoned the strength to preach at All Souls.

Love and death persisted as his central pulpit themes, but from time to time he also reported on how he was coping with cancer: "I try to resist the temptation to crouch in a defensive posture. After all, odds are that this will be my last spring, and I don't want to let it slip by unnoticed. I wish to honor it with my wonder. I wish to revel at its strangeness and glory . . . The chemo's going well, by the way. My tumors are shrinking. Time is being bought. The cancer is incurable, but it can be held at bay . . . Most of the time, I'm happy to report, I feel very much myself." And he publicly acknowledged his debt to steroids. "For two or three days after every treatment, I was flying . . . I haven't been so high since the late sixties!"[7]

The good news was that chemo was shrinking the tumors, but high spirits and humor could take Church only so far. He had read Gibbon's multivolume *Decline and Fall of the Roman Empire*, followed by Marguerite Yourcenar's *Memoirs of Hadrian*. In one passage in the Frenchwoman's great novel, the Roman emperor reflects on his triumphs and defeats: "Each of us has to choose, in the course of his brief life, between endless striving and wise resignation, between the delights of disorder and those of stability, between the Titan and the Olympian . . . To choose between them, or to succeed, at last, in bringing them into accord." These words, Church e-mailed me, "hit me right between the eyes and in a strange way summed up the psychic rhythms of my own life."[8]

Between endless striving and wise resignation Church forged a more supple middle ground based on his mantra. Want what you have. Do what you can. Be who you are. He was neither raging against the dying of the light nor spinelessly abandoning hope. He was living, as best he could, in the moment.

This discipline was never easy for him, and it could be even harder for the family. He and Carolyn spent Easter weekend at their Shelter Island home, the first time in nearly thirty years he was not in the pulpit on Easter Sunday. After returning from her morning jog, she confessed to her husband that her sobbing was so intense that she had to stop and collect herself three times. Ordinarily very calm and in control, Carolyn had been brought low in anticipation of grief.

Bethine Church called twice a day from Idaho, urging her son to be sure to eat. But under the impact of the disease, his appetite dwindled, and by early May he had shrunk from his normal 190 pounds to 140. In an effort to boost his weight, he subsisted on Big Macs, mashed potatoes, and macaroni and cheese. For the time being, none of it added a pound.[9]

Later that month, Church flew to Denver to join a celebration of his mother-in-law's eightieth birthday. His admiration for Minna Buck was boundless, and he enjoyed the round of parties. But the several days of intense activity strained his body. "Coming home was hell," he e-mailed me. "The destroying the village to save it project finally hit with full force." Back home, he endured the most harrowing ten days of his disease. "It felt terminal, really brutal," he said. He was exhausted and feverish, due, it turned out, to a declining white blood cell count. He was admitted to the hospital and had to be catheterized. Then the catheter didn't work and had to be reinserted several times.[10]

Nonetheless, Church was determined to attend the UUA's annual General Assembly, held this year in Fort Lauderdale, Florida. By late June, his strength revived by temporary suspension of chemo and timely administration of steroids, he could make the trip. Nothing was going to prevent Church from missing the next leg of his "victory lap," as his wife called it. It had begun in April when the Roosevelt Institute presented him with its highest accolade, the Franklin Delano Roosevelt Freedom Award, at a ceremony in Washington, D.C., where other awardees included writer Karen Armstrong and Germany's former president Richard von Weizsacker. In New York, All Souls honored him with a book party for *Love and Death*. As usual, the pastor was more noticeably upbeat than his parishioners, many of whom wore long faces, wondering if they would ever see him again.

The General Assembly amounted to a love feast. In the question-and-answer session after Church's speech at the UU Ministerial Association, one minister declared, "You're a bright beacon of hope and will be for a long time." Another said, "Your beauty and your dignity and your wisdom shine through." To a standing ovation, the Unitarian-related Meadville Lombard Theological School presented him with an honorary doctorate. (Starr King School for the Ministry had done the same earlier in the year.) Afterward, Church read an excerpt from *Love and Death*. It was a well-paced, radiant, commanding performance, by a man very much alive. After another standing ovation, Church tossed kisses to the crowd and departed.

His crowning moment of glory came the next day, before a huge assemblage gathered to see him receive the UUA's Distinguished Service Award. Once again, delegates rose to their feet to applaud "the most widely heard Unitarian Universalist voice of his generation." At a luncheon afterward, a few friends gathered for a round of more intimate toasts. William Schulz hailed his longtime friend this way: "I knew him when he was drinking and I've known him when he was sober. I have never seen much difference. He was always witty, self-effacing, and possessed of a core of authenticity . . . The truth is, Forrest does not suffer fools gladly. But he suffers them with such grace and tenderness that fools do not know that they have been suffered. He knows we are all fools . . . My dear friend, my friendly fool, this also is an opportunity to return that tenderness and grace that you have given us."[11]

What meant even more for Church than these public honors was being able to attend the wedding ceremony of his daughter, Nina. She had actually been legally married at City Hall a year before, because her British fiancé, Thomas John Adams, needed a green card, but the occasion on August 3 amid family and friends within the green oasis of the Brooklyn Botanic Garden felt something like a miracle. Church got not only to walk his daughter down the aisle but to enjoy the traditional father-daughter dance.

"Everybody sort of rose to the occasion," Church said. "We spent three days, starting on Friday, intentionally bringing all the families together—Amy and her family, her husband's, Carolyn's, mine, and

Tom's. There were some people I hadn't seen for twenty years, members of Amy's family. They just were gracious beyond belief. It was almost a sacramental occasion."[12]

At All Souls, the celebration continued into late September as the church paid homage to its beloved pastor on two counts. His sixtieth birthday coincided with the thirtieth anniversary of his arrival from Harvard. His sermon that day led the congregation on a brief tour through his tenure, while adding the usual quips.

"After two or three poignant farewell sermons," he said, "I'm almost embarrassed to be seen in public upright."

Afterward, the church social hall was festooned with balloons and huge posters bearing facsimiles of the covers of his many books. Sparkling wine flowed, speeches were offered, and tears were shed. Time seemed to be running out. Then the festivities, as if they were taking place in some mystery novel, were abruptly cut short. An anonymous caller had contacted the police, warning that someone was walking around the church holding a gun. The hall was evacuated, until police decided there was no threat and most likely a hoaxer was playing a prank. Many parishioners were unnerved. Church, interviewed later at home by a *New York Times* reporter, had no idea who might have wanted to disrupt the occasion. He preferred to focus on the two thousand letters he had received since announcing his illness and his plans to continue preaching as strength allowed.

"I feel I've done what I needed to do. I look back without regrets, and I look forward without fear. I've never been more at home in the present."[13]

Church refused to let the disease get in the way of media appearances. He wanted to get the word out about *Love and Death*. When Bob Abernethy interviewed him in October on public television's *Religion and Ethics Newsweekly*, Church offered his message in pithy maxims that underscored his upbeat temperament and offered consolation to the dying and their families. "I don't pray for miracles," he said. "I don't pray to cure my incurable cancer. I receive and consecrate each day that I'm given as a gift. I have no idea what happens after we die, and so I go with Henry David Thoreau, who, when he was asked about the afterlife, said, 'Madam, I prefer to take it one life at a time' . . . One of the beautiful things about a terminal illness [is that] your friendships become stronger. Your loved ones become more vital and more present. Each day becomes more beautiful. You unwrap the present and receive it as the gift it is. You walk through the valley of the shadow, and it's riddled with light."

On public radio's *Fresh Air* with Terry Gross, Church proved as articulate and genial a guest as always, but *The Diane Rehm Show*, with its Q-and-A format, allowed his pastoral skills to shine. To each caller with a story of terminal illness, he dispensed compassionate advice tailored to the individual situation. Afterward, he took time to respond to e-mails from listeners, including one man asking how his wife should balance fighting her ovarian cancer with preparing for death.

"For me, not to fight does not and must not mean to give up," Church e-mailed the man. "On the contrary, I embrace my life with more appreciation and affection than I ever have before. For your wife, to fight must not turn the possibility of a victory by death (who always eventually wins) into a defeat for her. I've seen too many cases of people who do not simply die, but are vanquished by death and feel that they have lost a struggle that, had they only done things perfectly, they would and should have won. Fighting death as a full time preoccupation squeezes out opportunities to embrace life, as it is, as it comes, as a miraculous gift."[14]

In November, Church reported to his congregation that his four tumors remained small, and no new ones had appeared. "Having well outlasted the actuarial average for stage 4 esophageal cancer," he wrote, "like a particularly interesting game of football my life is now being played out in overtime." He had also regained some of the weight lost since beginning Erbitux therapy. Having met the goals he had set for himself at the beginning of the year—his daughter married, *Love and Death* published, and his sixtieth birthday reached—his spirits soared.

But Church's friends were in mourning. They could see their companion fading away and couldn't deal with his future absence. When they visited, it was Church who had to cheer them up.[15]

To counter the gloom, Robert Oxnam suggested that a circle of Church's close friends gather on Shelter Island in mid-December. They called it their "frat party." They were a diverse group of men, from different phases of Church's life. Some did not know each other, but the bonding over a weekend, based on their common love of Church, proved so intense that they came away with deep affection for one another. Peter Fenn, a Washington political consultant and frequent sparring partner of Pat Buchanan, the conservative pundit, on MSNBC, had known him since ninth grade. His Stanford classmate Patrick Shea later worked on Senator Church's staff, served as head of the Bureau of Land Management under President Clinton, and ran for the governorship and U.S. Senate in Utah. From Boise came Stanley Zuckerman, a psychoanalyst who had known Church since campaigning for his father in the late sixties. Oxnam, the China scholar who had presided over the Asia Society, was the only New Yorker. Jack Watson, once President Carter's chief of staff, a friend of Church via the Roosevelt Institute board, came all the way from his retirement home in Mexico.

Though each of the men realized that this was probably the only time they would all be together, they chose not to talk about that. Instead, they plunged into conversation about the political implications of Obama's historic victory, about Watson's jungle-fighting training with the Marines, about cutting-edge developments in science, about the Andrew Jackson biography Church had just read. They took long walks. They laughed a lot. They snapped photos of one another. Church took the occasional nap, or stretched out on a couch to rest. No time was spent watching sports, a rarity at male gatherings. Church coaxed them into playing Monopoly, then giggled with delight when he won.

"His mood was elated for most of the time," Zuckerman said. "It felt like he was kind of feeling, 'They're having a special party for *me*?!'

There was a positive feel to it right from the beginning through the end. Why drown in misery and sorrow?"

After Saturday dinner, Church, who was perhaps Amazon.com's best customer, gave each man a gift of two books. But the weekend's emotional climax came when Oxnam presented Church with an exquisite drawing of the Chinese character for friendship—two half moons reflecting each other's light. Created by a famous calligrapher on heavy paper speckled with gold, the artwork had room in the white space below, where each of the men inscribed a few sentences to their beloved friend. "I've only seen Forrest begin to cry three times in his life. That was one," said Oxnam.[16]

By January 2009, according to the doctors' odds, Church was about to die. He was surely dying—there was no stopping the long-term process—but death itself hardly seemed imminent. Buoyed by the embrace of family, friends, and the people of All Souls, he felt blessed. Still joking that he was embarrassed to be seen standing upright, he continued to preach once a month. He read Dickens novels, *Ivanhoe*, and presidential biographies. Music offered its soothing balm. There were good days and bad, but his spirits remained high.

To feel his exuberant self, all a stranger had to do was hear him in a public radio broadcast that month on *Prime Time Radio*. The AARP-produced show often ran interviews with authors of books of interest to its aging constituency. But AARP's producers felt that *Love and Death* was such rich material and its author such a winning personality that they decided, in addition, to create a series of videos based on it for the AARP Web site. *The Forrest Church Diaries: A Good Life to the End* grew out of conversations, begun in January and conducted weekly for several months, between Church and Carl Lehmann-Haupt, a New York–based graphic designer and writer. In seven videos, a camera pans over Church family photos and a soundtrack pulses reverently in the background, while the author, in a voice-over, talks about dealing with terminal illness. Church's voice is vibrant. He exudes warmth and compassion. Between bits of wisdom, he chuckles a bit, with Dalai Lama–like giddiness. Each video, released between October and December 2009, followed by an epilogue in June 2010, is only about five minutes long, but the cumulative effect is an inspiring, artful distillation of *Love and Death*.[17]

"Acceptance [of death] at one level has a flat meaning, letting go, let it be," he said. "I want my acceptance to be an embrace . . . You have to define what dying well means. For me, it's going gentle into that night."[18]

Going gently, however, could nonetheless feel like a roller-coaster ride. The highs were high, indeed. Years before, All Souls had shifted from in-house fund-raising for its community-outreach programs to a legally separate Heart and Soul Charitable Fund, with a high-profile auction usually held at Christie's. In February 2009, a beaming Church presented the fund's first annual Forrest Church Award for Humanitarian Service to former president Bill Clinton, who responded with a glowing endorsement of *Love and Death*. (Harvard Divinity School already was awarding an annual scholarship in his name, and later the annual Forrest Church Lectures in Liberal Religion and Politics would be established at Union Theological Seminary.) And in April, Church traveled to a black-tie gala in Washington, hosted by NBC's Chris Matthews, to receive the Buchwald Spirit Award for Public Awareness from the National Hospice Foundation for "inspiring millions through his latest book." Foundation trustees regarded *Love and Death* so highly that they bought five hundred copies for circulation among hospice leaders in every state.[19]

Still, Church admitted privately, chemo sometimes did "knock the wind out of me. About half the time, it doesn't matter since I'm not running any races. I lie down, I read." Then there were his teeth, rotting and turning brown, another victim of his chemo. "Finally I said, 'Geez, I'm going to outlive this. I'm going to look like John Adams with pointed teeth and whistle when I talk. I'm not going to do that.'" That he should get his teeth fixed to avoid a life-threatening infection seemed a ridiculous example of expensive American medicine needlessly prolonging life, but he agreed, after prodding by his wife, to begin the necessary dental work.[20]

In April, Church learned that the Erbitux therapy was no longer effective. His tumors, though small, were once again growing. From this point, he would be treated with a more conventional chemo cocktail. To his congregation, however, he insisted that his spirits were "splendid." That was especially so because he had just sent a completed, revised manuscript of *The Cathedral of the World* to his publisher. "It will be out in October. Reason for another party!"[21]

If the public face beamed, the private one possessed a candor and realism Church did not choose to share freely. "I can hear the clock ticking again," he told me a few weeks later. "There is a fatalism that has moved into the background. That was almost completely absent during that pink cloud time where time sort of stopped and eternity was almost always there for me to reach into."

He was certainly delighted that he had time to publish his final three books. Each brought a satisfying coda to his writing career, as historian, pastor, and theologian. But what troubled him deeply was an inability to console his wife:

"I don't feel sad and Carolyn does," he told me in May. "I feel a glow; I feel a fulfillment; I feel a rightness about everything, a deep and fundamental affirmation of being itself and my participation in it. She is understandably sad, and that places her in a situation where she will wall herself off a little bit because she wants to protect herself. It causes a distance which we both consciously work to bridge. And when we bridge it, we're even closer than before."[22]

On May 31, Church delivered his final sermon. Titled "The Summer of Our Content," it was surprisingly more scholarly, less emotion-laden than usual. At the close of the service, he was too weak to walk to the back of the sanctuary and shake hands, as he usually did. So he departed via a door at the front. As he left, he blew a kiss to the congregation. For most members of All Souls, this was the last glimpse of their minister.

A week later, he told me that he couldn't undertake his chemo "because my immune system is down to nothing. I don't have any energy at all."

After the success of the December "frat party," Church and his friends had hoped to reprise the gathering. The plan, to meet in the summer of 2009 at Watson's retirement city of San Miguel de Allende, depended, of course, on an optimistic forecast of Church's health. It did not happen. "I'm not able to hack it, I'm afraid," he e-mailed me in mid-July.

What he could hack, for the time being, was reading and listening to music. But he knew that eventually the disease would make even reading difficult. Music alone would accompany him on the final stages of his journey. But he turned this wish into another project; he didn't want to waste any precious time; he wanted to listen to nothing but the best, and he wanted to understand its context. So he called on the expertise of his friend from forty years before at Pacific School of Religion. From Bangkok, music critic Tim Pfaff e-mailed suggestions for CDs and books that would provide background information about composers and musical eras.

"I've set myself up with a crash refresher course from Mozart to [John] Adams," he e-mailed me, "building, for the first time systematically, on the knowledge base I had laid by the time I was 22 . . . I'm also selecting, slowly, the pieces I want to have on in the background when . . . the music will penetrate to my psyche even should I no longer be able actively to communicate."

Church's commitment to stay the course had its odd, mind-bending moments, too. A few weeks after this message came another: "I'm thinking seriously, by the way, of starting another book (*Overtime: Finding Meaning When Life Goes into Extra Innings*). Can't keep an old dog down I guess!" The will was there, no matter how recalcitrant the body.[23]

In early August, Church was able to fly to Boise to bid farewell to Idahoans he had known for decades. By the end of the month, however, he wrote to his congregation one more time: "After a magnificent three years enjoying a seemingly effortless high-wire act over the valley of the shadow, these past two weeks everything seems to be unraveling. A CT scan revealed that my second chemo treatment has failed, with the tumors in my liver in particular both multiplying and growing rapidly. I also have a new, extensive tumor in my throat . . . Death may approach silently on tiny cats' paws or sweep our loved ones (or us) away like a thief in the night. Hence, with our loved ones especially, we should never squander the opportunity when signing a letter, before setting the phone back in its cradle, or from the kitchen or bedroom before the front door slams shut of writing, speaking, or shouting out, 'I love you.' "[24]

On Labor Day weekend, Robert Oxnam, his wife, Vishakha, and her sister Chitra, visiting from India, were invited to dinner with Church and Buck Luce at their Shelter Island home. During the evening, Church lurched between bright attentiveness and nodding off. When Chitra asked him about his basic religious beliefs, Oxnam thought, "Oh God, is he up to this?" But Church shot up ramrod straight and talked about "love, death, and everything in between in a kind of semivigorous sort of distillation of his theology." Then he returned to the couch to doze. Up again later, he took Oxnam aside and said, "It's not far away. I'm going fast."[25]

By 2009, after surviving various degrees of adolescent angst, each of the Church and Luce offspring was carving out a healthy young adulthood. A graduate of Reed College, Jacob Luce served in Mayor Michael Bloomberg's administration. His younger brother, Nathan, was enrolled in a Colorado State University program combining his interests in ecology and business. Nina Church had graduated from Georgetown and was a small-business account manager for American Express in Manhattan. Frank Church, having completed a program at the French Culinary Institute in Manhattan, worked as a chef.[26]

Carolyn Buck Luce, a senior partner at Ernst & Young, had become enormously successful in business. She was one of the speakers, for example, at *Fortune* magazine's Most Powerful Women Summit at Pasadena in 2005. But she was increasingly focused on philanthropy and research on behalf of women. She served on the boards of the New York City Commission on Women's Issues and the New York Women's Foundation, a nonprofit whose goal is "sustained economic security and justice for women and girls." At Columbia University's School of International and Public Affairs, she taught a course, "Women and Power." With economist (and All Souls member) Sylvia Ann Hewlett, she co-wrote articles for the *Harvard Business Review*, including "Off-Ramps and On-Ramps: Keeping Talented Women on the Road to Success" and "Stopping the Exodus of Women in Science."[27]

Michael Luce, her ex-husband, moved to Alabama in the nineties, remarried, converted to Catholicism, and fathered more children. The former Bear Stearns executive became president of Harbert Management, an international investment management company based in Birmingham.[28]

Amy Furth returned to California in the late nineties. As noted earlier, she married Dennis MacDonald, a professor of the New Testament at Claremont School of Theology, whom she and Forrest had known at Harvard Divinity School. A minister ordained in the United Church of Christ, she now worked as a supervisor of hospital chaplains.

By September 12, Forrest Church had become weak and disoriented, and he had trouble breathing. He was admitted to the intensive-care unit of Memorial Sloan-Kettering and given a feeding tube and an oxygen mask. Morphine was administered to deal with his pain. When he was able, he listened to the music of Bob Dylan. Family members and friends came daily to comfort him, but gradually the conversations grew one-sided. As a tumor invaded and strangled his throat, one of the most gifted speakers of his day was deprived of his eloquence. The sounds issuing from "the man who made us feel good, better than we did before he spoke to us," according to one parishioner who visited him in the hospital, were no longer intelligible.

Still, there were tender moments beyond speech. "I put my hand on his, and he put his other hand on top," Robert Oxnam remembered. "And then I pulled out mine and put it on top of his. We were like little kids in a sandbox."

One afternoon, a new nurse approached Church's bedside. Somehow he communicated to her that he was a minister and author. "Our son Jacob happened to have a copy of *Love and Death* with him, and Forrest signed it for her," Buck Luce wrote. "It was the last time he wrote his name; but instead of his normal inscription, he wrote: 'With thanks and gratitude for the kindness and valor of your service. With love. Forrest.' After he gave her the book, she walked away but came back ten minutes later in tears. She told us that the book was a great gift, a turning point. One year earlier, she had given birth to twins who died within the day. She was hospitalized, close to death for a month. 'I have not been back in church since because I didn't think there was a God. I think I will go back now,' she said. Nina, Jake, Forrest, and I held her hands and we all cried."[30]

Forrest Church wanted to die at home. About one o'clock on the afternoon of September 24, the day after his sixty-first birthday, he was brought back to the apartment on East Eightieth Street overlooking the steeple of All Souls Church. He was surrounded by family members, his mother and mother-in-law, and a few close friends. He was apparently in no pain, but could not speak and labored to breathe. Robert Oxnam shaved his face and trimmed his beard. Buck Luce cradled his head and sometimes crawled in bed with him. To her husband, she kept up a steady, gentle stream of "It's OK, it's OK." She played a recording of one of Church's favorite songs, Tracy Chapman's "Change."

Just before Church died, about six o'clock, Buck Luce shouted, "God bless Forrest Church!" And then he stopped breathing. "My immediate reaction," she told an AARP interviewer later, "was to start clapping. And then everyone started to applaud. It just seemed like the right thing to do."[31]

Church's life and legacy were honored at a memorial service at All Souls on October 2. So many people came to pay homage that it was beamed by closed-circuit television into the church's social hall and chapel and to additional mourners gathered at a nearby synagogue. Those unable to attend could watch via live video stream on the All Souls Web site.

Some of Church's ashes were buried not far from his father's grave in

Morris Hill Cemetery in Boise. The rest were buried in the yard of the Church–Buck Luce home on Shelter Island. Over them, Buck Luce erected a flagpole bearing the American flag, a gift from Senator Kirsten Gillibrand, which had flown atop the U.S. Capitol on the day of Forrest Church's last birthday.[32]

NOTES

ONE: FREE-RANGE KID

1. The following account is drawn from Bethine Church, *A Lifelong Affair: My Passion for People and Politics* (Washington, DC: Francis Press, 2003), 64–74.
2. Author interview, Forrest Church, New York City, Feb. 6, 2008. (All interviews conducted by author, except as noted; all interviews conducted in New York City, except as noted.)
3. Genealogical Record of Frank Forrester Church [III], prepared by the Church of Jesus Christ of Latter-Day Saints, undated; genealogical charts of Clark family, undated; Nathaniel Philbrick, *Mayflower: A Story of Courage, Community, and War* (New York: Viking, 2006), 32–33, 79–89, 102, 163–68, 319–37, 357–58.
4. LeRoy Ashby and Rod Gramer, *Fighting the Odds: The Life of Senator Frank Church* (Pullman, WA: Washington State University Press, 1994), 11; Church, *Lifelong Affair*, 3–18, 28; F. Forrester Church, *Father and Son: A Personal Biography of Senator Frank Church of Idaho by His Son F. Forrester Church* (New York: Harper & Row, 1985), 14–20.
5. Ashby and Gramer, *Fighting the Odds*, 1–13.
6. Ibid., 5, 11, 16–34; Church, *Lifelong Affair*, 26–55.
7. U.S. Census, 1950, cited in Idaho State Historical Society Reference Series, Boise City and Urban Population, 1863–1980, no. 363, revised 1995; Merle Wells and Arthur A. Hart, *Boise: An Illustrated History* (Sun Valley, CA: American Historical Press, 2000), 113; Beirne Lay Jr., "The Cities of America: Boise," *Saturday Evening Post*, Jan. 18, 1947, 22–23, 109–11.

8. John Gerassi, *The Boys of Boise: Furor, Vice, and Folly in an American City* (New York: Macmillan, 1966; Seattle: University of Washington Press, 2001), 29–67, 176–79. Citations are to the Washington edition.

9. Ibid., 63–64, 23, 173.

10. Church, *Lifelong Affair*, 76.

11. Church, *Father and Son*, 34; interview, Forrest Church, Feb. 6, 2008; interview, Bethine Church, Boise, ID, April 15, 2008.

12. Interview, Forrest Church, Feb. 6, 2008.

13. Ibid.; Roosevelt School report cards, 1954–55 and 1955–56; interview, Bethine Church, April 15, 2008.

14. Ashby and Gramer, *Fighting the Odds*, 41–68.

15. Grade report cards, Roosevelt School (Boise) and Radnor School (Bethesda, MD), 1954–1963.

16. Interview, Forrest Church, Feb. 6, 2008.

17. Church, *Father and Son*, 41–42.

18. Church, *Lifelong Affair*, 112–13.

19. Interview, Bethine Church, April 15, 2008.

20. Church, *Lifelong Affair*, 88–92.

21. Forrest Church, *Bringing God Home: A Traveler's Guide* (New York: St. Martin's Press, 2002), 35–37.

22. LeRoy Ashby interview with Peter Fenn, Aug. 8, 1984, Frank Church Papers, Boise State University; Rod Gramer interview with Carl Burke, May 23, 1979, Frank Church Papers, Boise State; interview with Forrest Church, June 9, 2009.

23. Interview, Forrest Church, Feb. 6, 2008.

24. Telephone interviews, Jane Fairweather, Feb. 2, 2009; William Offutt, Jan. 31, 2009. The former is a veteran Bethesda real estate agent; the latter, a local historian.

25. Interview, Peter Fenn, Washington, DC, Feb. 8, 2009; Ray Eldon Hiebert and Richard K. MacMaster, *A Grateful Remembrance: The Story of Montgomery County, Maryland* (Rockville, MD: Montgomery County Historical Society, 1976), 352–53.

26. Interview, Bethine Church, Feb. 21, 2009, New York City; visit to 6704 Pemberton St., courtesy of current owner, Gary S. Lutzker, Feb. 8, 2009; Church, *Lifelong Affair*, 96–99. In 1964, Church voluntarily disclosed his income. Beyond his senatorial salary of $22,500, he earned about $2,000 a year in speaking and writing fees, held a modest savings account of some $6,800, owned no stocks or bonds, and owed more than $22,000 on his mortgage. U.S. Congress, Congressional Record, 88th Cong., 2d sess., 1964, vol. 110, no. 99. Bethine Clark Church held a half ownership of Robinson Bar Ranch, and, following the death of her parents, owned their house at 109 W. Idaho St. in Boise. Congressional Record, 91st Cong., 1st sess., 1969, vol. 115, no. 146.

27. Church, *Lifelong Affair*, 110–12; Bethine Church interviews, April 15, 2008, and Feb. 21, 2009; interview, Forrest Church, Feb. 6, 2008.

28. Report cards, 1961–1963; interviews, Peter Fenn, March 4, 2008, Washington, DC, and Feb. 8, 2009.

29. Bob Watkins, e-mail to author, March 13, 2008; Phil Dahan, e-mail to author, April 1, 2008. All e-mail is to author, unless otherwise indicated.

30. Petition, East Junior High School, Boise, 1963, in possession of Forrest Church. Interviews, Forrest Church, Feb. 6, 2008; Peter Fenn, Feb. 8, 2009; Phil Dahan, Feb. 8, 2009; Jim Bruce, April 18, 2008, Twin Falls, ID.

31. Interview, Forrest Church, Feb. 28, 2009.

32. Interviews, Forrest Church, April 4, 2009; Peter Fenn, Feb. 8, 2009; e-mail, Lisa Stratton, March 15, 2008.

33. George Bennett, "Memories of Walt Whitman," *Montgomery Journal*, 1992 (otherwise undated), and Linda VanGrack Snyder, "Whitman Plans Final Bash in Signature Dome," *Bethesda Gazette*, April 1, 1992, Montgomery County Historical Society, Rockville, MD; telephone interview, John Virden (former Whitman High School English teacher), Feb. 26, 2009; telephone interview, Barbara Steele (Whitman Class of '66), Feb. 5, 2009; Evaluation Handbook, Walt Whitman High School, 1965; "Best High School: Gold Standard List," Dec. 8, 2008, usnews.com/articles/education/high-schools/2008/12/04/best-high-schools-gold-medal-list; "The Top of the Class 2008," May 17, 2008, news week.com/id/39380.

34. Transcript, Walt Whitman High School, 1962–1966.

35. *Saga*, Whitman High School yearbook, 1966, 71; interview, Forrest Church, Sept. 8, 2008.

36. "My Future," Sept. 17, 1965, English IV, in possession of Forrest Church.

37. Church, *Father and Son*, 38–39; interview, Bethine Church, April 15, 2008; interview, Forrest Church, Feb. 6, 2008.

38. Interview, Peter Fenn, March 4, 2008; e-mail, Seiichi Tsurumi, March 26, 2008.

39. Ashby and Gramer, *Fighting the Odds*, 71–186. The quotation appears on 82.

40. Ibid., 167–220; Church, *Lifelong Affair*, 165.

41. Forrest Church to Carl Burke, Oct. 27, 1965, and Carl Burke to Douglas Walker (Stanford Director of Admissions), Dec. 3, 1965, Carl Burke Papers, Boise State University; transcript for Forrest Church, Walt Whitman High School, 1962–1966; *Saga*, Walt Whitman High School yearbook, 1966, 139; interview, Forrest Church, Feb. 6, 2008.

TWO: TICKING TIME BOMB

1. *Stanford Daily*, Sept. 23, 1966; Richard W. Lyman, *Stanford in Turmoil: Campus Unrest, 1966–1972* (Stanford: Stanford General Books, 2009), 43.

2. "Wallace Sterling; Led Stanford U.," *New York Times*, July 3, 1985; George Packer, *Blood of the Liberals* (New York: Farrar, Straus and Giroux, 2000), 194–99; Lyman, *Stanford in Turmoil*, 5–11; Rebecca S. Lowen, *Creating the Cold War University: The Transformation of Stanford* (Berkeley: University of California Press, 1997), 95–223.

3. Richard Todd, "An Eastern View of Stanford: From Ivy to Eucalyptus," *Harper's*, August 1967, vol. 235, no. 1407, 83–85; Lyman, *Stanford in Turmoil*, 5–11.

4. Todd, "An Eastern View of Stanford," 86; David Harris, *Dreams Die Hard: Three Men's Journeys Through the Sixties* (New York: St. Martin's Press, 1982), 17.

5. Harris, *Dreams Die Hard*, 157; *Stanford Daily*, Sept. 29, Oct. 21 and 24, Nov. 11 and 23, 1966.

6. Telephone interview, Hans Dankers, March 5, 2009.

7. Ibid.; interview, Christopher Norgaard, Feb. 21, 2009; interview, Patrick Shea, Salt Lake City, July 12–13, 2008; interview, Gary Maes, Oct. 6, 2008; telephone interview, Robert Yeager, March 7, 2009.

8. Interview, Forrest Church, Feb. 26, 2008.

9. Interviews, Christopher Norgaard, Feb. 21, 2009; Carla Berg Jolis, Sept. 11, 2008; telephone interview, Kim Dunster, Feb. 26, 2009.

10. Interviews, Forrest Church, Feb. 6, 2008, and April 14, 2009.

11. Interview, Patrick Shea, Salt Lake City, July 12–13, 2008.

12. Forrest Church letter to "Dad," undated; Frank Church to Forrest Church, Feb. 7, 1967, both in personal collection of Forrest Church; telephone interview, Kim Dunster, Feb. 26, 2009.

13. Harris, *Dreams Die Hard*, 166; *Stanford Daily*, March 9, 1967.

14. *Stanford Daily*, March 9, April 3 and 20, May 3 and 5, 1967: Hansen-Church undated press release, in personal collection of Forrest Church.

15. Forrest Church grade transcript, Stanford University; interview, Christopher Norgaard, Feb. 21, 2009, on Forrest's attitudes toward LASSU elections; Frank Church to Forrest Church, April 27, Sept. 13, and Oct. 23, 1967, in personal collection of Forrest Church.

16. Interviews, Forrest Church, Feb. 6, 2008; Patrick Shea, July 12–13, 2008; Christopher Norgaard, Feb. 21, 2009; and Winthrop Brown, Washington, DC, Feb. 9, 2009.

17. Interviews, Gary Maes, Oct. 6, 2008; Hans Dankers, March 5, 2009.

18. *Stanford Daily*, Feb. 21, 1967; interview, Robert Yeager, March 7, 2009.

19. Interview, Forrest Church, March 4, 2009.

20. Interviews, Shea and Norgaard.

21. Church, *Father and Son*, 64–65; interviews Shea, Norgaard, Dunster, and Jolis.

22. Church, *Father and Son*, 66–67.

23. Ibid., 64–68; interview, Forrest Church, Feb. 6, 2008; interviews, Shea and Jolis; Dalton Denton obituary, *Rio Grande Sun*, Espanola, NM, March 28, 1968.

24. Interview, Forrest Church, Feb. 6, 2008.

25. *Stanford Daily*, April 29–May 16, 1968; "Student Body," *Playboy*, September 1968, vol. 15, no. 9, 103–5; interview, Forrest Church, Feb. 6, 2008; telephone interview, Richard Lyman, March 5, 2009.

26. Interview, Forrest Church, May 20, 2008; interviews, Yeager and Shea.

27. Ashby and Gramer, *Fighting the Odds*, 253–56, 269–74.

28. Church, *Father and Son*, 74–75.

29. Telephone interview, Stan Zuckerman, July 22, 2008.

30. Interview, Zuckerman.

31. Church, *Father and Son*, 75.

32. Interview, Bethine Church, Boise, April 15, 2008; interview, Jerry Brady, Boise, April 18, 2008; interview, Peter Fenn by LeRoy Ashby, Aug. 8, 1984, Frank Church Papers, Boise State University.

33. Interview, Peter Fenn by LeRoy Ashby, Aug. 8, 1984; Ashby and Gramer, *Fighting the Odds*, 282.

34. Interview, Norgaard; interview, Winthrop Brown; telephone interview, Sarah Spaght Brown, Feb. 27, 2009.

35. Interview, Sarah Spaght Brown.

36. Interview, Maes.

37. Interview, Winthrop Brown; interview, Forrest Church, March 4, 2009.

38. Forrest Church grade transcript, Stanford University; interview, Forrest Church, Feb. 6, 2008.

39. Poems in personal collection, Forrest Church. They are undated and, according to Church, could have been written at any time during his Stanford years.

40. E-mails, Forrest Church, April 16 and July 31, 2009; Gordon Furth obituaries, *Point Reyes Light*, Aug. 17, 2006, and *Palo Alto Weekly*, July 26, 2006.

41. Interviews, Norgaard, Brown, and Spaght Brown.

42. *Stanford Quad* (yearbook), 1970, 67–68; Lyman, *Stanford in Turmoil*, 165–69.

43. Church, *Father and Son*, 76–77; Ashby and Gramer, *Fighting the Odds*, 307–42.

44. Interview, Forrest Church, March 4, 2009; transcript, Stanford University.

45. Interviews, Forrest Church, Feb. 6 and 26, 2008; Jan. 21, 2009.

46. Interview, Forrest Church, Feb. 26, 2008.

47. Church, *Father and Son*, 76–77; *New York Times*, May 31, 1970.

48. Furth-Church wedding vows, May 30, 1970, in personal collection of Forrest Church; Church, *Lifelong Affair*, 192–93.

49. Interview, Brady; Elizabeth Cobbs Hoffman, *All You Need Is Love: The Peace Corps and the Spirit of the 1960s* (Cambridge, MA: Harvard University Press, 1998), 205–7.

50. Essay submitted to Ada County Selective Service Board, July 26, 1970.

51. Frank Church to Elva Butler, Ada County Selective Service Board, June 29, 1970; Amy Furth Church, undated, to same; Wayne R. Rood to Local Draft Board No. 1, Ada County, June 27, 1970, all in personal collection of Forrest Church.

52. Church, *Father and Son*, 76.

53. Interview, Forrest Church, Jan. 29, 2009.

54. Interview, Forrest Church, Feb. 26, 2008.

THREE: SCHOLAR-IN-RESIDENCE

1. Wade Clark Roof, *A Generation of Seekers: The Spiritual Journeys of the Baby Boom Generation* (San Francisco: HarperSanFrancisco, 1993), 1–78.

2. Ibid., 89–91.

3. John Adams, *Hallelujah Junction: Composing an American Life* (New York: Farrar, Straus and Giroux, 2008), 66.

4. Interview, Forrest Church, Feb. 26, 2008.

5. Pacific School of Religion transcript for Forrest Church, 1970–1971; interview, Forrest Church, Feb. 26, 2008.

6. Robert R. Drovdahl, "Wayne R. Rood," Christian Educators, Talbot School of Theology, Biola University, www.talbot.edu/ce20/educators/view.cfm?n=wayne_rood#bio; interview, Forrest Church, Feb. 26, 2008.

7. E-mails, Timothy Pfaff, Feb. 12 and 27, 2008.

8. Interview, Forrest Church, Feb. 26, 2008.

9. Church, *Father and Son*, 88–89; Forrest Church, *Bringing God Home*, 167–69; interview, Forrest Church, Feb. 26, 2008.

10. Interview, Forrest Church, Feb. 6, 2008.

11. E-mail, Timothy Pfaff, Feb. 27, 2008.

12. Interview, Forrest Church, March 4, 2009; Church, *Father and Son*, 89.

13. Interview, Forrest Church, March 4, 2009.

14. Interview, Forrest Church, June 9, 2009.

15. Interview, Forrest Church, Feb. 26, 2008.

16. George Hunston Williams, "Three Recurrent Conflicts," 7–10, and Levering Reynolds Jr., "The Later Years (1880–1953)," in *The Harvard Divinity School: Its Place in Harvard University and in American Culture*, ed. George Hunston Williams (Boston: Beacon Press, 1954), 228–29; John A. Buehrens, "The Last Interview" (Dec. 6, 1999), Notable Unitarians, www.harvardsquarelibrary.org/unitarians/williams.

17. Andrew L. Yarrow, "Nathan Pusey, Harvard President Through Growth and Turmoil Alike, Dies at 94," *New York Times*, Nov. 15, 2001; "Paul Tillich Dies; Theologian Was 79," *New York Times*, Oct. 23, 1965; George H. Williams, *Divinings: Religion at Harvard, 1636–1992*, ed. Rodney L. Petersen (Newton: Boston Theological Institute, 2011), 1504–6, 1601–45 (page numbers are from prepublication manuscript version).

18. Williams, *Divinings*, 1524–58.

19. Dean Krister Stendahl, Divinity School, 1972–1973, 176, and 1973–1974, 279, Report of the President of Harvard College and Reports of the Departments; Peter Gomes, ed., *Foundations for a Learned Ministry: Catalogue of an Exhibition on the Occasion of the One Hundred Seventy-Fifth Anniversary of the Divinity School at Harvard University* (Cambridge: Harvard Divinity School, 1992), 24; Ann Braude, "A Shift in the Created Order: Fifty Years of Women and Transformation at Harvard Divinity School," *Harvard Magazine*, May–June 2006, www. harvardmagazine.com/2006/05/p-a-shift-in-the-created-o.html.

20. Stendahl, Divinity School, 1975–1976, 214, Report of the President of Harvard College and Reports of the Departments; telephone interview, Peter Gomes, Sept. 11, 2009.

21. Telephone interview, Robert A. Oden, May 4, 2009; telephone interview, Holland Hendrix, June 18, 2009.

22. Telephone interview, Dennis MacDonald, May 7, 2009; interviews, Oden, Gomes, and Hendrix.

23. John Noble Wilford, "John Strugnell, Scholar Undone by His Slur, Dies at 77," *New York Times*, Dec. 9, 2007; interview, Forrest Church, Feb. 26, 2008; transcript, Forrest Church, Harvard Divinity School, 1972–1974, and Harvard University, Graduate School of Arts and Science, 1974–1978.

24. Interview, Forrest Church, Feb. 26, 2008.

25. Interview, Oden.

26. Forrest Church, "George Hunston Williams: Historian of the Christian Church, 1912–2000," Notable Unitarians, www.harvardsquarelibrary.org/unitarians/williams; interview, Helmut Koester, Cambridge, MA, Nov. 12, 2008.

27. William Sloane Coffin, Jr., *Once to Every Man* (New York: Atheneum, 1977), 142; Williams, *Divinings*, 1534.

28. Interviews, Koester and Hendrix; interview, Forrest Church, Feb. 26, 2008.

29. Interview, Forrest Church, Feb. 26, 2008.

30. F. Forrester Church, "Sex and Salvation in Tertullian," *Harvard Theological Review*, vol. 68, no. 2, 1975, 83–101; F. Forrester Church, "Rhetorical Structure and Design in Paul's Letter to Philemon," *Harvard Theological Review*, vol. 71, nos. 1–2, 1978, 17–33.

31. F. Forrester Church, "The Munitioneer's Millennium: Sun Myung Moon's Theology in Historical Perspective," *The Unitarian Universalist Christian*, Autumn/Winter 1977, vol. 32, nos. 3–4, 51–58.

32. F. Forrester Church, "The Gospel According to Thomas Jefferson," submitted in partial fulfillment of the requirements for the degree of Master of Divinity, Harvard Divinity School, May 1, 1974, 30, 64, 80.

33. Interview, Forrest Church, Feb. 26, 2008.

34. Forrest Church to "Dad," postmarked Dec. 16, 1974, in personal papers of Forrest Church.

35. Ashby and Gramer, *Fighting the Odds*, 453–500; Church, *Father and Son*, 93–94.

36. Interview, Forrest Church, Feb. 26, 2008; e-mail, Feb. 25, 2009.

37. Telephone interview, John Cavanaugh, March 27, 2009; interview, Chris Burke, Boise, ID, April 16, 2008; interview, Joe and Mercedes McCarter, Boise, ID, April 17, 2008; telephone interview, Andy Litsky, Sept. 15, 2009.

38. Frank Church to "Dear Kids" (Forrest and Amy), Oct. 9, 1972, personal papers of Forrest Church; interview, Forrest Church, Feb. 26, 2008; interview, Joe and Mercedes McCarter.

39. Interview, Larry LaRocco, Boise, ID, April 17, 2008; interview, Forrest Church, Feb. 26, 2008.

40. Church, *Father and Son*, 123–26; telephone interview, Bill Hoppner, Sept. 15, 2009; telephone interview, W. Don Nelson, Sept. 15, 2009; interview, Forrest Church, Feb. 26, 2008.

41. Frank Forrester Church, "The Secret to the Gospel of Thomas," Ph.D. diss., Harvard University, 1978; Elaine Pagels, *The Gnostic Gospels* (New York: Random House, 1979), xiii–xxiii; interview, Forrest Church, Feb. 26, 2008.

42. Pagels, *Gnostic Gospels*, xv, xix; Church, "The Secret to the Gospel of Thomas," 1, 7, 116.

43. Interviews, Forrest Church, Feb. 26 and March 11, 2008; program, service of ordination, First and Second Church, Boston, April 13, 1975, in Archives of Unitarian Church
of All Souls, New York City (hereafter cited as AS Archive).

FOUR: UNITARIANS AND UNIVERSALISTS

1. David E. Bumbaugh, *Unitarian Universalism: A Narrative History* (Chicago: Meadville
Lombard Press, 2000), 7–19, 48–56.

2. David Robinson, *The Unitarians and the Universalists* (Westport, CT: Greenwood Press,
1985), 48.

3. Conrad Wright, ed., *Three Prophets of Religious Liberalism: Channing, Emerson, Parker* (Boston: Skinner House, 1986, 2nd ed.), 3–19, 49; Conrad Wright, ed., *A Stream of Light: A
Short History of American Unitarianism* (Boston: Skinner House, 1989), 24.

4. Wright, *A Stream of Light*, 19–33, 90–112.

5. Philip F. Gura, *American Transcendentalism: A History* (New York: Hill and Wang, 2007),
7, 212.

6. Wright, *A Stream of Light*, 62–70; Gura, *American Transcendentalism*, 274–75.

7. Wright, *A Stream of Light*, 71; Gura, *American Transcendentalism*, 295–301.

8. Wright, *A Stream of Light*, 108–10.

9. William F. Schulz, *Making the Manifesto: The Birth of Religious Humanism* (Boston: Skinner
House, 2002), passim; Mason Olds, *American Religious Humanism* (Hamden, CT: HUU-
manists Association, 1996, rev. ed.), passim.

10. Charles A. Howe, *The Larger Faith: A Short History of American Universalism* (Boston:
Skinner House, 1993), 2–5.

11. Ibid., 18–39.

12. Ibid., 45, 60.

13. Ibid., 52–60.

14. Ibid., 63–80.

15. Clarence R. Skinner, *The Social Implications of Universalism* (Boston: Universalist Publishing House, 1915), 5–47; Howe, *The Larger Faith*, 92–98.

16. Howe, *The Larger Faith*, 107–8.

17. Warren R. Ross, *The Premise and the Promise: The Story of the Unitarian Universalist Association* (Boston: Skinner House, 2001), 9–21.

18. Warren R. Ross, "Shared Values: How the UUA's Principles and Purposes Were Shaped
and How They've Shaped Unitarian Universalism," *UU World*, November/December
2000.

19. Robert B. Tapp, *Religion Among the Unitarian Universalists: Converts in the Stepfather's
House* (New York: Seminar Press, 1973), cited in Robinson, *The Unitarians and the Universalists*, 175–77.

20. Walter Donald Kring, *Liberals Among the Orthodox: Unitarian Beginnings in New York City,
1819–1839* (Boston: Beacon Press, 1974), 10.

21. Victor F. Escamilla, "The Quest for Religious and Community Identity: The Story Behind the Architecture and Moves of All Souls Church" (master's thesis, Columbia University, 2006), 63–87; Robert A. M. Stern, Gregory Gilmartin, and Thomas Mellins, *New York 1930: Architecture and Urbanism Between the Two World Wars* (New York: Rizzoli, 1987), 164.

22. Kring, *Liberals Among the Orthodox*, 45.

23. Ibid., 119–202.

24. Walter Donald Kring, *Henry Whitney Bellows* (Boston: Skinner House, 1979), 107–9, 259–320.

25. Walter Donald Kring, *Safely Onward: The History of the Unitarian Church of All Souls, Vol. III, 1882–1978* (New York: Unitarian Church of All Souls, 1991), 42–48; William F. Schulz, *Making the Manifesto: The Birth of Religious Humanism* (Boston: Skinner House, 2002), 30–33.

26. Kring, *Safely Onward*, 132–66; Kring, "What the Unitarian Denomination Ought to Be" (New York: Unitarian Church of All Souls, undated pamphlet).

FIVE: BRIGHT LIGHTS, BIG CITY

1. Interview, Forrest Church, March 11, 2008.

2. Interview, Forrest Church, March 11, 2008; Sue Bastion interview with Church, May 11, 1995, AS Archive; Nina Mende interview with Jane Levenson, March 12, 1997, AS Archive; Nina Mende interview with Jeanne Walton, no date, AS Archive; Rhys Williams to Bert Zippel, July 28, 1977, Archive of First and Second Church, Boston.

3. Interview, Jane Levenson; interview, Mary-Ella Holst, April 1, 2009.

4. Interview, Jane Levenson.

5. Interview, Forrest Church, March 11, 2008.

6. Bert Zippel to George H. Williams, Jan. 6, 1978; George H. Williams to Bert Zippel, Jan. 14, 1978; Helmut Koester to Bert Zippel, Jan. 12, 1978; George MacRae to Bert Zippel, Jan. 11, 1978; James Luther Adams to Bert Zippel, Jan. 21, 1978, all in AS Archive.

7. Interview, Forrest Church, March 11, 2008; interview, Walter Klauss, March 17, 2009; *All Souls Newsletter*, February 1978.

8. Population of the 100 Largest Cities: 1980, U.S. Bureau of the Census. www.census .gov/population/www/documentation/twps0027/tab21.txt; Jonathan Mahler, *Ladies and Gentlemen, the Bronx Is Burning: 1977, Baseball, Politics, and the Battle for the Soul of a City* (New York: Farrar, Straus and Giroux, 2005), 8, 30, 124, 175–256; Talk of the Town, *The New Yorker*, Sept. 4, 1978, 22–23; Ken Auletta, *The Streets Were Paved with Gold* (New York: Random House, 1979), 287.

9. Anthony Gronowicz, "Upper East Side," *The Encyclopedia of New York City*, ed. Kenneth T. Jackson (New Haven: Yale University Press and New York: New-York Historical Society, 1995), 1217–18; Anthony Haden-Guest, "Love and Death on the Upper East Side," *New York*, Sept. 11, 1978, 5, 42–48.

10. Directories of the Unitarian Universalist Association, 1976–1979; interview, Forrest Church, March 11, 2008.

11. Interview, Daniel Beshers, Jan. 11, 2010; telephone interview, Harris Riordan, Feb. 12, 2010; interview, Marietta Moskin, Jan. 5, 2010.

12. *Park East* magazine, September 1978, unpaged, AS Archive; Forrest Church to Alan G. Deale, Nov. 9, 1978, AS Archive.

13. George N. Marshall, *A. Powell Davies and His Times* (Boston: Skinner House, 1990), 3.

14. Robert Moats Miller, *Harry Emerson Fosdick: Preacher, Pastor, Prophet* (New York: Oxford University Press, 1985), passim.

15. Ibid., 342–43.

16. Interview, Forrest Church, March 11, 2008.

17. Interview, Forrest Church, March 11, 2008.

18. See, for example, the sermons "Meditation Upon the Rig Veda," Jan. 28, 1979; "The First American Amnesty Debate," Feb. 25, 1979; "Our Liberal Faith," Sept. 17, 1978.

19. Sermons, "The Gift of Life," Nov. 12, 1978; "Seizing the Day," June 10, 1979.

20. Sermon, "You Are Not Alone," June 3, 1978.

21. Interview, Mary-Ella Holst and Guy Quinlan, Feb. 18, 2010.

22. Kring, *Safely Onward*, 147; interview, Holst and Quinlan; *All Souls Unitarian Church Newsletter*, December 1977–June 1978.

23. Forrest Church, sermons, "Symbols of the Heart," Oct. 8, 1978; "Unitarian Democracy," Jan. 14, 1979.

24. *All Souls Newsletter*, Feb. 1979–June 1980; Sue Fuller, International Fine Print Dealers, www.ifpda.org/content/node/826.

25. Harris, ibid.; *All Souls Newsletter*, February 1979.

26. F. Forrester Church, *Born Again Unitarian Universalism* (Tulsa, OK: Cone-Lewis Printing Co., undated), 25–27, 83.

SIX: ONE NEIGHBOR AT A TIME

1. *The Hymn and Service Book* (New York: Unitarian Church of All Souls, 1957), passim; *Hymns in New Form for Common Worship* (Boston: Unitarian Universalist Association, 1982, revision of a 1979 edition), passim; interview, Forrest Church, March 11, 2008.

2. Interview, Forrest Church, March 11, 2008.

3. Interview, Forrest Church, March 11, 2008.

4. Forrest Church, sermon, "The Church of the Future," March 22, 1981.

5. Dorothy J. Gaiter, "Interfaith Alliance in Yorkville Initiates Grants to Aid Needy," *New York Times*, June 27, 1982; Annual Report, 1984, Yorkville Emergency Alliance, AS Archive; telephone interview, Hays Rockwell, April 16, 2009; telephone interview, Alanson Houghton, April 2, 2009; interview, Forrest Church, March 11, 2008.

6. Forrest Church, sermon, "Harvesting the Energies of Love," Nov. 21, 1982.

7. *All Souls Newsletter*, June 1983 and Summer 1986.

8. Sylvia Ann Hewlett, Children's Task Force fact sheet, undated but presumably 1987.

9. "Scoutreach for Kids Trapped by Poverty," *Scouting*, September 1989; Children's Task Force, "Boy Scout Activities in the Past Year," 1990.

10. Matthew Purdy, "Budding Scientist's Success Breaks the Mold," *New York Times*, Jan. 30, 1994; www.oeersweat.com/index.asp?page=biography.asp.

11. Ann Gronningsater, "Crossing 96th Street," *All Souls Quarterly Review*, Summer 1990; Twentieth Anniversary Program, Booker T. Washington Learning Center, 2006.

12. Forrest Church, sermon, "AIDS: A Religious Response," Sept. 29, 1985.

13. Forrest Church, sermon, "Link by Link: A Chain for Peace," Oct. 6, 1985; AIDS Task Force fact sheet, undated; Emile Nava, "AIDS: A Religious Response, the Beginning of the AIDS Task Force," *All Souls Quarterly Review*, summer 1995; telephone interview, Barbara Hosein, April 1, 2010; interview, Christina Bellamy, Feb. 9, 2010.

14. Interview, Inez Miller, Jan. 13, 2010; telephone interview, Barbara Hosein, April 1, 2010; interview, Barbara Lazear Ascher, April 1, 2010.

15. Telephone interviews, Margaret Blagg, April 1, 2010, and Richard Solomon, April 5, 2010.

16. Clare Ansberry, "AIDS, Stirring Panic and Prejudice, Tests the Nation's Character," *Wall Street Journal*, Nov. 13, 1987.

17. Interview, Bill Bechman, Jan. 19, 2010.

18. Ashby and Gramer, *Fighting the Odds*, 561–604.

19. Church, *Father and Son*, 157.

20. Ibid., 161.

21. Ibid., 178–79.

22. "The Best of the New Generation," *Esquire*, December 1984, 212.

23. Church, *Father and Son*, ix; telephone interview, George Rupp, March 31, 2010.

24. Bret Watson, "A Senator's Son Shuns Politics for the Pulpit," *Avenue*, March 1985, 150–54.

25. Church, *Father and Son*, 10.

26. Ibid., 184–85.

27. Marianne Means, "Frank Franking Privileges," *Albany Times-Union*, Nov. 8, 1985.

28. David Murray, *New York Times Book Review*, Nov. 17, 1985; Chalmers Roberts, "Mr. Church Goes to Washington," *Washington Post Book World*, Nov. 25, 1985; Rod Gramer, "Forrest Church's Book about Famous Father Illuminates the Lives of Two, Death of One," *Idaho Statesman*, Nov. 10, 1985.

29. F. Forrester Church, "A Father's Lessons on Living and Dying," *Chicago Tribune*, Dec. 1, 1985; Marian Christy, "The State of Rev. Church," *Boston Globe*, Jan. 1, 1986.

30. Terry Kelleher, "'Father and Son' Is One from the Heart," *Fort Lauderdale News/Sun-Sentinel*, Nov. 10, 1985; William F. Schulz, "The Churches," *Unitarian Universalist World*, May 15, 1986.

31. Bernice Kanner, "The Church Revival," *New York*, Nov. 4, 1985, 52–55.

SEVEN: LIBERAL EVANGELIST

1. *Time*, Sept. 2, 1985; quoted in Wade Clark Roof and William McKinney, *American Mainline Religion: Its Changing Shape and Future* (New Brunswick, NJ: Rutgers University Press, 1987), 186.

2. Robert Wuthnow, *The Restructuring of American Religion: Society and Faith Since World War II* (Princeton: Princeton University Press, 1988), 1–93; Roof and McKinney, *American Mainline Religion*, 27–69.

3. Telephone interviews, Dr. Nancy Ammerman, Boston University, May 14, 2009; Dr. Rhys H. Williams, University of Cincinnati, May 21, 2009.

4. George M. Marsden, *Understanding Fundamentalism and Evangelicalism* (Grand Rapids, MI: Eerdmans, 1991), 1–5; Susan Friend Harding, *The Book of Jerry Falwell* (Princeton: Princeton University Press, 2000), 77.

5. Interview, Ammerman.

6. Interviews, Ammerman and Williams; telephone interview, Dr. James Davison Hunter, June 10, 2009. Hunter, it should be noted, dissents from the view that higher birth rates were responsible for the growth of evangelical churches.

7. James Davison Hunter, *Culture Wars: The Struggle to Define America* (New York: Basic Books, 1991), 42–170.

8. Harding, *The Book of Jerry Falwell*, 12–14, 103–4, 147, 161.

9. Forrest Church, sermon, "The Problem with Being Right," May 10, 1981.

10. Forrest Church, sermon, "The Path to Peace: A Pastoral Letter," May 9, 1982.

11. Forrest Church, sermon, "The Politics of God," Oct. 7, 1984.

12. Forrest Church, "A Just-War Theory for Abortion," *The Christian Century*, Aug. 26–Sept. 2, 1987, 733–34.

13. Interview, Patrick Shea, Salt Lake City, July 12–13, 2008; Forrest Church, sermon, "Jesus and the Bomb," Sept. 16, 1984.

14. Forrest Church, sermons, "Truth and Consequences," April 21, 1985; "Terrorism," April 20, 1986.

15. Jeffrey Schmalz, "Church Returns State's 'Pork Barrel' Gift," *New York Times*, April 24, 1986; "Too Much Grease in Albany," *New York Times*, May 19, 1986.

16. Interview, Forrest Church, Oct. 27, 2008; interview, Mary-Ella Holst, April 1, 2009; telephone interview, George Rupp, March 31, 2010, confirmed Forrest's candidacy for the divinity school deanship.

17. *All Souls Newsletter*, March 1982, AS Archive.

18. Montgomery Brower, "Unitarianism Welcomes a Fresh Voice in Forrester Church, a Famous Son with a Fitting Name," *People Weekly*, May 19, 1986, vol. 25, no. 20, 76–79.

19. Bernice Kanner, "What Price Ethics? The Morality of the Eighties," *New York*, July 14, 1986, 30.

20. "Parents Are People," *Parents*, September 1986, 72; "5 Heartwarming Christmas Memories," *Redbook*, December 1986, 84–86.

21. The figures for All Souls are drawn from the annual directories of the Unitarian Uni-

versalist Association for the years cited. Membership in national religious organizations is notoriously unreliable. Institutions often find reasons to undercount or to exaggerate. Still, the best source is the Association of Religion Data Archives. For Unitarian Universalists, see www.thearda/Denoms/D_1403.asp. For comparative figures, see www .thearda.com/mapsReports/reports/US_1980.asp.

22. Robert Wuthnow, *After Heaven: Spirituality in America Since the 1950s* (Berkeley: University of California Press, 1998), 72–84, 123–31; George Gallup Jr. and Jim Castelli, *The People's Religion: American Faith in the 90's* (New York: Macmillan, 1989), 60–61, 72; Bruce Buursma, "Unitarian Chief Bows to Market," *Chicago Tribune*, June 5, 1987.

23. Edwin Scott Gaustad, "Did the Fundamentalists Win?" in *Religion and America*, ed. Mary Douglas and Stephen M. Tipton (Boston: Beacon Press, 1982), 175.

24. Cecile Holmes White, "Liberal Church Offers New Hope to Nation's Mainline Denominations," *Houston Chronicle*, Oct. 24, 1987.

25. Gustav Niebuhr, "'Evangelical Liberal' Preacher Will Hold Revival," *Atlanta Journal*, Oct. 3, 1987; Neal Gendler, "Unitarian Universalist Growth Potential 'Great,'" *Minneapolis Star and Tribune*, May 2, 1987; Don Duncan, "Dr. Church Outspoken for Liberal Religion," *Seattle Times*, March 21, 1987.

26. Interview, Tom Stites, Boston, Nov. 13, 2008.

27. "A Lion's Lament," reprinted in F. Forrester Church, *Everyday Miracles* (New York: Cornelia and Michael Bessie/Harper & Row, 1988), 53.

28. Forrest Church, "The [Im]perfect Primer, *Chicago Tribune*, Oct. 26, 1986.

29. Interview, Stites.

EIGHT: AUTHOR, AUTHOR!

1. Clayton Carlson to Forrester Church, June 19, 1985, personal collection of Forrest Church.

2. F. Forrester Church, *The Devil & Dr. Church* (San Francisco: Harper & Row, 1986), x–xi.

3. Ibid., 80–82.

4. Charles W. Bell, "Call Them the Books of Summer," New York *Daily News*, June 1, 1986; Bruce Buursma, "Exposing a Devil in Disguise," *Chicago Tribune*, June 10, 1986; Huston Horn, *Los Angeles Times*, July 27, 1986; unsigned review, *Presbyterian Outlook*, June 9, 1986; unsigned review, *United Methodist Reporter*, May 23, 1986; Peter R. Powell Jr., *The Christian Century*, Oct. 14, 1987, 895–96; Eliot Janeway, "Destroying Earthly Hells," *Commonweal*, Dec. 26, 1986; Marianne Hachten-Cotter, "Mixed Answers," *The World,* March/April 1987; Marilyn Sewell, *critical mass*, Fall 1986.

5. Clayton Carlson to F. Forrester Church, June 4, 1986, personal collection of Forrest Church.

6. F. Forrester Church, *Entertaining Angels: A Guide to Heaven for Atheists and True Believers* (San Francisco: Harper & Row, 1987), 10–11; Joanna Torrey, "Play Mystic for Me," New York *Daily News*, May 10, 1987.

7. Church, *Entertaining Angels*, 11–13.

8. Ibid., 29.

9. Ibid., 44.

10. Ibid., 78.

11. F. Forrester Church, *The Seven Deadly Virtues: A Guide to Purgatory for Atheists and True Believers* (San Francisco: Harper & Row, 1988), 11.

12. Ibid., 51.

13. Ibid., 33.

14. Ibid., 67.

15. Numerous letters to Forrest Church, AS Archive.

16. Interview, Terrence J. Mulry, April 30, 2009.

17. Interview, Forrest Church, Oct. 10, 2008; Robert P. Scharlemann, *Newsletter of the North American Paul Tillich Society*, vol. XIV, no. 2, April 1988, unpaged.

18. F. Forrester Church, ed., *The Essential Tillich: An Anthology of the Writings of Paul Tillich* (New York: Macmillan/Collier Books, 1987), 1–11.

19. Ibid., xiii–xv.

20. F. Forrester Church and Terrence J. Mulry, *One Prayer at a Time: A Twelve-Step Anthology for Those in Recovery and All Who Seek a Deeper Faith* (New York: Macmillan/Collier Books, 1989), ix–x.

21. Interview, Bill Moyers, May 17, 2010; Bill Moyers, *A World of Ideas: Conversations with Thoughtful Men and Women About American Life Today and the Ideas Shaping Our Future* (New York: Doubleday, 1989), vii–viii.

22. Moyers, *A World of Ideas*, 414–25.

23. Jefferson quoted in Forrest Church's introduction to Thomas Jefferson, *The Jefferson Bible: The Life and Morals of Jesus of Nazareth* (Boston: Beacon Press, 1989), ix; sales figures from e-mail, Robyn Day, assistant to the director, Beacon Press, March 8, 2010.

24. See, for example, "Hope, Faith and the Bluebird," *New York Post*, March 12, 1989, and "At 96, a Rhyme Against Time," *New York Post*, April 9, 1989.

25. Interview, John Buehrens, May 15, 2008.

26. Interview, Buehrens.

27. Interview, Forrest Church, March 11, 2008.

28. Interview, Buehrens; www.dartmouth.edu/~montfell/biographies/fellows_by_date.html; Edward Connery Lathem to Forrest Church, April 19, 1989, and Thomas L. McFarland to Forrest Church, April 19, 1989, AS Archive.

29. Interview, Buehrens; interview, Forrest Church, May 20, 2008; e-mails, Robyn Day, assistant to director, Beacon Press, March 8 and April 26, 2010.

30. Jack Mendelsohn, *Being Liberal in an Illiberal Age: Why I Am a Unitarian Universalist* (Boston: Beacon Press, 1985), 37; interview, Buehrens.

31. John A. Buehrens and F. Forrester Church, *Our Chosen Faith: An Introduction to Unitarian Universalism* (Boston: Beacon Press, 1989), xi–xiv.

32. Ibid., xviii.

33. Ibid., 5–15.

34. Ibid., 43–54.

35. Ibid., 98–101.

36. Ibid., 127–32.

37. Ibid., 158–64.

38. E. J. Dionne, Jr., *Why Americans Hate Politics* (New York: Simon and Schuster, 2004, 2nd ed., 2004), 14.

39. Publishing agreement, Simon and Schuster and F. Forrester Church, April 7, 1989, AS Archive; Forrest Church to Liz Perle, July 24, 1990, AS Archive; Church to Perle, Oct. 24, 1990, AS Archive.

40. F. Forrester Church, *God and Other Famous Liberals: Reclaiming the Politics of America* (New York: Simon and Schuster, 1991), xvi, 31.

41. Ibid., ix–x.

42. Ibid., xvi–xxi.

43. Ibid., 3–33.

44. Ibid., 94.

45. Ibid., 78–79.

46. Ibid., passim.

NINE: CHURCH OF THE HEAVENLY UNREST

1. AS Archive.

2. Mary-Ella Holst, journal, February 12, 1991.

3. F. Forrester Church, sermon, "Confessions," Feb 24, 1991.

4. Telephone interview, Minna Buck, April 17, 2009; interview, Carolyn Buck Luce, May 13, 2009.

5. Carolyn Buck Luce, "Carolyn Buck Luce," *Central New York Magazine*, March/April 2009, 33–34; interview, Minna Buck; Lois Chazen, "Who We Are," *All Souls Quarterly Review*, vol. IX, no. 3, Fall 2004; interview, Buck Luce, May 13, 2009.

6. Interview, Buck Luce, May 13, 2009; John Rothchild, *Going for Broke: How Robert Campeau Bankrupted the Retail Industry, Jolted the Junk Bond Market, and Brought the Booming Eighties to a Crushing Halt* (New York: Simon and Schuster, 1991), 22–187.

7. Interview, Buck Luce, May 13, 2009; Minna Buck interview.

8. Interview, Forrest Church, May 7, 2008; interview, John Buehrens, May 15, 2008.

9. Interview, Forrest Church, May 7, 2008.

10. Interview, Forrest Church, May 7, 2008.

11. Interview, Buehrens, May 15, 2008; telephone interview, Holland Hendrix, June 18, 2009.

12. Interview, Stephen Bauman, March 11, 2009.

13. Interview, Forrest Church, May 7, 2008.

14. Interviews, Bauman; Valerie Amsterdam, March 10, 2009.

15. All Souls Orders of Service, Jan. 15, Feb. 20, and March 10, 1991.

16. Interview, Forrest Church, May 7, 2008.

17. Interview, Daniel Beshers, Jan. 11, 2010; interview, Inez Miller, Jan. 13, 2010; interview, Marietta Moskin, Jan. 5, 2010; interview, Mary-Ella Holst, April 1, 2009; interview, Forrest Church, May 7, 2008.

18. Interviews, Beshers; Moskin; Holst journal, April 11, 12, and 13, 1991.

19. Telephone interview, Trudy Pojman, May 29, 2008.

20. All Souls monthly bulletins, January–April 1991; interviews, Beshers, Moskin, Miller, Holst; interview, Christina Bellamy, Feb. 9, 2010.

21. All Souls Order of Service, April 7, 1991; "According to Dick," *All Souls Bulletin*, April 1991.

22. Interview, Buehrens, May 15, 2008.

23. Interview, Forrest Church, May 7, 2008.

24. Rusty Unger, "Church of the Heavenly Unrest," *New York*, Oct. 14, 1991, 35–37; Guidelines, Unitarian Universalist Ministerial Association, 1988, 11.

25. Holst journal, May 19, 1991.

26. Board of Trustees minutes, May 13, 1991; telephone interview, Dennis MacDonald, May 7, 2009.

27. All Souls Order of Service, June 9, 1991; Board of Trustees minutes, June 10, 1991; Minister's Letter, *All Souls Bulletin*, June/Summer 1991.

28. Interviews, William Schulz, Fort Lauderdale, FL, June 28, 2008; Alison Miller, Morristown, NJ, April 22, 2009.

29. Nadine Brozan, "Another Sanger Leads Planned Parenthood," *New York Times*, Jan. 23, 1991; Lynne Tillman, *Bookstore: The Life and Times of Jeannette Watson and Books & Co.* (New York: Harcourt Brace, 1999), 1–50; www.barbaralazearascher.com.

30. Interview, Alexander and Jeannette Watson Sanger, Feb. 5, 2010.

31. Interview, Barbara Lazear Ascher, April 1, 2010.

32. Interview, Forrest Church, March 4, 2009.

33. Interview, Ascher.

34. Interview, Roslyn and David Will, Jan. 21, 2010.

35. Minister's letter, *All Souls Bulletin*, September 1991; Forest Church, sermon, "What I Did on My Summer Vacation," Sept. 22, 1991.

36. Interviews, Klauss, Moskin, Beshers, Holst, Bellamy, Sangers, and Ascher.

37. Board of Trustees minutes, Sept. 26 and 30, 1991.

38. Larry Sutton, "Minister Faces Flock's Fury When Illicit Affair Goes Public," *Daily News*, Oct. 4, 1991; Charlotte Hays, "Affair of the Heart Rocks Church's Soul," *Daily News*, Oct. 6, 1991.

39. Mary Papenfuss, "Randy Rev. Faces Church Vote," *New York Post*, Oct. 15, 1991.

40. Interview, Peter Steinfels, Jan. 7, 2010.

41. Peter Steinfels, "Pastor's Conduct Divides East Side Congregation," *New York Times*, Oct. 7, 1991; interview, Holst, April 1, 2009.

42. Unger, "Church of the Heavenly Unrest," 32–38.

43. Buehrens e-mail, June 11, 2010; Buehrens to Jeanette Watson Sanger, Oct. 7, 1991, Alexander Sanger Papers, Sophia Smith Collection, Smith College.

44. Forrest Church to "Dear Friends," Oct. 9, 1991; sermon, "Into the Woods," Oct. 13, 1991.

45. "Protocol for Congregational Meeting," All Souls Board of Trustees; Board of Trustees minutes, Oct. 7 and 10, 1991; telephone interview, Paul and Linda Frank, Feb. 19, 2010.

46. Buehrens e-mail, June 11, 2010; interview, Carolyn Buck Luce, May 28, 2008.

47. Marietta Moskin to Valerie Amsterdam, president of Board of Trustees, Oct. 3, 1991.

48. Sanger interview, Feb. 5, 2010; Sanger speech, delivered Oct. 15, 1991, Alexander Sanger Papers, Smith College.

49. Board of Trustees minutes, Oct. 15, 1991.

TEN: RETURN TO GRACE

1. Interview, Forrest Church, May 7, 2008.

2. Interview, Forrest Church, May 7, 2008.

3. Forrest Church, sermon, "Ministry," Oct. 20, 1991; Minister's letter, *All Souls Bulletin*, November 1991.

4. Interview, Forrest Church, May 7, 2008.

5. Interview, Christina Bellamy, Feb. 9, 2010.

6. Interview, Roslyn Will, Jan. 21, 2010.

7. Interviews, Will; Diana List Cullen, Jan. 21, 2010; Sangers, Feb. 5, 2010; Ascher, April 1, 2010.

8. Amy Church to the Trustees of the Unitarian Church of All Souls, Board minutes, Dec. 9, 1991.

9. Gail Birnbaum, "Preacher's Love Triangle Sparks Unholy Scandal in the Pulpit," *National Enquirer*, Dec. 10, 1991, 5.

10. Susan Wise Bauer, *The Art of the Public Grovel: Sexual Sin and Public Confession in America* (Princeton: Princeton University Press, 2008), 115–151.

11. Ibid., 2–3.

12. Interview, Forrest Church, May 7, 2008.

13. Letter from the UU Ministers Association to *UU World*, *UUMA News*, Summer 1992; statistics on female clergy cited in Qiyamah A. Rahman, draft of Ph.D. dissertation, Clark Atlanta University, "On the Shores of Babylon We Wept: An Exploration of the Institutional Response of the Unitarian Universalist Association to Clergy Sexual Misconduct Between 1991–2005," qiyamahinislam.blogspot.com/2007/07/by-shores-of-babylon-we-wept.html.

14. Telephone interview, Carolyn Owen-Towle, March 17, 2009.

15. "Rev. A. F. Perrino Resigns from the First Unitarian Church, Admits Added Extramarital Affairs," *The Plain Dealer*, Cleveland, Nov. 28, 1990; telephone interview, David Pohl, March 18, 2009.

16. Telephone interview, Rev. David Bumbaugh, April 9, 2009; telephone interview, Rev. Leon Hopper, March 20, 2009.

17. Interview, Rev. Lee Barker, Fort Lauderdale, FL, June 26, 2008.

18. Interview, Barker.

19. The Investigation of the Reverend F. Forrester Church, submitted Jan. 7, 1992, Andover-Harvard Theological Library Archives, cited by permission of Forrest Church.

20. Interview, Hopper; Highlights from the UUMA Executive Committee meeting, Jan. 15–19, 1992, *UU Ministerial Association News*, Winter 1992.

21. Forrest Church to Marilyn J. Abraham (his editor at Simon and Schuster), undated (from internal evidence regarding a forthcoming *New York* magazine article, the letter was clearly written in September or early October 1991); publicity schedule for Forrest Church in Washington, DC, Jan. 15–16, 1991, both in AS Archive.

22. Telephone interview, Dennis R. MacDonald, May 7, 2009; interview, Nina Church Adams, Dec. 24, 2008.

23. Interview, Church Adams.

24. Interview, Frank Church, March 11, 2009; John Dewey Academy, www.jda.asinsh.com.

25. www.mayoclinic.com/health/Klinefelter-syndrome/D501057/DSECTION=complications; Robert Bock, "Understanding Klinefelter Syndrome: A Guide for XXY Males and Their Families," NIH Pub. No. 93-3202, August 1993, www.nichd.nih.gov/publications/pubs/Klinefelter.cfm#xadol.

26. Interview, Jacob Luce, Feb. 3, 2009; interview, Nathan Luce, March 4, 2009.

27. Interview, MacDonald.

28. Interviews, Forrest Church, Sept. 8, 2008, and Feb. 28, 2009.

29. Based on firsthand observations by numerous Church–Buck Luce friends and the author.

30. Interviews, Robert Oxnam, Oct. 10, 2008; Sylvia Ann Hewlett, March 7, 2009.

31. Telephone interview, Rev. Bill Grimbol, July 7, 2010.

32. Interview, Alison Miller, Morristown, NJ, April 22, 2009.

33. Post, www.allsoulsnyc.org/Tributes-to-Forrest.

34. Telephone interview, Victoria Weinstein, Feb. 11, 2010.

35. Richard Ford post, www.allsoulsnyc.org/Tributes-to-Forrest.

36. Interview, Forrest Church, Sept. 8, 2008.

37. Forrest Church to Wendy Strothman, undated; Forrest Church to Joy Harris, Oct. 5, 1995, both in AS Archive.

38. Forrest Church, *Life Lines: Holding on (and Letting Go)* (Boston: Beacon Press, 1996), xv–xvii.

39. Ibid., 43.

40. Ibid., 84, 116.

41. Ibid., 151.

42. See, for example, Beacon Press tour schedules for Nov. 7–8, 1996, AS Archive.

43. Forrest Church, *Lifecraft: The Art of Meaning in the Everyday* (Boston: Beacon Press, 2000), 8–9.

44. Ibid., xi–xii.

45. Ibid., 30–31, 38.

46. Ibid., 73–78.

47. Ibid., 81–93.

48. Forrest Church to Joy Harris, March 30, 1993, AS Archive; telephone interview, Beth Walker, June 21, 2010.

49. Forrest Church, ed., *Without Apology: Collected Meditations on Liberal Religion by A. Powell Davies* (Boston: Beacon Press, 1998).

50. John Buehrens to Helene Atwan, Sept. 30, 1996; Atwan to Buehrens, Oct. 4, 1996, both in Beacon Press archives.

51. Buehrens and Church, *A Chosen Faith*, 185–98.

52. Interview, Forrest Church, March 24, 2008.

53. Telephone interview, Dennison Young, Jr., July 16, 2010; interview, Forrest Church, March 24, 2008; Forrest Church to Randy Mastro (Mayor Giuliani's chief of staff), simply dated 1995, AS Archive.

54. Telephone interviews, Lys McLaughlin, July 26 and 30, 2010; Dan Barry, "Sudden Deal Saves Gardens Set for Auction," *New York Times*, May 13, 1999.

55. Interview, Forrest Church, March 24, 2008.

56. Forrest Church to President Bill Clinton, April 7, 1997, AS Archive.

57. Forrest Church, sermon, "New Beginnings," Sept. 13, 1998.

58. Bill Clinton to Rev. Church, Sept. 22, 1998; Bill Clinton to Forrest Church, May 2, 1997; Clinton to Helene Atwan, June 12, 1997, all in AS Archive.

59. Forrest Church, "American Heroes Aren't Perfect," *Daily News*, Oct. 9, 1998.

60. Forrest Church, "Clinton's Sins: Impious, Not Political," *Newsday*, Dec. 3, 1998; Forrest Church to President Clinton, undated.

61. Forrest Church, sermon, "The God-Shaped Hole," Nov. 18, 2001.

62. Forrest Church, sermon, "It's Never Too Late," Jan. 17, 1982; "Giving Up for Lent," Feb. 21, 1982.

63. Church, *Everyday Miracles*, 12, 122.

64. Column proposal from F. Forrester Church and Dwight Lee Wolter, AS Archive; telephone interview, Tom Stites, Aug. 4, 2010.

65. Interviews, Forrest Church, May 20, 2008; Peter Fenn, Washington, DC, Feb. 8, 2009.

66. Interview, Forrest Church, May 20, 2008.

67. Interview, Kathleen Montgomery, Fort Lauderdale, FL, June 27, 2008.

68. George E. Vaillant, *The Natural History of Alcoholism: Causes, Patterns and Paths to Recovery* (Cambridge: Harvard University Press, 1983), 1, 44; Sarah Allen Benton, *Understanding the High-Functioning Alcoholic: Professional Views and Personal Insights* (Westport, CT: Praeger, 2009), 11–13; Caroline Knapp, *Drinking: A Love Story* (New York: Dial Press, 1996), 12.

69. Interview, Forrest Church, May 20, 2008.

70. Interview, Carolyn Buck Luce, May 28, 2008.

71. Interview, George Dorsey, March 19, 2009.

72. Interview, Bill Thompson, Feb. 25, 2010.

73. Interview, Forrest Church, May 20, 2008.

74. Interview, Forrest Church, Oct. 27, 2008.

75. Interview, Carolyn Buck Luce, May 28, 2008.

76. Interview, Stephen Bauman, March 11, 2009.

77. Telephone interview, Bill Grimbol, July 7, 2010.

ELEVEN: A NATIONAL PULPIT

1. Forrest Church, sermon, "Candlelighting Meditation," Sept, 12, 2001.

2. Gustav Niebuhr, "Religion Journal: Clergy of Many Faiths Answer Tragedy's Call," *New York Times*, Sept. 15, 2001.

3. *News Hour with Jim Lehrer,* Jan. 29, 2001, videotape, AS Archive.

4. *Good Morning America*, Sept. 14, 2001, videotape, AS Archive; CBS News, "Attack on America," coverage of National Prayer Service, Washington National Cathedral, Sept. 14, 2001, videotape, AS Archive; Hillary Rosner, "Attack on America," *New York*, Nov. 5, 2001, 53.

5. Interview, Forrest Church, Sept. 8, 2008.

6. Interviews, Forrest Church, Sept. 8, 2008; Tim Bent, Jan. 27, 2010; George Gibson, May 28, 2010.

7. Interview, Forrest Church, Sept. 8, 2008; Laurie Goodstein, "New York Cleric's Departure from Mosque Leaves Mystery," *New York Times*, Oct. 23, 2001.

8. Forrest Church, *Bringing God Home: A Traveler's Guide* (New York: St. Martin's Press, 2002), 237.

9. Ibid., 6–7.

10. Ibid., 20.

11. Ibid., 189–206.

12. Ibid., 8, 223–27.

13. Interview, Tim Bent, Jan. 27, 2010.

14. Forrest Church, *The American Creed: A Spiritual and Patriotic Primer* (New York: St. Martin's Press, 2002), xi–xiv.

15. Telephone interview, Christopher Breiseth, Aug. 24, 2010.

16. Forrest Church, *Freedom from Fear: Finding the Courage to Act, Love, and Be* (New York: St. Martin's Press, 2004), 66, 95–97.

17. Interview, Bent.

18. Church, *Freedom from Fear*, 209.

19. Church, *Life Lines*, 89; *Lifecraft*, 92–93.

20. Telephone interview, Gertrude (Trudy) Pojman, May 29, 2008; interview, Forrest Church, May 7, 2008.

21. Interviews, Diana Cullen, Jan. 21, 2010; Barbara Ascher, April 1, 2010; Alex and Jeannette Sanger, Feb. 5, 2010.

22. Interview, Ken Beldon, Fort Lauderdale, FL, June 28, 2008.

23. Interview, Marc Loustau, Somerville, MA, Nov. 14, 2008.

24. Interview, Alison Miller, Morristown, NJ, April 22, 2009.

25. Interview, Robert Oxnam, Oct. 10, 2008.

26. Interview, Oxnam.

27. Forrest Church letters to the All Souls congregation, Oct. 17, Nov. 16 and 19, Dec. 5, 2006.

28. Memorial Sloan-Kettering Cancer Center, "Esophageal Cancer: Risk Factors, Prevention & Screening," www.mskcc.org/mskcc/html/318.cfm; Peter C. Enzinger and Robert J. Mayer, "Esophageal Cancer: Review Article," *New England Journal of Medicine* 349:23, Dec. 4, 2003, 2241–52.

29. Forrest Church, sermons, "Looking Forward," Jan. 21, 2007, and "Beating the Odds," Feb. 18, 2007.

30. Forrest Church, ed., *The Separation of Church and State: Writings on a Fundamental Freedom by America's Founders* (Boston: Beacon Press, 2004), x–xi.

31. Forrest Church, *So Help Me God: The Founding Fathers and the First Great Battle Over Church and State* (New York: Harcourt, 2007), 42–49, 120–24, 225–30, 307–22, 365–66.

32. Ibid., 3–5.

33. Ibid., 12.

34. Tim Bent e-mail, Jan. 28, 2010.

35. *Tavis Smiley Show*, PBS, Oct. 25, 2007; *Kirkus Reviews*, August 2007; www.dailykos .com/story/2007/12/16/125924/04/221/422869; Elaine Jarvik, "Founding Fathers' Religious Intent Refereed," *Deseret News*, Oct. 20, 2007.

36. Jill Lepore, "Prior Convictions," *The New Yorker*, April 14, 2008, 71–75; Gordon S. Wood, "Praying with the Founders," *New York Review of Books*, May 1, 2008, 54.

37. Church wrote numerous drafts for this book proposal. See, for example, "In God We Trust: Religion and the American Presidency" (provided by George Gibson at Walker and Co.) and "The God of Abraham: How Lincoln Demolished Jefferson's Wall—The Battle over Church-State Separation from the Age of Jackson to the Civil War" (provided by Church's research assistant Justin Latterell). Copies of both are now in the All Souls Archive.

38. Forrest Church, *Love and Death: My Journey Through the Valley of the Shadow* (Boston: Beacon Press, 2008), 11.

39. Ibid., 34.

40. Forrest Church, *The Cathedral of the World: A Universalist Theology* (Boston: Beacon Press, 2009), 126.

41. Ibid., 99, 122, 158, 161.

TWELVE: THE MEASURE OF A MAN

1. Telephone interview, Peter Gomes, Sept. 11, 2009.

2. Jack Mendelsohn, *Channing: The Reluctant Radical* (Boston: Little, Brown, 1971), 146.

3. Interview, Rabbi Harold Kushner, Natick, MA, Nov. 13, 2008.

4. Interview, Christopher Walton, Boston, Nov. 12, 2008.

5. Interviews, Tim Bent, Jan. 27, 2010; Helene Atwan, Boston, Feb. 7, 2010.

6. Tim Bent e-mail, Jan. 28, 2010.

7. Interviews, John Buehrens, Fort Lauderdale, FL, June 26, 2008; William Schulz, Fort Lauderdale, FL, June 28, 2008.

8. Prof. Gary Dorrien, Inaugural Forrest Church Lecture, Union Theological Seminary, Sept. 23, 2010; Dorrien's interpretation of Church's Emersonian transcendentalism is also outlined in *The Making of American Liberal Theology: Crisis, Irony, and Modernity, 1950–2005* (Louisville: John Knox Press, 2006), 455–59.

9. Interview, Robert Oxnam, Oct. 10, 2008.

10. Mark Vonnegut, *Just Like Someone Without Mental Illness Only More So* (New York: Delacorte Press, 2010), 67.

11. Church, *Love and Death*, 139–40.

12. Telephone interview, Bill Grimbol, July 7, 2010.

THIRTEEN: LOVE AND DEATH

1. Forrest Church, letter to congregation, Feb. 3, 2008.

2. Carolyn Buck Luce, letter to congregation, March 6, 2008; interview, Forrest Church, Feb. 6, 2008.

3. Forrest Church e-mail, Feb. 29, 2008.

4. Interview, Forrest Church, May 7, 2008.

5. Interview, Forrest Church, May 7, 2008.

6. Interview, Forrest Church, May 7, 2008.

7. Forrest Church, sermons, "Love, Death and Easter," March 6, 2008; "Bedside Manners," April 6, 2008.

8. Forrest Church e-mail, March 21, 2008.

9. Interviews, Forrest Church, March 24 and May 7, 2008.

10. Forrest Church e-mail, May 27, 2008; interview, Forrest Church, June 18, 2008.

11. Author's notes, UU General Assembly, Fort Lauderdale, FL, June 26–29, 2008.

12. Interviews, Nina Church Adams, Dec. 24, 2008; Forrest Church, Sept. 8, 2008.

13. Cara Buckley, "His Death Postponed, a Minister Repeats His Farewell Sermon," *New York Times*, Sept. 29, 2008.

14. *Religion and Ethics Newsweekly*, Oct. 3, 2008; *Fresh Air*, Oct. 27, 2008; *The Diane Rehm Show*, Dec. 22, 2008.

15. Forrest Church, letter to congregation, Nov. 18, 2008; interview, Forrest Church, Oct. 27, 2008.

16. Telephone interview, Stan Zuckerman, Jan. 2, 2009; interviews, Forrest Church, Dec. 16, 2008; Robert Oxnam, Sept. 24, 2010.

17. Telephone interview, AARP producer Steve Mencher, Oct. 8, 2010.

18. *The Forrest Church Diaries*, "Acceptance," www.aarp.org/relationships/grief-loss/info-

10-2009/forrest_acceptance; "Death," www.aarp.org/relationships/grief-loss/info-10-2009/forrest_death.

19. Press release, National Hospice Foundation, May 19, 2009; telephone interview, Galen Miller, NHF executive vice president, Oct. 5, 2010.

20. Interviews, Forrest Church, Feb. 28 and March 4, 2009.

21. Forrest Church, letter to congregation, April 3, 2009.

22. Interviews, Forrest Church, April 14 and May 4, 2009.

23. Interview, Forrest Church, June 9, 2009; e-mails, July 12, 13, and 22, 2009.

24. Forrest Church, letter to congregation, Aug. 29, 2009.

25. Interview, Oxnam, Sept. 24, 2010.

26. Previously cited interviews with Church and Luce children.

27. www.timeinc.net/fortune/conferences/women05/speakers; Lois Chazen, "Who We Are," *All Souls Quarterly Review*, Fall 2004; Sylvia Ann Hewlett and Carolyn Buck Luce, "Off-Ramps and On-Ramps: Keeping Talented Women on the Road to Success," *Harvard Business Review*, March 2005; Sylvia Ann Hewlett, Carolyn Buck Luce, and Lisa J. Servon, "Stopping the Exodus of Women in Science," *Harvard Business Review*, June 2008.

28. Interviews, Nathan Luce, March 4, 2009; Jacob Luce, Feb 3, 2009; www.harbert.net/company/management-team.

29. Interview, Nina Church Adams, Dec. 24, 2008; telephone interview, Dennis MacDonald, April 7, 2009.

30. Galen Guengerich e-mail to All Souls leaders, Sept. 15, 2009; David Campbell, "Tributes to Forrest," All Souls Web site; interview, Oxnam, Sept. 24, 2010; Carolyn Buck Luce, letter to congregation, Nov. 30, 2009.

31. Carolyn Buck Luce, letter to congregation, Nov. 30, 2009; interview, Oxnam, Sept. 24, 2010; www.aarp.org/relationships/grief-loss/info-10-2009/forrest_epilogue.

32. Carolyn Buck Luce e-mail, Oct. 9, 2010.

SELECTED BIBLIOGRAPHY

Ashby, LeRoy, and Rod Gramer. *Fighting the Odds: The Life of Senator Frank Church*. Pullman, WA: Washington State University Press, 1994.

Bauer, Susan Wise. *The Art of the Public Grovel: Sexual Sin and Public Confession in America*. Princeton, NJ: Princeton University Press, 2008.

Benton, Sarah Allen. *Understanding the High-Functioning Alcoholic: Professional Views and Personal Insights*. Westport, CT: Praeger, 2009.

Bumbaugh, David E. *Unitarian Universalism: A Narrative History*. Chicago: Meadville Lombard Press, 2000.

Church, Bethine. *A Lifelong Affair: My Passion for People and Politics*. Washington, D.C.: The Francis Press, 2003.

Dorrien, Gary. *The Making of American Liberal Theology, Vol. III: Crisis, Irony, and Postmodernity, 1950–2005*. Louisville, KY: John Knox Press, 2006.

Fuller, Robert C. *Spiritual but Not Religious: Understanding Unchurched America*. New York: Oxford University Press, 2001.

Gallup, George Jr., and Jim Castelli. *The People's Religion: American Faith in the 90's*. New York: Macmillan, 1989.

Gerassi, John. *The Boys of Boise: Furor, Vice and Folly in an American City*. Seattle: University of Washington Press, 2001.

Gitlin, Todd. *The Sixties: Years of Hope, Days of Rage*. New York: Bantam, 1987.

Goldstein, Warren. *William Sloane Coffin, Jr.: A Holy Impatience*. New Haven, CT: Yale University Press, 2004.

Gura, Philip F. *American Transcendentalism: A History*. New York: Hill and Wang, 2007.

Harding, Susan Friend. *The Book of Jerry Falwell: Fundamentalist Language and Politics*. Princeton, NJ: Princeton University Press, 2000.

Harris, David. *Dreams Die Hard*. New York: St. Martin's Press/Marek, 1982.

Hodgson, Godfrey. *The World Turned Right Side Up: A History of the Conservative Ascendancy in America*. Boston: Houghton Mifflin, 1996.

Hunter, James Davison. *Culture Wars: The Struggle to Define America*. New York: Basic Books, 1991

Kelley, Dean M. *Why Conservative Churches Are Growing: A Study in Sociology of Religion*, 3d ed. Macon, GA: Mercer University Press, 1986.

Kring, Donald Walter. *Liberals Among the Orthodox: Unitarian Beginnings in New York City, 1819–1839*. Boston: Beacon Press, 1974.

———. *Henry Whitney Bellows*. Boston: Skinner House, 1979.

———. *Safely Onward: The History of the Unitarian Church of All Souls, New York City, Vol. III: 1882–1978*. New York: The Unitarian Church of All Souls, 1991.

Lyman, Richard W. *Stanford in Turmoil: Campus Unrest, 1966–1972*. Stanford, CA: Stanford General Books/Stanford University Press, 2009.

Mahler, Jonathan. *Ladies and Gentlemen, the Bronx Is Burning: 1977, Baseball, Politics, and the Battle for the Soul of a City*. New York: Farrar, Straus and Giroux, 2005.

Marsden, George M. *Understanding Fundamentalism and Evangelicalism*, Grand Rapids, MI: William B. Eerdsmans, 1991.

Marshall, George N. *A. Powell Davies and His Times*. Boston: Skinner House, 1990.

Mendelsohn, Jack. *Being Liberal in an Illiberal Age: Why I Am a Unitarian Universalist*, 2nd ed. Boston: Skinner House, 2006.

———. *Channing: The Reluctant Revolutionary*. Boston: Little, Brown, 1971

Miller, Robert Moats. *Harry Emerson Fosdick: Preacher, Pastor, Prophet*. New York: Oxford University Press, 1985.

Murry, William R. *Reason and Reverence: Religious Humanism in the 21st Century*. Boston: Skinner House, 2007.

Olds, Mason. *American Religious Humanism*, rev. ed. Hamden, CT: HUUmanists Association, 2006.

Packer, George. *Blood of the Liberals*. New York: Farrar, Straus and Giroux, 2000.

Phillips-Fein, Kim. *Invisible Hands: The Making of the Conservative Movement from the New Deal to Reagan*. New York: Norton, 2009.

Rasor, Paul. *Faith Without Certainty: Liberal Theology in the 21st Century*. Boston: Skinner House, 2005.

Robinson, David. *The Unitarians and the Universalists*. Westport, CT: Greenwood Press, 1985.

Roof, Wade Clark. *A Generation of Seekers: The Spiritual Journeys of the Baby Boom Generation*. San Francisco: HarperSanFrancisco, 1993.

——— and William McKinney. *American Mainline Religion: Its Changing Shape and Future*. New Brunswick, NJ: Rutgers University Press, 1987.

Ross, Warren R. *The Premise and the Promise: The Story of the Unitarian Universalist Association*. Boston: Skinner House, 2001.

Rothchild, John. *Going for Broke: How Robert Campeau Bankrupted the Retail Industry, Jolted the Junk Bond Market, and Brought the Booming Eighties to a Crashing Halt*. New York: Simon and Schuster, 1991.

Schmidt, Leigh Eric. *Restless Souls: The Making of American Spirituality*. San Francisco: Harper-SanFrancisco, 2005.

Schulz, William F. *Making the Manifesto: The Birth of Religious Humanism*. Boston: Skinner House, 2002.

Shibley, Mark A. *Resurgent Evangelicalism in the United States: Mapping Cultural Change Since 1970*. Columbia: University of South Carolina Press, 1996.

Traub, Marvin, and Tom Teicholz. *Like No Other Store: The Bloomingdale's Legend and the Revolution in American Marketing*. New York: Times Books, 1993.

Wilcox, Clyde, and Carin Larson. *Onward Christian Soldiers? The Religious Right in American Politics,* 3rd ed. Boulder, CO: Westview Press, 2006.

Williams, George Hunston. *American Universalism*, 4th ed. Boston: Skinner House, 2002.

———. *Divinings: Religion at Harvard, 1636–1992*, two volumes, edited by Rodney L. Petersen. Newton Centre, MA: Boston Theological Institute, 2011.

Wolfe, Alan. *The Transformation of American Religion: How We Actually Live Our Faith*. New York: Free Press, 2003.

Wright, Conrad, ed. *A Stream of Light: A Short History of American Unitarianism,* 2nd ed. Boston: Skinner House, 1989.

Wuthnow, Robert. *After Heaven: Spirituality in America Since the 1950s*. Berkeley: University of California Press, 1998.

———. *The Restructuring of American Religion: Society and Faith Since World War II*. Princeton, NJ: Princeton University Press, 1988.

———. *The Struggle for America's Souls: Evangelicals, Liberals, and Secularism*. Grand Rapids, MI: Eerdmans, 1989.

INDEX